Communication in Management

Many of the ideas contained in this book emerged as the result of discussion, debate and brainstorming with our late colleague, friend and brother, Colin Thomas Cecil Hargie. He gave us much inspiration, and always with a light, humorous, yet incisive touch. We therefore dedicate the book to his memory.

> He who binds to himself a joy
> Doth the winged life destroy;
> But he who kisses the joy as it flies
> Lives in Eternity's sunrise.

William Blake, *Eternity*

Communication in Management

Owen Hargie, David Dickson
and Dennis Tourish

Gower

Published by
Gower Publishing Limited
Gower House
Croft Road
Aldershot
Hampshire GU11 3HR
England

Gower
Old Post Road
Brookfield
Vermont 05036
USA

Owen Hargie, David Dickson and Dennis Tourish have asserted their right under the Copyright, Designs and Patents Act 1988 to be identified as the authors of this work.

British Library Cataloguing in Publication Data
Hargie, Owen
  Communication in management
  1. Communication in management
  I. Title II. Dickson, David, 1950– III. Tourish, Dennis
  658.4′5

  ISBN 0 566 07986 0

Library of Congress Cataloging-in-Publication Data
Hargie, Owen
  Communication in management / Owen D.W. Hargie, David Dickson and
  Dennis Tourish.
      p.   cm.
  Includes bibliographical references and index.
  ISBN 0-566-07986-0 (hc.)
  1. Communication in management.   I. Dickson, David, 1950–
II. Tourish, Dennis.   III. Title
HD30.3.H365   1999   98–46662
  658.4′5--dc21   CIP

Typeset in 10pt Century Oldstyle by Saxon Graphics Ltd, Derby and printed in Great Britain at the University Press, Cambridge.

Contents

List of figures and tables ix
Preface xi

1 Introduction: the communicating manager 1

Organizations 2
Management 7
Staff views on communication 11
What is communication? 13
The elements of communication 15
The structure of this book 18
Summary 22

2 The gentle art of persuasion: influencing others 23

Logical proofs 27
Emotional proofs 31
Personal proofs 34
Selecting an influencing strategy 39
Summary 43

3 Team-mates: building teams that work 45

Stages of team development 48
Characteristics of successful teams 50
Barriers to team development 57
Summary 62

4 Team-meets: managing productive meetings 65

When leadership is needed 66
Tasks versus relationships 67

	Leadership styles	69
	The role of meetings	71
	The role of the chair	75
	Summary	80
5	**Stand and deliver: making effective presentations**	**83**
	Types of presenter and presentation	86
	The presenter	89
	The audience	91
	Content of the presentation	91
	Delivering the presentation	98
	The setting	102
	Summary	102
6	**I think we've got ourselves a deal: negotiating and bargaining**	**105**
	Conflict at work	106
	Negotiation: characteristics and preconditions	107
	Negotiating strategies	110
	Stages in the negotiation process	112
	Skills of the successful negotiator	126
	Summary	129
7	**Selling the idea: the manager as salesperson**	**131**
	Step 1: opening the sale	132
	Step 2: establishing needs	135
	Step 3: making the sales presentation	138
	Step 4: overcoming objections	141
	Step 5: offering additional sales suggestions	144
	Step 6: closing the sale	144
	Summary	146
8	**Making the right connections: the telephone in business**	**151**
	Norms of telephone behaviour	154
	Differences between telephone and face-to-face interactions	155
	Telephone hates	159

Telephone communication problems   161
Making and answering calls   162
Summary   163

9   The word made permanent: putting it in writing 167

The strategic role of written communication   168
Evaluating written communication   170
The rules of high impact writing   172
Letters and memos   176
Writing reports   177
E-mail, snail mail, more mail   181
Dealing with complaints   183
Summary   185

10   It's your right: communicating assertively   187

Assertiveness and management   188
Communicating aggressively   192
Communicating submissively   196
Communicating assertively   200
Factors that shape assertiveness   206
Benefits of assertion   208
Summary   209

11   A problem shared: helping communication   211

Employee problems at work   212
What is counselling at work?   214
Incidence and effects of counselling at work 215
Who should counsel the workforce? The role of
    the manager   216
Qualities of helpers   217
Helping skills   221
Stages of the helping process   229
Summary   232

12 'Our most important asset': selecting people   235

The process of selection interviews   237
The behaviour description interview   240
Constructing a behaviour description interview 243

Planning and preparation   247
Conducting the interview   249
An interviewee's perspective   254
Summary   256

13   Feedback time: appraising performance   259

Biases in interpersonal perception   261
The principles of appraisal   265
The perils of feedback   266
Managing the feedback interview   267
Handling the interview   271
Summary   278

**14   More than words can tell: communicating
      non-verbally   281**

The importance of non-verbal communication   282
Non-verbal communication in management   283
Functions of non-verbal communication   284
Forms of non-verbal communication   286
Summary   302

**15   Ethics and audits: doing things right and doing
      the right thing   305**

The functions of communication in organizations 306
Communication ethics   307
Auditing communication   312
Audit measures   314
Developing a communication strategy   316
Summary   317

References   321
Subject index   341
Name index   345

List of figures and tables

FIGURES

1.1	The five directions of management communication	8
2.1	Persuasive communication outcomes	24
7.1	The sales model	133
7.2	Maslow's hierarchy of human needs	136
14.1	Seating arrangements and interaction	290
14.2	Office designs communicating power	291
14.3	Types of task and seating arrangement	292
14.4	Facial expressions and emotional states	293
14.5	Eye direction and thinking states	296

TABLES

7.1	Dealing with objections: the 10 As	143
8.1	Length of contact face to face and by telephone	157
9.1	Stress factors in management communication	168
12.1	Selection interview validity	240

Preface

This book has had a very long gestation period. For the past 25 years we have been working in the field of communications. During much of this time we have carried out research and consultancy work in the sphere of organizational communications. We have also designed and implemented numerous tailor-made training courses for a wide range of private and public sector bodies. These have spanned the full continuum from the 'hard' end of business in terms of training in negotiating and selling, right through to the 'softer' side of helping and counselling.

These experiences have informed our roles as educators. What we have learned from working with organizations has been carried back to university, and used to revise the modules which we teach to our undergraduate and postgraduate students. A recurring problem, however, has been finding a suitable text to meet the needs of managers on our training courses and our students in university. In our teaching to date we have used a variety of texts. Indeed, there is now a plethora of books on various aspects of business communication. These generally fall into two broad categories.

First, there are the 'how I did it' books by successful salespeople, chief executives, negotiators etc. These have a part to play in the total picture, and we can all learn from the success stories of expert practitioners in any field. However, the flaw which they also share is that they are usually anecdotal. They tend to be lacking in any generic research base, and the hints and tips they provide on how to deal with others are really only valid for one person (i.e. the author) in one situation. Indeed, the recommended courses of action may even be counter-productive when employed by managers of a differing personality, to meet an entirely different set of organizational demands. Furthermore, few texts by these gurus give as much weight to their failures as they do to their successes! Secondly, there are theoretically driven texts, usually written by academics in business faculties. While these are useful in furthering business studies as an academic discipline, they are not usually of much practical value to those seeking practical information and advice in the business sphere.

There is a dearth of books which bridge the divide between research and theory on one side and practical application on the other. Given this situation, we decided to embark upon the current text. This book is intended to provide a user-friendly, yet academically rigorous, analysis of the main communication factors central to effectiveness in management. It has been designed to meet the ever expanding demand for valid and generalizable information on how to relate to people in a business and management context. As such, it should be of interest both to practising managers, and to teachers and students of organizational communication.

The content of the book was determined by research and theory, and by firsthand experience. From working with practising managers and evaluating their central roles, and from analysing the work of other academics, we have selected 13 key areas for inclusion, namely: influencing and persuading, building teams, leading teams, making presentations, negotiating and bargaining, selling ideas, using the telephone effectively, writing skills, being assertive, helping and counselling, selecting staff, appraising staff and non-verbal communication.

In the opening chapter we place the study of these skills and strategies within the context of an analysis of the nature and functions of organizations, and the communicative role of managers therein. In the final chapter we underline the importance of regularly measuring communication within the workplace by using a communication audit approach. In this latter chapter we also emphasize the need for managers to communicate in an ethical fashion.

The core objectives of this book are to:

- examine the main communicative contexts within which managers operate
- identify and chart the key skills and strategies essential for effective managerial communication within organizations
- review research findings pertaining to each area
- help managers to apply the material to their own particular context
- enable managers to improve their day-to-day performance in their interactions with staff at all levels.

The style employed in all of the chapters enables the reader to interact with the content. Each chapter contains a series of boxed text which summarize key points. Exercises are provided to enable managers to put the material reviewed into practice. The text is supplemented throughout by bullet points, diagrams, tables and illustrations, coupled with relevant examples and case studies. All this is underpinned by a firm foundation of research findings. The referencing style employed, using superscript numbers and full references at the end of the book, enables the interested reader to identify and pursue the relevant source material. On the other hand, the reader whose needs are less 'academic' will not find the references impeding the flow of the text.

In writing this book the authors would like to acknowledge the assistance provided by Professor Jim Allen, Dean of Faculty, who organized teaching relief for research staff, thereby enabling us to devote more time to this particular task. A special word of thanks is due to Malcolm Stern, Gower's Consultant Editor, for all his help and advice. Words of gratitude also to Trevor Craig, Technician at the university, for his help in producing diagrams. Finally, we are indebted to our families who provided the necessary motivation, and who put up with us, throughout the production of this text.

Owen Hargie
David Dickson
Dennis Tourish

1 Introduction: the communicating manager

'Communications are terrible' – this is probably the most widespread complaint of those working in organizations.

Dave Francis, *Unblocking Organizational Communication*

Communication is a central phenomenon in organizations and is especially important for management. Certainly, as an activity it occupies a vast majority of a manager's time, and thus any increase in a manager's effectiveness or skill as a communicator should contribute directly or indirectly to improved organizational performance.

R. Klaus and B. Bass, *Interpersonal Communication in Organizations*

This book is about communication in organizations. More particularly, it examines the pivotal communicative role of managers, who play a significant part in maintaining information flow and promoting harmonious relationships within the workplace. Communication is necessary to effective management. Studies[1,2] have revealed that managers spend over 60 per cent of their working time in scheduled and unscheduled meetings with others, about 25 per cent of their time doing desk-based work, some 7 per cent on the telephone, and 3 per cent walking the job.

Furthermore, it has been shown that 'communication, especially oral skills, is a key component of success in the business world ... executives who hire college graduates believe that oral communication skills will become even more important for career success'.[2] One survey of British managers[3] highlighted a clear demand for more training in this field. Some 82 per cent of female and 69 per cent of male respondents expressed the need for more training in human relations skills such as leadership, team-building and assertiveness. This compared to a much lower expressed need for more training in technical/functional skills (18 per cent of female and 38 per cent of male respondents).

In this chapter we will use a travel analogy to introduce the book. We plan to take you on a journey around the whole world of the communicating manager. You will be introduced to the climates and cultures of different organizations and see how these affect the disposition and behaviour of the inhabitants. On our tour we will visit the different territories and terrains in which managers travail. We will witness how they can function as missionaries spreading the organizational gospel, and you will be encouraged to note the different styles they adopt and the relative zeal they display. Managers' relationships with their staff will be of particular interest.

While the main emphasis will be on verbal and non-verbal rituals in these often strange organizational environs, we will also examine the written forms of communication in which people engage. Among the interesting sights are new forms of technology (such as e-mail) which have transformed hitherto more primitive organizational hieroglyphics. To enhance our experience and inform our voyage, we will also hear positive and negative stories from other experienced travellers.

ORGANIZATIONS

One thing that is clear, as we begin our travels, is that organizations are everywhere; our social world is unimaginable without them. They come in all shapes and sizes. There are large ones and small ones; flat ones and steeply hierarchical ones; those which are long established (the oldest company being Weihenstephan Brewery, founded in Germany in 1040) and those which are new to business; some are geographically spread out and others are located in a single building. The wealth continuum ranges from the very small business going bankrupt to the huge conglomerate with immense cash reserves, enormous power and ambitious plans for expansion.

But what do we mean by the term 'organization'? We are all members of a whole host of organizations and often the closer you are to something the less you actually see. By taking a step back for a moment we can look at 'the organization' in broader perspective. A useful definition, which emphasizes the main features of organizations, is that they are 'social arrangements for achieving controlled performance in pursuit of collective goals'.[4] They involve:

- *Social arrangements*, where people come together to interact and organize themselves in a certain way.
- *Controlled performance*, which entails the setting of standards for outputs, measurement of performance against these standards, and the implementation of corrective action as required.
- *Collective goals*, wherein members work together to achieve shared aims and common objectives.

However, different organizations are formed for varying purposes and to achieve divergent goals. The function of the organization inevitably shapes its nature, form and structure, and in turn influences the types of people who will want to work there. The classification made by the social scientist Talcott Parsons[5] is useful, where organizations are divided into those which pursue:

1. *Economic production and profit-making goals* – these are primarily concerned with the market economy, in terms of maximizing income and accumulating capital. Both manufacturing and service sector companies are involved in seeking these private enterprise goals.
2. *Political goals* – these are determined by activities relating to the control and distribution of power in society. Examples here are government agencies, political parties, police and the military.
3. *Pattern maintenance goals* – these relate to the facilitation of education and the dissemination of culture. Those involved in this sphere include the family, schools and colleges, religious denominations and cultural heritage groups.
4. *Integration objectives* – these include the scrutiny of other groups and the mediation and resolution of disputes. This encompasses customer rights watchdogs, courts and legal offices, regulatory bodies, and citizens' advice agencies.

Organizations can also be evaluated by using the 'I-We-Them-It' principle:[6]

- *I* refers to how staff are regarded as individuals within the company. Are all staff treated as equals? Is there disparity of treatment? What are the pay differentials? What kind of people are rated most highly?
- *We* is concerned with how staff relate to one another. Is communication downwards only, or upwards and diagonal as well? Is there a rigid hierarchy through which communications must flow? Do managers encourage open and honest feedback from their staff? Is formal business dress required or is casual wear allowed? Is the firm one big happy family?
- *Them* reflects the way in which external publics are dealt with. Are customers valued or seen simply as profit targets? What steps are taken to monitor and improve customer care? Are suppliers paid on time and treated fairly?
- *It* represents how the organization feels about what it does. Is it proud of its products or services? What public face does it wish to display? Does it publicize proudly what it does, or are there aspects of its work it would rather hide and not talk about? Are staff proud of what they do and where they work?

Managers should examine these four dimensions of their business, the current value systems within each, their accompanying communication patterns, and how improvements could be effected.

As we traverse the organizational domain, it becomes obvious that the successful ones in any sphere are those which produce products or provide services that people want. They organize and manage their work efficiently, monitor costs and profits, market and publicize what they are selling, have good public relations, show concern for customers and suppliers, and continually evaluate their performance.

But one thing they all have in common is that they are composed of people. Organizations do not communicate – people do. Organizations do not have goals – the people who comprise them do. Organizations do not succeed or fail – their staff do. This means that any analysis of organizations is complex since, in the words of the old Yorkshire adage, 'There's nowt so queer as folk'!

For the organization, communication has been portrayed variously as:

- its life blood
- its oxygen
- its brain
- its central nervous system
- its arteries
- the highways along which its business is transacted
- the mortar/glue which binds its parts together
- the fuel which drives its engine.

All these metaphors emphasize the role of communication in enabling messages to be transmitted rapidly and in connecting the different 'bits' together. The larger and more complicated the organizational structure, the greater will be the need for effective and efficient communication. Problems caused by breakdowns in communication are legion and have produced effects ranging from, at one end of the continuum, job dissatisfaction and stress, damaging strikes, operating losses, bankruptcies, production line injuries, plane crashes and, at the other extreme, mass slaughter in the field of battle.

Communication is therefore paramount to business success. At this juncture, we will take our first excursion. This is to a company where the centrality of communication has been emphasized through strategies such as the use of first names for all staff, a casual dress policy apart from those directly interfacing with the public, a caring approach and an opportunity to interface directly with the boss (see Key point 1.1).

Comprehensive reviews of relevant research reveal the benefits of good internal communications,[7, 8] and these are summarized in Key point 1.2. A review of a range of leading companies including Federal Express, Xerox, IBM and AT&T identified the recurring best communication practices (see Key point 1.3).[9]

Key point 1.1   A senior manager speaks

Management cultures are changing. In order to be a fast moving company today, you have to be a people company. The old concept of familiarity breeds contempt is long gone. People are expected to work harder than ever before so they need to be supported by management. I believe strongly in the importance of making staff feel valued. In the end of the day they are the people making it happen, not the directors sitting in their ivory towers. If your staff are happy and motivated they will do a better job and customers will be happy. In the end of the day we are a business and we need to show growth and profitability, we are not taking our people-friendly approach because it makes us look good. It is very much an important part of our strategy to grow and develop the business. I have worked for companies where staff were in awe of management and spent most of their working day stressed out about their jobs or worried about their future because they didn't know what was going on. CableTel's approach is very informal and refreshing. A combination of focusing on the customer by focusing on each other. Communication is key to good management ... The communication must be a two way thing; that's why we have initiatives like breakfast with the boss. Once a month we pick eight people at random to go for breakfast and just talk about how the company is doing, how they are doing and what the company should be doing. Our associates (staff) are the people at the coal face. They are the ones that know if something is wrong and management need to get this feedback. At the same time if an associate has a problem with some part of his or her role, it is an opportunity to discuss it and get it fixed ... Yes, we have a budget for our initiatives, but it is directly related to our success. I am not sitting here throwing money at schemes just for the sake of it ... In any case it doesn't cost a lot to take the time to know your staff by their first names and to take an interest in their well being, which is the main thrust of our approach.

Source: Owen Lamont, Managing Director, CableTel, interviewed by Jacqui Quinn in *News Letter*, 7 October 1997, Business Section, p. 3. Reprinted by permission.

Key point 1.2 Benefits of effective communication practices

- Increased productivity.
- Higher quality of services and products.
- More staff suggestions.
- Higher levels of creativity.
- Greater employee job satisfaction.
- Decreased absenteeism.
- Reduced staff turnover.
- Less industrial unrest and fewer strikes.
- Reduced costs.

Key point 1.3 Best communication practices in top companies

- Clear communication targets are set company-wide, together with accompanying accountabilities for their achievement.
- Regular employee attitude surveys are conducted and the results and action plans widely communicated.
- Senior management have high visibility among all employees – managers make, and take, time to walk and talk with staff.
- Extensive face-to-face and two-way communication is fostered and employees are encouraged to communicate proactively with management; improvement suggestions are rewarded.
- There is a high use of technology, including heavy emphasis on videos and e-mail, to disseminate information and ensure it is understood.
- Communication training is an ongoing activity for all staff.
- All publications are carefully prepared and presented, each bearing in mind the specific purpose, goals and target audience.
- Management bonus takes cognizance of employee evaluations of communication performance and effectiveness.

MANAGEMENT

Let us now turn our attention to that strange creature known as the manager. Put simply, 'A manager is responsible for the work performance of one or more people in an organization'.[1] The plethora of titles for managers reflects the ubiquitous nature of the activity. In our travels we will meet this creature under a range of guises. Titles include supervisor, team leader, division head, chief executive, foreman, dean of faculty, administrative officer, unit co-ordinator, production manager, school principal, bishop, master chef, director of research, prime minister and president. Equally, staff may be called by different titles such as crew members (at McDonald's), associates (CableTel), cast members (Disney World), partners, colleagues, parish priests, shopfloor workers, employees, academics, technicians, secretarial staff and so on. The term used by an organization to describe its employees often reflects its position on the continuum from highly interpersonal and harmonious to highly authoritarian and discordant, which in turn affects employee satisfaction and productivity.

Managers can be divided into two broad categories – those who manage shopfloor workers, and those who manage managers. The former are first-line managers, who have titles such as section leader, floor manager or supervisor. They are the managers to whom a section of the workforce are immediately responsible on a day-to-day basis. In turn, they report to middle managers, who hold positions such as head of computer section, sales manager or marketing co-ordinator. At the top of the hierarchy are senior managers, in positions such as deputy director, chief executive or vice-chancellor.

Managers at all levels engage in four main types of activity:[1]

- *Planning* – deciding priorities, setting time-objectives and targets, and devising action plans to meet organizational goals.
- *Organizing* – the manager directs and co-ordinates the work of staff, makes decisions about their actual duties, monitors expenditure and allocates tasks to individuals and teams.
- *Leading* – motivating staff to work to their optimum level, directing and appraising them as they carry out tasks, maintaining good working relationships, and allocating rewards and sanctions to ensure compliance.
- *Evaluating* – in order to assess whether organizational goals have been met, outputs and work performance need to be measured, compared to the set targets, corrective action implemented to meet shortfalls and new plans devised as necessary.

Communication is involved at all four stages but is central to the organizing and leading phases of the management process.

Forrest identified five directions in which managers must employ their skills – upwards, downwards, across, outwards and self (see Figure 1.1).[10] Communication is necessary in each of the first four. Managers have to communicate effectively in writing, meeting face to face, and on the telephone, with superiors, subordinates, peers and people outside the organization. Furthermore, different forms of interaction will be required for each direction. An air of confidence is needed when managing staff, a more deprecating style may be appropriate when reporting to senior managers, a co-operative approach is best with colleagues and a professional manner should be displayed with customers.

Style of management is perhaps the ingredient which most determines the success of the organizational mix. Management can be regarded as a continuum between two styles.[11] These are:

1. Management by *suppression*. Managers perceive their role as directive. Decisions are taken by management and imposed on subordinates, who are expected to obey orders. Their opinions are regarded as unnecessary at best and subversive at worst, unless they concur absolutely with the version ordained by senior managers. Information is seen as the property of management, and staff are informed on a 'need to know' basis. Communication flows in one direction

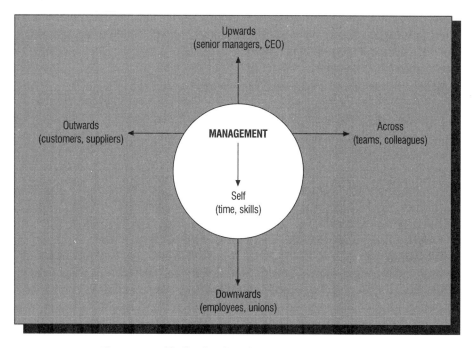

Figure 1.1   The five directions of management communication

only – downwards, and this flow rarely amounts to more than a trickle. This style can be summarized in the maxim 'workers work and managers manage'.

2. Management by *expression*. By contrast, in this style managers seek agreement. Information is not seen as anyone's prerogative, but is shared in such a way as to obtain the most satisfactory outcomes. Communication flows in all directions, and staff opinions are actively solicited and valued. The maxim here is 'working together to make it work'.

This division was recognized by the American psychologist Douglas McGregor, who argued that managers are guided by the assumptions they hold of employees.[12] He identified two diverse perspectives, which he called Theory X and Theory Y. Managers who adhere to Theory X believe that most people dislike work. They are basically lazy, have selfish interests, want to avoid responsibility, do not care about the organization, try to avoid making decisions and prefer to be given firm directions. They adopt a perspective on their dealings with the workforce somewhat similar to that of Lenin who advised: 'Trust them comrades, but check on the buggers!' Theory X managers, therefore, check up continually on people's work and enforce a rigorous system of control, backed up by threats and punishment. By contrast, Theory Y takes a much more benevolent view of human nature. The belief is that most people are responsible, wish to take an interest in their organization, and are eminently capable of self-direction. Given a conducive working environment, they actively seek responsibility, are industrious, like to make decisions and want to feel part of the organization. Theory Y managers do not threaten or coerce. They give employees encouragement to contribute, the freedom to be creative, and considerable delegated power and responsibility. By so doing, staff will give value-added performance in return.

Iron managers, from the Theory X school, who rule by suppression are likely to suffer from metal fatigue in the face of the corrosive power of continual negative staff reactions. Consensus management is eminently preferable. The Theory Y, management by expression, approach is characterized by the flow of communication in all directions, participative decision-making and a high degree of informality. Managers using this style are supportive listeners who ascertain and address the needs and concerns of staff, and discuss social as well as task matters. Actions which cannot be negotiated (e.g. legislative requirements) are fully explained. Organizations are seen as communicative systems whose effectiveness is dependent on good human relationships. All staff are encouraged to become active partners in the working enterprise, and to contribute to the operation. Success is a team game where all the players kick the ball rather than each another.

The Theory X style is no longer acceptable. Communication programmes in the past were often simply concerned with announcing management conclusions, and ensuring that management messages were both comprehensible and delivered to all relevant staff. This will not suffice, since the following objectives have also been shown to be of great importance:[13]

- Stimulation of thinking, participation and ideas.
- Networking of know-how and learning across the organization.
- Involvement of *all* staff in improving process.
- Identification of ways of providing added value to customers.
- Expansion of what all employees believe is possible.

To illustrate the validity of these points, let us take another short excursion, this time to a plant in General Motors (GM), to look at the effects of the introduction of a coherent, structured communication programme. Our guides here are McKeans[14] and Smith.[15] The GM programme included the following steps:

- Motivating senior colleagues to read about the basics of effective internal communications, so that at the outset they appreciated what the programme was about and the benefits which could accrue.
- Improving the existing newsletter, and introducing other publications including one jointly written and funded with trade union organizations.
- Setting up a communications review group which met monthly to review performance.
- Producing a quarterly video news magazine which was shown during working hours in scheduled meetings. This allowed managers to present business information on camera. These presentations served as a launch pad for subsequent discussions between supervisors and staff.
- Scheduling regular face-to-face meetings between managers and randomly selected small groups of staff, with the express purpose of facilitating open discussion on key issues.
- Implementing audits to track and chart the impact of the programme.

Performance improvements at this GM facility were quite dramatic:

- Within seven years sales had doubled.
- Budget savings were 2.8 per cent in the first year, 4.9 per cent in the second, then 3.2 per cent and 3.7 per cent.
- Within six years delays in delivering service parts had been eliminated.
- Suggestion savings per employee were $864 in the first year, $1 220 in the second year, then $1 306, $1 741 and $5 748.
- Before the programme began less than 50 per cent of GM employees said they believed the information supplied by management. After four years of the programme in operation, this figure had risen to over 80 per cent.

While no causal link can be proved in such interventions, it seems more than likely that the communications programme contributed to much of this improvement. A notable aspect of this case study is that the measures adopted were simple to implement, yet their effects were significant.

STAFF VIEWS ON COMMUNICATION

A range of staff surveys[8, 9, 16] have revealed four main features that staff value in terms of communication.

ACCESS TO INFORMATION

Employees want to be kept fully informed about important issues, especially those having a direct bearing on their jobs. Where this does not occur, they feel underinformed and undervalued. If there is an information shortfall, the bush telegraph works overtime to fill it, and credence is given to gossip buzzing along the lines. As communications deteriorate, staff tune in to the rumour mill, especially where they are subjected to the 'mushroom' method of management (kept in the dark and covered periodically with manure!). To prevent worst-case grapevine stories contaminating the organization, firm and credible communication channels must be established for the rapid dissemination of information. In organizations spread across geographical locations particular efforts need to be made to avoid this pitfall.

INFORMATIVE LINE MANAGERS

Satisfaction with communication is highest when staff feel they have good immediate line managers. In particular they appreciate managers who listen, share information openly, run meetings regularly and well, explain what is happening within the company, give regular feedback on performance in a sensitive manner, and seem to *care* for their staff.

UPWARD COMMUNICATION

Staff attach considerable significance to upward communication. In particular, they wish to report on initiatives taken in their area and request any information necessary for them to do their jobs effectively. They should therefore be encouraged to 'speak up' and managers should not get into a habit of 'talking down'. There should be a climate in which bottom-up communication is fostered and seen as positive. Regular staff attitude surveys and suggestions schemes are valued by staff who appreciate the opportunity to express their views on the organization. Information provided should be acted on, especially by senior managers.

Staff consistently express a strong preference for face-to-face communication with managers, yet in many organizations continue to rely heavily on written communication. Senior managers have frequently been encouraged to engage in activities designed to increase their 'visibility' and encourage communication with the workforce – for example, 'management by walking about'. However, there are several drawbacks to the latter approach. When prior notice is given, the manager is given special treatment and the exercise becomes something akin to a 'royal visit' with the decks being scrubbed and the desks polished before the senior manager 'inspects' the area. This becomes 'management by walking past!' Conversely, when the senior person arrives unannounced, such informal contacts may be viewed with suspicion by staff, interpreting this as a form of 'snooping'.

One solution is for senior managers to arrange regular meetings with groups of staff at which there is an opportunity for any issue to be raised. There should be a formal informality about these contacts – they should be round table, over coffee, for a set period (no more than one hour), beginning with a brief statement from the senior manager and opening out to allow anyone to raise any topic. This not only allows senior executives to 'address the troops', but also helps to foster a sense of openness and accessibility within the organization. There is a cathartic effect in meeting and being listened to by those in positions of power and this should be facilitated.

TRAINING

Staff recognize the importance of training in communication skills. They consistently express a wish for such training personally, and report a lack of effective interpersonal skills in their managers. Communication skills training, which has been shown to be effective across a range of professional contexts,[17] should be organization specific and should incorporate how interactions can be conducted in the most supportive and encouraging manner. Management development programmes should include the skills covered in this book.

Some of the other findings regarding communication are that:

- Staff readily assimilate information delivered on video – we live in the video age.
- Noticeboards are useful if they are located close to where staff work and are kept up to date and tidy – a specific member of staff should be given the responsibility for each particular board.
- Special display boards suddenly appearing in a central area of the workplace are a useful promotional device, since they secure instant attention – though if overused this medium loses its novelty appeal.
- Factsheets or bulletin sheets which deal with section-relevant information are preferred to glossy company newsletters containing more general information about the organization as a whole.

- Memoranda attached to payslips are read, but staff do not like this to be used as a regular channel – there is resentment about continual interference with what is seen as a personal correspondence.

In relation to employee satisfaction, the Gallup Poll organization has produced a scale (which they term Q12) comprising 12 questions which are rated by staff on a one to five scale. These are:

1. I know what is expected of me at work.
2. I have the materials and equipment I need to do my work right.
3. At work I have the opportunity to do what I do best every day.
4. In the last seven days I have received recognition or praise for good work.
5. My supervisor or someone at work seems to care about me as a person.
6. There is someone at work who encourages my development.
7. In the last six months, someone at work has talked to me about my progress.
8. At work, my opinions seem to count.
9. The mission/purpose of my company makes me feel my job is important.
10. My associates (fellow employees) are committed to doing quality work.
11. I have a best friend at work.
12. This last year, I have had opportunities at work to learn and grow.

As can be seen, much of this Q12 scale relates to communication by managers. From its database of surveys of more than one million employees in the USA,[18] Gallup found a significant link between scores on this scale and business performance. Organizations where staff scored highly outperformed their rivals on measures of productivity such as employee retention (by 22 per cent), profitability (28 per cent) and customer satisfaction (38 per cent). This again underscores the importance of good internal communications.

WHAT IS COMMUNICATION?

If we are to improve communication, we must first understand the process itself. In social science terminology communication is 'The scientific study of the production, processing and effects of signal and symbol systems used by humans to send and receive messages'.[19] This definition highlights three main dimensions:

1. Communication is amenable to scientific characterization. It is a process which is open to measurement, analysis, evaluation and improvement.
2. The study of communication centres on how messages are produced, how they are then processed or delivered (for example by face-to-face interaction, in writing or through technological mediation), and what effects they have on those who receive them.

3. The importance of signs and symbols is emphasized. All interpersonal behaviour potentially serves a communicative function and is judged on the basis both of verbal content and non-verbal signals. The overt message may be less important than the hidden meaning, or 'subtext'. For example, a manager may express support for a policy of informal dress on Fridays but, by personally arriving every Friday in full formal regalia, sends the signal that conventional apparel is preferred.

These elements of the communication process occur at four levels, namely intrapersonal, interpersonal, network/organizational and macrosocietal.

Intrapersonal communication is concerned with what goes on 'inside' the person – with the study of how individuals process, store and produce communication messages. This includes the elements of perception, cognition, emotion, beliefs, attitudes, self-image and self-awareness. How we interpret the behaviour of others and respond is shaped by these internal processes. If a manager believes that workers are inherently lazy and dishonest and need to be constantly scrutinized, this belief system will inevitably affect how the actions of individual staff are interpreted.

At the *interpersonal* level the focus is on the study of communicative relationships in one-to-one and group contexts. It includes the analysis of relationship development, maintenance and breakdown, the development of communicative ability and skills, communication dysfunction and the study of professional communication. While there is some debate about the exact nature of the process, it can be argued[20] that interpersonal communication is:

1. *Inevitable*, in that when we are in the presence of others we have to communicate. Even by saying nothing we are making a 'statement' non-verbally. The senior manager who appears unexpectedly on the shopfloor at different times of the day, says nothing, but carefully watches workers in action for five minutes, makes some notes on a sheet of paper and then leaves, is also making a 'statement'.
2. *Purposeful.* There is usually a reason for interaction, with the interactors pursuing definite goals. People may not be consciously aware of their goals as they communicate, but these nevertheless guide actions. The best managers will be more aware of the goals they are trying to achieve, and of what they need to do next to be successful.
3. *Transactional.* When we interact we simultaneously send and receive messages in a continuous process of mutual influence and adjustment. Manager and employee concurrently monitor the actions and reactions of one other as they interact, and moment by moment responses are affected by the ongoing behaviour of both parties.
4. *Multidimensional.* Communication occurs on many levels simultaneously. There is the actual content of conversation itself, but linked to this is the way in which it is discussed. Respect, liking and relational power are but three of the aspects

communicated by interactors. For instance, a common goal of employees is to impress their manager. Self-presentation and impression management concerns are therefore universal in organizations.

5. *Irreversible*, so that once we make an utterance or a non-verbal behaviour (e.g. a particular facial expression) we cannot hit the picture search reverse button and erase it. As the Roman poet Horace expressed it: 'Words once spoken can never be recalled.' We can apologize for what we have said or done, but in a very real sense the damage remains. Initial care with words and actions prevents lasting hurt and damaged relationships.

The third communication level is the *network and organizational* realm. Here, larger groups of persons are studied in the context of ongoing relationships. This encompasses the study of group norms and how they are developed, disseminated and enforced; the formation of organizational identity and its expression through symbols; value formation and the diffusion of values internally and also their external expression; formal and informal communication channels and networks; rewards and sanctions; processes which facilitate bonding and a sense of belonging; and the development of corporate image. The past decade has witnessed an explosion of interest by communication scholars in the world of work. Likewise, organizations are increasingly aware of the benefits of effective internal and external communications.

The final communication route leads to the *macrosocietal* or *mass* level – the communication properties and activities of large social systems. Examples of events studied at this level include: the nature, role, production and effects of the mass media; political structures and networks; dissemination and expression of national values, norms and identity; and the diffusion and continuity of language and culture.

THE ELEMENTS OF COMMUNICATION

As our gaze sweeps across the wider vistas of communication, we can observe a number of peaks which define the terrain. We shall now analyse each of these.

COMMUNICATORS

Communicators refer to the people involved. Personal attributes such as the age, gender, dress, physique and disposition of those involved influence both our own actions and our reactions to the behaviour of others.[17] An important attribute is what Goleman[21] termed 'emotional intelligence'. After examining studies involving hundreds of large organizations, he concluded that it was this dimension which characterized star performers. Emotional intelligence includes the ability to persuade and motivate others, to empathize and build relationships, to handle one's own and other people's emotions, to give open and honest feedback sensitively, to form alliances, to monitor one's own behaviour and to read organizational politics. It refers to the core skills of social awareness and communication. A working knowledge and understanding of the material covered in the present book will therefore enhance the reader's emotional intelligence.

MESSAGES

Messages are the signals and symbols which we use to convey what we mean. Communication messages are usually delivered in a visual, auditory, tactile or olfactory format. We are more conscious of the first three. Visual messages include written communication, as well as all of the non-verbal modes (clothes, jewellery, facial expressions, gestures, and so on) prevalent in social encounters. Auditory communication may be face to face or by telephone. Tactile communication refers to the use of touch and bodily contact (handshakes, hugs, kisses). Finally, olfactory messages include the use of perfumes, after-shaves, deodorants and all the other types of scent which serve to disguise our natural body odours and project a certain image.

CHANNEL

Channel describes both the medium and the means used to deliver messages. The 'means' of communication would include face to face, telephone, pager, written (fax, e-mail, snail mail, newsletter), radio and video. In face-to-face contact, communication occurs through the medium of the visual, auditory and olfactory channels, while the tactile channel may or may not come into play. A skilled communicator will select, and maximize the use of, the channel most appropriate to the achievement of the goals being pursued, bearing in mind that staff tend to prefer face-to-face communication with managers.[16]

NOISE

Noise is the term used to describe anything which distorts or interferes with meanings and messages. This includes:

- *physical noise* such as a pneumatic drill outside a window as you try to deliver a presentation or indeed the noticeable whispers of some members of the audience
- *psychological noise* such as the personal biases or stereotypes which influence how you 'hear' what a particular person (for example a racial minority member) is saying

- *semantic noise* where the actual meaning of what is being communicated becomes distorted due to language or cultural differences between the communicators.

While some degree of noise is inevitable in communication, the objective should be to reduce this to an absolute minimum.

FEEDBACK

Feedback allows us to evaluate our performance. We receive feedback both from the verbal and non-verbal reactions of others, and from our own responses. This latter process, which is known as 'self-monitoring', involves being aware of what we say and do in social encounters and of its effect on others. Skilled communicators are high self-monitors who continuously analyse and regulate their own behaviour in relation to the responses of others. The messages we receive have to be decoded or interpreted by us. Meaning is not an inherent quality of the message *per se*, but rather is something which is constructed in the mind of the recipient. For example, what we intended to be positive managerial feedback may be misconstrued as negative or patronizing. Likewise, feedback may be ignored altogether and, indeed, certain managers seem oblivious to the messages coming from staff – and to their meanings!

CONTEXT

Communication does not occur in a vacuum. Rather it is embedded within a particular context, which in turn will have a major impact on behaviour. A manager will behave totally differently when disciplining a member of staff in the office, as opposed to when calling at the home of the same person following the death of a child. In each case, the situation shapes the responses.

Culture is an aspect of organizational life that has been the focal point of much discussion and research.[22] There are four main aspects of organizational culture:[23]

- *Values* represent the philosophy and outlook of the organization, and employees are expected to share the corporate beliefs and behave accordingly. A broad distinction is often made between Eastern cultures which comprise collectivist values and Western cultures which are more individualistic. The former have tended to foster interdependence or a 'We' mentality, with importance placed on aspects such as roles, position, status, fitting in, being accepted and not offending the other's sensibilities. The latter encourage independence and an 'I' outlook, involving self-expression, assertiveness, and being 'up front'. However, care needs to be taken in generalizing these concepts, since in Eastern cultures there are people who are primarily individualistic in nature, while in Western society there are those who are more collectivist in outlook.

17

- *Heroes* are those members who best typify the company's values. They are the organizational equivalent of the guru or evangelist. Thus, Richard Branson epitomizes the dynamic, forward-looking and customer-oriented style of Virgin, while Bill Gates reflects the creative, laid back, yet serious about business, philosophy of Microsoft.
- *Rituals* are the symbolic ceremonies which are performed to celebrate and reinforce the organization's values. Employee of the month awards, aerobic exercises for staff before store opening, and university graduation ceremonies are all examples of rituals.
- *Networks* are the informal channels which are used to indoctrinate staff into accepting prevailing norms. The staff bowling club, a particular table in the canteen, or the pub down the road after work, are all situations where informal contacts are made, work roles and expectations are discussed, and gossip, opinions and information are exchanged.

With rapid developments in all forms of communication the world is now in many senses a global business village. Yet, differences in culture persist and are of great importance. Meanings can differ widely, as many multinational companies have discovered. For example, when Ford introduced the Pinto model in Brazil it flopped. The company, on discovering that Pinto was Brazilian slang for 'tiny male genitals', quickly changed the name to Corcel (horse). An awareness of cultural norms, meanings and values is clearly important to business success.[24] At a simple level, staff in those telephone call centres in the USA that handle consumer calls from the UK have to learn to refer to post codes rather than zip codes, and pounds and pence rather than dollars and cents. Furthermore, techniques which work in one society may be anathema in another. For example, it has been well illustrated[25] how consultants frequently recommend various business philosophies (or fads) which while appropriate at one time or in one culture yield disaster when implemented in another.

THE STRUCTURE OF THIS BOOK

This book contains a wealth of information about communication in management. It is divided into chapters, each dealing with a different facet of the managerial role. To avoid unnecessary duplication we do at times cross-refer to material explained more fully in a different chapter, but the intention is that each chapter is self-contained. Thus, before conducting an appraisal interview the manager can turn to Chapter 13, when planning a presentation the information is contained in Chapter 5, and so on. At the same time, when taken as a whole, the book offers a wide panorama of communication in action.

To continue with our analogy, in the course of our travels the attractions you will encounter as you explore each chapter are:

- *The persuasion river*. One of the main functions of verbal and non-verbal communication is to exert influence. Indeed, to be successful, managers must be persons of influence. The persuasion river runs across a variety of methods – both subtle and sometimes less subtle – which can be used to influence others. The core influencing and persuading strategies are summarized in Chapter 2, and the application of these techniques in one-to-one and small group situations explained. One important subsection here is the role of relationship-building skills in successful influence. To borrow a well-known book title, managers need to know how to win friends and influence people.

- *Team games*. Winning organizations develop effective teams for the specific game they have to play. Managers must ensure that staff actually feel they are part of the team, rather than feeling like substitutes on the bench or, even worse, spectators in the stand. Techniques for fostering the development of cohesive teams are the focal point of Chapter 3. It examines the stages involved in the formation of teams, the establishment of team identity, ways of encouraging loyalty, the role of 'celebration' and 'treats', and decision-making processes.

- *Leadership peaks*. It is true that the fewer the moving parts the less chance there is of anything breaking down. However, in large organizations delegation is inevitable. People must be given responsibility for specific areas of work, and for other staff. Meetings, while often portrayed as the *bête noire* of business, are unavoidable and, like the poor, they will always be with us. Indeed, there is considerable evidence[8,15] that staff wish to be consulted and have their say on decisions being taken. It has been said that meetings take minutes and waste hours but, as Chapter 4 illustrates, with effective leadership skills this is not the case. By climbing the leadership peaks, through gaining a knowledge of the key skills involved, managers will be able to chair useful (and even enjoyable) meetings.

- *The presentation performance*. Studies of adult fears consistently show that having to give a formal presentation is rated as one of the most feared activities in life.[26] Standing on your hind legs and performing in front of others considerably raises levels of anxiety. Yet, as discussed above, the main skills of effective public speaking have been analysed and written about for some 5000 years. There is no mystery about how to be successful in oral presentations – the expected performance can be well planned. Chapter 5 incorporates an analysis of presentational skills both in small groups (e.g. committees) and with larger audiences. It also offers useful advice on relaxation and anxiety-reducing techniques for those for whom stress may become distress.

- *The negotiation match*. Managers have to negotiate and bargain with their own staff as well as with those from other organizations. Indeed, these are important strategies in everyday life. Managers must understand the differences between negotiating and bargaining, and be cognizant with the different approaches to negotiation (such as win-lose, win-win). To be successful in the negotiating match the manager needs to be familiar with methods for producing concessions. The core skills and strategies of effective negotiation are detailed in Chapter 6.

- *The sales challenge*. Chapter 7 deals with the skills of selling. However, this chapter is not intended just for salespeople. Rather, it concentrates on selling as a challenge which all managers face regularly – selling ideas, enthusiasm, commitment and on occasions selling themselves. The well-established sales model of opening, establishing needs, presenting, overcoming objections, making additional points and closing, is presented as a template for action in many business situations.

- *Telephone land*. The fact that telephone calls are almost always much briefer than equivalent face-to-face encounters means that managers must know how to use this medium to best effect given the reduced time frame. Chapter 8 provides information on the norms of behaviour in telephone land, and outlines the communication differences between conversations on the telephone as opposed to face to face. It also deals with how best to make and receive calls, ways of facilitating immediacy, techniques for making impact, and advice on how to overcome what has been termed the 'coffee and biscuits problem' of the other communicator not actually being physically present.

- *Written plains*. The main differences between written communication and the spoken word are outlined in Chapter 9 where the specific requirements of the former are highlighted. This chapter includes an analysis of reports, letters, e-mail, memoranda and the design of forms. The role of fonts, spacing, diagrams, illustrations, forms of emphasis, abstracts, subsections, appendices and structure will all be examined. Given increased litigation, the importance of written information on appraisal forms, letters of reference, etc. will also be emphasized.

- *Assertion state*. Assertion is a state of mind rather than a trait of the individual. While once thought of as an American fad which had little applicability in Europe, assertiveness is now widely recognized as a skill necessary to the effective management of relationships. Standing up for one's own rights while recognizing the rights of others takes skill and tact. Assertive managers carefully tread the middle ground between aggression and submission. The techniques for achieving this are discussed in Chapter 10, where assertion as a response style is explained and distinguished from aggressiveness and submissiveness. The impact of factors such as situation, gender and beliefs is also discussed.

- *The helping melodrama*. Managers will sometimes have to deal with very sensitive personal issues. At times of crisis such as divorce, serious illness or bereavement, staff may need and wish to share the problems and concerns raised by these melodramas. When handled skilfully these helping encounters can enable the individual to cope better, while also strengthening the bond of loyalty and trust between manager and staff. Skills of reflection, listening, empathy and rewarding are analysed in the context of a helping format in Chapter 11.

- *Selection reefs*. When navigating the selection waters, care must be taken to avoid the many reefs on which decisions can flounder. In recent years there has been a great deal of research into the effectiveness of the employment interview and the identification of the main selection errors. These findings are summarized in Chapter 12. This is an important stage in any organization since the selection of staff involves a huge investment of money over a period of years and therefore mistakes can be very costly. At the same time, managers will also on some occasions be interviewees and so this chapter examines the selection process from the two perspectives of interviewing and being interviewed.

- *Appraisal mountain*. The appraisal precipice is one which must be climbed by manager and staff member acting in unison. Two important employee questions are 'How am I doing?' and 'Does anybody care?' Formal and informal appraisals offer an ideal opportunity to answer both, as well as allowing staff to answer the management question 'What can we do to help you do better?' Systems of appraisal are now part of the managerial operation of most organizations. The differences between and functions of appraisal, performance evaluation and discipline interviews are discussed in Chapter 13. An overview of research findings regarding appraisal systems is provided. The structure and content of this type of interview are outlined, together with the use of pro formas and the participation of the interviewee in the process.

- *Non-verbal world*. When we remove words from communication we enter a fascinating and at times strange world, where signs and symbols take on special meanings. More than any other aspect of communication, body language has attracted enormous interest and a torrent of research. We can derive considerable information from an analysis of personal space and touch, the way people orient themselves towards others, the manner and style in which offices are laid out, the facial expressions people adopt, how they dress, the postures they take up, their gestures and the patterns of their gaze. Chapter 14 takes the reader on a guided tour of this non-verbal world. The main functions of non-verbal communication are explained, the different types of non-verbal behaviour are charted, and clear guidelines are provided for managers wishing to use this often subconscious and subliminal communication channel more effectively.

- *The tour summary*. A concluding chapter ties together the various strands contained in the book. Most managers will have a 'feel' for how good communication is in their organization. However, this feel is often far from accurate, and so ways in which communication can be objectively measured using the audit approach will be explained. The chapter will also explore the ethical dimensions of organizational communication.

SUMMARY

It is clear that communication is of great importance to organizational life. Managers with good interpersonal skills will be better able to interact appropriately with staff at all levels. Research indicates that many benefits accrue. Working relationships are enhanced and staff feel a greater sense of belonging to the organization. A positive team spirit prevails and there is an increased readiness to innovate. As well as greater job satisfaction there are benefits in terms of reduced costs and higher levels of profit.

Yet, there is nothing mysterious or esoteric about good communication. Indeed, communication is now a recognized social science discipline in which a voluminous amount of literature has been published. A great deal of research and study has been carried out in the interpersonal and organizational domains, and the main skills, techniques and strategies which enhance social encounters have been charted. These are discussed in detail in the following chapters. As we end this chapter we will also use our final travel analogy – enjoy the trip!

2 The gentle art of persuasion: influencing others

> If you want to win a man to your cause, you must first convince him you are his friend.
>
> *Abraham Lincoln*

> Wicked men obey from fear; good men from love.
>
> *Aristotle*

The main attribute of good management is the ability to influence and persuade others to behave in certain ways. The *Chambers English Dictionary* defines a manager as 'one who organizes other people's doings'. To organize staff it is necessary to ensure that they complete specific tasks, behave in certain ways with other staff and with customers, and meet set targets. This does not mean that managers should be like little Hitlers, goose-stepping around the workplace and barking out orders which must be obeyed at all times. An important aspect of persuasion is the ability to gently encourage people and convince them (often in subtle ways) that your point of view has merit. Persuasion has been defined[1] as a process of 'guiding people towards the adoption of some behaviour, belief or attitude preferred by the persuader through reasoning or emotional appeals'.

The terms 'influence' and 'persuasion' are often used as synonyms. However, when we attempt to persuade others we do so consciously, whereas we can influence others unintentionally. For example, a pop star who smokes a cigarette during a television show may unintentionally influence young viewers to believe that it is 'cool' to smoke – yet no overt or conscious persuasion attempt was being made. A manager may *persuade* staff to work until 8.00 p.m. by openly asking them to do so, by offering them special rewards for so doing, by leaving dated/timed requests for information on the desks of those who have left earlier, or by only involving staff who stay late in important projects. A similar *influence* may well be effected simply by the manager always working to 8.00 p.m., thereby acting as a powerful role model which other staff feel compelled to emulate.

Persuasion techniques are used to achieve five main outcomes:

- *Adoption.* The aim here is to encourage the adoption of new responses – to persuade others to *start doing it*. This may involve retraining – for example, when a new computer system is being introduced.
- *Continuance.* Here, efforts are expended to reinforce existing responses; in other words to persuade others to *keep doing something*. When people are performing well, steps should be taken to maintain this level of performance. Such steps may include praise from managers as well as material rewards (bonuses, awards).
- *Deterrence.* The goal is to deter others from starting a new practice – that is to ensure that they *do not start doing it*. A company with an all male staff which is about to recruit females may run equality awareness seminars to explain to the existing workforce exactly what constitutes harassment, what the implications of such behaviour will be, and to prevent it from happening.
- *Discontinuance.* In this case the objective is to discourage existing responses – to persuade others to *stop doing something*. This is often very difficult, since 'old habits die hard', and once existing patterns of behaviour become habituated they are very resistant to change.
- *Improvement.* In this instance the purpose is to encourage greater efforts, that is to get staff to *do it better*. If existing targets are not being met in terms of quality or volume, then efforts need to be expended to rectify this situation.

Not all attempts at persuasion are successful. There are two main outcomes from any attempts by managers to persuade staff (Figure 2.1). First, the undertaking can

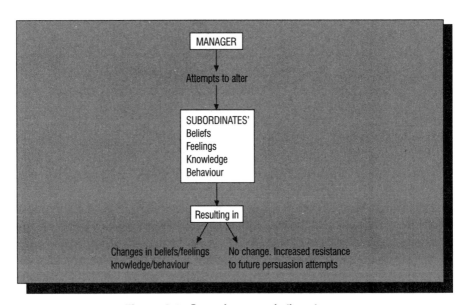

Figure 2.1 Persuasive communication outcomes

be successful. Second, it may fail, in which case a boomerang effect can occur with the target person likely to be more resistant to any future attempts at influence on this particular issue.

There is also a process known as 'inoculation', whereby the target becomes 'resistant' to and rejects a particular persuasion attempt. Managers can use this technique to strengthen their staff's resistance to persuasive messages from other sources, by providing them with relevant counter-arguments in advance. For example, if a manager is aware that rumours about closure are about to appear in the press, this could be countered by alerting staff to the fact that the story will be published and providing details of company expansion plans, to illustrate that the story is false.

Where an effort to persuade is particularly badly handled, the messenger may also be contaminated in that credibility is lost and the target becomes generally resistant to any future influence attempts by this person.

It is not always realistic to expect immediate compliance with persuasion attempts. There is what is known as the 'sleeper effect', whereby the target person initially rejects the attempt, yet after a period of time spent 'sleeping on it' eventually accepts the message. Such acceptance may be a subconscious process of incubation, with the arguments gradually sinking in to effect change. Thus, managers whose first persuasion effort fails should not despair. Given time, attitudes can and do change.

Successful long-term persuasion involves a number of sequential stages (Key point 2.1). These begin with the initial exposure to the message, and progress through attending to it, understanding it, remembering it and eventually adopting it. A distinction has been made[2] between *private acceptance* where an influence attempt leads to changes in your attitudes or beliefs, and *public compliance* which involves simply changing your behaviour without altering your internal attitudes. People can feign attitude change and display what they perceive to be expected behaviour. For instance, a highly autocratic manager may influence staff to behave in certain ways, through fear. However, at the first opportunity these staff will take delight in behaving in the contrary style. In other words, they will have internalized a resistance to that which they are forced to do. For enduring change, private acceptance is necessary, and so the goal of persuasion should be to alter attitudes as well as behaviour.

Key point 2.1   Sequential stages in persuasion

1. Exposure to the message.
2. Attending to the message.
3. Becoming interested in it.
4. Understanding it.
5. Learning how to process and use it.
6. Yielding to it.
7. Memorizing it.
8. Retrieving it when required.
9. Using it when making decisions.
10. Carrying out these decisions.
11. Reinforcing the actions.
12. Consolidating the decision based upon the success of the actions.

Source: Adapted from McGuire, W. J. (1981) Theoretical foundations of campaigns, in R. Rice and W. Paisley (eds) *Public Communication Campaigns*, Beverley Hills: Sage.

Exercise 2.1   Persuasive people

Think of the individual whom you regard as the most persuasive person you know. This should be someone who has successfully influenced you *personally*. What is it about this individual that gives them the power to persuade you? What interactive style does this person use with you and with others? How does this person present arguments? What is it about the presentation that makes it convincing? How does this person present him or herself in terms of dress, body furniture (watch, rings, necklace, bracelets, spectacles, ear studs), hairstyle and make-up? How do these contribute to the image?

A knowledge of the range of influencing tactics which can be used to increase compliance is clearly of importance for managers. The ancient Greek philosopher Aristotle was the first person to present a comprehensive analysis of persuasion. He categorized persuasion attempts as being of three types: those which emphasize the rationality of the message (*logos*), those which evoke the emotions of the listener (*pathos*), and those which underline the credibility of the persuader (*ethos*). These are now known respectively as *logical proofs*, *emotional proofs* and *personal proofs*. When using persuasion we can implement techniques from each area to maximize our case.

LOGICAL PROOFS

An appeal to reason and logic is the cornerstone of many persuasion efforts.[3] It is therefore useful to examine strategies which can maximise the impact of this approach.

LOGICAL ARGUMENT

Reason has been defined[4] as 'a strategy of influencing which relies on the presentation of data and information as the basis for a logical argument that supports a request'. There are well-established features of arguments, and of the way they are delivered, which increase their persuasive power (see Chapter 6):

- The message should be fully *comprehensible* – the meaning must be clear and unambiguous.
- The important aspects of the argument should be *emphasized*.
- The *advantages* of the recommended course of action, and the *disadvantages* of the alternatives, should be firmly stated and supporting evidence cited.
- Presentations benefit from the use of *case studies*, which has been shown to be a powerful technique for effecting influence.
- Whether the disadvantages of the recommended course of action should also be mentioned depends on the situation (see Key point 2.2). This is referred to as *sidedness* in message delivery. Two-sided messages while emphasizing the positive aspects of the message also recognize negatives, whereas one-sided messages are partisan and only accentuate the positive.
- Clear *conclusions* should be evident to the listeners.

Key point 2.2   Sidedness in message delivery

Two-sided messages are more effective with:

- those who are initially opposed to the message
- those with a higher IQ
- attempts to refute what the listeners have been told earlier
- those who will hear the opposing views later.

One-sided messages are more effective with:

- those who already support the message
- those with a lower IQ.

REPETITION

There is truth in the maxim 'something worth saying is worth repeating'. However, in management contexts, research has shown[5] that managers do not rate *persistent* tactics – which involve repeated reminders, continually checking up on whether something has been done and becoming a nuisance – to be advantageous. Instead *insistent* tactics, whereby requests are made in a firm, assertive fashion, are viewed as more beneficial (see Chapter 10). The lesson is that repetition needs to be used with care. When presenting a reasoned argument, it is useful to underline the main points through judicious repetition. However, someone who bombards others with repeated reminders of requests is liable to be seen simply as a pest!

RECIPROCATION

One way to exert influence is to use the 'trade-off' method, through an exchange of favours. This may take the form of *pre-giving* where the target person is 'buttered-up' by being given rewards before any requests are made. Persuasion is easier when both sides make reciprocal concessions, as opposed to the expectation that they should be one-way only. An exchange norm operates in human encounters, since we do not like to feel in debt to others. If someone buys us a drink in a bar, we feel obliged to buy a round of drinks in return. If someone discloses a piece of personal information to us, we feel under pressure to tell them something about ourselves. This tactic is used by sales companies when they give away free samples of their goods in the knowledge that this will (often dramatically) increase their sales.

The exchange norm increases the pressure on others to reciprocate, since they tend to feel indebted to the giver. In this way we are more likely to accede to requests from those who have previously done something for us. An alternative approach to reciprocation is *to make a promise* ('You do this for me now, I will do that for you later') before requesting something. Promises are more likely to be fulfilled where there is an existing close and trusting relationship between the interactors.

SCALE OF THE REQUEST

Two separate strategies have been identified in terms of scale of request. The first is *door-in-the-face* (DIF). This tactic involves initially making a large request, knowing that it will probably be rejected. The ensuing refusal is then followed by a scaled down request. This will often meet with more success since the target feels under pressure to reciprocate what appears to be a concession (indeed the DIF technique is also known as 'reciprocation of concessions') – the lesser request looks much more reasonable in comparison to its predecessor. For example, if a manager wants staff to work overtime for one evening, a DIF strategy would be to ask them initially to work overtime every evening for one week. When this is refused, the target request is introduced as a concession.

The second tactic is *foot-in-the-door* (FID). A small initial request is made and, if successful, further requests gradually increasing in size are made. Continuing with the above example, the manager may initially ask a member of staff to work overtime for one hour. When this is agreed the manager returns later, says how good it was for the person to agree to work overtime and how helpful it will be, and then asks if two hours would be a possibility. The FID tactic has been found to be successful providing the costs of later requests are not unduly high.[5]

Research has shown that both FID and DIF are effective sequential influencing strategies.[6] In change management, however, it is generally better to introduce changes gradually and so the FID approach is often most appropriate. In this sense, change has been found to be more likely to succeed when it is evolutionary rather than revolutionary.[7] It should also be 'devolutionary', in that responsibility for, and ownership of, the implementation of change should be cascaded down the hierarchy. We are, in general, more committed to a new course of action if we feel involved in its development.

SCARCITY VALUE

The scarcity principle dictates that opportunities become more valuable when their availability is restricted. The more restricted the item the greater its appeal. The fact that old masters are long dead and have produced a fixed number of paintings greatly increases the appeal and price of their works. Gold is scarce and therefore precious. Exclusive clubs charge exorbitant rates (Groucho Marx famously invoked the scarcity principle when he remarked that he would not belong to any club which would have him as a member). Collectors across a wide diversity of fields pay vastly inflated prices for particularly unusual or unique items. Firms publicize 'limited editions', 'time-limited' deals and 'once in a lifetime' offers to increase their appeal, urging customers to 'hurry while stocks last'. Managers can make staff feel important by telling them that the information they are about to receive is restricted and highly confidential.

One tactic used by retail salespeople who see a couple admiring a product in store is to approach them and tell them that the product is out of stock and the one on display has just been sold. This heightens their desire for it until eventually one of the customers asks whether another one could not be obtained. The salesperson, after underlining the difficulty of so doing, gets a commitment from the couple to buy at the display price if the product can possibly be obtained. After 'making some phone calls', hey presto the salesperson returns with a sales invoice having successfully located the item. Interestingly, at this point in the transaction it has been found that the customers' desire for the product decreases[8] but by then it is too late because they have made the commitment to purchase.

The effect of scarcity on behaviour has been explained in terms of what psychologists call *reactance theory*. Once something becomes scarce, our freedom of choice becomes threatened with restriction. We react against this threat to our freedoms by having an increased desire to have what has been presented as restricted. This desire is heightened when we are in competition with others for the scarce resource. For instance, people often bid more than they originally intended at auctions where others are bidding against them. Reactance can be seen in children from the age of two. At this age, a toy which is forbidden often provokes the child to scream for it unremittingly, until many parents capitulate in the interests of sanity!

Managers can make something appealing by selling it as a rare opportunity or a scarce resource. Access to the executive washroom, keys to certain doors, a personal computer or a larger office, can all become persuasive devices. Likewise, staff with special or scarce skills are in a position to wield greater influence. A study[9] by the Conference Board of Canada found that one-third of the companies they surveyed adopted special pay strategies to recruit and retain staff with scarce or 'hot' skills (such as computer programmers, scientists, and professionals with special financial knowledge). While 'average' staff received raises of some 2.7 per cent, those with special skills received 4.8 per cent increases.

A variant of the scarcity principle is the appeal of that which is new. Manufacturers repackage products as 'new improved', 'new faster acting', 'new formula' or 'new longer lasting'. They do so because it works – consumers are attracted by the novelty dimension. If something is both novel and scarce it therefore has considerable persuasive potential. Staff are more likely to accept a transfer if it is to a brand new 'think tank' section of the organization which will be limited to a small number of key specialists.

The attraction of a scarce resource can of course be abused. It was Lenin who said, 'Liberty is precious – so precious it must be rationed!'

EMOTIONAL PROOFS

While appeals to reason and logic can be powerful, emotions are also potent determinants of human behaviour. In this sense, appeals to the heart are every bit as potent as appeals to the head. The following are the main emotional aspects associated with persuasion.

THREAT/FEAR

The acceptance by a target of fear or threat messages is effective in influencing attitudes and behaviour.[10] The success of a fear appeal is dependent on four key dimensions:[11]

1. It should really *scare* the target.
2. There should be a *specific recommendation* for overcoming the fear-arousing threat.
3. This recommended action should be accepted as *effective* in removing the threat.
4. The target should feel *confident* about being able to carry out the recommended action.

If all four factors are present, the fear message will be very powerful. Equally, if any one is missing, the potency of the threat is diminished.

Threat and fear are not always successful. This is because at very high levels, fear distracts the target and increases anxiety, leading to a rejection of the message. In using this tactic, managers need to avoid a strategy which may be perceived as bullying their subordinates. The results of such a perception tend to be that the workforce are unhappy, will try to sabotage production and will take any opportunity to retaliate against the autocratic manager – including taking legal action against the bully.

One investigation[12] into the strategies employed by executives attempting to influence their superiors, found that with senior managers who interacted in an attractive fashion (were attentive, friendly, relaxed), reason was used most frequently. With those who interacted in an unattractive style, coalition formation with others to challenge the superior, and appeals to higher authority, were more likely to be used. In other words, the fear/threat tactic will be reciprocated by the workforce, who may also threaten sanctions such as going on strike or resigning.

As a policy, therefore, hectoring and harassment is not to be recommended. This was recognized by Peter Birse, the chairman of a large construction company in England, who had to take steps to change a culture of fear which had developed in his firm.[13] He noted: 'From the friendly family firm I had started in 1970 it had become a back-stabbing operation where managers ruled their fiefdoms with fear. No one learned from mistakes, never mind corrected them: instead there would be a witch hunt for a scapegoat and some poor innocent would be blamed'. Matters came to a head when the number of staff leaving each month reached 65 (out of a total workforce of 1000). Birse set about rooting out the bullies who ruled by fear, until he had 'weeded out the big egos, the arrogant bosses who got by on aggression'. The result was a much happier workforce, greatly reduced staff turnover and a massively increased £400 million annual profit.

AVERSIVE STIMULATION

This tactic involves subjecting the target to unpleasant experiences which are only removed when the requested action is carried out. An extreme instance is the use of physical or psychological torture during interrogation. A more common example is that of nagging by a spouse or child aimed at wearing down the resistance of the target. Advertisers recognize the value of this tactic when they pitch television adverts at children, in the knowledge that they will then continually request the product from their parents – a process termed *pester power*. The insistent manager referred to earlier can be successful by using a mild form of aversive stimulation, though clearly this technique needs to be used carefully lest one becomes labelled as a pest.

CONSISTENCY AND COMMITMENT

The consistency principle is a very powerful force in human behaviour. We like to be viewed as being true to our word and doing what we say – in other words we want to be regarded as *consistent*. Those who change their minds are seen as fickle, indecisive or weak. This means that we are more likely to continue with a course of action once we have made a public declaration of commitment to it. These twin towers of consistency and commitment can be used to 'move' people in a certain direction.

When the 'cooling off period' legislation was brought in to cover sales in various sectors, companies discovered that numerous clients were availing themselves of the opportunity to cancel the sale and receive a full refund. They found that one way to counteract this was to hand over the sales agreement form to the customer to fill out, rather than have the salesperson do this. The customer then felt greater ownership of, and commitment to, the deal, having actually written it out personally. The pressure to be consistent counteracted any later desire to revoke the sale. As a result there was a marked reduction in cancellations.

While writing it down on paper increases commitment to a course of action, this can be further enhanced by having people publicly read out what they have written. For example, in our interpersonal communication training programmes, we employ personal action plans for trainees. This includes having trainees at the end of the programme identifying and writing down their three main strengths and how these can be further enhanced, and three main weaknesses and how these will be remedied. Each trainee in turn then reads these out to the training group. We have found this to be a very effective motivator of future action.

Religious denominations employ various participation techniques (prayers, responses, chants, communal singing) to make their congregation feel a core part of the organization. Ceremonies (marriage, swearing in, initiations) include public declarations of intent. Entertainers are also aware of the importance of securing audience involvement, in the form of laughing, clapping or singing, for a successful show.

Those who are involved are more likely to enjoy the activity and their involvement represents a form of commitment. Their participation also means they are less detached and have less opportunity to objectively evaluate what is happening. Managers should therefore think of ways of involving staff in presentations, meetings and other public forums.

One large company we worked with had an open day for families of staff and members of the public. Some of the line managers were very sceptical about its worth. It was therefore organized in such a way that each line manager was given the task of preparing 'something special' in their department. At planning meetings, they were then asked to give a short presentation on what they were preparing and how it was progressing. At the evaluation meeting following the event, managers were asked to summarize and evaluate their input. By this stage every line manager, without exception, felt the open day had been a huge success.

MORAL APPEALS

The emotional impact of moral overtures can be very forceful. As summarized by Kleinke,[14] 'Research studies have shown that people can be induced to comply with requests if they are made to feel guilty'. This technique is learned at a very early stage, since even very young children invoke moral implications to influence their parents, with statements such as: 'It's not fair. You promised me'. 'But other fathers are taking their children'.

Moral appeals take a number of forms:

1. Reminding people that they have a *duty* to carry out certain actions. This technique is used by insurance companies to sell life policies, by highlighting to clients that they have a moral obligation to protect their family in the event of sudden death.

2. The use of *self-feeling* in either a positive ('You will feel good about yourself if you comply') or negative ('You will feel very bad about yourself if you do not comply') mode.
3. Emphasizing how *esteem of others* will either be positive ('You will be highly regarded if you do this') or negative ('People will not think much of you if you do that').
4. An appeal to *altruism*, which involves invoking the 'better side' of an individual ('Could you please help me? I wouldn't normally ask, but I am really in trouble').
5. *Altercasting* involves pointing out either that a good and caring person would carry out the proposed action, or that only a bad, uncaring person would not do so.

Few people like to be left with a feeling of guilt and so this is a potent ingredient in any influence mix. One drawback with this strategy is that we do not like to be made to feel guilty, and so tend to dislike the person who invokes this feeling in us. An interesting finding is that a mild insult about being uncaring from one person results in the target being more generous in the future, providing the next request is not made by the same person who made the insult.[14] People wish to 'prove' they really are caring individuals by acceding to the second request.

PERSONAL PROOFS

A significant feature of interpersonal influence is the nature of the persuader. If we are not convinced by the person, we are unlikely to be persuaded by their arguments. A number of the features pertaining to the persuader, and the relationship which exists with the target, will impact directly on the extent to which persuasion attempts are successful.

POWER

The possession of power is a potent weapon in the influencing armoury. The 'Iron Law of Power' means that people with great power tend to wield it, when necessary, to get their own way. This does not mean that force is the first influencing strategy used, but rather that if other tactics fail then the power card is likely to be played. Six different types of social power can be used to influence others.

Expert power

Managers are seen as experts in relation to the extent to which they possess expertise or knowledge that others do not have. For example, doctors are perceived to be medical experts and, so, can exert considerable influence over their patients.

The more a person is viewed as an 'expert' the greater their potential for influence. This is because we perceive experts to be more credible, competent and knowledgeable. Credibility is a main feature in persuasion. The higher we rate individuals on this dimension, the more likely we are to be persuaded by what they say. The two determining features of credibility are competence and trustworthiness. We are less likely to believe those we regard as untrustworthy, whatever their level of expertise. Likewise, if we perceive someone to be honest but lacking in knowledge we are unlikely to be influenced by their message. The impact of credibility is also affected by perceived vested interest. Someone who is seen to have a large stake in that which they are recommending will be viewed as less credible. For example, a Ford car salesman extolling the virtues of a Ford model will be seen as a less credible source of information on the car than a colleague at work who drives this model.

Particular sections of an organization have specialized language which is not readily understood by outsiders. This expertise sets them apart from the rest of the workforce. Expert power is underlined by what are known as the three *t*s – titles, threads and trappings. The use of *titles* such as 'product design engineer', 'systems auditor' or 'occupational psychologist', underlines the expertness of the individual. The power of titles is illustrated by the way they are sought and used. People often work much longer hours for very little more money when they are designated a new title such as 'unit manager'. Likewise, *'threads'*, that is clothes, convey expert power – ranging from the hospital white coat, the policeman's blue uniform and on to the priestly black. The well-tailored business suit has also been shown to positively influence others as to the wearer's credibility.[8] Finally, *trappings* convey expertise, in the form of diplomas on the wall, large tomes on a bookshelf or specialist equipment in the room. Other trappings, such as an expensive car, luxury house or private jet, also give the impression of power and status.

Information power

Here, the content of the message is the basis of the power. There is much truth in the maxim that 'information is power'. In organizations there can be a tendency for managers to control the flow of information on a 'need to know' basis. This may be due partly to fear – the belief that if subordinates know too much about what is going on then the manager will have less power over them. Yet, the available evidence shows that staff at all levels wish to be informed about what is happening within their organization, and that levels of satisfaction and commitment increase where information flow is swift and open. For instance, one study[15] of large organizations found that the most successful chief executives provided their workforce with reasonable and credible accounts of actions, together with appropriate technical and functional information.

A controlled study[16] of two worksites facing large-scale redundancies emphasized the importance of information. In one site the workforce was provided with comprehensive information about everything that was happening, while in the other existing levels of information were maintained. The result was that absenteeism and other stress indicators remained significantly lower in the former site throughout the redundancy period. Another study[17] investigated the impact on the staff of an organization which was being merged with a competitor to form a new company. Here it was found that employees valued most highly information which came from a known source and which gave them a sense of participation in the change process.

It is true that trade secrets should be kept from competitors, but it should also be remembered that employees are not competitors. In a range of audits of internal communication which we have conducted across a large number of organizations, one of the greatest consistent sources of dissatisfaction to emerge is an information shortfall.[18] While it may not be possible to disclose everything to all staff, the general rule is to *be as open as you can possibly be*. This increases a feeling of empowerment among staff and encourages ownership of issues.

Legitimate power

The power in this case emanates from the position occupied by the individual. A manager, by dint of job role, will have power over subordinates, but on retirement this is relinquished. The authority is vested in the role or position, not in the person. Interestingly, subordinates also have legitimate power over managers, in that certain procedures must be carried out by the latter in accordance with set guidelines (selection, appraisal, discipline etc.).

Referent power

We are influenced by those whom we wish to be like and whose group we want to be part of – our reference group. The process of emphasizing the acceptability of a course of action by having it recommended and used by significant others is a highly successful technique.[8] For this reason, advertisers use 'product endorsement' techniques whereby famous and admired people are used to sell products. Among teenagers there is enormous peer pressure to conform to certain types of behaviour and to follow current fashions. Similarly, in the workplace, there may be considerable peer pressure to follow set behavioural patterns (productivity rates, attitude to management). Reference groups are most powerful where two conditions apply. First, people are more likely to follow the actions of relevant others when they are unsure about what to do. Secondly, people are more inclined to follow the lead of *similar* others. This means that in a workplace dispute, shopfloor workers are more likely to follow the behaviour of fellow workers walking off the job, than that of senior managers staying at work.

Coercive power

This type of power is based on the extent to which someone has the capacity to punish others. Parents have considerable coercive power over their children ('If you do not finish your homework you will not be allowed to watch television tonight'). Managers will be able to wield coercive power to the extent that subordinates are concerned about receiving praise from them, or are dependent on them for other more material rewards ('If you get these contracts you will be in line for promotion, if not you will be spending the next year in the same job'). The further up the hierarchy, the more potential there is for coercion. Senior managers need to avoid overuse of power, since as noted by Edmund Burke, 'The greater the power the more dangerous the abuse'. While sanctions can be an effective ploy in the persuasion game, they must be used carefully, sparingly and preferably as a last resort. Repeated use of sanctions will lead to resentment or overt hostility. Furthermore, where they are brought into play they need to be followed through, since a failure to execute the stated sanction can lead to a loss of credibility – the manager will be seen as all gas and no flint!

Reward power

The corollary of coercive power is the capacity to reward others for performance. The power of reward is learned from an early age, and is again exercised by parents who have great reward power over their children ('If you behave today you can stay up late'). Likewise, a member of staff may comply with a manager's directives in order to receive a positive appraisal, and increase the chances of a bonus or promotion or other reward, such as being nominated employee of the month.

In relation to the administration of rewards and punishments, the advice given by Machiavelli in *The Prince* is worthy of note, namely that managers should 'delegate to others the enactment of unpopular measures and keep in their own hands the distribution of favours'. Remember that persuasion is a two-way process. Subordinates influence managers through rewards such as social approval (praise, non-verbal acknowledgement etc.), and by their work rate and volume of output and reprimands. Conversely they can punish managers by withdrawing verbal and non-verbal rewards and by reducing their work efforts. The introduction of formal systems of upward appraisal of managers in many firms has also increased the reward and coercive power of subordinates.

ATTRACTIVENESS

Personal attractiveness is a very important factor in the persuasion equation. Abraham Lincoln once said, 'The Lord prefers common-looking people – that's why he makes so many of them'. However, the vast majority of people clearly prefer beautiful people. There is truth in the old adage 'beauty may be only skin deep but its effects run much deeper'. Research shows[19] that physically attractive individuals as compared to their unattractive counterparts:

- are perceived to possess higher levels of favourable characteristics, such as intelligence, friendliness, popularity and being interesting to talk to
- are more successful in life, in that they achieve higher grades at school, are more likely to obtain secure employment, achieve higher earnings, date more frequently with (and marry) people of a high level of attractiveness
- have more positive effects on other people, who wish to spend longer in their company
- receive more positive responses from others – including requests for help
- are more persuasive – they have greater credibility, being rated higher in perceived expertise, trustworthiness and likeableness.

Given these findings, it is hardly surprising that people spend huge sums of money on fashion, jewellery, make-up, perfumes, hairstyle and plastic surgery, in an effort to increase their attractiveness. Ratings of beauty are consistent among judges and across cultures. In this sense it is not strictly true that 'beauty is in the eye of the beholder'. However, as with all aphorisms this one contains a modicum of truth, in that we all like different aspects of physical features, dress and embellishments. For example, some people find nose studs appealing while others abhor them. Furthermore, initial judgements of physical attractiveness are tempered by psychological, sociological, relational and contextual influences.[20] Features such as dress, perfume, sense of humour, attentiveness, sensitivity and shared beliefs, all affect ratings of attractiveness. Managers should maximize their level of attractiveness to those whom they wish to influence.

THE RELATIONSHIP

We are more likely to be influenced by people we like, are friendly with or for whom we have high regard. Indeed, research in the field of assertiveness shows that one of the most difficult tasks is refusing a request from a friend (see Chapter 10). Managers therefore need to develop and foster a positive working relationship with staff.

In large organizations the manager should develop a wide range of contacts across departments and, where possible, be at the centre of networks by introducing staff to one another. This will facilitate influence attempts when required. A useful piece of advice is to offer help and support to as many people as possible, so that they will in turn be ready to reciprocate with favours. Communication networks are also related to staff turnover, since research has shown that individuals who have formed larger networks are less likely to leave their employment than those with a smaller number of contacts.[21]

An important component of relational communication is the appropriate use of *praise* and compliments. The receipt of praise leads to liking for the sender, which in turn facilitates the process of influencing. Where the manager has *similar attitudes* and values to staff, or a common interest or hobby, this facilitates the relationship.

Similarity of language (accent, terminology etc.) has also been shown to aid compliance, and is part of what is known as 'communication accommodation'.

Using the person's *first name* is another useful strategy which, when not overused, leads to positive evaluations.[14] The judicious use of first name makes the person more attentive and also increases liking for the user. In the words of Rackham and Morgan,[22] 'The oldest sales trick known to man involves making maximum use of the name of any person you wish to influence'. In his best selling book, *How to Win Friends and Influence People*, Dale Carnegie advised using a person's name as one of the six rules for encouraging others to like us (the other five rules being: be a good listener, show genuine interest in the person, talk about the person's interests, smile, make the other person feel important). When elected as Prime Minister in 1997, Tony Blair made it clear to his colleagues that he wanted to be called by his first name. Despite the fact that the leader of the country wished to foster good working relationships with his subordinates by equalizing the use of names, this was not found to be widely practised in the workplace. A survey[23] of 557 workplaces in the UK employing more than 250 000 people in total, was conducted by the Manufacturing Science and Finance (MSF) union, also in 1997. This found that 33 per cent of senior managers expected to be addressed by staff as 'Sir' or by their title.

Another important dimension in establishing and maintaining relationships is the use of *humour*. The common denominator 'among those whom I love' for W. H. Auden was that, 'all of them make me laugh'. Furthermore, 'Studies of persuasion have revealed that humorous people are perceived as more likeable, and this in turn enables them to have greater influence'.[24] This is because greater liking is related to increases in the perceived credibility and authoritativeness of the source.

Finally, there is evidence to indicate that *eating with others* facilitates the persuasion process.[14] Eating is a vital part of human existence and necessary to survival. In Western society where food is plentiful we forget its importance. We are programmed to seek food and to protect it as necessary from others. This is the case with all animals – just watch the feeding frenzy of birds in winter fighting over scraps on a lawn! In countries where food is scarce and hunger is rife, human behaviour tends to revert to this basic form. This means that eating has a special significance. We usually only invite special people to dine with us (family, friends, sexual partners), and we use these occasions to help develop and cement relationships. Hence, the importance of the business lunch or working breakfast. This means that we can use the power of shared eating to help persuade others.

SELECTING AN INFLUENCING STRATEGY

Influencing as a strategy can be overt and hard or more subtle and soft. Kipnis and Schmidt[25] carried out a study involving 360 managers in the USA, Australia and the

UK, to investigate how and why they employed particular influencing strategies. Managers were asked to describe how they attempted to influence their subordinates, peers and superiors at work. The influencing tactics were then classified into three main strategies, namely hard, soft and rational (see Key point 2.3).

Key point 2.3   Influencing strategies

1. Hard influencing strategy: exemplar responses of managers

- 'I threaten to give an unsatisfactory performance evaluation.'
- 'I get higher management to back up my request.'

Hard tactics are more likely to be used when:

- the influencer has the advantage/more power
- resistance is anticipated
- the other person's behaviour violates social or organizational norms.

2. Soft influencing strategy: exemplar responses of managers

- 'I act very humble when making my request.'
- 'I make the person feel important by saying he or she has the experience to do what I want.'

Soft tactics are more likely to be used when:

- the influencer is at a disadvantage/has less power
- resistance is anticipated
- the goal is to secure personal benefits (e.g. time off work).

3. Rational influencing strategies: exemplar responses of managers

- 'I offer to exchange favours: "You do this for me, and I'll do something for you."'
- 'I outline the advantages of the recommended course of action.'

Rational tactics are more likely to be used when:

- neither party has a real power advantage
- resistance is not anticipated
- the goal is to obtain benefits for oneself and for the organization.

Kipnis and Schmidt found that people use different strategies depending on the situation and the target person. The choice of strategy was also determined by immediate objectives, relative power positions and expectations about the willingness of the other person to do what was being sought. When managers wanted a personal favour from their superior they tended to use soft tactics such as flattery and behaving in a humble manner. On the other hand, when they wanted to persuade their boss to implement a new procedure they were more likely to use rational tactics such as giving reasons and outlining the advantages. The interesting conclusion reached by Kipnis and Schmidt was that: 'people who rely chiefly on logic, reason and compromise to get their way are the most satisfied both with their business lives and with their personal relationships'.

In fact there are two cognitive routes involved in the processing of persuasive messages – the *central* and the *peripheral*. In the central route the individual engages in a careful and thoughtful consideration of the merits of the information as presented (asking questions, formulating counter-arguments, and so on). In the peripheral route, little conscious effort is devoted to message processing or analysis and the target may not be aware that a persuasion attempt is being made. For example, a television advert may sell a soft drink by presenting details of a research survey which found that in tests over 90 per cent of people preferred it to the taste of its rivals (central route strategy). An alternative approach would be to show attractive people having fun in sunny and glamorous locations, with the soft drink in hand and upbeat music playing, while the voice-over tells us that there is a 'whole world' in this soft drink (peripheral route strategy). The latter is an attempt to create a subconscious association between the drink and being happy. If this were processed centrally the viewer would be asking questions such as: 'What does it mean to say there is a whole world in a drink?' or 'Why are all these people grinning at nothing in particular?' However, the fact is that it does not tend to be processed this way but, rather, is dealt with through the peripheral cognitive route – and so it often succeeds.

Managers should be aware of the impact of both routes. Aspects such as the attractiveness of the persuader, use of the target's first name, smiles, humour, eating with the person, and so on can all affect the outcome of persuasion attempts. Yet, these dimensions are usually processed by recipients through the peripheral rather than the central route. We are not aware, when they are used skilfully and appropriately, that these tactics are influencing how we feel about an issue. Of course, if we do become conscious of an influence attempt we may begin to resent the fact that our first name is being used, that the person is being humorous or has invited us for lunch. In other words, the attempt may backfire. Skill and tact are therefore required when persuading others.

Exercise 2.2   Influence checklist

Think about recent occasions when you have used skills of influence and persuasion both at work and in other contexts. Using the checklist below, first rate how often (frequency) you used each tactic, along a 5-point scale ranging from 1 (never) to 5 (frequently). Secondly, rate how well (effectiveness) you think you used these tactics, again using a 5-point scale ranging from 1 (very poor) to 5 (very good).

Tactic	Frequency	Effectiveness
Reasoned argument	☐	☐
Pre-giving	☐	☐
Promising to reciprocate	☐	☐
Scarcity appeal	☐	☐
Threat/fear/coercion	☐	☐
Praise/reward	☐	☐
Receiving a written/public commitment	☐	☐
Moral appeal	☐	☐
Emphasizing personal expertise	☐	☐
Using the reference group	☐	☐
Giving information	☐	☐
Eating together	☐	☐
Humour	☐	☐
Use of first name	☐	☐

What does the pattern of scores tell you about your own persuasive style of influencing? Is your style hard, soft or rational?

SUMMARY

Persuasion tactics are valuable commodities in human interchange. Indeed, the ability to influence and persuade staff can be regarded as the *sine qua non* of management. If managers cannot encourage staff to follow directives, and use means other than force and threat to do so, they will inevitably fail.[26] There is a rich variety of techniques which can be used in a subtle yet genuine manner to produce desired and desirable outcomes. These have been summarized under the three main categories of logical, emotional and personal proofs. While these have been analysed separately, inevitably there is overlap between the three categories. This reflects the fact that effective persuasion often requires a combination of tactics which involve appeals to reason, emotion and personal relationship. The strategy used by a manager to exert influence will vary across situations and people. A wide repertoire of tactics, and flexibility in their usage, is therefore necessary to successful persuasion.

3 Team-mates: building teams that work

> We trained hard but it seemed that every time we were beginning to form up into teams, we would be re-organized. I was to learn later in life that we tend to meet any new situation by re-organizing, and a wonderful method it can be for creating the illusion of progress while producing confusion, inefficiency and demoralisation.
>
> *Gaius Petronius,* AD 66

Teams are groups co-operating to achieve jointly agreed goals. Members hold each other mutually accountable for success or failure. The underlying philosophy is that if one of them looks good, they all look good. Teams celebrate both personal and group achievements. Performance objectives are routinely exceeded. What was once considered impossible becomes viewed as inevitable. Given this, some leading researchers have argued that teams should be the standard unit of performance for most organizations, regardless of size.[1]

However, in the rush to develop highly productive and motivated teams, it is often assumed that groups are transformed into teams by a simple process of managerial decree: 'Let there be teamworking.' In reality, change in this area requires clear goals, time and supportive communication. The purpose of this chapter is to examine each of these requirements, and so help managers transform groups into teams.

This transformation is rarely easy. The quotation at the beginning of this chapter captures one view of teams, which we regularly encounter in our work within organizations. Many people find that working in groups causes them more anxiety than anything else they do in the workplace. As Sartre once said: 'Hell is other people.' Teams, committees and groups are often perceived as making poor decisions, while stifling innovation and creativity, and with spawning bureaucracy and inertia. As the well-known saying from the world's most prolific source of aphorisms ('Anonymous') puts it, 'A committee is a cul-de-sac down which promising young ideas are lured and then quietly strangled'.

On the other hand, teams are more widely used in the business world than ever before. Complex business processes foster interdependency. There may well be heroes in your organization, who regularly and single-handedly save everyone from catastrophe. But for every Superman there must be a network of supporting teams, well organized, highly motivated, trained and committed to the goals of the organization. Thus, interdependency inevitably leads to group development and the formation of complex relationships. The challenge for managers is to improve communication, transform groups into teams and free the human factor to fulfil its potential as the chief engine of business success.[2]

The human factor is paramount. Loyalty (on the part of employees, investors and customers) has been identified as more important in securing profitable growth than market share, scale, cost position or other business variables.[3] This supports the conclusion that the promotion of trust within the workplace – as well as with external customers and publics – is necessary for success.[4, 5] Teamwork is a powerful means by which trust and loyalty can be used to strengthen the foundations of your organization. It is underpinned by values which encourage listening, supportive communication, responding positively to the input of others and recognizing everyone's interests and achievements. With such values in place individuals, teams and the whole organization perform better. Teamwork is endangered by measures which threaten the underlying needs of employees. In that context, such management practices as downsizing (or, as it is sometimes termed, 'dumb-sizing') are inimical to the creation of trust and the promotion of loyalty within the organization.

Research has long established that well-managed and committed teams achieve much more than individuals working alone or in competition with each other. Key point 3.1 summarizes the findings of several empirical studies, where this effect has been conclusively demonstrated. This is because workers in self-managed teams have more autonomy and discretion in what they do, which provides greater intrinsic rewards and job satisfaction, improves flexibility and stimulates innovation.[6] As a result, more than 75 per cent of workers surveyed who were currently in traditional work groups said they would prefer to be organized in teams. On the other hand, fewer than 10 per cent of those currently in teams said they would like to return to traditional supervision and methods of organization.[7] Consequently, the transfer of staff into self-managed work teams has been identified as one of the seven core characteristics of what empirical studies suggest can be defined as high-performing organizations.[6]

Consider the example of quality teams in Hewlett-Packard (HP) (Key point 3.1). The most important point to be made here is that HP supervisors received 40 hours of training in team-building, and are allowed a great deal of autonomy in their day-to-day work. Success was due to training in main principles, intense communication and the empowerment of change agents.

Such points are necessary even for teams whose members are widely dispersed – what are known as 'remote teams.' For example, the Ford Motor Company has run

Key point 3.1   The achievements of teams

- Kanter[8] reported that Hewlett-Packard had restructured its organization around quality teams. Efficiency across the company improved by 50 per cent.
- Parker[9] listed a whole series of examples of the impact of effective teams – a plant in Ohio found that output increased by 90 per cent when production teams were created. Xerox headquarters reported that when a supervisory position was eliminated and the staff given more autonomy absenteeism fell by 75 per cent.
- Teamwork has consistently resulted in greater achievement, productivity, innovation, quality and work satisfaction than 'competitively' driven management environments. This has been demonstrated in studies ranging over scientists, airline reservation agents, business people, students and car assembly workers.[10]
- Nissan UK, based in Sunderland, has become one of the most successful manufacturing plants in the UK. At one point it had an absenteeism rate of 0.75 per cent compared to a national average of 4.7 per cent in manufacturing industry. Arnott identified teamwork as a main factor in this success. For example, at the start of every shift each day all employees met together in their work groups to discuss tasks for the day. Thus, people management and team-building skills were regarded as key requirements for potential supervisors.[11]
- A study of 128 claims adjusters from two insurance company offices found that the more employees communicated competently, listened skilfully and talked about the new computer system the more productive they were in using it. In short, the more formal and informal contact people engaged in with colleagues when a new process was introduced, the more quickly the new system was successful.[12]

a complex design and engineering process of 1000 people in five continents. The manager responsible sustained communication through fortnightly one-to-one telephone meetings, weekly video-conference meetings with 25 managers, and personal visits to each team at least once a year.[13] A rigorous approach and intense commitment to communication are vital to build effective teams.

STAGES OF TEAM DEVELOPMENT

Reorganizing in a team structure is an inherently risky venture. To succeed, new relationships must be formed and the structure of the organization will most probably need to be changed. There are hazards on every side – for example, if too much attention is paid to the task, people will feel neglected. But if too much attention is paid to relationships, the task will not be accomplished. Key point 3.2 lists a number of symptoms often found when teams have failed to strike the right balance on such issues.

Key point 3.2 Symptoms of team ruination

1. Members shirk responsibility. They constantly say 'This wasn't my fault.' 'Things were like this when I got here.' 'Why don't you ask Abu? That's his responsibility, not mine.' 'Here we go again.'
2. The team is always busy, but nothing ever gets done. There is no time for reflection or analysis. After all, reports have to be prepared for the higher-ups.
3. The team regularly fragments into subgroups. Members exchange stories about each other's failures rather than their successes. There are constant rumours of *coups* and counter-*coups*. Members spend their time recruiting reinforcements to shore up their own position. Secret treaties are regularly concluded, and instantly broken.
4. Members are terrified of making mistakes. They hope that when mistakes are made no one else will notice. New team members are taken aside and told to 'cover your back'.
5. Since nothing has ever worked before, everyone believes that disaster lies ahead whatever they do – a process that has been termed 'learned helplessness'.
6. Meetings start late and drag on past closure time. Members drift out before the end. The same items keep cropping up on the agenda, with nothing ever being decided. The chairperson decides nothing, but does so decisively.
7. No one else in the organization knows what the team is up to. Furthermore, they don't care. It keeps some more bosses busy and away from them, while the real work gets done elsewhere.
8. The team mascot is Homer Simpson.

The task for everyone involved is to steer team organization through such rapids, avoiding the rocks which lie round each new bend. This process is helped if the inevitable stages associated with the development of teams are anticipated. One of the best known contributions was made by Tuckman and Jensen,[14] who proposed that effective teams go through a number of clearly identifiable stages. These are:

- *Forming*. At this early stage team members are confronted with maximum uncertainty. Their task is unclear, while the personalities, abilities and hidden agendas of the other team members are relatively unknown. New members arrive in what is almost an arranged marriage, and see their prospective partners in this new role for the first time. People therefore try to define what the team's main task is, while also attempting to make sense of relationships between team members. All of this involves sharing information, discussing subjects unrelated to the task, and testing other members. Inevitably, misunderstandings occur and relationships sometimes become fraught. In fact, some would-be teams never go beyond such tensions – they sink as soon as they hit the water.
- *Storming*. Team members experience hostility and conflict as they struggle with the task. Defensiveness, competition and resistance to being a part of the team may occur. Internal conflicts break out over status, power and speaking or participation rights. Although our first instinct might suggest that this period, and conflict in general, is harmful the evidence suggests that it has a positive effect – if managed properly. For example, a study[15] of 44 members in 14 teams found that project teams which began with very harmonious interpersonal relations did not perform as well as those which had early disharmonies. It has been theorized that this may have been because early conflicts teach people how to solve interpersonal disputes and become task focused. However, it may also be that such conflicts helped the team avoid the natural tendency which also exists for the members to overconform with its emerging norms. This process will be discussed later in this chapter.
- *Norming*. There is growing acceptance by team members of each other's idiosyncrasies, and correspondingly less emphasis on enforcing absolute uniformity of thought or behaviour. A greater sense of belonging to the group is developed. New norms and methods of acceptable behaviour emerge. Co-operation and mutuality become more normal, in place of the conflict behaviours on display at an earlier stage.
- *Performing*. Team members work in a problem-solving manner to attain group goals. They also begin to evaluate their accomplishments and, if and when the team needs to disband, review their past achievements. The review process has been described as the stage where members often engage in the creation of heroic legends. This may in itself become an important part of the whole

organization's growth. Tom Peters and Nancy Austin[16] have argued that successful or excellent organizations are characterized, among much else, by legends of achievement and war stories of individual 'derring-do' which serve the purpose of illuminating and reinforcing the organization's underlying value system.

- *Adjourning*. All good things must come to an end and groups are no exception. Teams may cease to exist because their task has been completed and their goals have been achieved. Alternatively, the group may, over a period of time, begin to lose its attraction or success, resulting in gradual adjournment and slow disintegration as members progressively leave. Where a team is being disbanded suddenly, care needs to be taken to lessen the psychological impact on members. We become attached to groups to which we belong and termination can provoke bereavement-like symptoms.

CHARACTERISTICS OF SUCCESSFUL TEAMS

Building teams means moving a group of often disparate people through the stages discussed above, so that they all become committed to the group's goals, participate fully in decision-making, learn how to manage inevitable conflicts and feel complete ownership of the tasks in hand. At this point, team members will have found their sea legs. The research suggests[1, 17] that managing this transition requires concentration on a number of distinct issues as described below.

THE TEAM SHOULD HAVE HIGHLY SPECIFIC GOALS

The importance of clear goals is discussed in Chapter 13, in the context of individual appraisal. Similar points apply to team objectives. In the absence of a guiding sense of purpose teams become a bureaucracy, concerned with self-preservation rather than the achievement of the organization's objectives. Adherence to clear goals can be established and reinforced by ensuring that meetings regularly address the following questions:

- What did we achieve last week?
- What do we want to achieve this week?
- Who is responsible for what, when will it be done, and what will be different when they have finished?
- What specifically can we do better?
- What can we change in how we work?
- What can we change in the organization?
- What added value have we brought to this enterprise, this week?

This approach reduces emphasis on status, facilitates clear communication, maintains objectivity, assists evaluation and creates symbols of actual accomplishment.

Evaluation of the team's own workings is an important part of its growth and development. The suggestion is that such self-evaluation should be institutionalized into the team's workings, by ensuring that the above questions are openly addressed at each team meeting.

SUCCESSFUL TEAMS NUMBER BETWEEN TWO AND 25 PEOPLE, WITH MOST COMPRISING UNDER TEN

Team size supports constructive interaction, and enables an agreed concentration on real, achievable goals. People can snooze peacefully in a crowd of 50, but their snores will be noticed in a room of five. The smaller the team the harder it is to coast as a silent member. By facilitating involvement, small teams also reduce members' frustration – when people cannot participate they feel disempowered. Disempowerment ensures that, after team meetings, the main discussion point on everyone's agenda is the need to grumble about the chairperson rather than action to solve real problems.

EFFECTIVE TEAMS HOLD THEMSELVES COLLECTIVELY ACCOUNTABLE

Peer 'pressure' is much more effective than pressure that is external to the team. It promotes ownership, without which no cohesion or commitment is possible. Ownership is central to sustained effort and involvement: when, for example, did you last mow your neighbour's lawn in preference to your own? One researcher[18] has argued that such team accountability is also promoted if teams themselves devise relevant measures for their activities: in short, a genuinely empowered team will have the lead role in designing its own measures. This is because the main purpose of such measures is to help the team, rather than those outside its ranks (including top managers), measure its own progress. Furthermore, a team should adopt only a handful of measures. This keeps a few significant and achievable tasks to the fore. When teams have too much to do they do it badly or not at all while producing reams of paper to camouflage their inactivity. More is a mess, while less is best.

A GOOD START DETERMINES THE TEAM'S PROSPECTS

First meetings and actions create what is known as an 'expectancy effect' among team members. Is this a talking shop or an action forum? Are new ideas encouraged or punished? Will the team perform real work, or merely produce reports? First impressions and actions on these issues are important. Thus, teams should:

1. *Set some immediately attainable goals and then declare an early victory.* Good generals never give an order that cannot be obeyed. Such orders lead to defeat, and the fearful expectation of further débâcles to come. Likewise, teams need to know they have goals which can be accomplished and see steady progress towards them

unfold at an early stage of their development. In particular, a sense of achievement is certain if you set your sights on a few easily achievable goals, and then move quickly to declare victory.

2. *Set some clear rules of behaviour*. This would include issues such as confidentiality, punctuality, interruptions and the need to set action outcomes for all.

3. *Build evaluation of the team into all meetings*. This means habituating the team to ask questions such as:
   a) What did we do well here?
   b) What could we have been done even better?
   c) How can we promote greater participation at our meetings?
   d) What outside help can we get to improve our decision-making?

4. *Do something at the outset radically different to what members of the team would normally countenance*. Teams can unleash tremendous innovation, but only if a preparedness to change is the normal mindset of team members, and a characteristic of every task which they undertake. One management consultant expressed the position thus:[19] 'If you want change, if you want people to do something different, you must first stop them from doing what they are doing now. Once you do that, you have their undivided attention and it becomes possible to persuade them to do something else.'

ENCOURAGE TEAM INTERACTION

Successful teams spend a great deal of time together, engaged in both task and non-task activities. This investment in time promotes formal and informal communication, and so nurtures relationships. Expecting team members to view the team as an add-on to their real job ensures that they do not take it seriously. On the other hand, the quality of time spent together is more important than its quantity. As an old adage puts it, meetings take minutes but waste hours. Such a cynical view gains ground when teams lose sight of the task at hand. In short, meeting for hours while deciding nothing is akin to athletes gathering at the track but forgetting to run. All competitive edge will soon be lost.

EFFECTIVE TEAMS USE POSITIVE FEEDBACK

We are all heavily influenced by the power of social rewards. People are social beings, and the feedback which we receive from others helps shape our sense of who and what we are, and the broader social environment to which we belong. A number of social rewards have been shown to have a particularly powerful effect on us, and these are therefore likely to be especially appreciated by team members. Some of these are listed in Key point 3.3. Although these could be viewed as particularly useful for team leaders, their frequent use by all team members is a means of strengthening overall relationships.

Key point 3.3 How to use social rewards to build teams

- Make frequent use of praise and encouragement. Draw attention to people's successes. When a project ends with a setback, concentrate your feedback on what can be learnt from the experience, and what has been gained by the organization as a result of the things which still went well.
- Send out regular thank you notes to people, for jobs well done.
- Telephone people and thank them, when you hear that they have done something well.
- Have a regular 'employee of the month'.
- Bring up specific examples of good performance at team meetings.
- Live by the 90/10 rule: 90 per cent of your feedback should relate to positive performance, and 10 per cent (or less) should relate to problem areas in people's work.
- Direct praise and encouragement towards individuals rather than the group as a whole. Seek out individual instances of behaviour where such social rewards would be considered appropriate.
- Make rewards contingent on positive performance or behaviours. This increases the prospects that such behaviours will be repeated in the future.
- Apply rewards immediately after the behaviour has occurred, rather than after a long period of time has elapsed.
- Ensure that praise is sincere and appropriately varied. Use of the same expressions time after time diminishes their value, and is eventually seen as insincere.
- Encourage team members to engage in self-reinforcement and mutual reinforcement. Members should develop the habit of acknowledging when they or others do well.
- Utilize what has been termed 'response development'. This involves summarizing in your own words what other people have said, and generally has the effect of validating their contribution to group discussion.

Celebration is an important aspect of social reinforcement. It strengthens relationships among team members and ensures that achieving goals remains at the forefront of members' minds. Key point 3.4 lists ways in which celebration can be promoted. There is some evidence that successful organizations institutionalize such an approach into the daily routine of how they work. For example, the cosmetic company, The Body Shop, has a Department of Celebration at its main headquarters. The UK mobile phone company, Carphone Warehouse goes so far as to organize a 'beer bust' for some 600 employees one Friday evening each month. They are held in pubs and wine bars, when for a period of one and a half hours the company pays for all drinks, at a cost of some £4000. These 'beer busts' not only help team spirit, but have led to a number of romances and even marriage. The company also holds an annual ball for staff as well as specific team-building days. Results have been good. Turnover increased from £110 million in 1996/7 to £171 million in 1997/8, while a staff survey showed that 92 per cent of staff were proud to work for the company.[20]

Key point 3.4   Ways to celebrate

- Publicize your successes.
- Create posters and display them round the workplace.
- Circulate news-sheets advising of progress.
- Have award winners and ceremonies.
- Have wall charts showing levels of performance.
- Have a team lunch out.
- Plan evenings out, Christmas parties and team participation in charity fund-raising ventures.
- Create time and space for celebrations.
- Include celebration in your team agreement.
- At team meetings, regularly discuss what is good about the team and what could be even better.

DEVELOP THE PRACTICE OF SUPPORTIVE COMMUNICATION

In successful teams status differentials are noticeable by their absence. Communication is informal. Team members address each other by their first names. There is plentiful discussion, with everyone encouraged and expected to contribute. For example, a good team rule is that no one speaks twice until everyone has spoken once. Supportive communication facilitates civilized disagreement. The team is comfortable with this and shows no sign of avoiding, smoothing over or suppressing conflict. Key point 3.5 (page 56) lists some other commonly agreed characteristics of supportive communication. These represent behaviours which everyone, not just the team leader, needs to promote if the group is going to develop as a team.

Now turn to Exercise 3.1 (page 57). Give each member of your team a copy and ask them to answer the questions as frankly and honestly as they can. It will enable you to form some impression of the extent to which your communication among team members, and their communication with you, is either supportive or unsupportive.

BARRIERS TO TEAM DEVELOPMENT

We have looked, above, at some of the steps groups need to take in order to become teams. It also has to be acknowledged that a variety of problems commonly arise when such attempts are made. Human beings are the most complex phenomenon in the known universe. It is hardly surprising that anything which involves people requires a great deal of work to succeed. Some of the main difficulties, which have not so far been discussed, will now be considered.

COHESION VERSUS THE NEED FOR DISSENT

Teams need a consensus, on such issues as the nature of the task to be performed, how decisions are made, who performs various leadership functions and the extent of individual members' authority for different team functions. The resolution of these issues creates what are termed the norms of the group. It is also known that the quality of group decision-making is enormously improved when there is minority dissent. Nevertheless, groups have a tendency to suppress such dissent and punish, usually through the withdrawal of social rewards, those who challenge the conventional wisdom of the group.[22]

The benefits of minority dissent arise because decisions are improved when a variety of options are systematically explored and evaluated. Our first thought on a problem is rarely our best. Evaluation should occur at each stage of the decision-making cycle: for example, it pays for groups to return to first principles immediately before a final decision, and evaluate their options all over again. However, groups often avoid such debate and compel members to conform at an early stage to the perceived norms and values of the group. In short, it is difficult to play the role of minority advocate in a group of strong members already committed to a particular outcome. As Oscar Wilde put it: 'We dislike arguments of any kind; they are always vulgar, and often convincing.'

Key point 3.5   Principles of supportive communication

1. *Problem oriented, not person oriented*
   Characterized by: 'What can we do to solve this difficulty?'
   NOT: 'This is your fault, again.'

2. *Congruent, not incongruent*
   Characterized by: 'Yes, I am worried that we might not make the deadline.'
   NOT: 'Of course I'm not worried. Yes, I'm sure we'll make the deadline.'

3. *Descriptive, not evaluative*
   Characterized by: 'Well, this is what happened; this is how it made me feel; here are my ideas on how we can resolve it.'
   NOT: 'What you did was unforgivable.'

4. *Validating, not invalidating*
   Characterized by: 'What do you think needs to be done to solve this yourself?'
   NOT: 'This is a bit beyond you anyway, so I'll get Tina to look into it. Do you know where she is?'

5. *Specific, not global*
   Characterized by: 'You interrupted me three times at today's meeting.'
   NOT: 'You never show me any respect.'

6. *Conjunctive, not disjunctive*
   Characterized by: 'Right, you've raised whether we can meet the first deadline. I think this relates to ...'
   NOT: 'The deadline has to wait. The thing here is whether you are staying within your budget.'

7. *Owned, not disowned*
   Characterized by: 'I've decided not to support your proposal, because ...'
   NOT: 'I'd love to support your idea, and I fought hard for it, but the boss just wouldn't wear it. A pity.'

8. *Supportive listening, not one-way listening*
   Characterized by: 'Tell me what you think the problems are.'
   NOT: 'These sound like excuses. Let me tell you where you need to sharpen up.'

Source: Adapted from Whetten and Cameron.[21]

Exercise 3.1   Evaluating communication in your team

You will be engaged in a variety of communication acts with individuals within your team. Please circle the response which most sums up the general quality of communication with individuals who fall into the categories specified. A scoring system is given at the end of the chapter. Do not look at this until you have finished the questionnaire and completed this chapter.

1. When I communicate with other members of my team, we succeed in concentrating on the problem and reach a common agreement about what has to be done.

   Sometimes   Rarely   Frequently   Always   Never

2. When my team performs a task, I go away feeling positive about the way in which we have encouraged and supported each other.

   Sometimes   Rarely   Frequently   Always   Never

3. When I communicate with other members of my team, we would agree that the communication has been useful and helpful to all of us.

   Sometimes   Rarely   Frequently   Always   Never

4. When other members of my team communicate with me, they validate and encourage my work.

   Sometimes   Rarely   Frequently   Always   Never

5. I listen a great deal to what other members of my team have to say.

   Sometimes   Rarely   Frequently   Always   Never

6. Other members of my team listen a great deal to what I have to say.

   Sometimes   Rarely   Frequently   Always   Never

7. When other members of my team communicate with me, we concentrate on the problem and reach a common agreement about what has to be done.

   Sometimes   Rarely   Frequently   Always   Never

8. When I communicate with other members of my team, my communication validates and encourages the work of the individual concerned.

   Sometimes   Rarely   Frequently   Always   Never

A particularly important issue here is the extreme conformity which often settles on groups when they are involved in making important decisions, and which has been termed 'groupthink'. Janis,[23] who popularized the term, investigated a whole series of poor political and business decisions, and concluded that many of them could be explained by examining the decision-making process within the groups responsible. For example, the USA launched a disastrous invasion of Cuba's Bay of Pigs in 1961, using what was largely an army of Cuban exiles. On later reflection, it was apparent to many of those involved that they should have anticipated such a negative outcome. In explaining why they did not, Janis argued that the group taking the decision to invade shared the following characteristics:

1. *It was very cohesive.* Members valued being a part of the group, felt loyal to other members and to the leader (President Kennedy) in particular. This exaggerated their tendency to agree with each other. It takes more effort to disagree with someone than it does to agree. Moreover, it is harder to argue with a friend than an enemy.

2. *The group was relatively insulated from information outside its own ranks and had an inflated impression of its grasp of the facts.* The tendency to agree with other members also strengthened the members' view that they already knew all they needed in order to make a decision. The group developed illusions of infallibility, reinforced by the failure of its members to question the general drift of its deliberations. In short, even the most bizarre ideas begin to look credible if a group of people talk only to themselves. This has been identified as a significant factor behind the conformity to strange rituals and beliefs found in cult organizations, such as the Hare Krishnas and others.[24]

3. *Group members rarely looked systematically at alternative courses of action in order to evaluate their relative merits.* They put themselves under pressure to reach decisions quickly, which further predisposed them to 'agree' around a common position at an early stage of their deliberations. Their commitment to a decision reinforced their belief that it was right, since we all tend to seek positive reinforcement on decisions made. The group behaved like the man who leapt from the Empire State Building and was heard to mutter, as he passed each successive storey, 'So far, so good'.

4. *The group was dominated by a directive and charismatic leader – President Kennedy.* Group members therefore exaggerated the level of his insight, and this reinforced the natural tendency to agree quickly with what they thought was his main opinion. The spectacle of others agreeing further added to the spurious illusion that they were agreeing to something which made sense.

Various factors have been discussed earlier in this chapter which often prevent groups from gelling into teams at all. We are now more concerned with what happens when the team has developed beyond a group of disparate individuals. The suggestion is that the opposite problem might emerge – the team is so cohesive that it becomes a choir with no room for soloists. People no longer think for themselves. What can be done to avert these dangers? Key point 3.6 provides a number of suggestions, derived from the research literature, which all team members need to be aware of.

Key point 3.6 Measures to avoid groupthink

- The leader should adopt a more neutral role and avoid stating his or her views at an early stage of group discussion.
- Encourage the expression of dissident viewpoints.
- Assign the role of 'critical evaluator' to every group member.
- After every big decision, ask these questions: what's wrong with this decision? How could it be improved? What alternatives have we overlooked?
- Assign subgroups to independently develop proposals.
- Periodically bring in outside people or experts to review your deliberations.
- During important discussions, assign one member to play the role of devil's advocate.
- After formulating a plan, hold a 'second chance' meeting. Invite everyone to express residual doubts. Express doubts yourself.
- Always set tasks which involve everyone.
- Set clear performance goals for the group.
- Find a means of evaluating/measuring everyone's individual contribution.
- Encourage the expression of minority opinions. Cherish, reward and promote those SOBs who disagree with you.
- Provide rewards for individual as well as group effort.

TEAM PRODUCTIVITY

We are driven to work with others to achieve our goals, and frequently recognize that without such co-operation our efforts will not be as successful as they need to be ('Many hands make light work'). On the other hand, we also often find that the imagined benefits from such co-operation fail to materialize ('Too many cooks spoil the broth'). The questions arise of whether productivity losses are common in teams, why should they occur and what can we do to avert them?

First, the evidence does indeed suggest that productivity losses are common in team contexts. One of the early studies into this was conducted by a French agricultural engineer named Max Ringlemann at the turn of the century.[25] Ringlemann persuaded students to pull on a rope which was attached to an instrument capable of measuring the force exerted on it. The students pulled alone, and then in groups of either seven or 14. Ringlemann assumed that by adding up the individual scores for the level of force exerted by each member of the group he would have a total roughly in line with what the entire group would exert when it pulled. In actual fact, he found that the whole group only expended about 75 per cent of what the members' individual scores suggested should be its full capacity. A wide range of studies, varying the basic task, has tended to find the same: in groups, people do not work as hard.

In case you think that this might be a matter of co-ordination losses (after all, everyone must pull at exactly the same time, for the maximum force to be measured) it should be noted that Ringlemann's basic experiment was repeated in the 1970s.[25] The difference here was that only one 'real' subject was involved. He or she was placed at the front of the rope-pulling team, while the rest were instructed to make realistic grunting noises and only pretend to pull. Yet again, the luckless dupe at the front was found to pull at only about 75 per cent of his or her capacity when other people were involved. Studies of brainstorming have also found that people produce far more ideas on their own than they do when brainstorming in the company of others. This is explained by the phenomenon known as 'social loafing' – our apparent willingness when in the company of others to slacken our effort, in the hope or expectation that they will compensate for our reduced effort.

On a positive note, it should be borne in mind that the evidence suggests groups are more effective in problem-solving tasks, production tasks, and learning and memory tasks than individuals. They also learn faster, make fewer errors, recall better, and produce a higher quality product than individuals.[22] However, productivity per person is lower in groups – the individual commits less effort than they would on their own. Thus, groups are generally more effective than individuals but are less efficient.

But all is far from lost. Key point 3.7 contains some suggestions which if applied should ensure that social loafing can be eliminated, or at least drastically reduced.

Key point 3.7 Suggested measures for reducing social loafing

- The task should be one in which everyone must participate. For example, brainstorming works better if people come up with their own ideas privately, and then pool them in the group, rather than start the process off in the company of others.
- The group leader facilitates involvement, rather than simply promotes their own ideas or engages in the task without waiting for others. (See Chapter 4.)
- The team regularly evaluates its own performance in terms of achieving its goals, and functioning as a team. Issues of involvement, dominance and conflict are openly addressed.
- The task and the group are deemed attractive – by the participants. Remember that volunteers make more committed soldiers than conscripts.
- The task is intrinsically interesting. This tends to be the case when it impinges directly on the jobs of the people concerned, or what they regard as areas of core professional concern. For example, most nurses would be more likely to find the task of the team interesting if it is concerned with the quality of care on the ward, rather than the introduction of a computer system for monitoring personnel records.
- Social loafing is reduced if group cohesion is high. Social loafing decreases if members know each other well, interact informally before the task begins, and have some feeling of loyalty and durability about the group.
- Social loafing is less in evidence when the task of the group is more complex, since this tends to heighten involvement.
- Social loafing is reduced when the group sets its own performance goals and has the dominant say in devising its own measurement system.

SUMMARY

Business success is much more probable if people look forward to coming to work in the morning, if they are allowed to participate in decision-making, if they care about the people they work with, if they feel that the tasks they must carry out are worthwhile and if they feel loyalty towards the organization which employs them. The pay-offs are considerable. Participation is associated with less resistance to change and a greater likelihood of innovation. The greater people's involvement in decision-making (through having influence, interacting with others, and sharing information horizontally, vertically and diagonally) the more likely they are to be committed to decision outcomes and also to contribute ideas for more efficient and effective ways of working.

Team organization is a valuable means of promoting precisely such participation. Small teams, genuinely empowered to make decisions, have been shown to yield tangible results. In particular, self-managed work teams are a means of achieving a powerful competitive advantage. However, if they are to achieve their full potential such teams require extraordinary operational autonomy, and enormous flexibility in establishing their own reward, incentive and appraisal systems.[26] It is impossible to introduce effective teamworking into organizations while maintaining old-style command and control systems. Hierarchy, traditions of deference and status differentials are also inimical to the approach outlined in this chapter. Teams transform work, and how work is done transforms organizations.

On the other hand, Sinclair[27] has argued that:

> the team ideology ... tyrannises because, under the banner of benefits to all, teams are frequently used to camouflage coercion under the pretence of maintaining cohesion; conceal conflict under the guise of consensus; convert conformity into a semblance of creativity; give unilateral decisions a co-determinist seal of approval; delay action in the supposed interests of consultation; legitimise lack of leadership; and disguise expedient arguments and personal agendas.

This chapter has presented a radically different agenda for action. We are discussing teams as a further means of promoting empowerment within the workplace, to the mutual advantage of the managers and the managed. The measures which work have nothing in common with the type of pretence discussed by Sinclair: in the long run, and even in the short run, you cannot fake empowerment. The effort required to disguise coercion as consultation is such that it is actually easier, not to say more satisfying, to promote 'the real thing'. There is no point in urging change in how everyone else works and demanding top-class results, while remaining determined to sit astride the traditional organizational pyramid. Empowerment means managers identifying areas where they can relinquish power in favour of others – and then actually giving up those areas. Approached in this spirit building teams will be a powerful tool for liberating the workplace and improving competitive advantage.

Answers to Exercise 3.1

Score each answer as follows:

Sometimes (3)   Rarely (2)   Frequently (4)   Always (5)   Never (1)

Add up your scores for questions 1, 3, 5 and 8 (total A).
Then add up your scores for questions 2, 4, 6 and 7 separately (total B)

You now have two separate totals. The maximum score for each section is 20. Your minimum score is 4.

Total A is your own personal *perceived* level of communication effectiveness. The higher your score the more you perceive yourself to be a good, supportive communicator within your team.

Total B gives what you *perceive* to be the general level of communication effectiveness of the other members of your team. The higher the score the better you consider their levels of communication to be.

Points for discussion

If your team is functioning well you should find that:

1. Most team members score over 16 in each of the two categories.
2. Scores are very close for each respondent in both Total A and Total B. If most of you have scored over 16 in Total A but less than that in Total B, then it suggests that each of you think that individually you are very good communicators but that other members of the team are poor!
3. You now need to consider the following questions. Be as specific as possible in your answers. In the light of this exercise:
   a) What are your team's greatest strengths?
   b) What are your team's greatest weaknesses?
   c) What practical, detailed steps are required to overcome these weaknesses?

4 Team-meets: managing productive meetings

The best soldier is not soldierly
The best fighter is not ferocious
The best conqueror does not take part in war
The best employer of men keeps himself below them
This is called the virtue of not contending
This is called the ability of using men
The best chairman is not always conspicuously in control.

Tao-Te-King scripture, China, 6 BC

You must become the change you want to see in the world.

Australian aboriginal saying

For many managers, work is one uninterrupted meeting, with only occasional changes in personnel to freshen the scene. One researcher has estimated that middle-level managers spend up to 30 per cent of their time in meetings, rising to 50 per cent for top managers.[1] Mintzberg goes further, calculating that managers spend 59 per cent of their time in scheduled meetings and another 10 per cent in unscheduled meetings.[2] These are often profitable, productive and pleasurable. Unfortunately, many meetings are also held in a leaderless vacuum, in which all life forms perish. Roles are never defined. People feel powerless to influence events and eventually abdicate responsibility. Action is on permanent leave of absence.

Still other meetings are dominated by highly directive leaders who attempt to impose 'the one right' way of doing things on every discussion and on all participants. The result is the same in both cases: meetings feel like bad hangovers, rather than a forum for taking decisions and initiating action. Either way, dysfunctional meetings are one of the biggest costs which business has to bear – and one of the most avoidable. The purpose of this chapter is to outline techniques for managing meetings which enable organizations to achieve their goals, strengthen relationships and reach high-quality decisions.

Achieving this requires a judicious blend of intervention and non-intervention, organizational support, instinct, careful planning and good chairing skills. We will explore the extent to which the leadership of groups is necessary at all, and how different styles of leadership are appropriate in varied circumstances. We will then examine the role of meetings in group life and how managers can improve their chairing skills, particularly in the context of decision-making. Most of us rarely consider how to improve meetings, precisely because they have insinuated themselves so thoroughly into the fabric of our working lives. It is time to take a fresh look.

WHEN LEADERSHIP IS NEEDED

Most managers perceive leadership skills as one of the main requirements of their job. In one survey of 250 British chief executives, who were asked to identify the most important management skills, leadership emerged as the top ranked item.[3] (The other top skills listed were vision, people management, communications and financial literacy, in that order.) In the context of groups, leadership can be defined as one or more people committed to the goals of the group as a whole rather than to those of any one part of it, and who are therefore also committed to improving relationships between the group members. Leadership is necessary for continual group success.

Given that a variety of leadership roles exist (such *as clarifying the task*, *ensuring participation* and *improving decision-making processes*) it is also clear that more than one person can make a leadership contribution to the group's deliberations. Each of us may make many leadership contributions to our team's deliberations.

Group leadership is more important under certain conditions – for example, if the group is large.[4] In such groups there is a greater need to keep people informed, establish rules and make decisions. The job of leadership is made easier if the group believes it can achieve its goals, if it attaches value to the tasks being undertaken and if the tasks require co-ordination and communication. Since there is much emphasis on the supportive role of leaders, it is also appropriate to stress that leadership itself needs support in order to thrive. Introduced into an unhealthy climate, leadership will perish. People also prefer groups where leadership roles and functions are clear, since this reduces uncertainty, eases role confusion and relieves group members of such decisional nightmares as panicking about what to do next.

But how is such group leadership to be exercised? To appreciate this, we must explore the different styles of leadership and examine which are appropriate in different circumstances.

TASKS VERSUS RELATIONSHIPS

Leadership involves influencing the understanding, behaviours or decisions of other people. However, this need not become a display of overwhelming force deployed in order to ensure compliance from others. Subject peoples can never be fully conquered, but they will frequently revolt. Organizations faced with perpetual insurrection lose out in competitive global markets.

Thus, organizations are coalitions, which work best when power is shared rather than regarded as the privileged preserve of a minority. Pfeffer[5] has argued that

> virtually all of us work in positions in which, in order to accomplish our jobs and objectives, we need the co-operation of others who do not fall within our direct chain of command. We depend, in other words, on people outside our purview of authority, whom we could not command, reward or punish even if we wanted to.

As this suggests, the nature of leadership and management has been transformed. Management increasingly involves enabling others to take responsibility for critical thinking and decision-making, and so communication and human relations have assumed a higher priority. Thus, Kotter[6] has defined management as 'the process of moving a group (or groups) in some direction through mostly non-coercive means'. The language and paraphernalia of hierarchy, privilege and deference handicaps effective group functioning and meetings.[7]

This means that the successful management of groups and meetings entails empowerment. Key point 4.1 lists some of the signs which are commonly taken as indicating a feeling of empowerment among group members and wider layers of staff. It also contains a quotation from Lao-Tzu, which summarizes the attitude an empowered group could be expected to have towards its leaders and the group's own achievements. The choice of leadership style is an important factor in determining whether such feelings are generated.

Early studies[8] suggested that two types of leader tended to emerge in groups – those principally concerned with the completion of tasks and those focused more on the nurturing of relationships between group members. However, it has since become clear that effective leadership depends on matching leadership style to the characteristics of the group, the cultural constraints within which it operates and the task it is undertaking. Thus, groups always need to work at strengthening relationships, even if their primary objective is task oriented. At the same time, groups which are primarily of a relationship orientation (such as a therapy group) have work to do together, and must agree on objectives, how these will be achieved and how the group will evaluate its effectiveness.

Accordingly, more recent studies[9] look at how people have managed to integrate task and relationship maintenance, and concentrate on one or the other in line with the prevailing needs of the group. Achieving a balance between keeping the group on task while maintaining relationships is very important. Most of us have an inclination to emphasize either relationships or tasks, and it helps us adjust this preference more to the needs of the groups to which we belong if we can identify the leadership style to which we are most attracted, and why.

Key point 4.1   The symptoms of empowerment

- People believe that what they do makes a difference. Real work is done. People feel that they can influence the decision-making process.
- Learning matters. Mistakes are viewed as offering feedback and improving the group's ability to do better next time. Mistakes are openly discussed rather than desperately concealed. Top people talk about their mistakes, modelling openness. People who make mistakes are promoted.
- People feel that they are part of a community. This can be called brotherhood, sisterhood or even family. Informal get-togethers occur regularly.
- Work is exciting. People enjoy work and look forward to coming in each day.
- Informal discussions are characterized by the sharing of good news, rather than moaning about 'how terrible this place is'.
- Managers have a consistently supportive style of communication. They praise in public and criticize in private. The emphasis, in any event, is on praise rather than condemnation.

Thus, an empowered team should feel as follows:

Of the best rulers,
The people only know that they exist;
The next best they love and praise;
The next they fear;
And the next they revile.
When they do not command the people's faith,
Some will lose faith in them,
But of the best when their task is accomplished, their work done,
The people all remark, 'We have done it ourselves'.

Lao-Tzu, 6 BC

LEADERSHIP STYLES

Three main leadership styles have been consistently identified in the research literature.[9] Managers need to be familiar with these, and when they might be appropriate. The main styles are:

- *Democratic*. The democratic leader involves people during each phase of the decision-making process. A strong premium is put on consensus. Decisions are delayed until at least a majority of group members agree with them. A central goal is the maintenance of good relationships within the group. Sometimes, this looms larger than the immediate task, and sometimes such a stress on relationships is justified.
- *Laissez-faire*. A *laissez-faire* leader is fearful of making decisions. The group is left to set its own objectives, adopt a framework for decision-making and discover its own means of evaluating outcomes. The leader's responsibilities and those of other group members are never defined. Hard decisions are avoided or postponed, while initiative constantly waves a white flag to apathy. This could be termed the 'Let's cross our fingers together' school of leadership, in which closed eyes, hope and prayer attempt to compensate for foresight and planning. Order steadily surrenders ground to chaos.
- *Authoritarian*. An authoritarian leader is one who attempts to make the group's decisions for it, and whose definition of teamwork is 'lots of people doing what I say'. Such leaders have a strong sense of self-belief, and although they might sometimes be wrong they are never in doubt. When they shout 'Jump', they expect people to answer 'How high?' There is little emphasis on the relationship side of the leadership function, and this is combined with an obsessive and debilitating stress on tasks. Team successes are rarely acknowledged, but lead to the imposition of new and even more demanding challenges. The leader behaves like an angry god, sitting in perpetual judgement of lesser beings.

Although some of these labels might seem pejorative, the weight of evidence suggests that what constitutes an appropriate leadership style depends on the nature of the challenge facing the group.[9] There are also factors concerned with the norms and general culture of the group to take into account. For example, despite its problems, those elements of an autocratic style concerned with making rapid decisions without intensive consultation may actually be justified:

1. When a problem must be resolved quickly in the face of an impending catastrophe. If the Klingons have massed on the starboard bow and are preparing to fire, an elaborate debate led by Captain Kirk is not a sensible response.
2. When the meeting is dealing with a series of easy or routine items, such as agreeing the minutes. Not every issue invites controversy, needs comment or requires everyone's enthusiastic participation.

Exercise 4.1   Evaluating your leadership ability

1. In what situations do you perceive yourself as having a leadership role?

2. What are the behaviours you use when you are leading well?

3. Identify three different people whom you consider to be particularly successful group leaders.

   (i)

   (ii)

   (iii)

4. What behaviours do these people employ to empower the groups that they lead?

5. Identify the three main changes in your own behaviour which would enable you to behave more often as a leader rather than as a follower.

   (i)

   (ii)

   (iii)

6. Identify three specific changes in your own behaviour that you can implement immediately, which will improve your leadership of others.

   (i)

   (ii)

   (iii)

3. When higher levels of procedure and stronger control are needed in very large meetings. Such meetings are, in any event, often called solely to transmit information and do not need detailed plans designed to achieve active participation.

On the other hand, a democratic style is useful when:

1. Political, legal or representational reasons make decision by consensus necessary. Here, Captain Kirk can usefully seek the views of Dr Spock.
2. An informal atmosphere is needed in the meeting.
3. The quality of the decision is less important than its acceptability.

It has been suggested, for example, that concern for the task should predominate at an early stage of group development, and that when the group is functioning well interpersonally and achieving its tasks, a more relaxed leadership style is best. Deciding on which style to adopt therefore means analysing:

- the task facing the group
- the nature and qualities of the group members
- the past history of the group and those who comprise it
- the pressures and demands of the external environment.

Personal flexibility and an awareness of the entire situation produce a happy marriage, whose offspring is greater and greater success. The challenge is now to consider how this might be applied in meetings.

Exercise 4.1 is designed to set you thinking about the leadership roles and behaviours you routinely adopt in groups, and how they might be developed to widen the range of leadership behaviours you find yourself employing.

THE ROLE OF MEETINGS

Research has shown that people are more likely to comply with a decision if they have been involved in its development.[10] Communication audits carried out by us have found that meetings often have a high personal value to people, and that there is a widespread desire in the workplace for more face-to-face contact with immediate and senior managers.[11, 12] In short, it seems that people view meetings as an important means of participating in the decision-making process. The evidence suggests, incidentally, that involvement and participation improves an organization's prospects of success in the marketplace.[10] Thus, meetings are both unavoidable and an important means of fulfilling fundamental human needs. The issue, therefore, is not one of going without meetings, but of how to manage them more effectively. Such management requires an understanding of when meetings should be called, the types of meetings appropriate for each occasion and the chairing skills which dismantle barriers to involvement while bringing people together.

WHEN TO CALL MEETINGS

People become frustrated when meetings are convened inappropriately – for example, when information could have been conveyed by phone or memo, when important players are not prepared, when all of the relevant people cannot attend, or when the meeting has been arranged solely as a matter of routine. We all grow exhausted and quarrelsome during a voyage from nothing to nowhere. The 'Monday morning meeting' should never be held simply because it has always been held. By contrast, Key point 4.2 lists some of the circumstances when meetings are generally deemed productive, and can usefully be called.

The weight of the evidence suggests that most successful meetings are characterized by participant involvement, with the exception of very large meetings convened solely for the transmission of information. Involvement may be achieved through subgroups formed to look at particular issues, in brainstorming sessions, or through straightforward debate. The role of the chair is indispensable, in facilitating participation, discussion and constructive disagreement. Critical success factors include:[14]

- Goals are considered separately to maintain objectivity. The emphasis of the discussion is on agreeing *action* to achieve concrete goals.

Key point 4.2   When to call meetings

- *There is real work to be done*. For example, important decisions must be made, or a work project needs to be reviewed.
- *There is a cause for celebration*. Celebration in the workplace motivates and empowers. Meetings are a useful forum for public praise.
- *Good news needs to be shared with everyone*. When this is done at meetings managers acquire a reputation for openness, gain some of the credit for the good news they are spreading and create another occasion for celebration.
- *Uncertainty has to be dispelled*. When rumours are rife, silence adds to the impression that there is something to hide.
- *In the midst of a crisis*. When people are given information, even in the face of unsettling news such as an impending merger, they retain a much higher level of commitment than those kept in the dark.[13]

- Participants feel utilized in a meaningful manner. Their contribution makes a difference. People are allowed to speak, contribute their ideas, disagree with the group leader and decide on objectives.
- Between meetings, real progress is made on important issues. Reviewing this generates an infectious feeling of achievement, which provides the rocket fuel for yet further success.
- Members feel that they have some personal responsibility for the success of the meeting. They are allowed to participate in the discussion, and a norm prevails that action outcomes will be declared for all participants.
- People learn something new and interesting. Ancient topics are not brought out of retirement, and compelled to jump over the same boring old hurdles – again. Action leads to success and new challenges.
- People enjoy themselves. Fun sparks creativity, comradeship and commitment.
- There is an atmosphere of commitment. The US banker, Walter Wriston, has defined commitment as a dream with a deadline.[15] Meetings should allow for the development of creative, innovative ideas – but then translate them into firm action plans, with time limits.

BLOCKS TO EFFECTIVE MEETINGS

Unfortunately, not all meetings are successful. A number of barriers to effective meetings have been identified,[8] and include:

- *Domination by a single member*. One person occupies centre stage and elbows everyone else into the wings. He or she attempts to keep the spotlight trained on his or her main object of veneration – themselves. Meanwhile, the real business of the meeting goes unrehearsed. Other participants become frustrated. Attempts to staunch the verbal flow are thwarted. Key point 4.3 lists a number of typical behavioural problems of this kind, adapted from the work of Whetten and Cameron,[16] and suggests various responses which might help to curtail them.
- *Critical norms*. This concerns the ratio of negative to positive comments made. Group solidarity disintegrates under a blitzkrieg of criticism, probably initiated by the leader. There is a relentless emphasis on difficulties and what has not been achieved, rather than what has. People fear that an ambush party lies in wait, wherever they turn. They lose all faith in the possibility of finding a different and more constructive way of doing things. Eventually, they turn their anger on each other. The problem-solving abilities of the group are culled to the point of extinction.
- *Vested interests*. The group has lost sight of its collective identity and responsibility to concentrate on organizational goals. Everyone is in the same vehicle,

Key point 4.3 Suggestions for interrupting destructive behaviours

Type	Behaviour	Suggested response
Hostile	'This is rubbish.' 'I'd expect a finance person to obstruct manufacturing in exactly that way.'	'Lets look at the evidence before reaching a decision.' 'How does everyone else feel?' 'I propose that we avoid labelling each other's ideas, and instead identify how they might or might not be helpful.'
Know it all	'As an expert in philosophy, perhaps I could be allowed to say ...' 'No one knows more about Gizmos than me.'	'Everyone is here because they have something useful to say on this.' 'We need everyone's input to make the best decision.' 'What are the facts?'
Dominator	Speaks at length on everything and anything. Brings in pet hobby horse, regardless of topic.	'Can you try to summarize your main point?' 'Right, Jeff has now spoken twice and if I can summarize his main point as follows ...'
Informal chatterer	Whispers to neighbours. Forms subgroups.	Stop talking, and create a silence. Ask everyone to pay attention to speaker. Point out that the rest of the group will be at a disadvantage if information is not shared with everyone.
Disrupter	Comes in and out of meeting. Receives faxes, messages and memos from secretary. Arrives late, mutters apology, and leaves early, possibly before important decision.	Establish ground rules such as no interruptions at an early stage. Agree that all should switch off bleepers or mobile phones throughout meeting. Establish finish time at the beginning, and obtain commitment from participants to stay.
Non-contributor	Sits silently, never speaks.	Address questions directly to person. Bring up an area of special concern to them.

but they have each seized the wheel and are attempting to drive off in different directions. Individuals or subgroups place a higher priority on their own needs, which may involve blocking constructive suggestions when they emerge from unapproved sources. Meetings become a war of attrition, with constant battles over strategy, tactics and the allocation of resources. Members leave bloodied and exhausted, rather than exhilarated by a feeling of accomplishment.

- *The dilemma of new members*. New members are generally expected to conform to the norms of the group, rather than express innovative new ideas of their own, particularly if such ideas challenge the conventional wisdom of the group. It is difficult to speak out, particularly when people feel that they are novices in the company of experts. However, groups often grow blasé and sometimes need corrective input from fresh sources.
- *Physical structure and space*. Non-verbal behaviour is an important ingredient in management communication, including during meetings. We can simply note here that physical structure helps to determine whether the meeting invites participation and sustains free-flowing dialogue between group members. Main needs include: comfortable seating arrangements; moderate heating; circular tables, with no 'head of table' position – this is most facilitative and promotes equality of status; physical proximity – this generates closeness, as sports teams huddling together before a match can testify.

THE ROLE OF THE CHAIR

In one sense, presiding over meetings is straightforward. There are a variety of functions which the chair is routinely expected to fulfil. These include:

- Opening the meeting.
- Moving through the agenda, when one exists, in an acceptable time.
- Providing people with sufficient opportunity to express their views.
- Ensuring that decisions are taken, are agreed and that responsibility for their implementation is allocated.
- Conducting votes on resolutions, where necessary.
- Upholding the rules, constitution or 'standing orders' of the organization.
- Regulating the discussion.[17]

How these functions are executed is fraught with ambiguity. For example, discussions at meetings on important issues improve when the chair is neutral, at least initially. This prevents the emergence of groupthink and facilitates the expression of minority dissent (see Chapter 3). On the other hand, the chair is also in charge of the discussion, and has a responsibility to ensure that the goals of the organization are realized. It would seem that successful chairs require the agility of a circus acrobat, as well as the verbal skills of a ring-master and the thick hide of a performing elephant in order to succeed!

Meetings pass through a number of stages during which the role of the chair is particularly important. These are planning, helping group members get acquainted, managing the discussion and formulating decisions. Each of these is examined in depth below.

STEPS TOWARDS GOOD PLANNING

Like many management activities the quality of the outcomes generated by meetings is correlated with the amount of effort invested in preparation beforehand. Planning for meetings is necessary, especially if it is anticipated that important proposals will meet with opposition, if members are likely to turn up with serious grievances or that radically new proposals will be discussed. Key point 4.4 lists a number of the most important steps which will help with this process.

HELPING GROUP MEMBERS TO BECOME ACQUAINTED

As discussed above, problem-solving and long-term group cohesion are improved when steps are taken to improve relationships as well as keeping in mind the group's tasks.[18] Thus, it is useful if:

1. Before the first meeting, and if the members are relatively unknown to each other, the chair sends each member a biographical sketch of the other members, alongside some description of the group's origins, role and its intended outcomes.
2. Again, just before the first meeting, the members should socialize, perhaps over coffee. We have worked with some public sector organizations where there is a policy that coffee is no longer provided at meetings, in order to save money. However, the evidence clearly shows[18] that the informal dialogue which springs up around such social outlets improves the quality of group decision-making. Chairs should expand opportunities for social interaction, not curtail them.
3. At the first meeting, each member should be introduced by the chair, or should briefly introduce themselves. Care needs to be taken to prevent the proceedings becoming bogged down in exaggerated self-eulogies, or lengthy perorations in favour of pet projects. Among the advantages of the chair performing such introductions are that:
   a) A useful opportunity is created to publicly praise excellent performance.
   b) This makes the recipient feel good.
   c) The status of the manager delivering the praise goes up.
   d) Control is asserted at the outset.

Key point 4.4   Steps towards successful planning

Understanding the participants

- Who does each of the participants represent?
- Why exactly have they been chosen for this group?
- What is known about their goals and needs, their ego, their vested interests?
- What special skills do they possess which may help the group achieve its goals?
- What are their biases on the issues which this group will confront?
- How do they feel about the group leader, and indeed about the organization as a whole?
- What are their strengths and weaknesses?
- What is their track record in group work?
- Are they what the advertising guru, David Ogilvy, referred to as 'extinct volcanoes', from which no further sign of life can be anticipated?

Assessing the history of the group

- How did everyone leave the last meeting? Was there a feeling of accomplishment, or one of learned helplessness?
- What will people's expectations be of the next meeting?
- What caused any problems, and what can be done about them?

Setting realistic goals

- Have goals been set that are achievable?
- Have goals been set that are within the 'terms of reference' of this group, or has the group gone off at an interesting but futile tangent?
- Have goals been identified that meet the group's collective needs, and the wider needs of the organization?
- Will the goals adopted by the group command significant support within the organization?
- What opposition to the group's goals can we anticipate?

4. During long meetings breaks should be provided, enabling members to resume the social conversations with which they began. This reinforces the human bond which underlies successful task performance.

MANAGING THE DISCUSSION

Early research[19] identified 31 excellent chairs by observation, expert judge ratings, track record and the views of people they chaired. This found that successful chairs made more proposals about managing the group discussion than other group members, expressed less support for various positions which emerged during debate, used a very high level of testing understanding and summarizing, disagreed less frequently with members' ideas, were high in their use of information seeking and were relatively low in information giving. It appears that success occurs if the chair is aware of the value of neutrality early in group discussions, and encourages members of the group to express their real opinions. A range of chairing skills have been identified, and these can be summarized as follows:[14, 17, 20]

- Begin the process before the meeting. For example, circulate important papers, and consult with key individuals. Prior activity improves the rate of discussion and enhances levels of satisfaction with the process. Key point 4.4 has already listed a variety of tactics which help to achieve this.
- Begin your meeting on time.
- Clarify or refine what has been said when the discussion is under way. Use paraphrasing, summarizing and probing questions as key skills. Show that you are paying attention to speakers.
- Ensure that all items on the agenda are discussed during the meeting for which they are scheduled. It is also generally good practice to ensure that the chair does not raise items for discussion under 'Any other business', although it is legitimate for others to do so. Otherwise, it is possible to be seen as someone who manoeuvres controversial topics through, while allowing other participants insufficient time for preparation.
- Bring in non-participants and shut down those who attempt to dominate the discussion. A norm can be established that everyone who attends is expected to speak. Planned subgroups help with this and enable people to feel that they have contributed to the eventual outcome. Time limits on contributions and presentations may also be necessary.
- Use 'key questions' to promote discussion. Ask open-ended questions rather than questions that can be answered with 'yes' or 'no.' Thus, say: 'What are your opinions about the plan to increase production?' Do not say: 'Do you agree with the plan to increase production this month?'
- Use rewarding behaviours and attentive listening to encourage greater participation.

- From time to time, stay silent. The chair should not dominate the discussion or pursue pet hobbyhorses – others will quickly lose interest.
- Repeat statements that seem significant. Make procedural suggestions for closing or opening topics. Never let the discussion drift aimlessly, without reaching a decision.
- Summarize and clarify regularly. Tell speakers what you think they mean – it might be right or wrong, but avoids post-meeting confusion. Use examples from your own experience to illustrate a topic.
- Ask group members for reaction to each other's points. When appropriate, involve group members in answering a question addressed to you.
- At the end of the meeting, summarize the points made, the decisions reached and indicate the way ahead. Decide on 'immediate next steps' and list action outcomes for all participants. This is a particular chairing skill, and group members become aggrieved if the role is left to another participant in the meeting.
- End the meeting on time, or even shortly before your scheduled cut-off point. If you go over an agreed deadline your fellow participants will have already vacated the room mentally, thereby rendering continued discussion pointless.
- Stick to the agenda and a rough order for items. Develop, and keep, a long-range schedule.

FORMULATING DECISIONS

Teams exist to solve problems. This suggests an action framework within which the team:

A. Decides what it has to do.
B. Discusses how this will be done, how the team will conduct itself and how it will evaluate its efforts.
C. Starts doing it!

Our own observations of many groups suggest that most of them are inclined to start at point C. Teams tend to have such a thirst for 'action' that they engage in frantic (and usually chaotic) activity at the outset. This is often caused by external pressure, such as a boss screaming for instant results. After a further period of upheaval, teams then begin to discuss how they should be going about their task. Only after yet another period of fruitless but demanding activity do they begin to consider what it is they should be doing in the first place – a sequence, it will be noted, of C→B→A, rather than A→B→C. A review of group decision-making concluded that: 'One of the common dangers to group effectiveness is becoming "solution minded" too soon; that is, generating solutions before a full understanding of the problem is available.'[21]

A main responsibility of the chair is to ensure that the group has sufficient awareness of its own behaviour to implement an A→B→C, approach to decision-making.

This understanding can be promoted if the chair ensures that issues are discussed in the following fashion:

1. What is our goal on this particular issue?
2. How are we going to go about generating solutions?
3. What is the action that we have agreed to take on this issue?
4. When will it be done?
5. Who is going to be responsible?
6. What did we do well in this meeting?
7. What could have been done better?

SUMMARY

Leading groups is an exciting but often frustrating challenge for managers. However we feel about it, leadership is an unavoidable component of the management job. Success depends on a range of skills, attitudes and behaviours which encourage participation, generate excitement, inspire hope and result in concrete change. According to Warren Bennis,[22] one of the main researchers into leadership in management, this is facilitated if leaders possess the following characteristics:

- *A guiding vision.* There is a clear idea of where the leader wants to go. The vision is persisted with, in the face of temporary setbacks or obstacles.
- *Passion.* Enthusiasm energizes, inspires and fortifies people in the face of adversity. Key point 4.5 contains Henry Ford's views on this subject: one of the most powerful testimonials to enthusiasm ever produced.

Key point 4.5   The power of enthusiasm

You can do anything if you have enthusiasm.
Enthusiasm is the yeast that makes your hopes rise to the stars.
Enthusiasm is the sparkle in your eyes, the swing in your gait, the grip of your hand, the irresistible surge of will and energy to execute your ideas.
Enthusiasts are fighters. They have fortitude. They have staying qualities.
Enthusiasm is at the bottom of all progress.
With it, there is accomplishment.
Without it, there are only alibis.

Henry Ford

- *Integrity.* The three main components of integrity are self-knowledge, candour and maturity. There is a breadth of learning, going beyond the basics of balance sheets, organization design or marketing strategies. Broad perspectives are held and introduced into the group.
- *Curiosity and daring.* Life becomes a ceaseless quest for new knowledge and new ways of doing things. Innovative approaches to problem-solving are introduced or encouraged in others. Stagnation is not an option.

These qualities lift meetings out of the humdrum, giving them purpose and sparkle. Leadership should be fun, as well as productive, and leadership in groups is a skill which can be studied, learned and improved. Adopting the range of approaches discussed in this chapter will help to improve the quality of the meetings in which we are all destined to continue spending so much of our time.

5 Stand and deliver: making effective presentations

> The scientist must sometimes move out of the laboratory, the accountant from the office, the boffin from the drawing-board. They are forced into battle with overseas competitors who often have a far more practical, intelligent, informed and structured approach to presentation – formal or informal, public or private – than our old fashioned world of the public school and the ancient university where the learning of presentation skills bears the taint of the ill-bred.
>
> Greville Janner, *Janner on Presentation*
>
> Good speakers have a way of moving audiences: great speakers have a way of moving generations.
>
> *Anon.*

We live and work in a world that is subject to the increasing effects of information technology in all its forms and guises. Information is relayed quickly and effortlessly by telephone, fax, voice mail, internet and e-mail, to name but a few. Some of the skills and techniques for enhancing the effectiveness with which these tools are put to use in the office, form the content of other chapters in this book. But despite the many different options that technology affords, the oral presentation has an enduring quality and appeal as a means of delivering ideas directly and with impact. One study[1] surveyed 500 managers in retail, wholesale, manufacturing, service industries, public administration, transport and insurance and finance. Oral communication emerged as the type of competency felt to have the greatest currency for graduates entering the workforce. Furthermore, when the actual skills that constitute this competency were distilled down, those to do with making presentations were found to rank highly in both importance and frequency of use.

Many successful careers have been founded on the ability to catch the eye of those in senior management. For junior staff, making an impressive presentation in

Exercise 5.1 Effective presentations

This exercise is intended to help you identify some of the features of effective oral presentations, and the extent to which you make use of them. There are three stages:

1. Think back to a presentation that readily comes to mind as having been really well handled. It stays in your memory perhaps because it was so useful, interesting, expertly delivered, and so on. Using the headings below, jot down a few comments that sum up what you experienced. Make a note of any other attributes that you feel made it successful, but which are not mentioned in this list.

Presenter

Well informed

Well prepared

Credible

Presentation

Clear purpose

Good introduction

Relevant

Structured

Integrated

Exercise 5.1 (Cont'd)

Concise

Right pace

Good visual aids

Effective closure

Delivery

Engaging

Dynamic

Articulate

Appropriate language

Appropriate style

Audience

Reactions

2. Select the last presentation that you gave. Using the same headings, together with any additional features that you feel are important, analyse it in a similar way.

3. Based upon a comparison of your two lists, jot down three areas where you feel you are generally strong and three that you feel need improving.

Strong

Need improving

the form of a briefing or a report is a prime opportunity to get noticed by those in a position to advance their progress in the company. Research carried out at Stanford University found that the best predictor of success and upward mobility was positive attitude towards, and effectiveness in, public speaking.[2]

Presenting also features prominently in the day-to-day schedule of executives in more elevated corporate positions. It can be a means of increasing staff morale, and directing and co-ordinating effort. When targeting chairpersons and board members, presenting typically forms part of the decision-making process whereby policy is shaped. In the context of external relations, new business approaches demand high-quality presentations in such areas as market research and advertising.[3] Not only are contracts secured in this way, but when the job is done, findings are commonly delivered in some form of presentation. We could continue with further examples but the point has been adequately made. Giving oral presentations which can vary in purpose, formality, privacy, and size and composition of audience is an unavoidable part of successful management.

On occasion, though, many fail to make the most of the opportunities afforded by giving a presentation. Through a combination of causes including unmanaged anxiety, lack of planning and preparation, weak structure, and poor judgement of audience interests and need, what is delivered is often nervy and discomforting, convoluted and confusing, or dull and insipid. There is evidence that managers prefer business communication to be direct, easily understood and succinct.[4] Oral briefings mostly fail because they are confusingly organized, contain too much technical jargon, are too long-winded, include too few examples and are unattractively delivered.[5] But it need not be this way. Having the capacity to make a successful presentation is not a natural gift. It is a set of skills and techniques that can be learned, practised and refined with further experience. While some are destined to be better than others, everyone can improve.

At this point let us pause for a moment's deliberation. Exercise 5.1 is included to encourage you to think more deeply about presentations, assess your own current performance and reach decisions about your strengths and weaknesses.

TYPES OF PRESENTER AND PRESENTATION

Advice on public speaking has a well-established tradition in literature. The ability to capture the attention of an audience and express one's message in such a way that it is received with respect and changes beliefs, opinions and actions, has been valued down the ages. But the prospect of having to face such an undertaking can be extremely emotionally taxing. According to research cited by DeVito[6] between 10 and 20 per cent of American college students suffer from severe and debilitating apprehension at the thought of communicating formally in public. A further 20 per cent are sufficiently affected in this way that their normal performance is interfered with. Furthermore, surveys of the adult population have found that fear of public speaking consistently ranks above that of heights, snakes, ill health and even death. For some, having to make a presentation can literally be a fate worse than death! But not all react in this distressed way. A few, at the other extreme, relish the opportunity. Where do you place yourself on this continuum?

Steve Mandel, a well-known organizational communication consultant, has identified four categories or types into which most of us fit when it comes to reacting to making presentations:[5]

- *Avoiders* – those who will go to any lengths to avoid having to make a presentation, including going sick, or even finding another job.
- *Resistors* – those who are extremely reluctant to carry out duties of this type and for whom doing so causes considerable negative emotion.
- *Acceptors* – those who give presentations reluctantly, for the most part. They seldom volunteer to do so, but sometimes may enjoy it and feel good about what they have achieved.
- *Seekers* – those who actively seek out opportunities to appear before groups. They can turn initial anxieties into positive forms of energy and work at promoting competence in this area.

We can also recognize different types of presentation. There are three main kinds:

- *Informative*. The primary purpose is to deliver a body of material, including data together with interpretations and judgements, in such a way that it is fully comprehended. The aim is to promote understanding.
- *Persuasive*. In this case, attitudes, beliefs and opinions of the audience are targeted. The objective is to affirm and strengthen existing positions adopted by participants in relation to some issue, or try to bring about a change in the opposite direction. In either case the intention has to do with influencing attitudes and held positions on issues. Much of what has already been covered in Chapter 2, can be put to use here.
- *Energizing*. Here the presentation serves to mobilize the group and spur them to action. It is a 'call to arms'. To be considered successful, the audience must leave with a firm commitment to do something – and then do it! Ideally it should be done with enthusiasm: the course of action should be warmly embraced. Needless to say, this can often be the most difficult of presentations to deliver. It requires generous measures of rhetoric and emotion, and is at its best when served with great charismatic appeal.

We will now move on to consider the different components that make up the presentational process. In all cases, and simply put, there must be a presenter who presents to an audience in a particular setting. The presentation itself comprises content which must be suitably delivered. Each of these five elements – presenter,

Key point 5.1 Qualities and characteristics of successful presenters

The more audiences perceive presenters in the following terms, the more receptive they are likely to be, both to the presenters and to their message:

- *Poised.* The audience should be assured that the presenter is in control of him or herself and the situation. If not, members become uneasy and lose interest.
- *Competent.* The audience must be convinced that the presenter has some acceptable level of expertise in relation to the topic.
- *Trustworthy.* The audience must be able to believe that the presenter is fair, reliable, honest, honourable, truthful and mindful of their interests rather than merely seeking self-gain. Trustworthiness is frequently something that develops over time with a group.
- *Committed.* The presenter must show commitment to the message delivered and, where applicable, to the course of action advocated. Being prepared to 'go the extra mile' with the group is one way of displaying commitment.
- *Dynamic.* Dynamism carries its own message about energy, enthusiasm and forcefulness. It is displayed in words and actions. Non-verbally, it requires a more animated style in bodily movement and voice amplitude and variation. Dynamism is one of the attributes of that more ephemeral quality, charisma. It is particularly important in presentations designed to persuade and energize.
- *Sincere.* Dynamism without sincerity is worthless. A trickster with a livelier patter is simply seen as a bigger charlatan! The successful presenter must come across as believing totally in what is said. As noted in Chapter 14, incongruities between verbal and non-verbal messages can signal deception.
- *Respectful.* The presenter must show respect for the audience, its views, opinions and knowledge base. Inexperienced presenters, often in an attempt to conceal their own feelings of anxiety and vulnerability, sometimes sound superior, even arrogant. An audience treated in this way is likely to be defensive, perhaps antagonistic.
- *Attractive.* For the most part, more physically attractive presenters command greater attention, and are more likely to have their case

Key point 5.1 (Cont'd)

accepted and acted upon. But there are limits. If the attractiveness of the presenter exceeds expectations for that sort of event, it can have a boomerang effect. The 'blonde bimbo' mindset can be triggered!

Apart from sheer physical attraction, the more similar the audience thinks the presenter is to it in values, attitude and outlook (but not expertise in the area of the presentation), the more attractive that person will be perceived to be.

audience, content, delivery and setting – deserves close attention. The remainder of the chapter will discuss each in turn.

THE PRESENTER

Unless the presenter is perceived and received in an accommodating way, especially at the outset, it is highly unlikely that much attention will be paid to the message, let alone that the message will carry sufficient gravitas to have the impact intended. Here we can think of judgements made by the audience based on:

- *How the presenter looks and sounds.* Initial impressions of, for instance, cues to do with dress, deportment and level of anxiety will be quickly formed. These lead to estimations of expertise, confidence, and sincerity.
- *What the presenter says and does.* Presenters, as part of the introduction, can enhance their credibility by mentioning, for example, prestigious companies that have called on their expertise, professional associations of which they are members, qualifications obtained, books they have written and research that they have carried out on the subject, and so on. As with all attempts at impression management, they must be subtle if they are to work. Read as moves to ingratiate, they will invariably backfire and defeat the purpose. Without doubt, however, it is in how the main body of the talk is handled that the most enduring impressions are created.
- *What the audience already knows or is told about the presenter.* The situation where the presenter's name and reputation are already known to the audience and are held in high esteem, is a happy starting-point to any delivery. Short of that, it is usually acceptable to make the person who will introduce you to the group, familiar with some of your achievements. It is always more compelling to have someone else trumpet your successes.

Information gleaned in these ways will form the basis of impressions of personal qualities, dispositions and attributions such as outlined in Key point 5.1 (pages 88–89). Many of these concern the fundamentally important issue of accepting the credibility of the presenter.

MANAGING ANXIETY

One of the qualities of an effective presenter, mentioned in Key point 5.1, is poise. Handling dysfunctional anxiety, as we have already seen, presents the greatest difficulty for many. But the point needs to be made that experiencing *some* level of stress when about to present is neither abnormal nor dysfunctional. It is often even desirable. Without it we probably would not be sufficiently able to give of our best. Keeping stress within constructive boundaries is what matters.

Extreme distress at the prospect of having to speak in public has a number of causes with associated implications for how to go about overcoming it. The three most important steps that can be taken are:

1. *Find out how to present effectively and become more skilled at it.* Often fear is a consequence of knowing or suspecting that you have not the resources to put on a competent performance.
2. *Learn to relax.* There is no obvious reason why so many should be afraid in this way. Anxiety is something that is learned. This may be from:
   a) listening to parents or watching, as children, others' faltering attempts
   b) being humiliated in this way at school
   c) giving a presentation that went horribly wrong, so that extreme trepidation has become associated with this activity.
   But learning to relax is easier said than done. Key point 5.2 (pages 92–93) offers some guidelines.
3. *Don't talk yourself down.* Often those who are cruelly tormented at the thought of having to talk in public, engage in an internal chatter that runs along the lines of 'I'll never be able to do this! I'll make a complete fool of myself. They will see right through me, and think that I'm stupid. I'll dry up in the middle of it. My mind will go blank! I'll never be able to face them again!' and so on. In other words these people 'talk' themselves into believing that they are going to do poorly, and then get extremely agitated at the prospect. This serves to make them even more certain that failure is inevitable: and in truth under these circumstances it probably is. Negative ruminations must be replaced with constructive alternatives.[7] Concentrate on your strengths and factors that can be exploited to your advantage. Substitute negative self-talk with reassuring reminders such as:
   a) 'I know this report back to front'
   b) 'I am well prepared and know exactly what I intend to do'
   c) 'The presentation will run smoothly, just as I have planned it'.

THE AUDIENCE

Success in presenting is measured not on a scale of how much is given, but rather how much is received. Each talk must be tailored, therefore, to the idiosyncrasies of the particular group to which it is delivered. The presenter must find out as much as possible about who will attend, at an early stage of planning. A useful starting-point is with those who arranged the event. They might have a list of names of participants with some details on each. Information to gather includes size of group, age, sex, occupation and position in the company, background knowledge on the topic and attitude towards it. Gleaning further details during the course of the presentation is also a wise step.

What participants know about the topic and their attitudes towards it, prior to attending, are particularly useful pieces of information. Attitudinally, audiences seem to fall into one of four types as outlined in Key point 5.3 (page 94). But ultimately they are made up of individuals and, at that level, members are likely to react differently within the group. For a start, it is usually unrealistic to expect all of those present to be constantly and totally in agreement with what is being said. The fact that some show signs of losing interest, can adversely affect the inexperienced presenter. Some participants adopt a confrontational stance, not because they dislike the speaker, or even disagree strongly with the content of the presentation, but simply to show that they are discerning.

CONTENT OF THE PRESENTATION

We now look at steps such as preparing the material to form the substance of the presentation, structuring it in an organized way best suited to increasing coherence and adding impact, and deciding which visual aids to utilize.

PREPARING CONTENT

The principal reason why presentations fail is inadequate planning. Nor should it be thought that this stage can be skipped because the talk will be brief. In fact, having a short space of time within which to explain complex ideas, or make a compelling case, puts an added premium on careful preparation. Winston Churchill is reputed to have said that he would spend ten minutes making ready a two-hour speech, but two hours if the speech was only ten minutes!

The preparation stage comprises the following.

Identify the aim and clarify the objectives

A natural point of departure in this venture is establishing firmly why the presentation is being made and what precisely it is intended to achieve. A useful way to think

Key point 5.2 Learning how to relax about presentations

1. Find a quiet, dimly lit, comfortable room where you will not be disturbed for 15 to 20 minutes.
2. Take off your shoes and lie on your back with your body straight, arms by your side. Make yourself comfortable. You may want to place a folded towel under your head. Turn you palms upwards and let your toes flop outwards.
3. Breathe steadily and evenly. Now, beginning with your feet and calf muscles, take a deep breath and hold it as you tense those muscles. It is important that the rest of your body stays as relaxed as possible. Hold it for a count of four, breathe out and relax the muscles. Repeat three times, each time feeling more tension ease away with your out breath. (If you find this difficult, you may want to start with the right leg first, then the left.)
4. Do the same for your thigh muscles, again keeping the rest of your body relaxed.
5. Move on to the buttocks and repeat, then the stomach muscles, hands and forearms, biceps, shoulders and chest, neck and face.
6. Now tense the whole body and relax with an out breath as before. Repeat several times. Your whole body should now feel quite relaxed. Check it for signs of any parts where tension may still be lurking.
7. Continue to lie quietly for a few minutes simply being aware of your slow even breathing (without trying to control it) and your state of relaxation. You should have no other intrusive thoughts.

After sufficient repetitions of steps 1–7, over a number of sessions, to enable you to quickly establish a state of bodily relaxation, move on to step 8. You are now ready to begin to introduce some thoughts about that troublesome presentation while in your new-found state of relaxation.

8. Draw up a list of situations in which you will find yourself when conducting the presentation. Arrange them in order from the least to the most anxiety provoking (e.g. collecting material for the presentation may be the easiest, getting dressed the morning of the presentation more difficult, getting to your feet and actually beginning to speak, the most anxiety provoking).

Key point 5.2 (Cont'd)

---

9. Begin with the least anxiety provoking. Work through steps 1–7 to establish a relaxed state. While in that state, begin to imagine yourself doing that task. Check for signs of tension. Stop if they become difficult to manage and return to steps 1–7. Once you can visualize yourself completing the task relatively free of anxiety, tell yourself that you can do it. This begins the process of replacing negative self-talk with more positive statements.
10. Once you have mastered the least difficult task, move on and repeat the next most difficult, and so on, always returning to the previous one if anxiety becomes intrusive.
11. Arrange to give a presentation to a small group of people whom you know will not be overly critical on a topic that you feel extremely comfortable with.

---

of objectives is to specify in detail what changes the presentation should make to the audience. These changes can be in their (1) knowledge, (2) feelings/beliefs/attitudes or (3) behaviour, and it is important that these be teased out and clearly sighted or it is highly unlikely that success will be achieved. While a single presentation may have more than one type of objective, each points quite naturally to a contribution that should be primarily informative, persuasive or energizing.

Knowing the audience plays a pivotal part in preparation, as does establishing the length of time available for the address and finding out where it will take place. The latter will be returned to later in the chapter. As far as the length of the presentation is concerned, if this is left entirely to the speaker to decide, something in the order of 20–25 minutes should be aimed for. Given that attention tends to wane after about 15 minutes, it will be difficult to keep the group engaged if this sort of time frame is much exceeded.

Research the issue

Once the purpose has been established, the next task is to decide what the audience needs to be made aware of in order for those objectives to be met. Above all else, it is imperative that the presenter 'masters the brief'. Audiences can be, and generally are, quite forgiving, but not if vast holes in that person's knowledge base quickly develop. This does not mean, of course, that *everything* must be known – few people do, about any topic – but the speaker should appear to be well-informed. If not, why is he or she there?

Key point 5.3   Types of audience

1. *Indifferent.* This audience is probably present under duress. They do not appreciate that they have a need, let alone a want, that can be met by anything that you have to say in this situation. The introductory part of your presentation has to succeed in quickly capturing attention and increasing motivation. This type of audience presents a particular challenge when the intention is to deliver an *energizing* type presentation.
2. *Uninformed.* The audience may know little about what you intend to cover and have developed no particular attitude towards it. This makes a persuasive presentation easier. It requires careful planning though in the case of the *informative* presentation.
3. *Undecided.* Unlike the previous, this group has information at its disposal but has not reached a position on the issue at hand.
4. *Antagonistic.* In this case, the audience is opposed to the line being taken in the persuasive presentation. This poses fairly obvious challenges to the presenter intent on dragging the group through 180 degrees in their thinking. It can also mean that the presenter may have less credibility in the eyes of those present and will possibly be less well liked. In these circumstances, it is important that the presenter is not too ambitious in the objectives set. Perhaps a lessening of audience entrenchment is the most that can be realistically hoped for at this stage.
5. *Supportive.* This is the presenter's dream: a group that already holds a position on the issue, in keeping with that of the presenter. There is potential here for an energizing presentation to succeed in mobilizing the gathering into effective action. There is also scope for an approach relying heavily on emotion to be well received.

Researching the issue does not just mean collecting evidence to support the case being advocated. It must also cover alternative perspectives and possible counter-arguments, together with refutations. This does not mean, however, that all that has been found out must be included in the presentation. The aphorism 'the mind can only comprehend what the backside can tolerate', should not be dismissed lightly!

Select the method of delivery

It is one thing to be familiar with the content, another to decide how to deliver that material with best effect. How formal should the presentation be? Should it be all talk and if so should you, as presenter, be the only one doing it? Does the topic really require, perhaps, a process to be physically demonstrated? Should you have visual aids? Should you try to actively involve the audience? The actual process of delivery will be returned to later in the chapter.

Prepare visual aids

Most presentations benefit from visual aids in one form or other. These can range from physical objects and models, to pictures, tables, charts, graphs, diagrams, etc., shown on video, film, computer, slides, flip chart, or overhead projector (OHP). People take in information using different sensory channels. Some favour listening, others looking. Visual representations can, therefore, support the spoken word and, by introducing greater variety, make for a more attractive experience for the group. Presenters who use visual aids are perceived more favourably by their audiences, take less time to present concepts and enable greater retention of what is learned.[8]

In preparing visual aids, avoid:

- having too many
- cluttering each with too much information
- using a font size that is too small
- letting the technology take over – remember these are just aids.

Decide how to handle questions

Quite often inexperienced presenters look forward least to this element of the talk. The feeling is that at this juncture they are less in control and may be 'caught out' with an unanticipated query. But a question and answer session holds much potential for obtaining feedback, clearing up misunderstandings, consolidating learning, underscoring the position advocated and securing a commitment to change.

The options are to establish ground rules whereby either all questions are kept to the end or they are dealt with during the course of the delivery. Although the former reflects a more formal style with reduced audience involvement, it does make it easier to control the progress of the presentation so that everything is covered in the allotted time. The other possibility is simply to field questions as they arise. Incidentally, when a sensible answer does not come to mind it is invariably better to admit it and suggest responding to the questioner later, rather than trying to bluff. Remember, the speaker will not be expected to know everything.

ORGANIZING CONTENT AND STRUCTURING THE PRESENTATION

A simple, but useful, structuring model is to think of the presentation in three phases. The first is the introduction, the second is the main body, the third is the conclusion.

Introduction

This first phase should not be overlooked or treated in a perfunctory fashion. Remember the importance of creating favourable first impressions. The introduction serves a number of purposes, as outlined in Key point 5.4. Useful opening gambits that are 'attention-grabbers', depending on circumstances, include:

- asking a challenging question
- providing an interesting piece of information that has relevance for the group
- using humour
- relaying a significant event or happening
- recounting a riveting story or dramatic event
- making a novel prediction
- citing an engaging quotation from a respected source
- stressing the importance of the material for members.

The main body

An adequate researching of the issue, as part of the preparation of the presentation, should reveal main points that need to be recognized, understood and accepted if

---

Key point 5.4   Functions of the introduction to the presentation

Introductions can serve to:

1. Make yourself known to the group and begin the process of building rapport.
2. Stimulate interest and gain attention.
3. Arouse motivation.
4. Create a suitable mood/climate for the meeting.
5. Outline clearly what the presentation is about.
6. Map the structure and progression of your talk.
7. Invite the audience to play a particular role, by suggesting activities that may be included for them.
8. Establish a common base with the group in terms of shared knowledge as a point for departure.
9. Project yourself and take control.

---

the objectives are to be reached. These key points will be located amid other supporting information and evidence. They must be identified. Having done so, the next concern is with how best to sequence them in the context of the delivery, to provide a cohesive, persuasive and well-formed address. The preferred organizing structure will depend both on the nature of the material and the purpose to which it is being put. Some strategies are listed in Key point 5.5.

Key point 5.5 Some strategies for organizing content

1. *Topical arrangement.* Here the issue is analysed into related topics and subtopics to be presented: the key elements. These have no particular relationship to one another apart from shared relevance. The order in which they are covered is typically shaped by going from (i) the known to the unknown, and (ii) the simple to the complex.
2. *Chronological sequence.* Here the key elements of the material are ordered in relation to a sequence of time (e.g. describing how the company evolved to its present state) or progression (e.g. outlining the steps involved in a manufacturing process).
3. *Logical sequence.* There are two alternatives. The deductive sequence moves from general principles to what needs to be done in certain specific cases which need to be considered by the group. The converse, inductive sequence begins with specific cases and from them moves to the derivation of broad principles that should be accepted and applied.
4. *Causal pattern.* The material is ordered in terms of a sequence of cause–effect relationships that explains events, for the audience, and why they came about. It can be extended into the next possibility.
5. *Problem and solution.* This option structures the presentation into two sections. The first sketches the nature of the problem. The second maps the solution.
6. *The motivated sequence.* This is a more elaborate strategy than 5 above. Like 5, it is particularly suited when the intention is to change attitudes, beliefs or practices. It follows the sequence of gaining attention, establishing need, outlining how that need can be satisfied, helping the audience to visualize the satisfied need and, finally, stipulates what has to be done to accomplish that state.

The conclusion

It has been found that audiences tend to remember more of what was said at the beginnings and endings of talks, than of the bits in the middle.[7] The conclusion, therefore, offers a valuable opportunity to contribute something that will be taken away, retained and used to shape thinking or action. Quite often 'the sleeper effect' works: it is only some time later after mulling over what was said that a member decides to accept it. Furthermore, the presentation should not come to an abrupt and unexpected end. Rather it should be flagged, so the audience realizes what is about to occur. The following tactics should form part of this stage:

- Review and summarize the key points.
- Pull together any loose threads.
- Reaffirm the conclusion reached and its importance (it can, sometimes, be highly effective to draw the 'inescapable' conclusion from the audience).
- Elicit commitment to advocated courses of action (if the intention is to energize the group).
- Obtain feedback.
- Suggest ways in which the issues dealt with could be extended.
- Clarify how the presentation will be followed up (if appropriate).
- Disengage by thanking the group for their attention and co-operation.

DELIVERING THE PRESENTATION

We now consider styles of delivery and the techniques that can be used to make the presentation more attractive, comprehensible and impactful.

STYLES OF DELIVERY

Basically there are four main types of delivery to choose from:[6]

1. *Impromptu*. An address is given without any prior planning. This is best avoided if possible, especially for the inexperienced and unconfident. Having said that, an effective style is often one that *seems* impromptu, in the sense of being relaxed and conversational – the well-rehearsed ad lib!
2. *Extemporaneous*. This requires the presenter to generate the presentation, as it progresses, around main points and headings available in the form of notes or cue cards.
3. *Memorized*. In this case, a set script is memorized and regurgitated. While it is largely unfeasible for all but the shortest of presentations, there can be advantage in memorizing your introductory statement to move 'off the mark', as well

as particularly pertinent points throughout that need to be delivered verbatim for reasons of accuracy or impact.

4. *Read.* This involves reading from a prepared manuscript. Unless done by a trained actor it quickly degenerates into tedium. It is best avoided despite the fact that it offers the greatest degree of control over the proceedings. In the case of highly technical presentations where accuracy is at a premium, it is best to cover the main findings using visuals, and if necessary provide the rest in the form of a hand-out.

TECHNIQUES OF EFFECTIVE DELIVERY

It is sometimes mistakenly thought that good speakers are born. The corollary is that if one has not been predestined in this way at birth, there is little that can be done to retrieve the situation. Nothing could be further from the truth. There are quite simple pieces of advice that can vastly improve the quality of an address:

- *Appropriate language and avoidance of jargon.* If the audience cannot understand most of what is being talked about they will become detached, then bored and resentful. Jargon *per se* is not a problem. All professions have their stock in trade and this communication register eases information transfer amongst the discerning few. The problems arise when these professionals overlook the fact that the rest of humankind does not share with them this form of talk. Under these circumstances jargon serves to mystify, confuse and alienate.

- *Suitable pace of delivery.* Inexperienced presenters tend to speak too quickly. This 'rush response' can be a nervous reaction. The feeling is that the sooner it is all over with the better. On the other hand having the audience mark time while you catch up is a recipe for boredom. The pace to aim for is that with which the participants seem comfortable. As a rough guide, it has been suggested that listening can become difficult when the rate of speech exceeds 300 words per minute or drops much below 125 words per minute.[9]

- *Visual aids.* These are an immensely powerful tool for delivering the presentation in an illuminating and attractive manner.[10] Established devices such as video, slides and OHPs are now complemented by the enormous versatility of computer graphics packages. It must never be forgotten, though, that even the best of these are only aids to assist the speaker.[11] They should never be permitted to take centre stage thereby relegating the hapless presenter to the wings.

- *Subsummaries and transitional statements.* It can be helpful, with complex material and convoluted arguments, to pause at transitional points in the flow of ideas to briefly summarize the material covered. Explaining how this 'chunk' of information links with what comes next helps to signpost the path through the presentation and increases its coherence. Like all helpful signposts along the way, it shows where one is, the place that has just been visited and the next destination.

- *Emphasis of key points*. Any given body of information contains points that can be graded in importance, as they apply to the audience. Participants cannot always be expected to instinctively appreciate the relevance of a piece of detail. If they could they would not need to be at the talk. It is therefore the role of the speaker to emphasize those aspects that really must be grasped.[12] This can be done verbally (e.g. 'It is vital that you recognize ...', listing main points, repeating core elements), non-verbally (e.g. gestures, changes in posture and position) and vocally (e.g. altering volume, speed of delivery, tone of voice).

- *Verbal fluency*. Good public speakers do not have to be word perfect. Nevertheless, many 'umms' and 'ahhhs', unfinished sentences, false starts and lack of fluency erode personal credibility and the group will lose interest.[13]

- *Concreteness and precision*. As a general rule, speakers should strive to be precise in what they have to say rather than appearing vague and indefinite in the detail offered.[14] The latter style is, at best, unhelpful in enabling sensible decisions to be taken by participants. At worst, the speaker is seen as putting up a smokescreen to hide a lack of real knowledge on the topic.

- *Dynamic*. Impressive public speakers perform dynamically.[15] Their irrepressible enthusiasm and compelling commitment makes them powerful agents of influence. Contrast this with the most boring speaker that you have ever had the misfortune to be forced to listen to. Noticeable differences in punchy rhetoric, vocal variation and non-verbal animation will become quickly apparent.

- *Stimulus variation*. Try to introduce variety into your address. Intersperse your talk with graphs, slides or clips of video that the audience can look at, as a break from listening. If appropriate, encourage some discussion as an alternative to one-way communication. Asking the audience to work on a brief exercise, is a further way of introducing variety and increasing their active participation.

- *Appropriate examples*. Relevant examples act as a bridge between what the listener knows and is familiar with and the new material being offered by the speaker.[16] These examples must have a firm foundation on the audience's side if the breech in understanding is to be spanned. Too often they collapse through being supported on one side only – that of the presenter.

- *Immediacy*. This has to do with engaging interpersonally with the audience: being a real presence for them. It can be done by referring to individuals by name (if that is appropriate under the circumstances); using the type of language and forms of expression that resonates with those of the group (without appearing patronizing); removing unnecessary barriers, such as tables, between the speaker and participants; moving close to them without making them uncomfortable; and using suitable patterns of direct eye contact.

- *Avoiding distractions*. These can be caused by pacing around, playing with a pen or pointer, and overuse of certain stock phrases or forms of expression. Not only do these inhibit listening to the content, they can become intensely irritating for an audience.
- *Appearing natural and uncontrived*. To work as intended, all of the above pieces of advice, which are summarized in Key point 5.6, must be acted on in such a way that the presenter does not seem artificial. They must become incorporated into the presenter's own style. This can take some time and practice.
- Finally, before the delivery takes place, the presenter is well-advised to *rehearse what is going to be said*.[10]

Key point 5.6   Features of effective deliveries

Effective deliveries tend to:

- use appropriate language and avoid jargon
- be suitably paced
- use visual aids without placing them centre stage
- make use of subsummaries and transitional statements
- emphasize main points verbally, non-verbally and vocally
- be verbally fluent
- be concrete and precise
- be dynamic
- be varied
- include carefully chosen examples
- avoid distractions
- seem natural and uncontrived.

THE SETTING

If possible, it is always worth looking at the location of the presentation in advance and the actual room which has been set aside.[17] The size and position of the room, type of furniture and facilities, and available equipment should be noted. They can all influence levels of comfort and conduciveness to learning. They will also shape what it is possible for you to do with the group. Factors to consider include the following:

- *Location*. Make sure you, as presenter, know precisely where you have to go on the day of the presentation. Arrive early so that you can relax and meet the members as they arrive.
- *Size and shape of room*. It is usually better to have a room that is slightly larger than the bare minimum to accommodate the numbers attending. The actual shape may make some layouts difficult. (Issues to do with seating arrangements, and so forth, are covered in Chapter 14.)
- *Acoustics*. Are the acoustics suitable? Does the room have carpet and heavy curtains that can attenuate the sound? When full of people, will you be heard easily at the back? Do you need a microphone?
- *Equipment*. How is the room equipped? Can other equipment be provided? Will it be there on the day *and in working order*? Can you operate the equipment? Do you know where the various controls are? Will there be technical assistance to hand?
- *Power sockets*. The position and type of power socket should also be noted if it is intended that equipment be used.
- *Furnishings*. How is the room furnished? Is the seating comfortable and in keeping with what you intend to do? Best to avoid fixed seating unless for extremely large gatherings.
- *Decor*. Is it bright, airy and stimulating or have you been offered a dull, drab and rather sorry room? If the latter, your task of stimulating the group can be made more difficult. It sends all the wrong signals at the outset.
- *Lighting*. Is the lighting adequate? What type is it? Natural lighting often creates a more attractive ambience than the fluorescent alternative.
- *Temperature*. Is the room sufficiently well ventilated and can the temperature be adequately regulated.

SUMMARY

A successful presentation can be one of the best ways of getting your ideas across to others and influencing them.[18] It is also one of the most conspicuous ways of demonstrating your competence to those who matter in the organization. For many, however, it is an unpleasant ordeal to be rid of quickly, or an unacceptable part of an otherwise fulfilling job that eventually leads to a radical career reappraisal. But everyone can benefit from paying greater heed to their presentations and how they are delivered.[19]

A useful framework for approaching this task, as we have seen in this chapter, incorporates the presenter, the audience, the setting and the case to be presented. The importance of preparation and planning cannot be overstressed. Ways of structuring and organizing the material to be put across must be considered. The possible use of visual aids to help convey the message and enliven the performance should also be recognized. Finally, techniques of delivery, during the introduction, main body and conclusion of the presentation can make all the difference between a well-received, stimulating address and an insipid talk with little or no lasting impact.

6 I think we've got ourselves a deal: negotiating and bargaining

To jaw-jaw is better than to war-war.

Winston Churchill

Nobody ever saw a dog make a fair and deliberate exchange of one bone for another with another dog. Nobody ever saw one animal by its gestures and natural cries signify to another, this is mine, that is yours: I am willing to give this for that.

Adam Smith, *An Inquiry into the Nature and Causes of the Wealth of Nations*

Cast your eye over the landscape of management practice. There can be few tracts where, from even a cursory look, negotiating in some shape or form is not a significant feature of the terrain. In certain regions it may be conspicuously present in the imposing, majestic peaks of industrial relations settlements or mega-buck corporate take-over deals: in others, the paltry hillocks of the day-to-day business of life at work with its myriad clashes of interest, disagreements and frustrations. Nevertheless, an organization depends on the proper handling of such everyday situations. When recognized and dealt with astutely they do not compromise the smooth running of the organization – indeed it may even be enhanced. When ignored or mishandled, however, the whole operation may come to a standstill.

Negotiations, or at least opportunities for negotiating, are an ever present part of the world of management. Although being a shrewd negotiator does not guarantee managerial success, the more accomplished you are in this sphere the more likely you are to manage well, regardless of work context. As written by O'Hair and Friedrich in their book *Strategic Communication in Business and the Professions*,[1] 'Negotiation is a skill that you will need throughout your career whether you work in a corporate setting, a volunteer or non-profit organization, an academic field, a profession such as law or medicine, or a service industry'.

But what is a negotiation? For the moment it can be thought of as a discussion between two or more parties, each of whom is to some extent reliant on the other, with the aim of satisfying what seem to be incompatible goals. For example:

- Management proposes a wage restructuring for sales staff to reduce the standard element in favour of the performance-linked component; union representatives mount bitter opposition.
- Suppliers issue notice of a sharp rise in the price of their component parts in line with increased import costs; buyers complain that they can neither absorb such increased charges nor pass them on to the consumer due to the depressed state of the market.
- Your line manager would like you to accept an extension of your duties on the strength of a vague promise of promotion at some indeterminate point in the future; you regard this as unreasonable and resist.

In all three cases, each party has plans which are at odds with those of the other. Furthermore, each is dependent on the other to make their plans work, producing a classic negotiating situation.

In this chapter we will consider the circumstances that give rise to negotiations and the contrasting approaches that can be taken to them. The stages which negotiators work through as they move towards a resolution will also be addressed. A considerable part of the chapter will be devoted to revealing a range of tactics and techniques that can be used, especially in bargaining.

CONFLICT AT WORK

Why should negotiating be such a ubiquitous feature of the role of the manager? The answer has to do with the pervasiveness of conflict in and between organizations. Indeed Robert Bolton, the President of Ridge Consultants, a New York based firm that specializes in improving human performance, goes even further, asserting that discord is an ever present aspect of life in general: 'To be human is to experience conflict.'[2] Be that as it may, conflict without doubt is endemic at work. It arises when 'one party perceives that the other has frustrated, or is about to frustrate, some concern of his.'[3]

But the prospect of work being conflict-ridden should not distress us unduly. Early thinking, along the lines that disharmony is grit in the bearing of an otherwise smooth-running machine, all traces of which must be removed before permanent damage is caused, is now accepted as unrealistic and unjustifiably alarmist. Indeed some hold that even if this were possible, it may not be desirable. Conflict may be good – at least in moderate doses! It may promote increased effectiveness, strengthened relationships and further goal achievement.[4] The trick is to maximize its constructive potential. Negotiating has an important contribution to make to conflict management.[5]

NEGOTIATION: CHARACTERISTICS AND PRECONDITIONS

Those who have defined the term 'negotiation' have done so in slightly different ways, emphasizing various aspects of the process. Therefore, searching for the stock defining statement is a somewhat futile exercise. The following, however, are commonly recognized as the main factors of the negotiating process:[6, 7]

- *Incongruency of interests, ideas or objectives*. A precondition for negotiation is the presence of conflict, or at least the perception of conflict. Unless parties view their positions as contrasting and incompatible, there will be no need to contemplate negotiating. Differences when probed can turn out to be more superficial than substantial, and this should not be overlooked. What initially seems to be an intractable impasse can sometimes be resolved speedily and amicably, once the issues have been more fully explored. (See the example in Key point 6.1.)
- *Joint resolve*. Negotiation may resemble debate, group problem-solving or shared decision-making and, indeed, may sometimes encompass aspects of all three. What sets it apart, however, is the unique dynamic of forces that surrounds it, some antagonistically pulling the parties apart, others collaboratively pushing them together. While, at one level, there may be conflict of interests, at another both sides strive towards the same goal, *if they are negotiating in good faith*.
- *Shared interests*. Sometimes opposing parties will not be at odds on *all* issues. More characteristically, areas can be found where they are at one. When these are overshadowed by points of disagreement, the results can be bleak for all concerned. Even in the supposedly cut-throat world of business, rivalry is rarely untrammelled. Brandenburger and Nalebuff[8] coined the term 'co-opetition' to describe the judicious blend of co-operation and competition that best serves present-day business relationships. When companies are sucked into all-out war, there are few victors. For example, it has been estimated that the price war in the years between 1990 and 1993 cost the US airline industry more revenue than it had previously made since the days of the Wright brothers.[8]
- *Interdependency*. For a negotiation to take place, each side must be reliant on the other to meet its requirements. If this were not the case, each could simply disengage at the first realization that their requests were not being acceded to, and seek alternative routes to their fulfilment. The dynamic of such a situation of interdependency empowers all parties. No resolution of the situation is

Key point 6.1   Message in a bottle

They grabbed the bottle of wine at the same moment, each unaware of the other until then. They looked surprised, then embarrassed, then annoyed.

'I think I had it first,' he said.

'No,' she insisted 'I saw it before you,' realizing quickly that it was the last bottle of Chateau Duplonk 92 on the shelf.

'But you don't understand,' he protested, 'I simply must have this wine.'

'I've been looking all over for a bottle of Chateau Duplonk 92,' she persisted, 'and now that I've finally found it, I'm not prepared to let you simply walk away with it.'

'I'll buy you any other bottle of wine in the shop – forget about the price,' he pleaded.

'You can have two, any two, but not this one,' she retorted.

On hearing the rising commotion, the shopkeeper intervened, 'Can I ask sir, why this rather modest wine matters so much to you?'

'Well you see, my wife and I shared a bottle on the night we met and tomorrow is our first wedding anniversary. I've tried everywhere and had almost given up. I really must have it.'

'And you, madam?' the shopkeeper asked.

'I collect unusual wine bottles and I really need this one to complete my collection.'

'So you don't want the wine, as such?' the shopkeeper confirmed.

'No, can't really stand the stuff.'

'And you sir', he persisted, 'What do you intend to do with the bottle, once you and your wife have enjoyed the wine?'

'Probably throw it out,' came the reply.

'Can I suggest that you share the cost of the bottle and exchange addresses,' mused the shopkeeper.

possible unless and until each is prepared to say 'Yes'. Of course, not all sides are empowered equally.

- *Trading concessions*. Negotiating depends on those entering being prepared to accommodate each other, if necessary, through 'give and take'. Indeed it has been suggested that, 'The basis of negotiation is exchange: every party gains and gives concessions until they reach agreement'.[9] This does not mean, though, that making concessions is inevitable, as we shall see. What is important is that, ultimately and if required, all parties tacitly commit themselves to compromise if that is what it takes to reach a settlement.

- *Communication*. Obtaining and giving information lies at the heart of the negotiating process. The negotiation has been described as being, 'by nature a communication encounter, not a physical encounter (like war) or a mechanical encounter (like voting) ... Controlled communication is the essence of negotiation'.[10] Information can be obtained indirectly, 'picked up' through inference and 'reading between the lines' or, where levels of trust permit, can be exchanged more directly and openly. Indeed the process tends to operate most successfully when this is possible.

   Information is exchanged to promote understanding. It also influences the other party to make concessions and shift their position. Indeed, this is seen as the basis of negotiations, by Fisher and Ury, authors of the highly acclaimed book *Getting to Yes*, who regard them as encounters 'in which two or more parties are communicating, each for the purpose of influencing the other's decision'.[11]

   Parties should be able to communicate directly, and preferably face to face, although negotiating through a representative may be an option. Involving a third party in a mediating role is also a possibility, if negotiations reach an impasse. When that third party is empowered to propose a settlement, we move into the area of arbitration.

- *Misrepresentation*. Following on from the latter point, negotiating often has a dark side of hidden secrets and half-truths. While rules differ from culture to culture, blatant lying is usually regarded as 'breaking the rules' and, if discovered, seriously jeopardizes the whole process. A commonly held assumption, especially when the transaction is a 'one-off' with strangers, is that not all will be revealed and that what is revealed will probably carry a strategic spin: 'parties struggle to exploit asymmetries of interest and power, each knowing that the other may disguise or misrepresent their real position'.[12]

Key point 6.2   Preconditions for a negotiation

Negotiating depends upon:

- an initial incompatibility (or perceived incompatibility) of interests
- each party requiring the co-operation of the other to meet their needs
- all parties regarding negotiating as a more satisfactory way of resolving the conflict than any possible alternative
- being able to interact and communicate with the other side, preferably face to face
- each considering it possible to influence the other to modify their position
- each having some degree of power and influence over the other side
- each being prepared to accommodate the other's requirements, to some extent
- all being hopeful of an outcome acceptable to them in some measure.

NEGOTIATING STRATEGIES

There is no one best way to negotiate, nor a single strategy that guarantees success. How one approaches the task should be shaped by the circumstances of each encounter. The skilled negotiator must ultimately be strategically flexible, and certain approaches are more likely to lead to success that others. Four negotiating strategies are discussed below.

COME IN PEACE

The plan is to readily concede ground from the outset to appease the other side and fully accommodate their demands. This may be done for a number of reasons, such as:

- extreme discomfort in the face of conflict and an abiding desire to simply get it over with and get out
- a belief that doing so may send a 'friendly' signal to the other side
- an overriding concern with relationship matters at the expense of material outcome
- a move to make the other party feel obligated to reciprocate
- lack of assertion (see Chapter 10).

Whatever the thinking (or lack of it) that informs the decision, unilateral concession is a highly dubious approach to take. In most cases it leads to 'giving the store away', as it is euphemistically put in US circles.

This approach is likely to fail because:

- if you are allergic to conflict you should not be negotiating – ask someone else to do it for you
- an unforced concession will be read as weakness, naïveté or inexperience, rather than as an amicable gesture
- the relationship is unlikely to be strengthened, in reality, in a situation where the other obtains everything
- there is no reason why the other party should feel compelled to match a concession that you have volunteered unconditionally.

GO TO WAR

This is probably the strategy traditionally associated with negotiating. Indeed many people still believe that it is the only option. Here the aim is to defeat the other side: to win more from the transaction than they do. It is commonly premised on a 'zero-sum' distribution of pay-offs, where a gain to one side represents a correspondingly direct loss to the other. Think of a game of poker as an example. If both players start with £100 and at the end of the evening, one walks away with £160, the other must be down £60. They cannot both win! For this reason this strategy often leads to 'win-lose' negotiations.

But 'go to war' can also lead to neither side achieving much from the negotiation. Take the case of two adjacent supermarkets involved in a price war. While one may attract more trade than the other, neither may have much profit at the end of it all. They have got themselves embroiled in a 'lose-lose' situation.

SMASH AND GRAB

The intention is not necessarily to beat the other side, but merely to get as much from the negotiation as possible. The motive is purely egotistical. It may lead to you 'scooping the pot' and leaving the other party with little. Indeed one of its negative aspects is the complete disregard for the outcome to the other party. But negligence in this regard can prove short-sighted, especially if you find yourself in further negotiations with the same party at some point in the future.

BROTHERS IN ARMS

The thinking is radically different from what we have considered so far. The strategy relies on co-operation, co-ordination and the integration of effort – both sides working together to solve a shared problem to their mutual benefit. The enemy is not the other side, it is the obstacle that stands in the way of their joint progress and is consequently common to both. It is the problem not the person that must be defeated.

The mindset here is therefore 'win-win' and is accomplished by:

- accepting, as a goal, the best possible arrangement for both sides
- separating the people from the problem – the latter rather than the former is the enemy
- building trust
- avoiding entrenched positions
- exploring the needs behind the demands – sometimes those demands can be met in other ways
- looking for new options that have added value for both sides rather than trying to grind the other side down in the concession-making mill
- trying to reach agreement based on reason and principle, rather than the sheer weight of emotional pressure.[11]

There are four possible outcomes from these strategies:

1. There may simply be no agreement with the negotiation breaking down.
2. One side achieves everything, while the other is left with nothing. This is the most likely outcome of the 'come in peace' strategy.
3. A compromise solution may be worked out in which each side wins less than they had initially hoped for. 'Go to war' usually produces this result.
4. An integrative agreement is arrived at in which both sides enjoy higher joint benefits than could have been delivered through compromise. This is more probable when parties adopt a 'brothers in arms' strategy.

Where possible to achieve, this fourth outcome has obvious attractions underscoring the advantages of the 'brothers in arms' strategy.

STAGES IN THE NEGOTIATION PROCESS

It is common to think of negotiations evolving through a recognizable series of stages or phases. Bill Scott,[13] the international management consultant who specializes in the field of negotiating, proposed six sequential steps:

1. Planning and preparation.
2. Getting started.
3. Exploring.
4. Proposing.
5. Bargaining.
6. Reaching settlement.

STAGE 1: PLANNING AND PREPARATION

Abraham Lincoln declared, 'If I had nine hours to cut down a tree, I would spend six hours sharpening my axe'. This division of time is reflected in the attention that we will devote to the present stage. Never be ill prepared, in an impetuous charge to clash antlers with the opposition over the negotiating table. Planning and preparation have been described as 'the most important parts of negotiation'.[14] Indeed, being skilled in this area was regarded, by a group of professional negotiators in the USA when asked, as the most important attribute that they possessed.[15]

Planning and preparation should covers goals, obstacles to the achievement of those goals and possible ways of overcoming these obstacles.[16] These concerns are reflected in a more detailed way in the following suggested components of the planning stage.

Clarify purpose and establish goals

It is pointless going into a negotiation with only the vaguest of ideas as to why you are there or what you hope to come away with. Ask yourself the following questions:

1. *Is negotiation necessary?* Can I get what I want in some other way? If I must negotiate, is this the most appropriate party to get involved with? You may discover, with some reflection, that you are less dependent on the other side to achieve your needs than either you or, indeed they, had initially thought.
2. *What must I come away with at the end in order to satisfy my needs?* This question deserves some careful thought. It requires you to identify precisely three positions:
   a) Your *target point* or *target range*. This is what you aim to get from the transaction, being optimistic, but realistically so. It can be conceived as a precise amount (target point) or as falling within limits (target range).
   b) Your *resistance point* or *'bottom line'*. This is the point beyond which you are not prepared to concede. For this reason it is sometimes called the 'walk away' point. As far as you are concerned, beyond this point, a deal will not be done.
   c) *BATNA*. This is your Best Alternative To a Negotiated Agreement.[11] It is a response to the question, 'What if we can't reach an agreement?' and should never be left for consideration until a breakdown actually takes place. Identifying what your best option would be if the negotiation fails, will help you position your resistance point. Remember, a poor settlement, from your point of view, may be worse than no settlement at all. Perhaps you simply cannot do business with these people at this time.

Of course you should bear in mind that the other party will probably have target and resistance points. The space between the two sets of resistance points will set the parameters for a settlement, as exemplified in Key point 6.3.

Key point 6.3   Target points, resistance points and settlement range

Bob has just changed job. He now works out of town which involves commuting to and from work, thereby incurring a cost both in fares, time and energy. Property prices in the town where he works are comparable to those where he presently lives, as are amenities and quality of life so Bob decides to put his house on the market. He decides that it is worth £130 000. This is his target point. Would he accept less? Yes, but he feels that anything under £100 000 would be giving it away, with the property market as it is. This is his resistance point. But what if he can't get a buyer to offer at least £100 000? Having done his sums, Bob decides that his BATNA would be to continue commuting until the spring and put the house back on the market then.

Along comes Bill. He sees the house and is pleased with what he sees. He feels that the house could be bought for £110 000. This is his target point. In any case he could not raise a mortgage of more than £140 000. This is his resistance point. His BATNA would be to wait for another similar house in the area to come on the market and rent accommodation in the meantime.

Their settlement range lies between £100 000 and £140 000 and, therefore, it is likely that the house will change hands.

Identify the issues

Time spent teasing out the issues to be negotiated on is always time spent well.

1. *What are the different considerations that could or should be introduced into the process?* A negotiation that centres around just a single issue can prove extremely difficult and prone to deadlock. There simply are no other variables that can be brought into play and used to get around the main obstacle. However, few negotiations are inherently as limited as this when the negotiators step back from the main concern, for a few moments, to view the wider picture of their difference. Key point 6.4 provides an example.

Key point 6.4 Widgets and things

Betty is in the business of making and selling widgets. Beth needs widgets for her gizmo plant. Beth offers Betty £10.00 per widget for her produce. Betty demands £20.00. Betty finally comes down to £16.00. Beth increases her offer to £14.00, but neither is prepared to concede further – deadlock!

What other issues could have been introduced to broaden the negotiation and that could have been perhaps traded off, one against the other, in reaching an agreement? The list might include such variables as:

- volume discount – more for less
- quality of product
- extended product guarantees
- payment terms and conditions
- assisted financing
- transport
- time/place of delivery
- packaging
- insurance
- installation costs
- buy-back arrangements
- options on further contracts.

---

2. *Are some issues more important to me than others?* The next step is to rank the variables in terms of their importance. Which issues are central, which more peripheral? Probe beneath the variable to recognize the actual need or value that it represents. Often this need can be satisfied in other ways, introducing greater scope for manoeuvre once the negotiation gets started.

3. *Are issues linked? Can they be offset one against the other, if need be?* Depending on the other party's needs, it may be possible to concede on what to you are peripheral concerns at no substantial cost. It has been recommended that you locate target, resistance and satisfaction points at the outset, for each of the variables isolated.[17] You then have a basis for calculating where you stand as the picture changes in situations of intense bargaining where there is considerable linkage amongst the issues.

Gather information

It is impossible to be too well informed approaching a negotiation. That does not mean, though, that you cannot or will not be required to seek further detail once the negotiation gets under way. However at this stage two types of question can usefully be posed:

1. *Do I know as much as I need to about my own position?* Make sure that you are fully briefed on the background to all relevant issues, including implications which various concessions might have for finance, production, sales or human resources. What are the arguments in support of the position that you will take? What is the supporting evidence for them? What are the areas of weakness and the counter-arguments? How can they be refuted? How long do you have to complete the negotiation? Must you reach a settlement and are you authorized to do so?

2. *Have I unearthed as much information as I can about the other party?* Find out all that is possible about the other side, who they represent and the type of deal they are after. What is their track record? What style do they prefer – highly competitive or co-operative? Which tactics tend to be introduced – brinkmanship, bluff, time pressures? In terms of personal qualities are they, for example, honourable and trustworthy, impetuous and unpredictable, rational and calculating, patient and unflappable, or the opposite of these? What power do they have to agree a settlement? Could this negotiator simply be a stalking horse, sent in advance of the proper negotiation to reconnoitre your position?

As far as the negotiation itself is concerned, the greater your vision of the other party's position, the more successfully you will be able to anticipate possible areas of agreement, conflict and compromise. What are the likely issues from their position? What are their underlying needs? Which issues are core to them and which more tangential? If necessary can you make concessions that will be valued highly, but at little cost to yourself? What are the strengths and weaknesses of their position as you understand it? What do they probably know of your position?

Identify areas of potential agreement and conflict

It is always wise to stake out common ground that you seem to share with the other party. It offers areas that can be retreated to, if the negotiation begins to falter, to affirm the basis of a settlement and strengthen spoiling relationships.

Areas of likely conflict must also be spotted. What is the crux of the difficulty? What are the possible avenues for overcoming conflict? What concessions can be made? Under what conditions will they be offered and accepted? Are there areas that can be conceded at perhaps no great loss, but that could lead to significant movement in more central areas?

Decide on the type of negotiation to pursue

Given what you know of the other party's approach, the background to the negotiation and possible deals which it may spawn in the future, the issues involved and potential for conflict resolution, a decision has to be made about the approach to adopt. The basic choice is between competing with the opposition in a zero-sum battle of might, played out under win-lose rules, to see who can wring the most from the other side and ultimately emerge victorious, or collaborating with them in a joint quest to find the best possible mutually beneficial outcome in the spirit of win-win co-operation. The latter strategy is preferred where circumstances permit.[6, 11, 13, 17] Conditions which promote collaborative negotiations include:

- trusting the other side not to take advantage of your willingness to co-operate.
- being involved with the other side in a long-term negotiating relationship, or being in a situation which has this potential. In such an arrangement it may be in neither party's best interests to engage in a protracted war in which either may go under[8].
- seeing beyond a narrow zero-sum distribution of pay-offs.
- coming from a particular cultural background. The Japanese, for example, tend to be much more accommodating of win-win arrangements than are the Russians.[6]

Formulating an agenda

You should now be ready to draft a tentative agenda for the negotiation. This should list the issues that you want to introduce and the order in which you would like to consider them. Is it in your interests to negotiate item by item, or do you prefer to negotiate on a broader front? Being prepared to be flexible in the order in which issues are tackled is advisable. It has been found to separate successful from less successful negotiators.[18]

It should be appreciated, of course, that the other party will also have ideas about the shape of the agenda. Indeed, the agenda may be subject to preliminary negotiations. For this reason, it has been suggested that the agenda be drawn up jointly, as a collaborative exercise.[17] General ground rules, deadlines and such like can be clarified as well.

Agreeing a settlement

Settlement details are sometimes overlooked with the result that the deal ultimately unravels. To omit issues of how the settlement should be documented, formalized and implemented as part of the initial stage of preparation can often lead to disaster when least expected, just as participants are beginning to congratulate themselves on reaching a workable agreement.

Choosing a location

Where the negotiations take place also has to be agreed. Custom and convention may take care of this. It is more likely that the person selling will visit the buyer, than vice versa. Many negotiators feel more comfortable negotiating on 'home territory'.[19] Alternatively, there may be advantage in seeing people you intend to do business with in their 'natural habit'. One can quickly learn more about them and their standing in the company.[6]

As a final option, negotiations may be held on neutral territory. Indeed this is a favoured compromise in political negotiations which are particularly intractable and prone to breakdown.

Rehearsal

If the negotiation is particularly important you may want to have a dry run at it, as a culmination of your planning and preparation.

STAGE 2: GETTING STARTED

The parties meet at the negotiating table to begin the transaction. This stage can be more difficult than might be imagined. The objectives are to establish a suitable climate, begin to build a conducive relationship and orient proceedings to the business at hand.

Create a suitable climate

What type of climate is most likely to favour the negotiation and bear fruit? This will vary somewhat depending on the type of negotiation envisaged, but for the most part it should be courteous, co-operative and businesslike.[13] The assumption is that, where circumstances permit, you should flag the opportunity to negotiate within a win-win framework. Such an atmosphere can be worked at in a number of ways:

- Initial contact involved in agreeing an agenda will set the tone and should strive to be positive and as non-confrontational as possible.
- The room set aside for the negotiation should be pleasant and comfortable with space available where people can mingle in a less formal setting.
- Use 'we' language which suggests that parties have common concerns and are working together, 'We seem to be moving to a stage where ...'.
- Distractions, such as mobile phone calls or intruding secretaries should be minimized.

Build a conducive relationship

This is sometimes referred to as establishing rapport[20] and is related to the previous task. Relationship work can include:

- spending some time over rituals such as personal introductions
- respecting the other party's concerns and showing a commitment to taking them on board
- emphasizing the shared nature of the difficulties faced
- listening to what the other party has to say
- sending the correct signals non-verbally as well as verbally
- avoiding gamesmanship to gain initial advantage. This tends to be seen as just that and can quickly sour the relationship.

Orient proceedings towards business matters

It is common for this stage to be brought to a close by both sides acknowledging, ratifying, and proposing modifications to any earlier agreements drawn up in an agenda. Each may sketch the issues of concern and their stance in relation to them. In doing so they present their opening positions. The negotiation is now ready to move into the next phase.

STAGE 3: EXPLORATION

This stage is a natural progression from the preceding one. In it parties begin to explore in greater depth issues merely stated in Stage 2, and to seek a fuller appreciation of them. If these are dealt with fully, it may be possible to short-circuit the bargaining phase and move the negotiating process expeditiously towards a win-win settlement. If not, at least each party should be in a position to make proposals and counter-proposals from a more fully informed background.

Probe beneath the surface level of wants and positions

Underlying needs and values are explored, enabling seemingly incompatible stances to be accommodated and opportunities for collaborative negotiation recognized. What the other wants may, on closer inspection, not be what they really need. Needs can often be met in a variety of ways which neither party had recognized before they began to share deeper thoughts about the issues surrounding the negotiation. Going back to Key point 6.4, Beth wanted to buy widgets for no more than £14 each. However, what she really needed to operate in profit was to have the widgets installed in the gizmos that she manufactured at or beneath a particular cost. This realization would have made the other variables listed in Key point 6.4 relevant as potential opportunities to enable her to go beyond £14 on the amount paid for each item. For example, let's say her trucks already made deliveries close to Betty's factory, coming back empty. Transport could, therefore, have been taken care of at very little cost to Beth. In return Betty, for whom having to deliver the goods would have been quite expensive, could have looked more closely at her per item price.

This stage of exploring is pivotal in mutually beneficial integrative negotiating.

Do not rush

The exploratory phase should never be rushed. In some cases, had more time been spent exploring each other's requirements, bargaining could have been avoided or at least marginalized. Time saved exploring is often wasted tenfold as the negotiation subsequently gets bogged down in dogged and protracted bargaining with characteristic deadlock and occasional breakdown.

Seek a panoramic view of the other's issues

Gain as broad a picture as possible of the totality of what matters to the other side.[17] The unexpected introduction of a raft of new concerns later in the negotiation drags the whole process back to the stage of exploration, and is highly frustrating.

Look for areas of complementarity

Areas of agreement should be carefully noted when exploring. Furthermore it is often possible to identify, from the different values attached to variables introduced by parties, ways in which both could benefit from particular outcomes.

Acknowledge areas of conflict

What seem to be areas of conflict also need to be noted and perused. Sometimes the conflict turns out to be more illusory than real, but not always. Unpack such issues without being sucked into a process of bargaining on them. That comes later.

Listen to what the other party has to say

This may seem too obvious to be worth mentioning, but opposing positions tend to quickly spiral out of control because neither side is willing or able to listen properly to the other. Listening, which is covered more fully in Chapter 11, is not just hearing but being as fully receptive to the total message given by the other person, as possible. It involves tuning in to how things are said, as well as what is said. Noting what is not said can also be highly illuminating.

STAGE 4: PROPOSING

Having achieved a fuller appreciation of where each other stands, and being mindful of the fact that the other side may not have been completely open or honest, the next stage is where a firm bid is made or proposal for a settlement put on the table. Opening stances need to be carefully thought out and presented appropriately.

Opening proposals should be high (or low)

Classic win-lose negotiation stresses the importance of beginning with the highest possible *realistic* asking price (if you are selling) or the lowest possible offer (if you are buying). In both cases parties must be realistic and credible in the stances that they take. If other houses in your street have sold for around £200 000 recently, your house is comparable and the property market has not changed significantly in the interim, there is no point putting your house on the market at £300 000. Opening positions cannot be so high or low that you appear ridiculous, ignorant of the market, unscrupulous or plain greedy. With that proviso, opening high (or low) has the advantages of:

- shifting the goalposts in your favour. The other party may be forced to modify its target point in your direction
- providing ample space between where you begin and your target point, to enable concessions to be made if necessary
- revealing information about the other's target point. For example, do they seem shocked and reject your offer out of hand or do they seem nonplussed?[6]
- making the final settlement, when it is reached, seem even more attractive to the other side.[13]

Opening proposals should be clearly stated

The other side should be left in no doubt as to what precisely your opening position is. There should be no confusion or uncertainty. Switching perspectives, it is important if you are on the receiving end to check the details of what is on offer.

Opening positions should be presented firmly

It is pointless making a high opening bid if it is presented in a weak, apologetic manner. If it is read as 'I want £8 000 for my car – but realize that there is no way that I will get it and am prepared to accept substantially less if at all pressed', you will probably find yourself at your 'bottom-line' in double-quick time.

Going first or second

The concern is whether to make an opening bid, or wait for the other party to make the running. There are advantages and disadvantages attached to each.[6]

121

Advantages of opening the bidding are that you:

- take the initiative
- force the other to possibly rethink their starting-point
- put the other party on the defensive.

On the other hand, disadvantages of the strategy could be that you:

- misread the situation and don't start high (or low) enough
- are the first to make concessions
- are put on the defensive by the other side as they probe your position.

Conditional proposals

Mills[19] points to advantages in making conditional proposals. For example, 'We would be prepared to let you have that grain for £120 per ton if you can agree to pay in full within ten days of delivery'. While in win-lose negotiations, beginning in this way might confuse the deal, there are obvious advantages for win-win arrangements.

STAGE 5: BARGAINING

Once parties begin to yield their opening positions and trade in compromise, bargaining has begun. Bargaining has been defined as 'the successive adoption and relinquishment, through concession, of a sequence of positions with the intention of arriving at a mutually acceptable alternative'.[11] A concession represents a change in offer by party A in the direction of party B's interests that reduces the level of benefit accruing to party A. It is done with the intention of bringing the parties' positions closer together but does not unerringly have that effect, if mishandled.

Being able to win concessions from the other party is a powerful weapon in the armoury of the bargainer caught up in a competitive negotiation. Some of the tactics that can be used will now be mentioned.[6, 13, 17, 19, 21]

Impose deadlines

Here the other is made to believe that unless they are prepared to accept quickly the offer on the table, it will be withdrawn to their disadvantage.

Utilize the friendly relationship cultivated

Parties are more likely to be prepared to compromise if they have developed a positive relationship which neither wants to jeopardize.

Appear resolute

Perceptions of firmness can be enhanced through decoupling concessions from perceived weakness by:

- stating the one-off nature of a concession
- showing that the concession is a result of a unique circumstance ('I need the space for new stock')
- combining the concession with a strong move ('I'll lower the price if you take double the amount').

Reduce the other's resistance to making concessions

This can be done by using:

- persuasive arguments
- the promise of benefits (e.g. a trade union may argue that a pay rise will lead to increased productivity)
- reference to objective criteria (the 'book' price of a car; the pay of other professionals)
- an appeal to the disadvantages to the other party were an agreement not reached
- an ultimatum – unless they are prepared to reconsider, the negotiation is over (this brinkmanship is a high-risk option to be used very carefully).
- face-saving devices that make it easier for the other side to concede without appearing to lose.

Salami

The significance of the title is that if you ask someone for a whole salami they will invariably refuse. Ask them for a single slice and they will probably comply. If they comply often enough, you end up with the whole salami.

Logrolling

This is trading off pairs of issues which differ in importance to both parties. For example, the purchaser may agree the asking price of the car if the dealer is prepared to service it free for a year (a big saving to the purchaser but of little cost to the dealer).

Good guy/bad guy

This tactic can be used in team negotiations where one member is particularly tough and uncompromising, another much more accommodating. If used subtly, accommodating the 'good guy' comes to be seen as the only way of working with the other side.

Sometimes the 'bad guy' is a third party who has to be placated ('unless I get £135 for each, my boss will fire me on the spot as soon as he hears').

Fait accompli

This is based on the principle of 'act now and negotiate later'. Workers may come out on strike before negotiations with management get under way. One party has taken direct action in advance of the negotiation designed to put the other party on the defensive and make it more likely that they will concede.

In distributive bargaining situations, where each is concerned with winning as much of the cake for themselves as possible, it is inevitable that there will be give and take. Your concession-making should be governed by the golden rules of conceding listed in Key point 6.5.

Key point 6.5 Golden rules when making concessions

Do:

- trade concessions
- concede slowly
- grant small concessions
- monitor your concession-making.

Don't:

- give concessions unconditionally
- set inappropriate expectations by starting off with sizeable concessions
- be the first to make significant concessions
- concede too early in the bargaining process
- make concessions without having worked out their value to you and, to the best of your calculations, the other party.
- engage in tit-for-tat concessions. The fact that the other party has dropped its demand by £50 does not mean that you must reciprocate as a matter of course.

STAGE 6: REACHING SETTLEMENT

Sensing that a settlement is within reach and moving in to grasp it is an impressive skill in its own right. If snatched at too early, the other party can feel pressured and resist. If delayed too long you can end up having to concede further, or missing the deal altogether.

Some of the moves which can be employed to secure an agreement[19] will now be considered.

Cues suggesting that the other side is ready to agree

They may begin to tidy up some papers, summarize points and confirm them, look excited, look tired or raise issues to do with implementation.

No further concessions

Convince them that it is not possible for you to concede further – that they have wrung the last drop of blood from your veins! If they feel that you still have a bit more to give, and it has been an uncompromising negotiation, they may not be satisfied until they have it.

Trial closure

This is a technique used in selling to test if the customer is ready to buy. It may take the form of asking, say in a house sale, which child will claim which bedroom, or if an appliance, whether the extended warranty will be taken up.

Summary closure

What has been agreed so far is summarized. Concessions and benefits that the other party has obtained are emphasized, and significant losses suffered were the deal not to go ahead highlighted. This is a way of finally clinching the deal.

Concession closure

Some negotiators hold back a final small concession which can be granted if all else fails. The trouble with this is that you might attract a reputation of always having something extra to give even when you protest that you have not.

Splitting-the-difference

This is commonly seen as a way of finally clinching the deal. While it seems to be a fair and equitable way of getting to 'Yes', this may be more illusory than real. For a party that has conceded relatively little to that point, splitting the difference is quite attractive. For the other side which has given considerably more, it will be less so.

Positive endings

A successful negotiation is one from which all parties feel that they have come away with a good deal. It is important therefore that negotiations end on an upbeat note:

that no one feels they have lost out. This is important not only for future contacts but for agreement implementation.

Documenting the agreement

Most agreements are formalized in a written contract and are legally binding. Settlements that cannot be enforced are of little value.[6] Pursuing disputes through the court, though, is a costly option and to be avoided. Therefore, all parties should be clear on precisely what has been agreed. Go over the arrangements that have been hammered out making sure that interpretations are shared and differences of opinion resolved. Pay heed to the fine detail. Then ensure that the written document reflects this level of understanding.

Implementation

Ultimately, an agreement is only as good as its implementation. Good settlements, therefore, explicitly address these issues by considering difficulties that may be encountered at this stage and how these should be resolved if they do arise. Most contracts include grievance and arbitration elements, but these should be invoked only as a last resort.[19]

SKILLS OF THE SUCCESSFUL NEGOTIATOR

There is considerable agreement about what good negotiators should do, some of it based on research evidence.[18, 22] The skills that successful negotiators tend to employ will now be considered.

BEHAVIOUR LABELLING

Skilled negotiators often give notice of their intention in speaking, by labelling. Instead of just asking 'How many units are there?' they preface this with: 'Can I ask you a *question* – how many units are there?' Other examples of behaviour labels include: 'If I could make a *suggestion* ...', and 'Could we *compromise* here by ...'. This process of labelling is advantageous in that it:

- focuses attention on the behaviour to follow
- puts social pressure on the other side to respond accordingly
- slows the pace of negotiation
- allows both sides to focus on what will follow
- reduces ambiguity by making clear what the behaviour will be
- introduces rationality into the encounter.

However, poorer negotiators are more likely to label instances of negativity, such as 'I disagree with that because ...'. By comparison, skilled negotiators, under these circumstances, give reasons why they cannot concur. These reasons are in themselves expressions of disagreement, but they avoid the need to state overt dissent.

TESTING UNDERSTANDING AND SUMMARIZING

The function of both these behaviours is to reduce the possibility of misunderstandings about what has been said or agreed. Skilled negotiators often use these behaviours to facilitate the eventual successful implementation of any decisions. The less skilled tend to ignore ambiguous points rather than confront them directly – their main concern is often with immediate agreement, even if this is likely to raise problems at the implementation stage.

Skilled negotiators use:

- *reflections* to check for immediate understanding. Examples of reflections in negotiating include: 'So your main worry here is ...'; 'This aspect seems particularly important for you ...'; 'What you are saying is that this option is simply not acceptable'.
- *summaries* in the form of compact statements at the end of discussion, to check that both sides concur about exactly what has been agreed.

SEEKING INFORMATION

The skill of questioning is necessary to successful negotiation. Skilled negotiators ask significantly more questions of different types than average negotiators. Questions are used to:

- ascertain the expectations of the other side and any constraints they may have (time, resources, etc.)
- gather specific necessary information
- maintain control of the interaction
- keep the other side active and reduce their thought time
- give yourself a breathing space to plan strategy
- avoid overt statements of disagreement.

REVEALING INTERNAL INFORMATION

Perhaps surprisingly, skilled negotiators tend to be more disclosing of feelings and emotions as the negotiation unfolds, than their less skilled counterparts. In particular, the former are more likely to use a 'feelings commentary' by revealing their affective states about what is happening.[22] Such feelings may be real or mentioned for effect, but this openness serves to reassure the other party that motives and intentions are explicit and above board.

AVOIDING IRRITATORS

These are words or phrases used by one side which cause annoyance to the other. Examples of irritators include 'generous offer', 'fair and equitable arrangement', 'reasonable' (these imply that the other side is ungenerous, unfair or unreasonable). Skilled negotiators use significantly fewer of these. While few negotiators will directly insult or antagonize the other side, using irritators can produce the same (unintended) effect.

RESISTING COUNTER-PROPOSALS

In negotiations, when one side puts forward a proposal it is often met by an immediate counter-proposal from the other. However, skilled negotiators are less inclined to follow such practice. Using counter-proposals in this way is not recommended in negotiation because they:

- are put forward at a time when the other side is least receptive
- complicate the negotiation by introducing a new issue or option before the previous one has been dealt with
- are likely to be perceived as a blocking tactic or disagreement rather than a genuine proposal.

ARGUMENT DILUTION

Skilled negotiators give fewer reasons to back up their proposals. The more reasons given to justify an argument, the more likely it is that the other side will find (and exploit) weaknesses in one of them. Skilled negotiators have been found to advance a single reason insistently and only if they begin to lose ground do they introduce a subsidiary argument.[22]

DEFEND/ATTACK SPIRALS

Since negotiation typically involves conflict, there is a danger of the encounter becoming heated, with Side A attacking the other using emotional terms ('It's your fault that these difficulties arose in the first place', 'Don't try to blame us for that'). Side B is then likely to defend in similar vein, which in turn will be viewed as an attack by Side A and defended likewise – and so the spiral continues. Such events are not helpful and, not surprisingly, skilled negotiators are significantly less likely to become involved in this practice.

SUMMARY

Conflict in some form seems to be part of organizational life. The process of management invariably involves keeping this disharmony at a level where it does not interfere with the smooth running of the operation. Negotiating is one approach to accomplishing this task and managers are unlikely to be successful if they are weak in this area. Negotiating is typically seen as an antagonistic activity in which those engaged play the roles of opponents or enemies, each out to defeat the other. But it does not have to be this way. In most negotiations there is scope for co-operation to secure a win-win outcome for the benefit of all.

Nevertheless, the strategy adopted has implications for the shape of the negotiation and the characteristic stages that it passes through. Generally the process should begin with planning and preparing, and move through phases of getting started, exploring issues, making proposals, bargaining and, finally, reaching settlement. Ultimate success is dependent on the level of skill of the participants. Skilled negotiators tend to engage in labelling behaviour, testing understanding, summarizing, seeking information and disclosing their feelings and intentions (real or otherwise). They avoid the use of irritators, defend/attack spirals and immediate counter-proposals.

7 Selling the idea: the manager as salesperson

Everyone lives by selling something.

Robert Louis Stevenson

Selling products, services, or ideas occupies a great deal of time in organizational life.

D. O'Hair and G. Friedrich, *Strategic Communication*

No business will survive without the ability of its people to sell. While some individuals earn their living as salespeople, for all managers it is necessary to 'sell' to others, whether what you are selling is in the form of an idea, or something more tangible such as a service level interdepartmental agreement. At times we specifically have to sell *ourselves* – the obvious example being at selection interviews (see Chapter 12). However, in all instances where we are making a presentation (or sales 'pitch') others will evaluate us[1] as well as what we are promoting – in other words they will 'buy' or reject us.[2]

Managers often have to demonstrate good sales skills. Examples include selling a new system to superiors, selling one's own ideas to peers, selling management decisions to subordinates and selling the importance of change to staff at times of innovation. The process of selling is therefore a more specialized form of influencing and persuading[3] (see Chapter 2 for a fuller discussion of these techniques). Indeed, the main abilities of effective salespeople as identified in a number of studies[4-8] are all relevant to the role of management in general (Key point 7.1). It is therefore no surprise to learn that good managers can 'sell'.

Selling is the process of persuading others that your product, service or idea is what they need and will be of benefit to them. There is a well-known sales model[9] which, as illustrated in Figure 7.1, comprises six main processes or steps: opening the sale, establishing needs, presenting, overcoming objections, giving additional sales suggestions and closing the sale. The operation of this model can best be examined by considering each of these steps separately.

Key point 7.1   Key selling abilities

- Ability to learn.
- Adaptability with different people.
- Capacity to handle rejection.
- Confidence.
- Creativity.
- Empathy/rapport building.
- Enthusiasm/motivation.
- Flexibility with different people.
- Integrity and trustworthiness.
- Knowledge and expertise.
- Likeability.
- Observation and listening skill.
- Organizational skill.
- Perseverance.
- Persuasiveness.
- Questioning skill – especially in relation to client needs.

STEP 1: OPENING THE SALE

The opening move is an important stage of any interaction. Psychologists have clearly shown that the first (primacy effect) and last (recency effect) events in any sequence tend to be best remembered. This means that the opening and closing stages of any sales attempt offer greater opportunities to make an impact on others. The importance of effective opening is recognized in phrases such as 'Well begun is half done', 'You don't get a second chance to make a first impression' and 'Start off as you mean to go on'. The initial perceptions which a target audience forms of the salesperson will influence the likelihood of success. How the individual is dressed, the posture adopted, facial expressions used, and all the other forms of body language employed, will affect judgements made on dimensions such as trust and confidence, which in turn influence buying decisions.

In sales terms the opening phase involves the processes of meeting, greeting, seating and treating. For example, a manager who calls a meeting at which a 'sales pitch' will be made should be there in advance to *meet* others as they arrive, *greet* and welcome them (preferably using first names), smile, shake hands and engage in

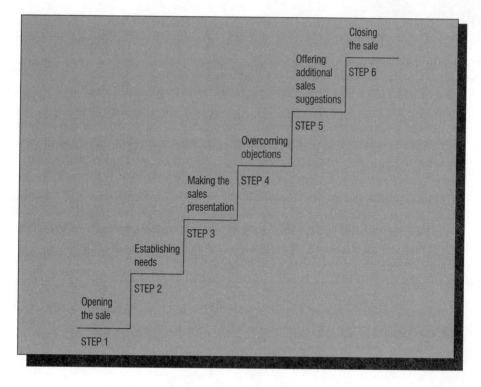

Figure 7.1 The sales model

some small talk, have suitable and comfortable *seating*, and offer *treats* in the form of tea/coffee/drinks/sustenance as appropriate for the time of day and occasion. Time spent in the opening phase is a good investment. The greeting and parting rituals are very important to human discourse. From an early age children are taught how to meet and part from others – told to say hello and goodbye, shake hands, smile and wave. These behaviours therefore become imprinted on us and we expect them. Those who use them effectively make a positive (often subconscious) impression on us. We ignore them at our peril. In the sales situation, the task and social aspects are inextricably linked. The task of completing a successful sale is made much easier by the smooth lubricant of good social skills.

Making a good opening impression is part of relationship-building. Effective salespeople are rated highly in terms of sociability and likeability – this is a prerequisite to successful social persuasion. In their book, *In Search Of Excellence*, Tom Peters and Robert Waterman discuss one way in which the 'likeability' tactic was used by Joe Girard, the top car salesman in the USA for 11 years running. Every month he sent out over 13 000 cards to his customers, wishing them, for example, Happy George Washington's Day in February or Happy St Patrick's Day in March.

The front of each card simply read 'I like you'. This tactic worked. The customers loved the cards, and by association, Joe, who in a typical year sold twice as many units as the salesperson in second place.

After the initial 'social' stage of opening, comes the process of motivating others in preparation to receive your message. This involves gaining their attention and arousing interest in what you are about to say. The methods used to achieve this with larger groups (see Chapter 5) will differ from those appropriate when dealing with one or two others. In both situations, however, it is useful to mention a *tentative benefit* early in the encounter. For instance, the authors of this book were invited by the Chief Executive of a large organization to make a sales pitch at a board meeting of the senior management team to run an audit of communications. Our opening gambit was as presented in Key point 7.2, where the benefit mentioned very early in the process was that an objective audit by independent consultants was the best way of discovering the reality of what was happening with communications.

Key point 7.2   Opening phase of a sales pitch for a communication audit

'All of you here today are managers. You all communicate with your staff and you control how communications operate within your Department. But do staff tell you the truth when they deal with you? How do you know they do?

There is a process called "The Boss's Illusion" which means that subordinates tell their superiors what they think they want to hear. Do you always tell the whole truth to the Chief Executive? No one wants to be a dead messenger.

Yet if you don't know the real truth about the state of communications how can you remedy deficits and effect improvements? If you have a false diagnosis then the prescribed treatment is not likely to work! So, how can we obtain information about what is *really* happening in terms of communication within departments.

There is a valid and reliable way of achieving this and it is called a communications audit. What an audit does is tell you exactly what is really happening on the ground. It will give you a clear picture of current strengths, weaknesses, blockages, overall patterns of communication ...'

Key point 7.3   Approaches to opening

- Compliment the customer, e.g. 'We know you are all committed managers who recognise the importance of good communications.'
- Ask a question leading in to what you are selling, e.g. 'How do you currently measure the effectiveness of your communications?'
- Give a tentative benefit of what you are selling, e.g. 'A communication audit will enable you to make quite dramatic improvements on present practice.'
- Emphasize that what you are selling is up to date, e.g. 'We use the most recent approach to auditing, which involves a combination of methods.'
- Show a picture/sample, e.g. graphs of reductions in absenteeism, increases in staff suggestions, improved productivity etc. following an audit.
- Show the acceptability of your product, e.g. 'Large companies, such as Wizzo, AOK, and Wheeker, all now use audits on an annual basis.'

At this motivational stage the salesperson should check and probe for receptivity. Is the message being fully accepted – or totally rejected? Is the 'customer' interested? Do some people seem supportive while others are more hostile? Information gleaned at this stage can facilitate how the sales pitch will progress. It allows decisions to be made about which people to target and in what ways, and which ones may be allies who could be brought into the frame later to help clinch the sale. Approaches for opening a sale are outlined in Key point 7.3, together with examples pertinent to the above example of selling an audit of communications.

STEP 2: ESTABLISHING NEEDS

Having set the scene, this is the next important stage of the sales process. Kossen[10] suggested that salespeople should remember the acronym FUN to emphasize the importance of 'First Uncovering Needs' before making a sales presentation. Human behaviour is driven by motivation which in turn is determined by needs and wants. Once we know what another person needs or wants then we can adapt our sales pitch to emphasize how what we have to offer will help to satisfy these. One of the most common errors made by ineffective salespeople is to attempt to make a sales presentation before identifying the real needs of the client. Questioning skills have been shown[11] to be valuable in determining needs.

Open-ended questions should be used at the outset to obtain maximum information (e.g. 'Could you tell me about how you presently do X?') followed by more close-ended questions to check for accuracy (e.g. 'So you obtain some information through that method but you would like more?'). Throughout this stage listening skills are very important (see Chapter 11 for more details on effective listening). In his analysis of the social skills of selling, Poppleton[12] identified the sequence used by demonstrably successful salespeople as that of asking initial questions, listening, then asking further questions, without embarking too early on the sales pitch.

The best known analysis of human needs is Maslow's hierarchy (Figure 7.2). At the bottom of the hierarchy and therefore most important are physiological needs, which are essential for the survival of the individual. Thus, if we are very hungry, cold or thirsty, we will be highly motivated to rectify this deprivation and our goal will be to seek food, heat or water. If these needs have been satisfied, the next most important are those connected with safety, security and protection from harm. We meet these needs by a whole range of methods including locking our doors at night, purchasing insurance policies, or obtaining secure and permanent employment.

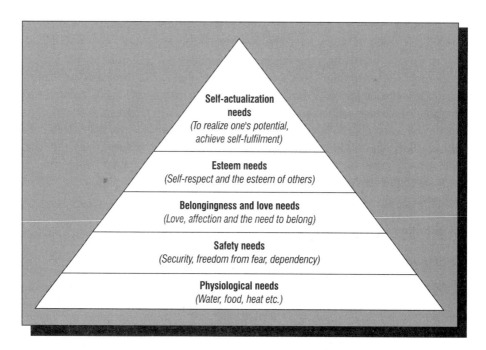

Figure 7.2   Maslow's hierarchy of human needs

At the next level are belongingness and love needs, such as the need to be liked and accepted, and not to be lonely or isolated. Making and keeping friends, maintaining good relationships at work, joining clubs, getting married and having a family are all ways of satisfying needs at this level. After these are esteem needs which are met through occupational status and other achievements. Finally, there is the ultimate wish for self-actualization by realizing one's true potential. People continually seek new challenges (such as running marathons or pursuing courses in education), need to feel their talents are being fully recognized and utilized, and want to realize their full potential.

Maslow argued that only when the basic needs are met will the individual become concerned with needs further up the hierarchy. Thus, someone who is starving will usually seek food at all costs, even risking personal security, and will show a lack of concern for self-esteem by begging. Equally, someone in secure, salaried employment may resign in order to open their own business and become 'self-actualized'. However, people can be manipulated either by promises that important needs will be met, or by threats that these needs will be unfulfilled. Politicians promise to reduce the 'appalling' crime rate and make the streets safe again for the people; insurance salespeople offer to remove worry about the results of horrible events which may occur; and company management threaten a whole range of needs by warning that if workers go on strike the company may close and their jobs will be lost.

In Western society many people have achieved most or all of these needs and they become more concerned with wants. I may not *need* a surround-around stereo system, but the fact that I *want* one is more important than the fact that I could live without it! Thus, both needs and wants can be related directly to buying motives. Someone whose house is very cold is liable to be more susceptible to a sales pitch by a central heating company, while a lonely person will be more likely to pay attention to someone extolling the virtues of a dating agency. Also, different types of need are more important for some people than for others. Advertisers therefore employ a variety of advertisements to encourage people to 'buy' their product – each advertisement will appeal more to some people than to others. For example, different advertisements for a fast-food chain encompass those which emphasize:

- the quality, size and speed of their food and drink (physiological needs)
- the pure nature of their products, the hygienic environment and the attention to detail at their outlets (safety needs)
- the friendly staff, the fun people who go there, and the great parties which they provide for families and friends (belongingness needs)
- the *pro bono* work for worthy causes and charities which they engage in – so supporting them also has a wider good (esteem needs).

The key buying motives are presented in Key point 7.4. Again, some of these will be more important than others for any particular individual. Thus, 'obtaining value for money' may be an overriding motive for a miserly individual, who may be less concerned with 'having the best'. Managers, in making sales presentations, should attempt to ascertain and chart the level of needs and wants of the target audience before moving on to the next part of the sale. Furthermore, as the following two quotations illustrate, a key component of effective selling is the ability to recognize what people will be prepared to buy:

Who the hell wants to hear actors talk?

H.M. Warner, Warner Brothers, 1927

We don't like their sound, and guitar music is on the way out.

Decca Recording Company rejecting the Beatles, 1962

Key point 7.4   The top ten buying motives

1. Self-preservation.
2. Attractiveness enhancement.
3. Emulation of the successful.
4. Being in-style and up to date.
5. Having the best.
6. Being liked or accepted.
7. Gaining knowledge and skills.
8. Fulfilling a dream.
9. Obtaining value for money.
10. Revenge motives ('showing them').

STEP 3: MAKING THE SALES PRESENTATION

Having opened the sales encounter and established customer needs, the next step in the sales process is to present a product or service which will meet the identified needs. In making such a presentation a distinction must be made between *features* and *benefits*. Features refer to those characteristics inherent in what you are selling. They describe its attributes. Benefits refer to the advantages to the customer of what you are offering. Each of the features described should be converted into a benefit. In his book on the 'supersalesman', Davis[13] has shown how people 'buy' benefits rather than features. In particular, where the benefits are shown to directly meet the needs (or wants) of clients, they are more likely to buy. When making presentations managers should therefore aim to convert features into benefits. For instance a salesperson selling an automatic camera to a customer may mention the following features and benefits:

Features	*Benefits*
• This camera has a built-in lens cover.	• This means you don't have the nuisance of looking after the cover each time you want to take a picture. Nor is there any danger of losing the cover.
• It also has automatic focus.	• So you don't need to worry about adjusting for focal length. You just point and shoot, and your pictures will always be in focus – no more fuzzy pictures!
• It has a built-in automatic flash.	• You don't have to bother with the nuisance of having to carry a flashgun. Also, the camera decides from the prevailing light whether the flash is needed – so you get the correct lighting for any situation. No more dark pictures!

The following lines vividly illustrate the power of benefits over features:

1. Don't sell me gas lights.
   Sell me attractiveness, soft lights and full time service.

2. Don't sell me gas ranges.
   Sell me modernity, fluffy cakes, savoury roasts, juicy steaks.

3. Don't sell me gas water heaters.
   Sell me temperature, sufficiency, reliability all day and night.

4. Don't sell me gas furnaces.
   Sell me heating comfort, cleanliness, labour-saving convenience and health.

5. Don't sell me air conditioners.
   Sell me trouble-free comfort cooling, efficiency and simplicity.

6. Don't sell me industrial fuel.
   Sell me controlled heat, speed, production,
   quality and greater profits.

7. Don't sell me Btu's.
   Sell me benefits and intangibles to convince me that I get more than I pay for with gas.

North Thames Gas Board

This distinction between features and benefits is important. Exercise 7.1 should therefore be completed at this stage. Detailed information on the skill of presenting is provided in Chapter 5, but in general a well-planned sales presentation has three main objectives:

- to create and sustain interest and attention
- to demonstrate how what is being offered can meet and satisfy established client needs
- to ensure client understanding.

Exercise 7.1   Benefits or features?

Indicate (✓) next to each of the following statements whether it is a feature or a benefit.

	Feature	Benefit
1. This video-recorder has a built-in satellite receiver.	❏	❏
2. Your promotion means you now have a key for the executive washroom.	❏	❏
3. This risograph makes 100 dry, high-quality, copies from an original every minute.	❏	❏
4. The new structure will mean one boss for every 10 staff as opposed to the present 19.	❏	❏
5. These jackets are fully waterproof.	❏	❏
6. You will receive one free tape with each purchase of a pack of five.	❏	❏
7. Our communications audit will provide you with a set of clear approval ratings.	❏	❏
8. This new machine works at twice the operating capacity of the old version.	❏	❏
9. With our computer system you will be automatically connected to the Internet.	❏	❏
10. Our system has a full one-year parts and service warranty.	❏	❏

See Answers at the end of this chapter.

Key point 7.5   The top ten objections to change
attempts

1. 'We're not ready for this.'
2. 'We have too many other problems at present.'
3. 'It is far too expensive/a waste of money.'
4. 'Our staff will never agree.'
5. 'We've been through all this before.'
6. 'Our existing methods work perfectly well.'
7. 'We will have to change our whole system of operation.'
8. 'That doesn't apply to us.'
9. 'We can use the facilities at Head Office.'
10. 'We're far too busy to get involved in this.'

STEP 4: OVERCOMING OBJECTIONS

Following (or sometimes during) the sales presentation clients may raise objections or reservations regarding what is being offered (although objections may also occur at any stage of the sales process). For example, the ten most commonly stated general objections to any attempts by management to introduce change are shown in Key point 7.5. Handling objections is an important part of the selling process, since they can serve a number of useful purposes (see Key point 7.6).

In considering the importance of objections as a core part of the sales process, Williams[14] noted: 'If you think a sales objection is worrying, consider the implications of the prospective buyer who says nothing!' When handling objections the techniques found to be used by effective salespeople are to:

1. Listen carefully and let the person finish the objection without interruption.
2. Observe how strongly the person expresses the objection and, if in a group context, how many others offer verbal or non-verbal support.
3. Check for agreement about the exact nature of the objection and show understanding by verbalizing it in summary form (e.g. 'So am I right in saying your main concern is ... ?').
4. Provide some credibility to the objection and recognize its importance for the person raising it (e.g. 'I can see that this is a genuine concern and you raise an important issue ...').

Key point 7.6   Advantages of objections

Objections:

- *indicate buyer attention and interest.* If the person is able to make objections this means they have listened to the sales presentation and are at least not apathetic.
- *give insight into buyer attitudes.* The nature of the objection and the way in which it is expressed provide valuable information about what the person making the objection regards as important and what level of needs or wants they have.
- *allow for the provision of reassurance* and correction of any misunderstandings. The objection may be based upon a misconception of what was being sold.
- *are a useful form of feedback* as to the effectiveness of the sales presentation. For example, if all objections are based upon misconceptions then changes need to be made to the information provided and the way it is delivered.
- *suggest potential product disadvantages* which need to be dealt with in future presentations.
- *create further selling opportunities* in overcoming them. Some theorists argue that if there are no objections then the customer is buying rather that the salesperson selling! Where the buyer does not raise any objections the salesperson may do so and proceed to overcome them (e.g. may say 'Some people think that this is rather small, but in fact that is an advantage ...'). This approach has the added advantage of dealing with possible hidden objections which are felt but not overtly expressed.
- *offer the opportunity to empathize and sympathize with the client.*

---

5. Prepare stock phrases to counter every possible objection.
6. Answer the objection directly and truthfully giving the minimum amount of information necessary to overcome it; do not go on at length since this may raise suspicions that you are 'trying too hard'. The objective is to neutralize the objection, not to win a debate.
7. Avoid becoming embroiled in a lengthy argument on any one objection.
8. Use it as an opportunity to clinch the sale, or to learn what to change in future presentations.

A distinction can be made between *logical* and *psychological* objections. Logical objections include:

- cost (too expensive)
- negative product characteristics (too difficult to use, too slow, etc.)
- no need for it (if I am a vegetarian I won't want pork chops!)
- dissatisfaction with the source (e.g. 'We have had a lot of problems with The Dodgy Computer Company in the past').

Psychological objections are more difficult to deal with since they may not even be fully recognized by the client. They include:

- a preference for established habits and a high resistance to interference in these
- negative feelings towards anyone who tries to 'sell' anything
- a tendency to resist what is perceived to be a persuasion/dominance attempt
- a general dislike of decision-making.

While decisions can quickly be made about whether logical objections can be overcome, psychological objections usually take longer to deal with.

A variety of techniques can be employed to deal with genuine objections (Table 7.1). It should be realized that buyers may be well motivated towards what is on

Table 7.1   Dealing with objections: the 10 As

Technique	Purpose	Example
Acceptance inducing	To show the widespread acceptability of what you have to offer	'All the major agencies are using it. WISE & Co have had this system for the past six months.'
Adapting	To convert the objection into a reason for buying	'It does seem expensive but it lasts twice as long and so saves money in the long run.'
Advocating the advantages	To underline the benefits of what you are selling	The benefits as opposed to features should be stated or restated
Agreeing and neutralizing	To empathize with the buyer while overcoming the objection	'Yes, it involves change and I appreciate that this will cause you some difficulties, but it will make life a lot easier for you in the long run.'
Anticipating the objection	To overcome likely objections before they are stated	'You may be thinking that this is rather expensive, but ...'
Apprehension-raising	To underline the dangers of not buying	'Your competitors will be one step ahead of you ...'
Arguing logically	To appeal to logic	'Let me summarize the main reasons why you should buy this.'
Asking for a trial	To encourage the buyer to give it a try	'Give it a month and we can review what you think of it then.'
Attractiveness enhancing	To inspire confidence in the buyer towards the salesperson	Smart dress, good grooming, appropriate use of scents etc.
Authority stating	To inspire confidence in the buyer	'I have been in this field for over 15 years and I know what works.'

offer, but want to be fully persuaded – or at least reassured – that their decisions are appropriate. Alternatively, objections may be raised to test how convinced the salesperson is in the quality and appropriateness of the product. Dealing patiently and fully with objections therefore offers the opportunity of reinforcing the buying decision.

STEP 5: OFFERING ADDITIONAL SALES SUGGESTIONS

This step is not always necessary or appropriate in every sales encounter. However, in many situations opportunities arise to make additional 'linked sales' associated with the primary item. This is quite common in retail selling. For example, having selected a pair of shoes in a shoe shop, the customer at the point of sale may be asked 'Would you like some cream/polish with these?' Another example comes from a meeting of the senior management team in one of our consultancies with a large corporation. Here the Communications Manager, having persuaded his colleagues and the Chief Executive of the advantages of setting up an internal communication project team, proceeded to successfully sell the linked idea of having the chairperson appointed from junior management.

A useful piece of advice, however, is do not push things too far at this stage. It is the main sale which is important. If the linked sale might in any way jeopardize this, then it should not be attempted or should be quickly and gracefully abandoned.

STEP 6: CLOSING THE SALE

The 'close' is the process wherein the salesperson motivates the client to make an affirmative decision regarding purchase and proceeds to terminate the encounter in a smooth, friendly fashion – thereby facilitating future interactions. This is perhaps the most important step in the selling process, yet it is the one that often causes the most difficulties.[15] Some of the main difficulties faced in closing a sale are shown in Key point 7.7. It should be realized that the close is an integral part of the process of sale, and not divorced from it.

The salesperson needs to be aware of – and act on – buying signals. These include questions such as 'When would this be available?', statements like 'That sounds very useful', non-verbal responses such as agreeing nods, smiles and receptive facial expressions, and physical actions including handling the product possessively or trying it out (e.g. trying on a dress or using a new computer package). In relation to the latter response, a jeweller trying to sell a bracelet to a woman will ask her to wear it and then compliment her on how well it looks and how much it suits her.

Key point 7.7 Main closing difficulties

- Lack of confidence in asking directly for a commitment.
- Not wishing to appear 'pushy'.
- Fear of rejection of sales suggestions (and by implication oneself).
- Accepting first 'no' without persevering.
- Inability to recognize and act upon buying signals.
- Buyer not ready to close because:
  - needs have not been fully established or met
  - poor presentation has not been convincing
  - objections have not been adequately dealt with
  - he or she is over-talkative and cannot make a decision.

Similarly, a salesperson attempting to sell a piece of equipment will encourage the customer to use it while simultaneously highlighting its benefits. This is why car dealers encourage prospective buyers to take a test drive.

To expedite a close the salesperson can make trial closures using what are known as 'assumptive questions'. The assumption is made that the buyer has decided and the question focuses on the formal close. Examples include 'How many do you want?' 'Would you like it wrapped?' as well as what are called dual positive assumptions, such as: 'Do you want to pay by cash or credit card?' 'Would you prefer the blue or the red?' When used skilfully these questions place subtle pressure on the client to agree to the sale.

The close is important in that it offers a final opportunity to reinforce and reward the buyer's decision.[16] All changes cause some degree of stress. When people make significant change decisions they therefore experience anxiety, or what psychologists have termed *cognitive dissonance*, about whether they have decided correctly. The greater the investment in time and cost the higher this will be. Such dissonance can be reduced by the salesperson providing reassurance and support, to ensure that the person stays committed to the buying decision and does not resolve the dissonance by abandoning the change and resorting to the original behaviour. Statements such as 'Your staff will be delighted when they hear about this', 'You will wonder why it took you so long to obtain this' or 'You have made an excellent choice', are all examples of dissonance-reducing interventions.

SUMMARY

Managers do not have to earn their living as salespeople, but they do need to be able to sell. They have to convince their superiors, peers and subordinates of the benefits of courses of action which they propose. They have to persuade all of these 'customers' to 'buy' what they are recommending. The importance of good sales skills is recognized at the highest levels of business. As one review[17] expressed it: 'you will now hear chief executives talk about their role in the selling of products, services, ideas and even the company'. In making such sales attempts, a knowledge of the process and techniques of selling will be very useful. The sequential structure outlined in this chapter – opening, establishing needs, presenting that which will meet these needs, overcoming objections, making linked sales suggestions and closing – offers a template for action. This model of sales has been usefully summarized within the organizational context in a format known as Monroe's motivated sequence[18, 19] (see Key point 7.8).

Exercise 7.2 provides a useful checklist which you should employ before you attempt to make a sale.

The skills and techniques discussed in this chapter within each stage of the sales process are useful in the many contexts where managers have to influence and persuade others. We will end the chapter with a final word about interactive style. Buyers prefer sellers who are trustworthy (dependable and honest), task-oriented (main focus on the business in hand rather than on unrelated small talk), and composed (comfortable and relaxed) in their approach.[20, 21] Buyers also wish to be treated with warmth and respect, and favour a co-operative to a competitive approach by the salesperson. This suggests that, in most instances, a 'soft' sell is preferable to a 'hard' sell. Managers should bear this in mind as they use the skills covered in this chapter.

Key point 7.8   Monroe's motivated sequence

Step 1: gaining attention

Arousing listener interest in the topic.
Focusing the listener's attention on the message.

Step 2: showing the need – describing the problem

Explaining what is wrong with the current situation. (statement)
Clarifying the problems with examples. (illustration)
Showing the extent and seriousness of need. (ramification)
Relating the problem directly to the listener. (pointing)

Step 3: satisfying the need – presenting the solution

Stating the proposed changes from the present. (statement)
Explaining the mechanics of the solution. (explanation)
Showing how the solution solves the problem. (demonstration)
Showing that the proposal is workable. (practicality)
Answering objections to the proposal. (rebuttal)

Step 4: visualizing the results

Describing future benefits if the plan is adopted. (positive projection)
Describing future consequences if the plan is not adopted. (negative projection)
Describing both positive and negative projections. (contrast)

Step 5: requesting action or approval

Describing specific actions for listeners to take.
Asking for commitment from the listeners.

Exercise 7.2   Planning the sale

Think of a situation that you will have to deal with in the near future in which you will have to persuade others to 'buy' something that you will be advocating. Now consider each of the following questions:

- What will be the key techniques you will use at the *opening* stage?
- How will you establish fully the *needs* of those whom you will have to persuade?
- In what way can you tailor your *presentation* to clearly meet these needs?
- Exactly what *objections* are you likely to face and how will you handle each of these?
- If your sale is successful, is there is an opportunity for a *linked sale*?
- How will you *close* the sale to reward the buying behaviour and ensure that any cognitive dissonance is reduced?

Answers to Exercise 7.1

They are *all features*. Each can be converted to a *benefit statement* and, indeed, the reader may already have done so when reading them. However, no benefits are stated in any of the items. In sales contexts the benefits must be clearly laid out for the customer. Thus, the *benefits* in each item are emphasized in the following statements:

1. This *saves you money* and is *much more convenient*. You do not have the expense of buying a separate satellite receiver, nor the inconvenience of finding space for two separate pieces of electrical equipment – the combined one is more compact and less cluttered.
2. This gives you *convenient access to a scarce and desired resource*. It also gives you *higher status* than most of your colleagues.
3. The speed of this machine *saves you considerable time* and gives you a much *higher quality product*.
4. *Access to the boss will be easier* and *your chances of promotion are greater*.
5. *You do not have to worry about the weather* since you *will stay dry should it rain* – no need to bother with an overcoat.
6. This is a *direct saving for you of £4* on each pack of five.
7. You will *have a direct quantifiable measure for judging current performance* to act as a *benchmark against which to measure future performance*.
8. This *saves you both time* and *money*.
9. It gives you all of the *advantages of the Web* (including e-mail) *without any further costly equipment* or connections.
10. This means you have complete *peace of mind* and *security*.

8 Making the right connections: the telephone in business

> The far is near. Our feeblest whispers fly,
> Where cannon falter, thunders faint and die.
> Your little song the telephone can float
> As free of fetters as a bluebird's note,
> Quick as a prayer ascending into Heaven.
> Quick as the answer, 'all is forgiven'
> The Lightning writes it, God's electric clerk;
> The engine bears it, buckling to the work
> Till miles are minutes and the minutes breaths ...
>
> Benjamin Franklin Taylor, *The Wonders of Forty Years*, 1886

The above lines, written over a hundred years ago, extol the benefits of the then new system of communication, and exemplify one of the many poems which have been written about this now taken for granted device. The word 'telephone' is derived from the Greek words for far (tele) and voice (phone). It was invented by Alexander Graham Bell, a Scotsman who had emigrated to America and who transmitted the first spoken sentence by telephone in Boston in 1876. Since then it has gradually yet inexorably become part of our daily lives.

This chapter provides background information regarding the development of the telephone as a communication device, examines the norms of telephone behaviour and discusses the main differences between telephone and face-to-face communication. It also outlines the main problems which occur when using the telephone and discusses techniques designed to solve them.

Shortly after its invention, the potential development of this innovation was summarized as follows:

> This 'telephone' has too many shortcomings to be seriously considered as a means of communication. The device is inherently of no value to us.
>
> *Western Union internal memo*, 1876

My department is in possession of full knowledge of the details of the invention, and the possible use of the telephone is limited.

Engineer-in-chief of the British Post Office, 1877

So much for the skills of scientists as niche marketers!

The telephone system has developed rapidly. For example, the percentage of households with a telephone in the UK increased[1] from 42 per cent in 1972 to 92 per cent in 1992. In the developed world, most private homes now have more than one telephone, many of which are cordless or include a 'handsfree' facility, and mobile phones are commonplace. Users are no longer 'tied up' to a base unit, and this in turn has helped to encourage its phenomenal growth. In the UK, in 1985 there were only 25 000 mobile phone users, but by 1998 this number had risen to 9 million. In 1997 in the UK, some 40 million people called mobile phones from fixed lines spending a total of 5 billion minutes on the line, and these numbers are rising by 40 per cent a year.[2] The miniaturization of mobile phones, coupled with the use of satellites as well as terrestrial transmitters, has further enhanced their popularity – it is not surprising that this is the fastest growing part of the telecommunications sector.[3] In addition, systems such as videophones will develop the information-giving potential of this communication network.

Paradoxically, the increased availability of telecommunications has had the effect of encouraging many people to seek shelter from the electronic storm. The exponential growth in use of voicemail, mobile phones, pagers, faxes, e-mail, and so on, has heightened the danger of what has been variously termed 'techno stress', 'information fatigue syndrome', 'future shock' or 'multiphrenia'. In other words, we become overloaded and overwhelmed with the wide range and volume of communication information being sent to us. Not surprisingly, some people then take steps to protect themselves. One example of restricted access is shown in the fact[4] that the proportion of ex-directory numbers among residential telephone owners in the UK rose from 24 per cent in 1991 to 37 per cent in 1998. This trend is greatest in cities, where the level of such communications tends to be highest, so that 56 per cent of residential telephone users in London and 49 per cent in Birmingham elected to stay out of the book in 1998.

In the business context it is impossible to imagine life without the telephone. The Direct Marketing Association has estimated that some 80 per cent of all financial transactions are carried out by telephone. Telecommunications is currently a trillion-dollar business (that is 1 000 billion dollars). This has been encouraged by the growth in freephone usage, a system pioneered by the telecommunications company AT&T in 1967, in which year Americans made a total of 7 million toll-free calls. By 1997 AT&T alone carried 20 billion such calls.[5]

This growth is likely to continue. The Henley Centre's *Telecultures Future* report found that customers view a freephone provision as a sign that a company is professional and wants their business, since this minimizes the inconvenience and removes the cost of telephoning them. They also estimate that freephone numbers in adverts result in increases in customer enquiries of up to 140 per cent. One negative aspect of increased usage of freephones is their misuse. For example, in the UK every day some 47 000 people call the emergency services 999 number when it is not an emergency,[6] causing potential delays in dealing with the real distress calls. However, the benefits of freephone services far outweigh their drawbacks.

Economic wealth is dependent on many factors, one of which is the effectiveness of communication between people in organizations. The telephone is of importance here since it facilitates instant communication, within and between organizations, across time and distance. Indeed, the correlation between gross national product (GNP) and telephones per head of population is very high – for all countries and even for states within countries.[7] It is, however, unclear whether an increase in telecommunications somehow contributes to an increase in GNP, or whether greater wealth leads to the purchase of more luxury goods such as telephones. That this correlation does not hold for other electronic goods (such as televisions) tends to support the view that there is a causative relationship between total number of telephones and growth in industry.

In his book on the subject, Frey[8] concluded that: 'The telephone is a technological innovation that has altered our social relations perhaps more than any other device.' Psychologists have clearly shown a strong relationship between physical closeness and the formation of friendships. We are more likely to become friends with the family next door, or opposite, than the family living on the other side of town. Within the workplace, higher trust evaluations are given to those with whom we interact more often.[9] Another finding is that increases in physical distance have been shown to impair friendships.[10] However, with the advent of mass usage of the telephone this is now no longer necessarily the case. Friends and family can maintain regular contact, provide topical informational updates and share experiences over distance without any great effort or expense. Although research shows that we tend to express a higher degree of liking for those we have met face to face rather than those we have only spoken to on the telephone,[11] friendships can and do develop over the telephone without the participants ever having met face to face (as tele-dating agencies have discovered).

Furthermore, what is known as the 'synergistic effect' means that an increase in one medium of contact stimulates demand for contact through other media, i.e. the desire for synergy increases. Thus, for example, the opening of the first Severn Bridge linking South-West England with South Wales soon resulted in the jamming of telephone trunk routes between these areas. Once we have made contact with others we want to communicate more and through all available media. Having met someone we are more likely to telephone them, write, send e-mails, and so on. Likewise, having talked to someone on the telephone we are more likely to take any available opportunity to meet them.

There are over 1 billion telephones in use in the world and billions of person-to-person telephone calls are made every year. In many cities there are now more telephones than people. Yet comparatively little attention is paid to the effects of this medium on interpersonal behaviour. Paradoxically it is usually those at a lower level in the organizational hierarchy who receive training in telephone skills. Thus, secretaries, receptionists and those handling consumer complaints or making tele-sales will be given training in how to improve their skills in the use of the telephone. However, middle and senior managers are somehow expected to be naturally skilled in its use – a state of affairs which is patently not the case. Indeed in reviewing this area, the social psychologist Michael Argyle[12] concluded that 'The telephone ... is a different communication skill, which has to be learnt'. In order to manage communications effectively, a knowledge of telephone conventions and techniques are very important.

NORMS OF TELEPHONE BEHAVIOUR

1. *The ringing phone creates inner tension*. When a telephone rings our arousal level increases and we have an inner urge to 'answer the call'. The noise is intrusive and cannot easily be ignored – it *demands* attention. Indeed, people often actually *run* to answer the telephone. The reasons for this are a matter for speculation. It has been suggested that the noise of the telephone ringing is akin to a distress call – for example the cry of a child or the alarm bells of an ambulance, police car or fire engine – and that we are therefore conditioned to respond. Thus, there is a compulsion to answer and even disrupt other activities. Sales assistants in smaller businesses (for example in travel agencies) will often interrupt face-to-face interactions to answer a ringing telephone. Why does this occur? This brings us to the second norm of telephone behaviour.

2. *There is a mystery about a ringing telephone*. Not to answer may mean the loss of a reward or the receipt of a later punishment. As a result, tension increases. Who was that? Was it someone important? Will they call back? Should I have answered? This means that tele-sales staff have the advantage of knowing that at the very least their call is likely to be answered (since even if they have caller display, householders will not recognize the caller's number and so the mystery is further heightened).

3. Another norm is that in most interactions *the initiator shall terminate the call*. This is because hanging up by the recipient amounts to 'interaction homicide'. It is also a form of bad manners. In a sense a telephone caller is analogous to someone arriving unexpectedly. The caller becomes our guest. Norms of civilized behaviour dictate that we should be hospitable to guests and not ask them to leave unless they have upset us. We may drop broad hints about their leaving in

the hope that they are sensitive enough to act on them, or we will make excuses as to why we are ending the interaction ('I have to go to a meeting', 'I am picking up my daughter'). To do otherwise will result in the guest feeling annoyed and offended.

As a result, few respondents to a telephone call hang up without speaking. Rather, we negotiate our intention not to participate, or give a reason or excuse for being uncooperative. This may be done rather quickly – for example if we receive a cold call from a double glazing company we may simply say 'No thanks I already have double glazing. Goodbye'. Interactional norms place pressure on recipients to participate at some level, since few of us like to be intentionally rude. Of course, tele-sales staff can make use of these learned norms of politeness to try to establish a rapport with the recipient during that initial window of opportunity at the start of the call. Thereafter, those skilled tele-sales staff who can give length and life to the call will increase their opportunity for a sale.

This norm also means that if someone whom we do not want to talk to for a long period phones, we should make an excuse such as, 'I'm tied up with someone just now. Can I call you back in about five minutes?' Then when calling back, the norm is that *we* determine when the call will be terminated. This process also conveys the impression that we are very busy and helps to reduce what the other person will perceive to be the expected duration of the call.

4. *Most person-to-person calls begin with a position of equity* and callers then use what has been termed 'image vending' to highlight their importance, impress the other person and sell their message. This norm can be changed, of course, by having one's secretary ring so that when the actual person-to-person call begins, the caller is already at a position of advantage (I am of high status – I have a secretary) – unless of course the call is mediated for the recipient by another secretary in which case the equity norm applies again.

DIFFERENCES BETWEEN TELEPHONE AND FACE-TO-FACE INTERACTIONS

When we use the telephone we change our behaviour in a number of often subtle ways. These include the following.

1. We increase our use of what are called 'filled pauses'.[13] Linguists have identified two types of speech dysfluencies – 'Ah' and 'Non-ah'. Non-ah dysfluencies include stuttering, stammering, slips of the tongue, incompletions, Spoonerisms, and so on. The Ah category, also known as 'filled pauses', includes all those ubiquitous vocal fillers such as 'ums', 'ers', 'ams' – and of course 'ahs'. It is in this latter domain where differences arise, with filled pauses four times as

likely to occur during telephone calls than in face-to-face interactions. This is because we use filled pauses to communicate to the other person that we have not finished what we want to say and that therefore we wish to continue speaking. In face-to-face interaction (and especially when making formal presentations) a high number of ahs would be negatively regarded and seen as poor presentational style, but this is not the case in telephone encounters. The following is taken from an actual telephone communication and in this ten-second excerpt it can be seen that the speaker uses three filled pauses to maintain the floor:

> I could have it for you by Friday ... ah ... but there would be a cost implication ... ahm ... in that this would mean overtime for staff ... uh ... and re-organizing the production schedule.

It should be noted that this is an example of the skilled use of filled pauses, since each one occurs just before a new and important issue is raised. Their use here allows the speaker not only to keep the floor but also to signal an important upcoming piece of information. This is an effective telephone technique since, when they are used skilfully and systematically, filled pauses help recipients understand and remember what immediately follows their use.

2. There are fewer interruptions on the telephone and what is known as 'turn-taking' is smoother. In any interaction those involved have to negotiate who speaks when, and at what point one person stops and the other takes over. In face-to-face encounters this turn-taking process is signalled by the speaker dropping voice volume, ending the use of gestures, looking directly at the listener and pausing. However, there can be confusion in that these behaviours may occur when the speaker wishes to continue and is just checking for feedback that the listener is still interested. At such points both people will begin to speak. On the telephone, however, where the speaker wishes to continue, an 'ah' filler will tend to be used as a clear indicator of more to come, and so there is less likelihood of confusion. In this way, the absence of visual cues actually reduces the opportunity for interruptions.

3. What are known as 'guggles' are of great importance when using the telephone. Guggles refer to all those vocal indicators of listening such as 'Uh huh', 'Hmmm', 'Mm hm'. These are part of what is termed 'backchannel behaviour',[14] whereby the listener provides feedback to the speaker in an ongoing but unobtrusive manner. Backchannel behaviour includes guggles, as well as non-verbal cues (head nods, eye gaze, facial expressions). Since on the telephone there are no visual cues to indicate how the other person is receiving our message, we judge interest on the basis of vocal cues. If no such vocalizations are forthcoming there will be a query such as, 'Hello, are you still there?' The power of guggles also means that they can be used to 'shape' the behaviour of the other person. Since they are a form of reward, they can be used subtly to encourage the other person to talk

about certain topics but not about others. Giving more guggles and sounding more enthusiastic in the way they are used when the topic is of interest is a way of shaping behaviour. When done skilfully the other person will not be aware that this shaping process is happening.

4. Single utterances are on average longer when using the telephone, yet as a whole interactions are much briefer. In this sense, telephone conversations are more 'businesslike' and economical. For example in one study[15] of a total of 705 employees in 72 firms in central London, involving 1544 meetings and 5266 telephone calls, the results were as shown in Table 8.1. As can be seen, almost all of the telephone contacts lasted for less than ten minutes. This finding was confirmed by us in an audit which we carried out on managerial communications in the health service context.[16] Here, we found that the average length of all telephone contacts between managers was well under five minutes.

Table 8.1 Length of contact face to face and by telephone

Length of contact	Telephone (per cent)	Face to face (per cent)
2–10 minutes	87	19
10–30 minutes	12	29
30–60 minutes	1	19
1–2 hours	0	18
Over 2 hours	0	15

By contrast, when people meet they tend to ramble on. In Table 8.1 over 50 per cent of the face-to-face encounters lasted for more than half an hour and 15 per cent were longer than two hours. The message is clear. If time is limited and something needs to be decided quickly, use the telephone. This does not mean that all telephone calls are always brief, as readers with teenage children will testify! Thus, social usages of the telephone involve a longer period of contact, although again by comparison they will be shorter than comparable face-to-face meetings. One other finding is that length of utterances between people on the telephone is positively correlated. The duration of a telephone conversation can therefore be reduced by employing briefer utterances.

5. Another part of the business edge associated with telephone calls is that they involve less chit-chat, are more formal, more task-centred and less personal. There are fewer jokes and less humour in telephone interactions than face to face. In addition, more questions are asked during telephone interactions and, not surprisingly, a greater proportion of utterances are replies to questions. Many of these features make it more difficult to develop relationships. Therefore, when the relational dimension is important, managers should make deliberate efforts to use humour, engage in small talk and so on.

6. Some studies[7] have shown that attitudes change more readily as a result of telephone communications. It is argued that during such encounters we pay more attention to the actual *message* and are not distracted by the *person* delivering it. In face-to-face interaction we make judgements based not only on the content of what is said but also on the look and general non-verbal behaviour of the person delivering the message. If we do not like the cut of a person's jib then we are more likely to reject what they are saying.

7. It is easier to refuse a request over the telephone. For example, in surveys refusal rates to sensitive questions are higher on the telephone than in face-to-face interviews.[8] Indeed, studies show that for almost all interactions people express a preference for face-to-face contact *except* when they are required to be assertive (such as in refusing a request), when the telephone is preferred.

8. The incidence of aggression and rudeness is greater on the telephone. One review[17] of this area quotes a 9 per cent and 65 per cent chance of rudeness respectively for face-to-face and telephone communication. Part of the reason for this is distance and anonymity. It is easier to be aggressive with people we do not know and with whom we are interacting from a distance. In face-to-face situations, being rude or aggressive may lead to physical violence. However, on the telephone there is no such danger and so it is easier for either party to 'up the ante' without any imminent physical threat. Also in face-to-face communication, other cues (such as facial expression, physical attractiveness) may help to take some of the potential heat out of the encounter. Managers should be aware of the temptation to become aggressive on the telephone and consciously avoid so doing. There is truth in the old adage that if you lose your temper you lose the argument.

9. One study[18] found evidence that the telephone is used most often in lateral communication between those at the same level in an organization, rather than in upwards or downwards communication, where other media (face to face or written) are preferred. It was also found that managers rated the telephone as the most potent communication medium for influencing others.

10. A problem with telephone interaction is that it must be synchronized in that the other person must be there to answer the call. An analysis[19] of intracompany calls in the USA conducted in 1983 found that only one out of every four business calls was completed at the first attempt, resulting in what is known as 'telephone tag' where callers were chasing round trying to 'catch' the recipient. The cost of each call, including unsuccessful attempts, was calculated at $13. This is very wasteful. In fact, a US survey[20] of 200 corporate vice-presidents estimated that one month out of the executive's working year can be lost through unnecessary or unproductive telephone communications. Increasingly, people end up communicating with each other's voicemail.

While the lack of visual cues causes communication problems, information-giving and problem-solving are often as effective on the telephone. We can also accurately judge from vocal cues alone whether the other person is smiling, and we are able to make accurate estimates of their age, gender, emotional state and level of extraversion or introversion.[21, 22] There is also a device on the market which purports to measure whether the caller is telling the truth. This is based on voice stress analysis and uses sophisticated electronics to measure microtremors from the caller's vocal chords. However, there is continuing debate over the accuracy of such a system for measuring deceit.

As discussed in Chapter 5, explanations can be improved through the use of several well-established techniques. On the telephone the most relevant of these are to:

- State the most important points at the beginning and end.
- Emphasize the main points. This can be achieved through the use of changes in voice and by making good use of filled pauses.
- Use a logical structure.
- Present in a fluent style.
- Move at the other person's pace.
- Repeat main points and if necessary spell important words.
- Summarize what has been agreed.
- Check for understanding.

TELEPHONE HATES

A number of surveys have revealed what people dislike most when using the telephone. From these it is possible to compile the top ten most annoying telephone experiences (see Key point 8.1). These need to be addressed, since a survey by British Telecom in 1997 revealed that the reaction of nine out of ten customers who experienced unanswered or poorly dealt with calls was to simply stop dealing with that organization. They further estimated that some 4.6 million clients have been lost by firms in the UK as a result of negative telephone experiences. Conversely, and not surprisingly, if someone telephones a company with a problem which is then efficiently resolved, that person is much more likely to use the company's services in the future.

The top hate is a delay in the call being answered. In a survey conducted by the *Financial Mail* in 1997 the length of time taken by companies to answer a call ranged from one second at best to 7 minutes 30 seconds at worst, and more than 25 per cent of calls took longer than a minute to be answered. In the same year, a survey by British Telecom revealed that 31 per cent of calls to small businesses in the

---

Key point 8.1   The ten most annoying telephone experiences

1. A delay in your call being answered.
2. Being greeted by voicemail rather than being dealt with in person.
3. Being left 'hanging on' for a long time.
4. Being put through to the wrong person.
5. Being passed from pillar to post until being finally put through to the correct department.
6. People who interrupt the telephone conversation to talk to someone at their end.
7. People who deal with you in an offhand manner, and do not treat your call professionally.
8. Leaving a message on voicemail and no one returning your call.
9. The call being terminated without being told what the follow up will be.
10. Listening to 'muzak' when put on hold.

---

south of England went unanswered (the cut-off point in this survey was 15 rings). Many companies have recognized that this is unacceptable. For example, Citibank, also in 1997, discovered that over 500 calls a day to the bank's London office were not being answered within target times of between ten and 30 seconds. They then installed new equipment at a cost of £120 000 with the result that 95 per cent of the 5 000 daily calls to the bank were answered within ten seconds. The benefits of an effective telecommunications system have been well demonstrated by Direct Line, which launched its telephone insurance business in the UK in 1985. By 1997 it had become Britain's biggest insurer with 2.2 million customers, employing 4 000 staff at call centres in six cities. With automatic call distribution systems, 3 000 calls can be answered simultaneously within a second.

After delays in calls being answered, customers next dislike the call not being dealt with in person. Indeed in an NOP poll in 1997 of what most irritated members of the public the third most frequently cited irritation (mentioned by 33 per cent of the sample) was 'companies where the telephone is answered by recorded messages'. (As a matter of interest the top hate was 'junk mail' and the fourth was 'people who use mobile phones in public places'.) The most disliked system has been termed 'voicemail jail' which is the situation where the caller is told by a recorded voice: 'Press 1 for X, Press 2 for Y ...' Studies in the USA show that such electronic answering services have on average a 67 per cent 'slam down' rate.

A related hate is the use of muzak when put 'on hold'. One survey revealed that the most hated piece of 'muzak' was Vivaldi's 'Four Seasons'. However, David Marr of the telephone service company Information on Hold has estimated that it is difficult to win here since the muzak any company chooses is likely to drive at least 80 per cent of its callers 'absolutely barmy'! The problem, of course, is that callers simply do not like having to wait and the muzak becomes linked to the annoying delay, with the result that a conditioned negative association occurs.

The lesson for companies is clear – answer calls quickly and in person. Avoid voicemail where possible, and especially 'voicemail jail'. An awareness of this fact has resulted in many businesses employing specialist call handling centres to deal with their calls. British Telecom estimated that in 1997 the UK had 5 000 such centres employing some 250 000 staff. Large companies have their own centralized call centres. For example, computer giant IBM has located its European, Middle East and Africa help centre at Greenock, Scotland. Here, some 500 staff handle enquiries from business customers and users in 16 countries, using 11 different languages.

TELEPHONE COMMUNICATION PROBLEMS

The problems posed by telephone communication are all part of what has been termed 'the coffee and biscuits problem'.[7] In most business encounters when people meet there is an initial social stage at which time refreshments are usually provided, there is some small talk, and the participants begin to settle in to the encounter. During this period, each side sizes up the other and makes judgements about aspects such as the receptivity and warmth of the other person, the degree of formality likely to ensue and whether rapport can easily be established. This makes it easier when the conversation moves on to the business side of things. On the telephone, of course, there is no coffee and biscuits. Even on a video-conference link where both sides are simultaneously engaging in refreshments the social dimension is lost – socialization tends to occur with those face to face at each end of the link.

Three related theories have been put forward to explain the problems normally associated with mediated communication.[7] These have been termed 'cuelessness', 'social presence', and 'immediacy'.

1. *Cuelessness* refers to a reduction in social cues (visual contact, physical presence) which increases the psychological distance between the interactors. Thus, in face-to-face communication more cues are available (from non-verbal communication and the environment) than in telephone interactions. As cuelessness increases,

the content of any interaction becomes more depersonalized, the interaction is likely to be task-centred rather than social, and the interactive style becomes more formal and less spontaneous. In other words, it is argued that the lack of social cues makes communication more stilted and less free-flowing. Interestingly, in telephone counselling,[23] such cuelessness helps to increase the anonymity of the conversation (as compared with face-to-face contact), which facilitates 'psychological proximity'. Callers feel less embarrassed, since the counsellor cannot see who they are, and feel better able to discuss intimate problems. The discussion content can then more readily become personalized. This is an important advantage for helpline services such as the Samaritans.

2. *Social presence* refers to the degree of presence of the other person in the interaction – the extent to which the other person is 'there'. Communication media vary in the degree of presence which they afford. A descending scale of social presence occurs from face to face, to video, audio and, finally, written communication. On the telephone therefore the problem can be summarized as the absence of presence! Of course, one reason for this is the decrease in social cues along this scale, and so this theory has close links with the cuelessness perspective.

3. *Social immediacy* refers to the degree of psychological distance between sender and receiver. The more information a medium can transmit the greater the 'technological intimacy'. For example, someone two doors away in the organization may telephone rather than drop in. This decreases the social immediacy and will shorten the duration of the interaction. Increased cues and greater presence help to increase immediacy, and so these three theories are all closely interrelated. With the telephone, immediacy can be increased through the use of first name, references to family and friends, social chit-chat and gossip, non-task comments and the use of humour. An awareness of the importance of employing such immediacy-enhancing tactics on the telephone helps to compensate for the lack of coffee and biscuits.

MAKING AND ANSWERING CALLS

Studies of caller openings[24] have shown that we may use one or more of six main categories of behaviour at the beginning of a call:

1. A *greeting term* such as 'Hello' or 'Good morning'.
2. *Identification of the recipient* ('Who am I speaking to?' 'Is that James?').
3. A *reference to the recipient's 'state'* may be made ('Did I wake you?' 'Are you with someone?').
4. A *'switchboard' request* may be necessary ('Is Joan there?' 'Can I speak to the manager?').

5. *Self-identification* ('This is Mr Jones speaking' 'It's me').
6. A *joke introduction*, in the social rather than business sphere. For example, asking 'Is that the undertakers?' or using a funny voice or accent when phoning a friend.

There are five categories of recipient opening behaviour. As above, the first of these is a greeting ('Good morning'). Second is departmental identification ('Marketing Department'), or in social calls this may just be the person's telephone number (954765). This is followed by personal identification ('Mrs Fyfe speaking'). Fourth is an invitation ('How may I help you?'). As with caller openings, in social calls there can be the recipient joke introduction ('Joe's cafe').

Answering and making telephone calls are a necessary part of any business and so it is important that all staff have good telephone skills. The main areas to bear in mind in making and receiving telephone calls[25, 26] are summarized in Key point 8.2 (page 164) and Key point 8.3 (page 165).

SUMMARY

The telephone is now a ubiquitous piece of technology. In a relatively short space of time it has moved from being the preserve of the rich to being an integral part of everyday life. Advances in technology, a reduction in unit costs, and the user-friendly nature of the product have contributed to an exponential growth in usage of the telephone.[27] It is a communication device which has now been adopted and embraced by all levels of society and in all walks of business. Because we all use the telephone, however, it does not follow that we all use it wisely or well. The fact that most of us will have had personal experience of appalling telephone technique is testimony to this fact. In the business sphere the implications of such ineffective usage can be financially damaging. Staff members in any organization should make good use of the telephone both internally for the accurate transmission of messages between colleagues to ensure the smooth operation of the business, and externally with customers and others in the public arena.

In relation to the latter, a large part of the work of most businesses will be transacted by telephone. How these calls are handled will be important to the public perception of the company itself. A firm which answers calls promptly and pleasantly, connects callers quickly with the right department, listens to the caller's concerns and explains what action will be taken, by whom and when, will leave the impression of efficiency and competence. Return business is likely to ensue. By contrast a company where calls are not answered for long periods of time, where the caller is dealt with in an offhand manner, transferred all over the place and eventually receives little direct advice or satisfaction, will be perceived as slipshod and inefficient. Any return contact is likely to be in the form of complaints or notice of termination of business.

Key point 8.2   Answering the telephone

- Answer promptly – within three rings.
- Start the call by giving a greeting ('Good morning'), the Department ('Human Resources Department'), your name ('This is Mrs Jones') and position ('... Departmental Administration Officer'), and offer an invitation ('How may I help you?'). Also, smile as you answer (remember this can be accurately judged by the other person) and sound interested/motivated/enthusiastic.
- Establish the reason for the call.
- Ascertain and use the caller's name early in the conversation.
- If the call is inconvenient or you cannot deal with the enquiry, explain why, take the name and number of the caller, and arrange exactly what will happen next and if appropriate when you will call back.
- Most departments have a pro forma for logging calls – remember to use it. Do not hesitate to suggest alterations to it if it misses out important points.
- If taking a message for someone else, again there should be a 'messages' pro forma. Remember to log the name of the caller, time and date of call, summary of message or topic of enquiry, and when the caller will be available to take return calls. Indicate to the caller when the person is likely to be available to return the call. Be accurate – check with the caller the spelling of names and addresses, repeat numbers, facts and so on.
- Take notes during the call and read back main points so that the caller knows you are taking the call seriously. This also allows for an accuracy check.
- Show verbal and vocal signs of listening ('Uh huh' 'Hmmm' 'Yes' 'OK').
- Explain fully what you are doing if the caller is required to 'hang on'.
- If dealing with a complaint, do not interrupt. Allow the caller to ventilate. Treat the call as a problem to be dealt with, not as a personal attack (unless of course it is!).
- End the call by recapping on what exactly has been agreed and what each side will do next.
- Thank the caller and give 'action' reassurance that the call will be dealt with.
- Remember, callers like to close so try to structure the call to make it seem that *they* are closing.

Key point 8.3   Making telephone calls

- Make notes before you make the call. What are your goals? Exactly what information do you require? Have a checklist of points to be covered. In case you have to leave a message with someone else, have the main points distilled.
- Start the call by stating your name (first name is important for relationship establishment), your organization/department, your position and the main purpose of your call.
- Establish to whom you are speaking, and if not the right person ask to be put through to the latter.
- Use the person's name – and try to get on first name terms (though be sensitive to feedback here).
- Sound pleasant and motivated.
- Make your requests and have them answered or, if not, find out why they cannot be dealt with.
- End the call by summarizing what exactly has been agreed and what each side will do next.
- Remember the norms are that you made the call, therefore you will close the call.
- Use reinforcement if appropriate ('Nice talking to you', 'You have been most helpful').
- Anticipate having to leave a message with voicemail. If leaving a message on voicemail, itemize what your main points are, speak at a slower rate, repeat main details (for example your telephone number), emphasize the importance of a return call and give suitable times for this. If really important, try to connect with someone else (who may be able to contact the person) or telephone back to leave more than one message on the voicemail.

Exercise 8.1　Telephone technique

Think of the person you deal with who in your opinion has the *best* telephone technique you have encountered. How does this person:

- open calls (a) when phoning you, and (b) when answering your call?
- establish rapport and reduce social distance (through humour, use of first name, personal conversations about family, holidays)?
- conduct the business side of the call?
- terminate calls?

How many of these techniques do you currently use? Which of them should you incorporate into your telephone style?

Now think of the person you deal with who in your opinion has the *worst* telephone technique you have encountered and answer the above questions. How many of the mistakes that this person makes do you make?

Finally, think carefully about how, and in exactly which ways, you need to change you present telephone style to maximize your communicative potential. Identify three specific improvements you could make in (a) making calls, (b) receiving calls, and (c) terminating calls.

Analyse your telephone manner carefully over the next ten calls you make and receive, and produce a list of your strengths and weaknesses.

9 The word made permanent: putting it in writing

> If language is not correct, then what is said is not what is meant; if what is said is not what is meant, then what ought to be done remains undone.

Confucius

> Abraham Lincoln became America's greatest Precedent. Lincoln's mother died in infancy, and he was born in a log cabin which he built with his own hands. When Lincoln was President he wore only a tall silk hat. He said 'in onion there is strength'.

> Bach was the most famous composer in the world and so was Handel. Handel was half German, half Italian and half English. He was very large. Bach died from 1750 to the present.

> *Exam howlers produced by children in a London comprehensive school*

The ability to communicate in writing has been one of the earliest and most significant achievements of human civilization. Indeed, postal systems were first used by the Egyptians in 2000 BC. Since the invention of printing in the fifteenth century, written communication has enabled us to disseminate ideas and information widely, cheaply, clearly and (with the advent of e-mail) instantaneously. Increasingly, it is seen as a necessary means of attracting and retaining customers. In consequence, it has become all pervasive, and so absorbs a great deal of any manager's time. One study of 60 front-line supervisors at a Midwest US steel manufacturing plant[1] found that 70 per cent of them spent between eight and 14 hours per week in writing-related activities. These involved producing disciplinary action reports, clarifying job procedures, dealing with formal grievances, writing memos, producing instructional documents to subordinates, drafting incident reports and writing external letters or reports to customers. Managers also spend a significant amount of time responding to the written communications of others.

Written communication causes many people a great deal of stress. The survey discussed above disclosed a number of stress factors in managerial writing (Table 9.1).

Table 9.1 Stress factors in management communication

Major problems in the writing of documents	% of managers identifying difficulty
Meeting deadlines	76
Identifying appropriate information for document	68
Organizing information in document	65
Writing instructions that workers understand	58
Summarizing information from other sources	46
Understanding grammatical and stylistic conventions	33
Creating effective tables, graphs and charts	18

It is, therefore, imperative that managers reduce such stress factors, while monitoring and improving the written communications in which they engage. This chapter seeks to facilitate this process by examining the strategic role which written communication plays in dealing with a business's internal and external customers. In particular, we look at how written communication should be evaluated, to ascertain whether it is doing its main job – enabling a receiver to understand, internalize and act on the sender's message. We then discuss steps which managers can take to improve their written communication – producing reports, memos, letters and dealing with complaints. We also increasingly live in an era of e-mail communication. Therefore, a special section of this chapter is devoted to the main trends in e-mail use, and how it can support rather than undermine business goals.

THE STRATEGIC ROLE OF WRITTEN COMMUNICATION

Written communication activates customer recognition, purchases and loyalty. The reasons for this are clear. In one study, 70 per cent of businesses claimed to look forward to receiving their post.[2] Clearly, there is a pleasure factor in anticipating the plop of a letter hitting the mat. Most people rush to receive their mail in the morning. This reflects our profound sense of curiosity about the unknown, to the extent that we are generally curious about the contents of mail intended for others. Two thousand people were surveyed on this point by the Royal Mail in the UK. One-third admitted to reading mail addressed to their partner, relatives or other people, while one in six even claimed to steam such letters open.[3]

This sense of curiosity can be used to attract and retain customers. The Henley Centre for Forecasting found that 68 per cent of customers actively wanted information from the companies they dealt with and 60 per cent were more likely to buy from suppliers who kept in touch.[4] This may be an illustration of what has been dubbed 'the availability factor':[5] information about something which is readily known to us is more likely to inspire action than information which requires considerable effort to access. Maintaining contact ensures that knowledge about products and services is more available to customers than what is on offer from competitors. Thus, sending newsletters, cards, calendars, circular letters and directly addressed letters activates the availability factor, cements customer loyalty and improves profits.

This effect is also achieved since written communication can engage what has been termed the norm of reciprocity (see Chapter 2). Once we feel that a positive attitude has been displayed towards us we are motivated to respond by expressing similar feelings to the other person. We might, for example, feel obliged to return a favour, even to a much greater extent than the one we originally received. Ninety-four per cent of respondents in one survey agreed that when they received a letter from someone they felt that the sender had put time and thought into its contents.[4] Clearly, this predisposed them to feel favourably towards the sender, and respond in like fashion to what was perceived as a positive act. Thus, simply staying in touch influences people – and attracts their business. The one exception is what is perceived to be junk mail. This is detested by many recipients precisely because its impersonal character conveys the impression that the receiver's individual needs were not considered when it was produced.

Retaining customer loyalty by writing to them is cost efficient. The Office of Consumer Affairs has calculated that it costs six times more to win a new customer than to keep an existing one.[5] Such findings put the costs of sustained communication in a proper perspective. It has also been found that small changes in presentation enable your written communications to stand out from the crowd. For example, the Henley Centre estimates that 80 per cent of people are more likely to open a personally addressed white envelope than a manila one.[5] As an illustration, the owner of a small family company which won an export award, Tanice Slater, reported that when she uses direct mail the envelope is handwritten to give it a personal touch. Regular customers receive a birthday card.[3]

Such findings suggest that the impact of direct marketing mail can be intensified if you:

- handwrite the envelope
- use a white envelope rather than a manila one
- use the receiver's name in your opening line
- include as many personal details about the recipient as possible.

Written communication is also a powerful means of rewarding people, publicly disseminating praise and encouraging an atmosphere of celebration inside an organization's own ranks. Tom Peters[6] gives an example of a manager at Marriott's in New Mexico, who made a firm policy of sending out 100 'thank you' notes a month to members of his staff for jobs well done. But such notes, or other efforts at promoting written communication, do not in themselves yield results. Personal competence matters, and will be covered later in this chapter. However, a systematic approach to evaluation matters more, and should form an integral part of a planned and systematic approach to written communications.

EVALUATING WRITTEN COMMUNICATION

What is effective communication? It is useful to explore some of the most pertinent myths we have about written communication, and which prevent us from accurately estimating its impact.

MORE COMMUNICATION IS BETTER COMMUNICATION

This assumption often leads to the circulation of multiple photocopies or indiscriminately circulated memos and e-mails, about everything. In reality, these are usually produced to protect the sender rather than inform the receiver. There is some evidence that communication between senior managers may be particularly prone to this fault.[7] In organizations where the dominant urge is to 'cover your back', paper is used to camouflage the lack of real communication. People drown in ink while gasping for facts. The result is information anxiety. One respondent in a communication audit conducted by us, a senior manager, complained bitterly of 'death by memo'. Typically, those working in such organizations are uncertain about what messages to attend to, and deal with this uncertainty by filtering out most communication emanating from senior managers. A blizzard of paper causes snow blindness, ensuring that the business's main aims and objectives continually drift in and out of focus. The result is inertia, internal feuding and missed business opportunities.

WRITTEN COMMUNICATION EQUALS A FULFILLED OBLIGATION

The assumption is that if a message is received, it is read, understood and acted on. The sender can then always claim: 'But I told you about this, in paragraph 23 of my 14-page memo of last January!' In reality, *repetition* of key points (albeit in as *concise* a manner as possible) is as important as their initial transmission in determining impact.

INFORMING SOMEONE IS THE SAME THING AS PERSUADING THEM

Most of us assume that more people agree with us than actually do, and that our opinions are more correct than is really the case.[6] We also assume that our arguments are more attractive to other people and hence more persuasive than they actually are. An additional difficulty is that people often view the needs of the reader as less important than their own credibility, possible financial rewards and scope for promotion.[8] In short, the writer's own agenda and ego needs override the requirements of the audience. A golden rule is that the information needs of the receiver should be clearly established before messages are transmitted.

In one study, investigators[9] found that roughly half of keyboard and secretarial staff who regularly used erasing fluid did not know the content of the warning label on the bottle. Thus, even if information is presented it is not necessarily attended to, understood, retained or acted on. Real communication involves mutual feedback. It is vital to build opportunities for this into our written communications.

USING ONE CHANNEL OF COMMUNICATION IS EFFICIENT – IT SAVES MONEY

The consequence here is that important issues are often only mentioned once, perhaps in a company brochure, newsletter or an internal memorandum. In reality, good communication requires us to:

- employ multiple channels for important information
- use written channels several times
- engage in the systematic, planned repetition of main themes and messages.

In one survey,[10] a selection of women undergoing a hysterectomy and who received a booklet providing information about how to cope with anxiety and what to expect in hospital, experienced less postoperative pain and stress than those who did not. They also left hospital more quickly. In short, people can obtain added benefit when they receive written communication, even if the information it offers has already been made available to them by other channels.

CHANNEL PROLIFERATION EQUALS INCREASED INFORMATIVENESS

This is the opposite but equally destructive mistake to that identified above. Particularly with e-mail technology, an abundance of communication creates the illusion that real information exchange has occurred and that messages have been understood, agreed with and acted on.

Many surveys have shown that employees have a strong preference for face-to-face communication, above all else. The more vital the issue at stake, the more important face-to-face communication from immediate and senior managers becomes.[11] Written communication should reinforce contact between people, rather than paper over its absence.

Key point 9.1 contains a number of evaluation criteria, which you are encouraged to apply to the written communications in which you engage.

Key point 9.1 Evaluating channels of communication

1. Feedback potential: How quickly can the receiver respond to the message?
2. Complexity capacity: Can this channel effectively process complex messages?
3. Breadth potential: How many different messages can be disseminated through this channel?
4. Confidentiality: Can the communicators be reasonably sure their messages are received only by those intended?
5. Encoding ease: Can the sender easily and quickly use this channel?
6. Decoding ease: Can the receiver easily and quickly decode messages in this channel?
7. Time-space constraint: Do senders and receivers need to occupy the same time space?
8. Cost: How much does it cost to use this channel?
9. Interpersonal warmth: Does the channel have the potential to communicate interpersonal warmth?
10. Formality: Does the channel imbue a sense of formality?
11. 'Scanability': Does the channel permit the message(s) to be easily browsed or scanned to find relevant passages?
12. Time of consumption: Does the sender or receiver exercise the most control over when the message is consumed?

Source: Clampitt, P. (1991) *Communicating for Managerial Effectiveness*, Sage, p. 135. Reprinted with permission.

THE RULES OF HIGH IMPACT WRITING

Effective writing does three main things:[12]

1. *It attracts the recipient's attention.* Ignored messages fail to persuade. Worse, messages submerged in the small print lose any sense of urgency, purpose or conviction.
2. *The arguments in the message must be understood.* This means that arguments should be simple, repeated, short and to the point. Waffle muffles your voice in cotton wool, and sends your audience into a trance.

3. *The recipient must learn the arguments contained in the message and come to accept them as true.* This means that the argument should promise the reader a benefit. We scan written messages with one question foremost in our minds – what is in this for me? Thus, the sender should keep the needs of the reader clearly in view, answer this cardinal question at once and repeat this answer several times.

In general, a 'high impact' style includes stating your main objective in an opening paragraph, using bold type headings and constructing simple but dynamic sentences. A more traditional bureaucratic style is characterized by abstract language, no personal pronouns and the general lack of an explicit purpose.[13]

In the quest to develop a high-impact style there is no substitute for quality writing and vivid presentation. The following steps will enhance this effort:

- Five times as many people read headlines in advertisements as read the body copy. Headlines in quotes increase recall by around 28 per cent.[14] Headlines on memos, notices, e-mails or most other forms of written communication grab attention, without which no real information exchange occurs. As Sam Goldwyn reputedly once remarked: 'A good movie should start with an earthquake, and then work up to a climax.' Get the promise, claim you are making or the main point of the issue into your headline, reaffirm it in the opening paragraph and repeat it at intervals throughout.
- If you start your text with a large initial letter readership is increased by 13 per cent. Large initial letters attract the eye, symbolize the importance of your case and Announce to an audience that your argument is worth hearing.[15]
- Insert frequent cross-headings – that is, short headings to break up your text – and summarize the main issue of the next section. An army engaged in a long march needs regular stops for rest and refreshment. Cross-headings create curiosity, but should also convey the gist of what is to follow in order to prepare the reader for the message to come. They improve both comprehension and recall.[15]
- Insert illustrations. Pictures and cartoons convey a human dimension to your message and attract attention. People love stories, however brief, about other people.[16] As discussed in Chapter 2, case studies are more effective than statistics in persuading an audience of your case.
- Use bullets, asterisks and marginal marks.[17] This is particularly important when you are listing a number of disparate points on a range of issues, as we are doing here.
- Use concrete words rather than abstract words and sentences.[17] Do not say 'collateral damage was inflicted on his upper personage by an object'. Do say 'a brick hit him on the head'.
- Indenting the first line of a paragraph increases speed of reading.[15]
- Type should be at least 10 point in size – this type is 14 point, while this is much smaller at 9 point, this is in 10 point, and 12 point immediately looks much better.[15]

- *Printing in italic reduces the speed of comprehension, although it is effective for short passages of emphasis.* [17]
- State presuppositions explicitly rather than refer to them implicitly. For the most part, people can only understand evidence when they know what it is aiming to prove. Thus, lawyers tend to begin summing up by saying what they intend their evidence to mean ('My client is innocent'). Open with your big sell, and then reiterate and refine it throughout. [17]
- New information is more easily understood if it is related to what people already know. Thus, put new information at the end of a sentence and old information at the beginning. [17]
- NEVER WRITE AT LENGTH IN CAPITAL LETTERS, *or prolong your use of italics, PARTICULARLY IN CAPITALS* – IT IS MUCH HARDER TO READ, ESPECIALLY IN A LONG MESSAGE. THAT IS WHY NEWSPAPERS ARE NEVER PRODUCED IN THIS STYLE! [16]
- Make your writing vigorous, direct and personal.
- Never use a metaphor or other figure of speech which you are used to seeing written down or spoken aloud. [18] Metaphors should create a visual image for the reader, and so assist them to sharpen their thinking on the topic at hand. Clichés begin as an arresting image ('We need a level playing field'), but lose all colour, subtlety and shade through overuse. Why arrive at a dinner party in someone else's cast-offs, when you can wear a designer outfit of your own? Dress to impress.
- Avoid vague modifiers. [16] These are imprecise expressions which leave an audience puzzled about what you expect them to do. Never use a long word or sentence where a short one will do. [18] Padding illuminates an argument in the same way that a burnt out candle illuminates a darkened room. Instead, use specific, concrete language. For example, 'interface' means *meet*. Key point 9.2 contains two examples of writing which contain many vague modifiers, and then how they might appear if translated into a more vigorous style. Be ruthless while pruning your prose, and clear messages will bloom in the imagination of your readers.
- Avoid errors in typing, spellings, in numbers and dates, and misplaced apostrophes. [19] Presentational blunders suggest the presence of a sloppy thinker. Readers will reason that your careless attitude towards small issues betokens a careless attitude towards bigger issues: you are frequently judged by the clothes you wear.
- Use the active rather than the passive style of writing. [18] The active is more direct, more forceful, tends to use fewer words and is more likely to conjure up a clear picture of what you are talking about. Consider the following sentence: *The building was destroyed by the storm*. The subject in the sentence (building) receives the action, and is hence described as passive. However, this could be amended to read: *The storm destroyed the building*. In this case, the subject

---

Key point 9.2   The poor impact of vague modifiers

Sample 1

Although an appropriate budget had originally been established, a slight financial overrun has been caused in the short to medium term, due to the consequences of unanticipated industrial action in our main supplier industry.

Total words: 34

Translation:

The project is now overspent. This is because of strikes in the machine tool industry.

Total words: 15

Sample 2

He has a talent for self-aggrandizement, obfuscation and indolence, leavened only by the transparent nature of his intentions which renders it distinctly questionable whether his obvious ambitions will be realized.

Total words: 30

Translation:

He tells lies and is lazy. His main aim is self-advancement, but since everyone knows this he will never be promoted.

Total words: 21

(storm) does the destroying, and is therefore described as active. The overall impact is more vigorous, and the reader will be more likely to assume that such energy is a normal characteristic of the writer.

- Consider at all times the importance of accuracy, brevity and clarity.[20]

A significant contribution to the campaign for clear writing has been made by the Plain English Campaign. This has identified many examples of bureaucratic or otherwise mystifying jargon in company and government documents, and urged the use of plainer English as a means of more clearly communicating meaning. In addition to many of the points listed above, the Campaign urges the following in written English:

- an average sentence length of about 15–20 words
- everyday English (e.g. words such as 'we' and 'you' rather than 'the insured', 'the applicant')
- conciseness
- an average line length of between seven and 23 words
- plenty of answer space and a logical flow (on forms).

In 1990 the Campaign introduced its seal of approval – the Crystal Mark. This is now a much sought after symbol among organizations who wish to use it on their documents. An excellent book-length discussion of how to write in plain English is available, and readers interested in exploring this issue in more depth are encouraged to read it.[21]

LETTERS AND MEMOS

Written memos and letters should follow the guidelines listed above. They have a definite purpose, a specific target audience and convey clear information in as succinct a fashion as possible. When they are required to do more than simply impart information, they should use an appropriate blend of the levers of persuasion discussed in Chapter 2 to argue a case. One of their most important characteristics is length. The arteries of even the healthiest organization tend to become clogged with paper. Readers therefore respond with gratitude towards short communications in which the primary point is nevertheless made absolutely clear. Elegant formula and captivating excursions have their place, but their primary role is to make the ultimate sacrifice in the interests of brevity. A partial exception arises with paragraphs. There is some evidence to suggest that one-sentence paragraphs are much harder to read, and should therefore be avoided.[22] Exercise 9.1 is designed to help you put these principles into practise, and so produce urgent, informative and persuasive memos.

Exercise 9.1 Dynamic writing

Read the following memo carefully. Then rewrite it, adhering to the guidelines for dynamic writing outlined previously. An alternative is contained at the end of this chapter, but you should first draft your own before reading it. Cheating is not allowed!

To: All employees of Rite Manufacturing Corporation

From: Managing Director

Date: 28th June, year

I am happy to advise you that representatives of the Board will be available next Friday 5th July to acquaint you with information about additional voluntary contributions to our existing occupational pension scheme. This will help all of you to plan for a comfortable retirement, and should take no more than a few minutes of your time. Feel free to contact my office for further details. The meeting with the Board representatives will be at 11.30 a.m. in the Boardroom. In addition, experts from our finance department will be on hand to deal with any detailed queries you may have on this issue. I hope to see you there.

Total words: 123

WRITING REPORTS

Most managers are called on to produce reports during their careers. The ability to do so frequently determines whether your career progresses upward, or whether it stalls on the launch pad. Reports have been defined as 'an organized presentation of information to a specific audience for the purpose of helping an organization achieve an objective'.[23]

In general, reports should be:

- *Timely.* This refers to both the production of the report, and its contents. Ideally, it should arrive before it is due (but certainly no later), and contain the most up-to-date information available on the problem at hand.
- *Well written.* The report should be clear, concise and interesting; it should capture the reader's attention and hold it throughout; it should avoid errors in grammar, spelling, punctuation and its factual content. One factual error damages the

credibility of your whole case, much as a single episode of adultery shatters a reputation for fidelity. Above all, it should be driven by a bias towards action, which solves a problem, identifies the next steps your audience can and must take, and relates to the underlying business objectives of the organization.

- *Well organized.* A good report is designed to be read selectively, so that the reader can pay attention only to its most necessary parts. Most reports have multiple audiences, and will have few readers interested in its entire content. For this reason, with long reports, an executive summary is obligatory.
- *Attractive.* It should be clearly labelled, arrive in good condition, and be presented with an attractive typeface and layout. First impressions count. They shape expectations about the overall impact and import of the report. Thus, many of the issues concerning the power of attractiveness in communication between people which we discussed in Chapter 2 also apply here. A well-presented report projects a favourable impression of you, and creates an aura of attractiveness around your propositions.
- *Cost-effective.* The report's recommendations should be designed to solve real problems facing its readership, and should be clearly explained, possible to implement, and cost-effective. Although there are no guidelines on the maximum number of recommendations it should contain, it is important to remember that an organization with 40 priorities in reality has none. On the other hand, a small number of proposals is known as an action plan.
- *A report begins before the beginning*, with the terms of reference set for its production. These identify the problem(s) it will be expected to solve, set explicit limits on the range of issues to be addressed, and identify specific outcomes towards which the report should aspire. Key point 9.3 provides examples of terms of reference which aim to produce reports and recommendations which achieve these aims.

You are also asked to consider the terms of reference outlined in Exercise 9:2, and contrast them with the examples offered in Key point 9.3.

Standard formats exist for the structure of a report, which will normally contain the following:[23, 24]

1. Title-page.
2. Contents.
3. Acknowledgements.
4. Executive summary.
5. Introduction.
6. Methodology.
7. Findings/conclusions.
8. Recommendations.
9. Appendices.
10. References.

Exercise 9.2   Writing for objectives

Study carefully the terms of reference shown here, and then answer the questions listed below:

To produce ideas which will enable the Board to refine a strategy for innovation in certain key resource areas, thereby increasing market penetration in our most important markets, enhancing quality, improving the efficient use of resources and increasing profits in the next financial year.

Issues for consideration:

- List as many of the objectives contained in the above terms of reference as you can.
- Consider whether the objectives identified are compatible or in conflict with each other.
- Pick what you think are the top two objectives. Consider the criteria which influenced your decision. Would other people in your organization employ other criteria, and reach different conclusions?
- Translate your main two objectives into terms of reference which match the style and specificity of those on offer in Key point 9.3.

Key point 9.3   Examples of terms of reference

1. Complaints from customers. To investigate why the rate of complaints from customers about the new payment system has increased by 20 per cent in the last three months and to recommend changes in procedure which will solve this problem.
2. The current computerized personnel management information system (PIMS). To explore alternative systems currently available, conduct a cost benefit analysis of the various options, and recommend whether to upgrade the present system or to keep it for a specified period.
3. Absenteeism. To establish our current level of absenteeism, compare it to industry-wide norms, investigate its causes and recommend measures which will significantly reduce it.

- The *Acknowledgements* are an opportunity to identify important change agents within the organization who have helped you with the most important aspects of the report's production. By sharing the credit you gain a valuable reputation as a team player. You also spread the responsibility for awkward issues raised and difficult decisions proposed: it is harder for people to reject your conclusions outright, if you can identify the Chief Executive as a key figure in drawing up your terms of reference and gathering your data. But avoid 'Oscar night syndrome': the urge to thank everyone, down to your remotest ancestors, who has made the tiniest contribution to your moment of glittering triumph. This tempts readers to reach for the off-switch before your performance reaches its climax.

- The *Summary* should outline the main findings and recommendations. Busy senior staff will read only this section. However, the rest of the report lends authority to the summary. Readers who query a particular finding or recommendation can delve into the appropriate section in more depth, to reassure themselves that you have done your homework, and that your conclusions rest on solid evidence rather than an unstable mixture of hope and hype. Such supporting testimony is excised from the summary, which needs to combine brevity with a comprehensive account of the most salient issues.

- The *Introduction* should explain who commissioned the report, who was responsible for the project or issue it is discussing, the purpose of the report, the method of inquiry which has been adopted and the terms of reference which have been set. It should also explain how the data have been assembled and arranged, how the report is structured and whatever general background factors you consider to be most important. In general, this means identifying the importance of the issue to the organization at this stage. The temptation here is to assume that, since the issue is by now over-familiar to you, it will be equally familiar to everyone else.

- The *Methodology* sets out in detail the steps which you took to assemble your data – for example, who you interviewed, what questionnaires you used (and why), what other reports you relied on, what tests you carried out and what other organizations you studied. Each measure taken should be explicitly related to your starting terms of reference. This helps you to build a convincing series of steps towards your grand design – the recommendations which you want the organization to implement. They should appear logical, rest on irrefutable facts and be supported by a wealth of impressive detail. Would you buy a house if the builder had used only wood-shavings in its foundations?

- The *Findings/Conclusions* section details precisely what you have discovered. It should also present your analysis of their significance. If 70 per cent of your customers express a hostile attitude towards your new product, and a favourable attitude towards that of your main competitor, what precisely does this mean for your marketing strategy? Add interpretation to the facts. Draw clear conclusions.

- The *Recommendations* are the heart of any report, and should emerge clearly from the findings, rather than appear unintroduced in the middle of your conclusions. Your principal finding (judged by its importance to your organization, and as identified in your terms of reference) should attract the most emphasis in the recommendations. Remember also that too many recommendations produce paralysis rather than action. Anything which irritates your readers or does not support your case distracts from it. Thus, you should resist the urge to drag your own hobby-horses centre stage: other people never find your children as fascinating as you do. Above all, answer this cardinal question: what can the organization do differently to what it already does, and how will this make a difference to the main problem which it currently faces?
- The *Appendices* should contain supporting material which is important to your case, but which does not belong logically in the main body of the report. These include examples of data collection instruments (e.g. questionnaires), tables which are of interest to some readers but are marginal to the main issues being explored, or more lengthy extracts from interviews with people who have been surveyed.
- The *References* is a list of main sources cited in your text – books, reports, newspaper articles, journal articles or official statements. This reassures readers that your methods, findings and recommendations rest on a solid body of research and experience. It also enables anyone who wishes to explore in more detail a particular issue you have raised to do so by following up some of the sources you have cited. If they do, this is also likely to reinforce their interest and hence commitment to the issues raised in your report.

E-MAIL, SNAIL MAIL, MORE MAIL

The Internet has transformed business communication. At one point during the 1990s, there were 20 million US e-mail addresses, and more than half of these had gone on line during one calendar year: a phenomenal rate of expansion.[25] Worldwide on-line sales were calculated to rise over 20 times in one four-year period, bringing the number of people connected to the Web to 550 million.[26] This has speeded up the flow of information, but also increased its volume. When the e-mail communications of one *Fortune 500* company were investigated it was discovered that 60 per cent of the messages they received by this means would not have been received via other channels.[27] Thus, people increasingly regard it as a necessary link in the information chain, and as a measure of the importance which managers attach to communication, both internally and externally. One respondent in a communication audit conducted by us, in an organization where e-mail had not yet been introduced, commented: 'We need e-mail around here. Without it I feel like the Flintstones.'

There is some evidence that staff view superiors as less intimidating in e-mail settings (possibly, again, because many of the non-verbal signals that we normally rely on to decode status are absent). Hence, some surveys have found that detailed and frank discussions are more likely to take place using e-mail than with more conventional forms of communication.[27]

But all opportunities also bring dangers. More than half of the 1 000 users who responded to one survey had received abusive e-mails (so-called 'flame mails'), which irreparably damaged working relationships.[28] Fifty-four per cent of antisocial e-mails were from managers to their staff and one in six of all respondents reported being officially disciplined via e-mail. Interestingly, flame mails were five times more likely to be written by men than by women. Forty-six per cent of respondents also said that e-mail had reduced face-to-face communication in their workplace, and that this had led to less co-operation, greater internal conflict among colleagues, bullying and a more unpleasant working atmosphere. In short, e-mail lacks the non-verbal and tonal cues of face-to-face communication, on which we rely to interpret meaning. The rapid nature of e-mail also means that it provides for instant communication, at a time when tempers are running high and both parties require a cooling-off period.

It has been suggested[28, 29] that these problems can be reduced if we follow the simple guidelines contained in Key point 9.4. Additional guidelines are also included, to improve general e-mail usage.

A clear danger with e-mail is the assumption that more communication is better communication. This can transform computer screens into slag heaps of discarded information, through which people forage in a futile quest to find something useful. The outcome is more likely to be isolation and despondency, rather than cohesion and enlightenment.

Quirke[30] reported precisely such a difficulty with Apple Computers, which developed a culture of people having a computer on their desks. Everyone loved the technology and came to rely on it so much that face-to-face communication was neglected. Apple's response was to hold a series of conferences for different levels of management, specifically to promote face-to-face communication. This led to systems for face-to-face briefings, the development of national publications and the convening of cross-functional communication meetings. The lesson is that the role and impact of e-mail should be carefully monitored, to ensure that it supplements rather than supplants the old 'technology' of people talking to people.

Key point 9.4 Composing e-mails

1. Resist the temptation to respond to the e-mail of another person when you are still angry.
2. Wait until you calm down before replying.
3. Consider whether you would say what you want to say to someone's face.
4. Do not use abusive language: a message cannot be rescinded once it has been transmitted, and the more discourteous your tone the more likely it is that this will become the issue, rather than whatever it is you should really be discussing with the other person.
5. Temper your enthusiasm for e-mail with an awareness of its defects and hazards.
6. Consider whether a face-to-face meeting might be more appropriate, or at least a useful follow up to your e-mail message.
7. Invest the same care in composing your message that you would do in writing a formal letter or memorandum.
8. Set the e-mail aside for an hour and then review it, before finally sending it.

DEALING WITH COMPLAINTS

An area where written communication is particularly pertinent is in dealing with complaints. A study by the Henley Centre for Forecasting[4] found that 95 per cent of complaining customers preferred their grievances to be dealt with in writing. Evidently, this reassures them that the issue is being treated seriously and in most cases, has the effect of discouraging further action, including litigation. Guidelines have been suggested by various writers[4, 31] on this question, and these are summarized in Key point 9.5. In general, complaints are viewed as a litmus test of an organization's commitment to genuine customer care. This holds true for 'internal' customers, as well as those outside its own ranks. Adherence to these guidelines is a means of nurturing those relationships most necessary to success.

Key point 9.5 Dealing with complaints

1. Don't delay – reply today. It is human nature to postpone tasks we find unpleasant; it is equally human nature to seek a fast response when we feel aggrieved. Rapid action short circuits customer disillusionment.

2. Remember that it is easier to fire missiles in missives than it is face to face. Resist the temptation to declare war on the enemy.

3. Personalize your reply. Use the complainant's name. Otherwise, they are liable to feel they have received a standard form letter and that their complaint is not being taken seriously.

4. Thank the person for bringing the problem to your attention, however annoyed you feel by the complaint or however irrational you assume it is. This might calm troubled waters: you must also reckon with the possibility that whatever you write will be read by many people other than the addressee. If people see you in full Desertstorm mode they will assume that this is your natural state, and take their business elsewhere.

5. Inform the complainant that you understand his or her point of view. Do this even if you think they are wrong – you can then explain the other point of view. However, most people want to be treated seriously and feel that they are understood. Acknowledging that you hear their grievance deflates aggression.

6. If an apology is on order, then express it wholeheartedly. Communicate your genuine desire to make amends.

7. Ensure that the letter is signed by the most senior person possible.

8. Resist the temptation to be curt. If a detailed reply is necessary to deal adequately with the issue – write it.

9. If the problem lies with some other department in your company avoid catching the virus of 'blameititis'. Customers detest organizations which treat complaints like an unexploded bomb, to be lobbed from department to department.

10. Err on the side of accepting responsibility, offering restitution and making placatory noises.

SUMMARY

Communication must add value to information, rather than simply distribute it. Written communication, as this chapter has shown, has the potential to accomplish this in multiple ways. It can become a permanent form of recognition, and thus has high reward potential for staff. E-mail binds an organization tighter together, speeds up the flow of information, increases its quantity and facilitates more rapid contact between an organization and its customers. Well-crafted reports create a bias towards action, and help promote their authors' careers.

Meanwhile, the ability to write cogent, clear and persuasive letters and memoranda remain vital ingredients of career and business success. As an Australian solicitor, Christopher Balmford, has said: 'Lawyers who use plain language know it doesn't just make good sense, it makes good cents.' Most of us can improve our written communication with practice, and attention to the guidelines outlined throughout this chapter. Remember – *writing matters*. Defective written communication leads to congestion on the information superhighway, causing traffic jams, multiple pile-ups and outbursts of road rage. Effective written communication keeps the traffic flowing freely, nurtures relationships and ensures a smoother journey towards business success. Used wisely, it will serve you and your organization well.

Answer to Exercise 9.1

To: All employees of Rite Manufacturing Corporation

From: Managing Director

Date: 28th June, year

Come and find out how you can plan for a more comfortable retirement by taking out additional voluntary contributions to our existing pension scheme.

Date: Friday 5th July

Place: Boardroom

Time of meeting: 11.30 a.m.

Total words: 49

---

10 It's your right: communicating assertively

> ... to be 'umble to this person, and 'umble to that; and to pull our caps off here, and to make bows there; and always to know our place, and abase ourselves before our betters.
>
> Uriah Heep in Charles Dickens, *David Copperfield*

> When people won't let you alone, it's because you haven't learned to make them do it.
>
> David Seabury, *The Art of Selfishness*

We tend to react in predictable ways when confronted by situations that we find threatening: we are inclined to either go on the offensive with all guns blazing or withdraw from the battlefield without firing a shot, to seek the sanctuary of a safe bunker – what is called the 'fight or flight response'. Down through the aeons of evolutionary time, this physiological and behavioural predisposition has been passed from generation to generation. When confronted with a woolly mammoth or sabre-toothed tiger, there was obvious survival value for our ancestors in being well prepared for intense physical activity.

In the twentieth-century world of business, commerce and public service, the threats to which managers are exposed are of an altogether different kind. Their jungle is the boardroom, the shopfloor and the boss's office. What is at stake is not life but monetary success, personal advancement, reputation and respect. In place of predatory animals are myopic directors, ambitious colleagues, wayward staff and unfaithful customers. Injury is sustained through rejected visions, sabotaged projects, unfulfilled commitments and broken promises. Still, when managers' antennae begin vibrating to danger signals in workplace dealings with others, the likely and natural reaction is the time-honoured fight or flight response, though it is now acted out in a form different from its origins. Violent physical attack (although it still does happen) has been reshaped into an aggressive verbal mauling: running away by withdrawal into a sullen quiescence.

Despite the fact that these two options of fight or flight are, in a sense, the reflexive way to react when confronted with conflict situations at work, both are often strikingly ineffective. Verbal attack often triggers reciprocation or the victim makes an escape. Either way, the precipitating problem is left unresolved. Likewise, metaphorically fleeing from the situation, while bringing a temporary respite and sense of relief, does not help to achieve a workable solution. But these two are, thankfully, not the only options. We are not *compelled*, in such instances, to fall victim to our evolutionary heritage. We are not helpless prisoners of earlier generations. In the place of aggression and submission, assertion is an alternative way of dealing with people problems that is likely to lead to more successful outcomes all round and a more committed and productive workforce.

Assertion is a way of expressing one's needs, feelings and opinions honestly, openly, directly but respectfully, without being racked by negative emotions such as anxiety or guilt.[1] This chapter is about assertion and how it can advance more effectively communication in management. Assertiveness will be set against the contrasting styles of relating commonly found in work settings – aggressiveness and submissiveness. Causes and consequences of each will be explored. Verbal and nonverbal features of assertive behaviour will be outlined in some detail. The importance of knowing your rights in situations and moulding appropriate belief about yourself, others and what counts as acceptable conduct, will also be discussed. For the present, however, we will continue with some initial thoughts about assertiveness and why it is often the best way of dealing with people problems in management.

ASSERTIVENESS AND MANAGEMENT

Let us be clear at the outset what assertiveness is *not*. It is not about always getting your way through bullying and intimidation. Admittedly this is how the term has come to be commonly used. Describing a boss as being very assertive typically conjures up an image of a person who is loud, brash, arrogant, and thoroughly unpleasant.

It must be stressed, this is *not* how assertiveness is being thought of here. Indeed the above description sketches one of the contrasting styles of communicating that we will look at, that of aggressiveness. If aggressiveness is at one end of a continuum with submissiveness and passivity at the other, then assertiveness falls somewhere in the middle.[1]

So what is assertiveness? One of the earliest definitions, by Lazarus,[2] pointed to four key attributes. It is being able to:

- refuse requests
- ask for favours and make requests
- express positive and negative feelings
- initiate, continue and terminate general conversations.

Personal rights are also involved; the rights not only of the individual being assertive, but also of the other party. Lange and Jakubowski[3] stated that 'assertion involves standing up for personal rights and expressing thoughts, feelings and beliefs in direct, honest and appropriate ways which respect the rights of other people'. Indeed, this issue of acknowledging and respecting the rights of the person on the receiving end, was and still is recognized as marking a boundary between assertion and aggression.[4] Furthermore, Rakos,[1] a psychologist internationally known in the field of Assertiveness Training, believes that being properly assertive requires that the responsibilities attendant on those rights are also acknowledged and brought into play. We will return to the issue of rights and responsibilities later in the chapter.

As well as including the stipulation of exercising and acknowledging personal rights, the assertive individual should feel emotionally comfortable behaving in this way. Assertion 'enables a person to act in his or her own best interests, to stand up for herself or himself without undue anxiety, to express honest feelings comfortably, or to exercise personal rights without denying the rights of others'.[5] Seven types of scenario calling for an assertive response have also been suggested.[6] Three of these have to do with handling negative situations and are also described as conflict assertion: the remaining four with positive situations. These seven response classes are:

Negative

1. Expressing unpopular or difficult opinions.
2. Requesting change from others.
3. Refusing unreasonable requests.

Positive

4. Admitting personal shortcomings.
5. Giving and receiving compliments.
6. Initiating and maintaining interactions.
7. Expressing positive feelings.

People differ in the ease with which they deal with situations such as those above. For some they cause no great concern while others avoid them if at all possible. Before moving on to outline the role of assertion in management, it may be useful to pause at this point to consider your present levels of assertion. Using Exercise 10.1, decide if this style characterises your handling of social situations.

Those who read this chapter in the vain hope that it will enable them to dominate, control and subjugate their workforce more effectively will be disappointed. As explained, that is not assertiveness. But it is not only that they will not find this information – more importantly, they should not need it. In seeking out such advice they are completely misguided as to the communicative strategies and styles demanded by modern principles of good management.[4] The thinking in the 1990s contrasts starkly with that from an earlier era when management was all about taking decisions, often

Exercise 10.1 Check your assertiveness

Consider each of the following statements about yourself and respond to each by circling the number that *in general* best represents your position in relation to it.

Statement	Always	Often	Uncertain	Seldom	Never
I find it difficult saying 'No' to people.	1	2	3	4	5
I feel awkward meeting people for the first time.	1	2	3	4	5
I tend to comply with what others want.	1	2	3	4	5
I find it difficult talking about my feelings.	1	2	3	4	5
I avoid conflict at all costs.	1	2	3	4	5
Others take advantage of my good nature.	1	2	3	4	5
I hate having to complain.	1	2	3	4	5
I prefer to write rather than deal with awkward situations face-to face.	1	2	3	4	5
I avoid paying compliments because I find it too embarrassing.	1	2	3	4	5
I would rather drop hints that I am unhappy with others' performance than mention it outright.	1	2	3	4	5
I feel put upon by others.	1	2	3	4	5
I find it hard to get my ideas accepted.	1	2	3	4	5

Exercise 10.1 (Cont'd)

Statement	Always	Often	Uncertain	Seldom	Never
I generally don't obtain the respect that I deserve.	1	2	3	4	5
I dislike having to ask others for favours.	1	2	3	4	5

Now calculate your total score. This may range from 14 to 70. The lower the score the less assertive you are likely to be in general. As a rough guide, a score under 45 suggests that a much more assertive style could substantially improve your present levels of interpersonal effectiveness.

with little or no consultation with the rest of the workforce, and then expecting total compliance. Power and strength of leadership were measured in these terms. Communication was top down, from boss to staff. Workers acquiesced resentfully, left or were sacked. They did what they had to do but, typically, with little enthusiasm, commitment or dedication. Many managers were slow to recognize that this was scarcely the way to obtain the best out of staff.

Changes in work that have heralded a new set of values and principles shaping how management and the workforce should organize their relationship in their mutual best interests must be recognized. These have direct and very potent implications for how communication should be conducted.[4, 7] They include:

- The flattening of organizational structures and the devolution of responsibility leading to the greater autonomy of small teams of workers.
- The deconstructing of once powerful institutions and authority figures has been accompanied by the erosion of worker respect that was once expected and provided unquestioningly. The emperor undressed is a much less imposing figure.
- The present generation entering the workforce is less prepared to reverentially obey orders, as previous generations have done, merely because they come from someone on a higher rung of the organizational ladder.
- A better educated workforce is more fully prepared and keener to become involved in the decision-making process that directly affects its livelihood.
- Modern workers are perhaps less content than their parents and grandparents to accept merely monetary rewards for their effort. Having a sense of ownership of their work and developing feelings of personal fulfilment are demands that must be met.

- The growing internationalization of industry has led to the wider dissemination of alternative management practices at odds with those that were practised in the first wave of industrialization and persisted in many quarters until recently.

All of these changes point in the direction of new styles of management with an emphasis on participation, facilitation and empowerment. Influencing workers rather than controlling them through subjugation is what counts. Maximizing available resources and expertise in decision-making leads to more effective outcomes. Communicating in an open, inclusive and honest way that is direct yet respectful, is what is required. This calls for a style that is assertive rather than aggressive or passive.

Before moving on to examine assertiveness in greater depth, it will help to focus it more firmly if we briefly contrast it with the other two contrasting styles already mentioned – aggressiveness and submissiveness.

COMMUNICATING AGGRESSIVELY

An aggressive style ignores, threatens or violates the rights of other people. Managers acting aggressively operate in accordance with just one set of personal considerations – their own. The working assumption is that their needs are more important, their concerns more pressing, their opinions more valid and their feelings more acute than those of the person being put on. Aggressive types are out to get what they want rather than what is best for all concerned. The objective is to have things their way, to win at all costs. This may be done through bullying, threatening or making empty promises. It inevitably trades on the misuse of power and the exploitation of weakness or vulnerability. In addition to being strategically short-sighted, aggression is also ethically dubious.

Aggressiveness can be explicit and direct or implicit and indirect.[8] We tend to think of it as the former, for the most part, and expressed in shouting, dire threats, red faces and savage looks.

DIRECT AGGRESSION

We have all most probably witnessed, experienced or perhaps even perpetrated an aggressive attack on someone at work, at some time or other. In the most extreme of cases this can take a physical form. But short of that, being present when a colleague is subjected to sustained verbal aggression can also be quite upsetting: being on the receiving end, even more so. The hapless member of staff is left scarred and shaken. Direct verbal aggression, in its extreme form, is not difficult to identify. But other instances which are less 'hot' may be less easy to notice. Remember though that the worker behaving aggressively denies or in some way violates the rights of others. This is the key. The sensitivies of the other person are infringed or denied: their needs are disregarded.

Aggressive individuals typically place themselves centre stage and try to dominate proceedings to the exclusion of others. They tend to be close-minded, opinionated and confrontative: they are right and all the others are wrong and should be made aware of the fact. They are poor listeners, finding it difficult to place themselves in the position of the other person or to appreciate how things might look from that angle. Forceful, arrogant, demeaning and abrasive are other descriptors.[9] Typical verbal and non-verbal accompaniments of this style are noted in Key point 10.1.

Key point 10.1 Responding aggressively

Verbal cues

- Threat: 'If that report is not on my desk by four o'clock, you can look for a job elsewhere.'
- Ridicule: 'You never have your work done on time. I can never depend upon you to do anything.'
- Abuse: 'Come on you prat, get a move on.'
- Foul language: 'You f****** c***.'
- Demands: 'Get me the accounts for last year, and do it now.'
- Directives: 'Never leave your desk before it is cleared and always make sure that I know where you can be contacted.'
- Interruption: 'Stop right there! Before you say another word let me tell you what your rights are!'
- Blame: 'It would have worked perfectly if you had done it properly.'
- Self-opinionation: 'That is nonsense. The only workable solution is to move John into Sales, as I said at the start.'
- Intrusion: 'I heard you mention the ZX34 model, a fine machine. I worked on them for three years. What I don't know about a ZX34 isn't worth knowing. The name's Jones, by the way. Hope I'm not intruding, but let me tell you a thing or two about the ZX34.'

Non-verbal cues

- Tone of voice: loud, strident, yelling, intense, strained.
- Speed of speech: fast.
- Gaze: staring, unbroken, intimidating.
- Facial expression: glaring, frowning.
- Complexion: florid, blanched.
- Gestures: animated.
- Posture: expansive, tense.

There are several possible causes of aggression in the workplace:[10]

- Aggression may work *in the short-term*. It may be rewarded and therefore perpetuated.
- It could be modelled on the style of another senior figure in the organization.
- It may be a reaction to frustration. Frustration is a well-known precipitator of aggression.
- The aggressor may feel under attack. For whatever reason, situations and cues may be read as posing personal threat. The best defensive strategy becomes attack.
- Aggression is more likely to be displayed in situations where aggressors feel that they can get away with it. This is the bullying aspect. It is more likely to be directed at an underling than at the boss.
- Levels of personal control can be dysfunctional. People differ in the extent to which they can keep their hostile feelings in check.
- The aggressor may have been socialized into a work culture where aggressive behaviour is relatively common and largely tolerated.
- Aggression may be mistaken for assertion because acceptable assertive skills have never been learned.
- Hostility can be carried over from an entirely different situation. Due to 'deflected hostility', a manager may vent spleen on some undeserving junior member of staff in reaction to being castigated by the boss at an earlier meeting.

Regardless of why aggression occurs, an appreciation of its aftermath is very important. What are the consequences of this way of handling difficult situations and awkward people? Consequences are both short and long term and accrue to the perpetrator, the victim and the organization.[10, 11]

The perpetrator

Aggression may produce short-term advantages for the manager who adopts this style. The staff member whose rights have been trampled on in the attack, may acquiesce and comply with the demands made. The precipitating problem may be settled, after a fashion, and at least for the moment. This might lead to feelings of relief, perhaps even power and authority. The sheer reduction in tension that directly follows an aggressive outburst is also likely to be positively experienced. (It should not be forgotten, on the other hand, that attack can provoke instant retaliation by the other resulting in possible defeat.)

The longer-term consequences of aggression are largely unappealing. The emotional experience of the event may gradually be transformed, with positive feelings replaced by those of embarrassment, shame and guilt. There may be a growing paranoia that an enemy has been created with the person attacked now seeking opportunities to 'get even'. Perhaps more importantly there may be a justifiable concern about losing not only the goodwill, but the respect and trust of the workforce.

The victim

Depending on the severity of the attack, a recognized sequence of emotional reactions is likely to be experienced. This begins with stunned shock, then anger which gives way to shame, guilt and depression if the victim begins to accept some blame for what took place. A corollary of this emotional reaction is an acceptance of the perpetrator's right to act in this way. Repeated exposure to this form of abuse can eventually induce feelings of powerlessness and worthlessness. When the person on the receiving end refuses to succumb in this way, resentment is the most likely outcome, coupled with low morale and, perhaps the desire for revenge. Quality of work can suffer, sometimes through deliberate sabotage. Mistakes probably will not be reported or advice sought. Prospects for productive team-building are poor.

The organization

The effects of an endemically aggressive management style in an organization are devastating.[10] Many members of the workforce, usually the youngest and the brightest, leave while those who stay are less inclined to express their real opinions, present innovative ideas or take risks. Most of their time is spent 'covering their backs'. Few are prepared to pop their heads up over the parapet in case they attract enemy fire from the front line of management.

A further risk that is becoming increasingly common, is the possibility of legal action by a worker claiming compensation for damaged health. Workers exposed to unremitting harassment by rampantly aggressive managers leading to emotional collapse through intolerable levels of stress, usually have their cases looked on very favourably in the compensation hearing. Moreover, when the press covers the story, the reputation of the firm invariably suffers. As well as loss of business, increased recruitment difficulties are a probable result.

INDIRECT AGGRESSION

Aggression does not always have to be loud and oath-laden. The rights of others can be violated in more subtle and insidious ways through emotional blackmail, manipulation, sulking or pouting.[12] Take the following situation where a manager has a report to get ready for the next morning:

> *Manager*: Jane, I need you to work late this evening to finish off this report for Hawking. It should only take a couple of hours.

Secretary: I'm afraid I can't, Mr Blackstaff. I've got my drama group at 7.00 p.m.

Manager: Drama group ... I don't believe this! Hawking needs this report for 9 o'clock tomorrow morning but he won't get it. And why not? Because you have a bloody drama group! (*Direct aggression*)

or

Manager: Oh well! I must say that I'm disappointed in you, Jane. I have always tried to accommodate you when you have asked for time off. I'm only asking you to do two hours' extra work. It's not as if I ask to you to work late every evening. But if your drama group is more important than your work then I suppose I will just have to live with that. Mind you it will mean me being here to at least ten o'clock. I will just have to phone Mrs Blackstaff and tell her that I won't be able to take her out for her birthday celebration after all. She'll be very disappointed, but I suppose she will eventually get over it ... (*Indirect aggression using emotional blackmail*)

or

Manager: Oh that's most unfortunate, Jane, especially since you have already done so much work on the report and done it very well, if I may so. With you keen to achieve pro-motion and so on, it would have been good if you had been able to set the finished docu-ment on old Hawking's desk tomorrow morning. You deserve the credit. Still if you can't do it, you can't do it. I don't think Sally has left yet, I'm sure she will finish it off. I sup-pose it's really between the two of you as to who will fill Rosemary's post as old Hawking's PA. (*Indirect aggression using manipulation*)

Indirect aggression using these sorts of Machiavellian tactics, although less intensely emotionally charged than a direct attack, can be just as corrosive of trust, respect and loyalty. Feelings of anger or shame can be just as consuming. The quest for revenge can be pursued with equal vigour. Again, assertiveness tends to be the alternative approach which holds out greatest promise of a mutually satisfactory outcome to the problem. Before moving on to consider it in greater detail, however, let us take at look at a contrasting style of management at the other end of the spec-trum from aggression.

COMMUNICATING SUBMISSIVELY

People who are non-assertive due to over-passivity and over-submissiveness read-ily acknowledge the rights of others. This is not the cause of their problem. Their problem is that they do so at the expense of exercising their *own* rights in the situ-ation. They value the rights of others above their own and so go out of their way to accommodate others even when it means incurring unreasonable costs and incon-veniences. Typically they cannot say 'No' to the most unreasonable of requests. They hesitate to present their views and opinions and, when they do, it is in such a self-effacing manner that they almost invite others to discount them. The majority position is usually the one voiced regardless of what they really think about an issue. True wants and feelings are rarely expressed but, rather, those that are expected by others or in some way anticipated to be more acceptable to them. What is said tends to be expressed apologetically and with little confidence; apprehension, anxiety and threat are constantly lurking on the horizons of their emotional experience. Submissive people, therefore, play down their own rights or at best attempt to assert them in a very half-hearted and ineffectual way.

Managers lacking assertion are inclined to let problems and difficulties continue in the forlorn hope that they will sort themselves out if left alone. They adopt a generally low profile. Staff may comment, 'The manager ... you never see her! She could be on holiday most of the time, for all we know'. Neither can staff rely on support. A frequent comment is, 'I can't do anything, my manager won't back me up'.[12] Avoiding conflict at all cost is an abiding quest. Submissive people have a tendency to be diffident and indecisive. Despite a desire to please, they are often seen as weak and inconsequential. Characteristic cues of the submissive style have been identified[4, 9, 10] and some are listed in Key point 10.2.

There may be occasions when a submissive approach is the sensible course of action, just as there may be situations in which a more aggressive style is called for. It should not be thought that these contrasting ways of dealing with problems should never be contemplated under any circumstances. The point is that assertiveness is the option likely to lead to a successful resolution most of the time. The other two are usually little more than short-term palliatives that do little to cure the underlying pathology. Why then do some seem to inappropriately favour submissiveness as the preferred style? Amongst the reasons suggested[6, 7, 11] can be listed the following:

- *An ignorance of rights*. Submissive people may not appreciate that they too have rights deserving of respect or they may place greater emphasis on their attendant responsibilities. Alternatively they may 'know' in a remote, bookish way that they have rights, yet fail to embrace that knowledge sufficiently to act on it.
- *A desire to please*. The mistaken belief is that it is more important to be liked than to be respected. Over-submissiveness frequently leads to neither.
- *Avoidance of conflict*. The feeling is that confronting conflict only makes it worse. It's the 'ostrich with its head in the sand' mentality. Conflict is endemic in most organizations and gets worse if not managed effectively. There is a failure to distinguish between confronting the problem and confronting the person with the problem. A blind eye is turned to both.
- *Lack of self-efficacy and poor self-esteem*. An important factor in how we go about tackling difficult and challenging situations is the belief that we have the ability to cope successfully with them.[13] Without a sufficient sense of self-efficacy we may, in terms of the 'fight or flight' response, take flight. Doing so, however,

Key point 10.2   Responding submissively

Verbal cues

- Apologies *ad nauseam*: 'I really am frightfully sorry for bothering you with this trivial matter.'
- Hedges: 'I'm pretty well sure that the figures are accurate. On the other hand, they were done in a bit of a hurry.
- Waffle: 'The vast number of right thinking people in positions of authority in industry would be very unlikely to fail to accept the majority view of experienced senior managers ...'
- Prevarication: 'I know that I almost made a decision but I didn't quite.'
- Lack of self-referenced statements: 'It might be better if you got back to work. One would expect all staff to be working at this time.'
- Self-deprecation: 'I don't really know much about this and last time I made a bit of a mess of it.'
- Hesitations: 'Would it be possible ... uh ... um ... to take ... ah ... some time ... um ... to sort the ... ah ... whole thing ... um out?'
- Obsequious politeness: 'Excuse me, I hate to bother you but would you mind awfully moving your foot. You're standing on my toe.'
- Over-justification: 'I wouldn't ask normally, but if I don't know when you intend to take your holiday, I won't be able to arrange cover, you see.'
- Hints: 'I wonder who I could get to help me with the Rother's account.'

Non-verbal cues

- Tone of voice: soft, quiet, tailing off towards the end.
- Voice quality: weak, thin, strained.
- Speech pattern: hesitant, uneven rate, frequent false starts, dysfluencies or throat-clearing.
- Gaze: averted, downward.
- Facial expression: fear, unease, apprehension.
- Gestures: jerky, fidgety.
- Posture: small, hunched, tense.

reflects negatively on our sense of self-esteem. Next time round we will probably be even more convinced that we cannot cope with this sort of situation. Self-esteem will suffer further.

- *Cultural diversity*. It should be appreciated that what passes for submissiveness in one culture can be viewed, in another, as acceptable social protocol. Managers, in being 'submissive', are merely abiding by the dictates of that particular social order. There are no recognized benchmarks for gauging aggression, submission or assertion. Indeed, some feel that assertive ways of behaving in the USA, come across as aggressive in the UK.
- *Lack of assertive skills*. In circumstances where assertiveness is called for but not provided, it may be that the person simply has never learned the skills involved.

The consequences of a submissive style, in like manner to those of aggression, can be both short term and long term and affect the person, the other workers and the organization.

THE PERSON

Immediate effects of acting submissively can be quite positive. It may have prevented a 'nasty scene', it may have avoided the need to challenge the unreasonable demands of another, with corresponding reductions in anticipatory anxiety or guilt. Simply saying 'Yes' rather than 'No' is often the irresistibly easy way out at the time. In the longer term, however, submissiveness leads to broken promises, dishonoured contracts, unfilled orders or unsustainable workloads. Either way, standards of work will probably suffer, even leading to increased absenteeism through stress-induced sickness. Feelings about self are likely to be negative. What begins as a sense of relief and freedom from guilt, eventually creates an abiding and overwhelming feeling of powerlessness, worthlessness and self-loathing.

THE OTHER WORKERS

Again, how the submissive person is experienced typically changes over time, especially if that person is in a managerial role. Initially, and especially if the person is new to the job, there may be a reaction of benevolent sympathy. The gentler approach may be roundly welcomed. Not having someone constantly on top of you, checking your work closely, telling you what to do, often feels liberating. It can also be taken advantage of. In the long run, lack of guidance, support and direction produces a disgruntled, bickering, ineffective workforce with poor morale, that eventually turns its wrath on the manager they once embraced.

THE ORGANIZATION

An organization with a sizeable number of people in pivotal positions routinely behaving in a submissive fashion, cannot thrive. Important decisions will not be taken, there will be little sense of mission, dynamism will be absent and internal strife will be rampant but this conflict will be largely ignored. The approach to management must change quickly or the organization will fail.

Given that the long-term outlook is decidedly poor for those who routinely make use of aggression or submission to solve problematic situations with people at work, let us now consider assertiveness as a more promising alternative.

COMMUNICATING ASSERTIVELY

An assertive style emphasizes both the expression of personal wants, needs, feelings and preferences, on the one hand, and respect for those of the person being addressed, on the other.[4] An aggressive style cherishes the former but at the expense of the latter. By contrast, submissiveness maximizes respect for the other but trivializes personal concerns. As we have seen, aggressive people elevate their own rights in importance at the expense of those of others. Conversely, submissive people place the emphasis on the rights of others to the neglect of their own. Those acting assertively, however, uphold both their own and the other's rights in equal measure. Moreover, they acknowledge and accept the responsibilities that inevitably couple themselves to rights.

Assertive managers:

- make known their wants and needs
- express their ideas and opinions openly and honestly and do so comfortably without feeling awkward, anxious or guilty
- confront difficult situations that have to be dealt with rather than avoiding them
- attack the problem rather than the person
- seek the best outcome for all concerned (see Key point 10.3).

The objective is 'to try to ensure fair play for everyone'.[6]

ASSERTIVENESS, RIGHTS AND BELIEFS

Assertiveness demands an awareness of rights and responsibilities. Without an appreciation of what your rights are, or those of others, it is impossible to recognize when they are being violated, or what to uphold. It is a bit like being given a fully loaded rifle to defend the chicken coop from the fox, without ever having been told what the fox looks like. According to the *Concise Oxford Dictionary*, a right, in this sense, is 'fair treatment; a thing one may legally or morally claim; the state of being

Key point 10.3   Acting assertively

Acting assertively involves:

- being comfortable expressing personal needs, wants, opinions and feelings
- making reasonable requests of others without feeling awkward
- refusing unreasonable requests without being guilty
- being prepared to listen to others
- disagreeing with the views and opinions of others, if necessary
- giving and accepting praise and compliments without embarrassment
- refusing negative feedback considered unfair
- initiating, maintaining and terminating contact with others without experiencing undue negative emotion
- being open, honest and direct in dealings with others
- respecting self and others
- upholding the rights of self and others in equal measure
- confronting rather than avoiding difficult situations that have to be resolved
- being able to separate the person from the problem
- admitting mistakes and shortcomings, if necessary, rather than perpetuating a false façade of infallibility
- seeking the best possible outcome for all concerned, rather than blindly pursuing factional interests.
- acting non-assertively if it is felt that it is the best option under the circumstances.

entitled to a privilege or immunity or authority to act'. Many of those who have written about assertiveness have drawn up lists of those rights that legitimize this approach.[4, 9, 10, 14] While these differ to some extent, they are for the most part based on the United Nation's Universal Declaration of Human Rights. A composite of them is included in Key point 10.4.

These are universal human rights. We can also think of more specific sets of rights peculiar to the work setting. Some of these may be enshrined in general employment legislation, others may form part of particular contractual arrangements and differ from employer to employer. Assertiveness depends on a knowledge of where you

---

Key point 10.4   Just rights

You have the right to:

- hold and express views, opinions and ideas even though they may not be the same as those of others
- have your views, opinions and ideas listened to and taken seriously
- have and express feelings and emotions
- experience needs and wants
- request that these needs and wants be accommodated while acknowledging the right of others to refuse to do so
- refuse a request without feeling awkward or guilty
- respectfully disagree with the views, opinions and ideas of others without incurring attack or aggression from them or others
- order your own life, as long as it does not infringe the rights of others to do likewise
- be wrong sometimes; it is an unavoidable part of being human
- sometimes not know the answer to a question or problem; no one can know everything
- the respect of others, not necessarily on account of *who* you are, but rather *that* you are
- assert yourself
- not assert yourself, if you decide that this is best

---

stand in relation to them, so knowing your rights is necessary when it comes to acting assertively. Staff who are more assertive have a clearer view of their work role. They also tend to express greater levels of job satisfaction.[4]

The opposite of rights is responsibilities and obligations. While we may have a right to express our views, we also have an obligation not to shove them down the throats of others. Rakos[1] warns that we ignore these obligations at our peril. Indeed, he argues, merely stating our rights can come across as being aggressive. Rather, he suggests we have attendant obligations, in expressing ourselves assertively, to establish the rights and circumstances of others, consider how our assertive action might affect them and, if need be, explain our actions in order to avoid or minimize hurt or humiliation.

Knowing your rights, in a matter of fact, detached way, is one thing, but you must also be able to accept them. Some people 'know' their rights in this way, but fail to act accordingly because they have not fully owned them. Such individuals may be unable to embrace these rights and feel comfortable with them because this new knowledge fails to square with their beliefs about themselves, others and how the social world works. A strong assumption that intolerably nasty consequences will accrue unless the boss's demands are always complied with, can lead to permanent submissiveness. It has been found that assertive individuals believe that largely positive consequences will follow from their refusing an unreasonable request.[6] Their submissive counterparts, on the other hand, fully expect the consequences for themselves to be negative. They also tend to give themselves largely negative, defeatist messages. Their self-talk is along the lines of 'I'll sound awfully rude, if I say "No"', 'I'll become so anxious refusing, that I'll stutter and stammer and look a fool', and so on. It is only when more positive possibilities are recognized in assertive action that this style will be attempted.

VERBAL ASSERTIVE BEHAVIOUR

There are different verbal strategies for expressing assertiveness that can be put to use as circumstances permit.[3, 11, 12] A common theme is the assumption that one begins with the least assertive response calculated to have the desired effect, moving on to more potent alternatives only if required.

Basic assertion

This is a simple, straightforward statement of your wants, needs, views, feelings or rights, delivered directly and in a matter of fact fashion without elaboration or embellishment. In response to continual interruption, for example, basic assertion takes the form of a statement such as, 'I would like to continue with my point'.

Empathic assertion

A basic assertive statement can on occasion seem brusque. Sometimes embellishment is more acceptable. With empathic assertion, recognition is afforded of the circumstances of the other person, and the impact that your assertive stance might have. However, an apology should not be offered for behaving assertively. Remember it is your right to choose this course of action. Continuing with the example, the interrupted person might interject, 'I realize that you have strong views as well on this matter and that you want to share them, but I would like to continue with my point'.

Confronting discrepancies

Here the assertive approach hinges around pointing out to others how their course of action is at odds with what they have stated or agreed. This is done to best effect in a matter of fact way, without any hint at accusation or attachment of blame. Indeed all assertive behaviour accentuates fact and logic in preference to emotional outburst. Continuing with the above, as an exemplar, confronting discrepancy could take the following form: 'In debating this point, we agreed to abide by the normal conventions of turn-taking. Now, each time that I begin to speak, you interrupt. This flies in the face of what you agreed.'

Indicating *your understanding* of the agreement, can also be beneficial, since it enables problems due to misinterpretation to be identified at an early stage and ironed out. For example: 'In debating this point, I thought we agreed to abide by the normal conventions of turn-taking. Now, each time that I begin to speak, you interrupt. This flies in the face of what you agreed, as I understand it.'

Drawing consequences

This involves making others aware of what will happen if they persist with their course of action, e.g., 'If you continue to interrupt me, and I you, neither of us will be able to hear what the other has to say and both of our points of view will be lost'. This approach may take an even stronger form if you continue to the ultimate conclusion. For example, 'In these circumstances, with your persistent interruptions, I see no point in continuing our discussion and will therefore leave'.

Escalating assertion

A manager would begin with a basic assertive response, gradually bringing into play more powerful alternatives as and when required, in the face of a persistent violation of rights. For instance, unremitting interruptions can be dealt with using a basic assertive response, followed by empathic assertion, confronting discrepancies and finally drawing consequences.

Protective assertion

Three assertive tactics have been identified as a form of defence commonly used to counter hostility, manipulation, rudeness or unreasonable persistence.[15] They are called broken record, fogging and meta-level assertion:

- *Broken record.* This involves making a simple assertive statement and repeating it until it is complied with. It is as if the needle on the record had stuck.
- *Fogging.* Negative comment is apparently accepted but without the emotional snub that usually comes with it. The person using fogging seems to calmly 'hear the words' without rising to any emotional bait that may be dangled and without accepting any possible negative implications for self-concept or self-esteem. For example:

Director: You made an abysmal mess of that job for Seafirms.

Manager: It's true that it didn't go as well as I had hoped.

Fogging reveals to the accuser that the accused is not prepared to be emotionally put on in this way; to become involved in an argument or to engage in vigorous self-flagellation in a fury of self-blame. The consequence is quite often a shift to a more mature and assertive way of handling the situation.

- *Meta-level assertion*. In circumstances where it becomes obvious that the bone of contention cannot be resolved within the current confines of the problem, meta-level assertion suggests taking a broader view of the issue. Going back to our earlier example of persistent interruption, this reaction may indicate a deeper malaise in the relationship between the two people involved. In this case, a meta-level assertive response would be along the lines of: 'John, since you still persist in interrupting me, and I have been aware of this before in meetings, we need to look more closely at our working relationship together to see if there is anything there that makes it difficult for you to listen to my point of view.'

Three-step assertion

This is one of the most comprehensive statements of assertion. It is particularly useful in situations where person B's behaviour is unacceptable to person A and A would like it changed. The three steps referred to are:

- A factual description of B's troublesome behaviour.
- The consequences of this behaviour for A.
- The changes to B's behaviour that would resolve the difficulty.

In a situation where a member of the office staff begins taking excessively long tea breaks, the manager could employ the three-step approach as follows:

Manager: The morning tea break should last 15 minutes, Jane, but I notice that you are never back at your desk before 10.45 a.m. (*factual description of B's troublesome behaviour*). This means that Janet has to take the calls and deal with the desk and some calls don't get answered, which I find unacceptable (*consequences of this behaviour for A*). Could you make sure that you are back at your desk by 10.30 a.m. from now on, like the others in the office (*actual changes to B's behaviour that would resolve the difficulty*).

NON-VERBAL ASSERTIVE BEHAVIOUR

For assertive behaviour to have the desired effect, the non-verbal elements of delivery must be right. As with all communication, if the words spoken suggest one message while the rest of the body is signalling something entirely different, it is probable that the verbal message will be diluted or dismissed. People who find it difficult to be assertive in certain situations sometimes show their unease non-verbally. They use the appropriate forms of expression, but qualify them non-verbally in such a way that the impact is lost. Were the manager in the above example to deliver the three-step assertive statement with an apologetic smile, perhaps out of a sense of unease with possible conflict in the office, the chances of Jane changing her wayward behaviour would be greatly reduced. Non-verbal behaviour that promotes assertion is outlined in Key point 10.5, and the whole subject is explained more fully in Chapter 14.

Key point 10.5   Non-verbal assertive behaviour

- Tone of voice: intermediate modulation, relaxed but firm, confident.
- Volume of voice: medium, but slightly louder than that in normal conversation.
- Speed of speech: moderate, but tending towards the slow and deliberate.
- Response latency: a long pause should not be allowed to develop before the delivery of the assertive response.
- Gaze: medium levels – flexible and intermittent eye contact is most appropriate.
- Facial expression: alert yet avoiding uncontrolled movements or signs of negative emotion as well as smiles – consistent with what is being said.
- Complexion: normal.
- Gestures: smooth gestures while speaking, yet inconspicuous when listening.
- Posture: generally erect, avoiding shifting, shuffling or fidgeting.
- Head: erect, avoiding excessive head-nodding.
- Interpersonal distance: close enough to exert a presence but without gross violation of the other's personal space.
- Orientation: direct, face to face but not threatening.

FACTORS THAT SHAPE ASSERTIVENESS

Perhaps some readers find that they tend towards aggression or submission, rather than assertion. Having said that, there will be circumstances in which even the most aggressive individual adopts a quite submissive approach and, likewise, the submissive individual plays a more dominant part. We will now consider several personal and situational factors that have a bearing on the likelihood and the appropriateness of assertion.

- *Gender.* Traditionally, assertiveness has been more closely associated with masculinity than femininity. Contemporary social changes have largely eroded this stereotype, although both males and females may find it easier to be assertive to members of the same gender.[6] In professional circles, it seems that assertiveness is valued equally whether employed by male or female business-persons,[16] corporate managers[17] or lawyers.[18] Nevertheless, there is evidence that when females are assertive there is an expectation that they use more 'caring' techniques, such as empathic assertion.[6] No doubt, these norms will continue to change as women progressively occupy higher-status positions in society.

- *Relationship shared by those involved.* Expressing an unpopular opinion (as a form of assertion) tends to be more acceptable amongst friends than strangers. On the other hand, refusing a request from a stranger (another form of assertion) is viewed more positively than refusing a friend.[1]

- *Status.* It could be predicted that assertiveness by senior members in an organization would be more acceptable than similar behaviour by junior staff and there is some research evidence to this effect.[19] Acting assertively is also easier when directed towards those of lower rather than higher status.[19]

- *The setting.* Certain types of assertion appear to have greater currency depending on the setting in which they are employed. In the job interview, having the interviewee subsequently write a letter of thanks expressing continued interest in the position, for example, tends to be viewed by employers as increasing the chances of offering employment. Requesting a second interview with a different interviewer, by contrast, has the opposite effect. As far as ease of expression is concerned, it is usually less difficult to adopt an assertive pose in one's own, as opposed to the other's home or office.[6]

- *Culture.* Assertive behaviour is decidedly culture-bound. What passes as acceptably assertive in Europe and USA, may be perceived quite differently in countries with markedly different sets of norms and values. Even within European countries and the USA, ethnic minorities that have largely perpetuated the culture of the country of origin may abide by different standards of assertion. In the USA, Mexican, Japanese and Chinese communities report less use of assertion than do the Caucasian culture.

- *Age.* Many people feel more comfortable being assertive towards others who are younger, rather than older. In addition, there seems to be a positive relationship between age and assertive expression. As people grow older, this style of dealing with others appears to be more common.

BENEFITS OF ASSERTION

We have already seen that the two contrasting styles of relating, aggression and submission have some possible advantages in the immediate to short term, but that long term, the outcomes are counter-productive and frequently simply exacerbate the situation. The benefits of assertion are more enduring and are enjoyed by the manager, the staff and the organization.

THE MANAGER

Managers who adopt an assertive approach feel good about themselves. They do not evade the issue to be tackled, neither do they lose face through not controlling their temper, as often happens in an aggressive outburst. There is considerable truth in the claim that, 'The extent to which you assert yourself determines the level of your self-esteem'.[20]

While the issue to hand may not be 'resolved' instantaneously as sometimes seems to happen with an aggressive assault, the chances are that when it finally is resolved, the solution will be enduring and to everyone's satisfaction. Being assertive means communicating directly, openly, honestly, unemotionally and clearly. Therefore, the chances of a successful outcome to a situation of possible conflicting needs are strengthened.

A further advantage in this, of course, is that it enables the manager to move on to other matters with energy freed up to tackle them. The problem is not left festering to erupt once more at probably the most inappropriate time and demand attention that should be invested elsewhere. Nor is emotional energy consumed in ruminating on the possible aftermath of an aggressive assault, and the paranoia that this can engender. Indeed, difficulties handled assertively frequently strengthen the relationship amongst the participants, rather than erode it. As a result, the manager's confidence and motivation to extend this approach is enhanced.

THE STAFF

The word 'staff' is used to cover all those subjected to an assertive style. There can be no guarantee, of course, that the agreed solutions to the precipitating problems will always be *entirely* what staff want. Assertiveness is not a panacea. Those solutions will, however, be ones to which staff have contributed and by which they should be able to abide. Their views and concerns will have been give a full, even-handed and respectful hearing. In many cases, this alone goes a considerable way to placating the warring parties. Staff should, in consequence, recognize and appreciate the respect in which they are held by management.

If encouraged to act assertively, staff feel more at liberty to express ideas and opinions, to report mistakes, to ask for clarification when information is not understood and to make known to managers when they are struggling to cope, without having their stress added to by the fear of blame or ridicule. In this way difficulties can be dealt with at an early stage before they have an opportunity to cause worse problems.

THE ORGANIZATION

An organization in which assertiveness is the preferred management style is typified by good communication, high staff morale, vibrancy and commitment. Internal disputes are kept to a minimum and, when they do arise, tend to be resolved relatively quickly and to the satisfaction of most, if not all, parties. Such organizations characteristically enjoy an enviable reputation for good employer–employee relations, working conditions and quality of product or service. They are ones to which staff have a sense of commitment and involvement, a feeling of being valued and of having a say in the operation.

SUMMARY

When acting in accordance with the 'fight or flight' response, we often either metaphorically flee in the face of difficult problems and people, or we defend ourselves by going on the attack. These predilections give rise to two contrasting styles of communication in management, each of which is just as counter-productive as the other. While both may have possible outcomes which are positive in the short term, in the longer term consequences for the manager, staff and the organization tend to be negative.

In being submissive, one sets aside one's own rights in favour of those of the other party. Aggression, on the other hand, entails violating the rights of the other in favour of one's own. By contrast, assertiveness typically upholds the rights of all, accepts attendant responsibilities and leads to positive benefits for all parties sharing the problem or experiencing the difficulty. Exercise 10.2 is designed to help you identify occasions at work when you have difficulty acting assertively and how these might be handled more effectively.

Exercise 10.2 Assertiveness at work

This exercise is intended to help you identify assertiveness opportunities at work.

1. Think back to a situation at work in which you inappropriately lost your temper and behaved aggressively.
2. Jot down how you could have handled the issue in a more assertive manner, thinking of both verbal and non-verbal elements.
3. How might the outcome have differed, both immediately afterwards and long-term if you had acted in this way?
4. Were the situation, or one similar to it to recur, what would *help* you to act assertively and what would *hinder* you doing so?
5. Now think back to a situation at work in which you were overly submissive.
6. Again, jot down how you could have handled the matter in a more assertive manner, thinking of both verbal and non-verbal elements.
7. How might the outcome have differed, both immediately afterwards and long-term for both you and the other person involved, if you had taken an assertive stance?
8. Once more, were the situation, or one similar to it to recur, what would *help* you to act assertively and what would *hinder* you doing so?

11 A problem shared: helping communication

The world of the happy is quite different from the world of the unhappy.

Ludwig von Wittgenstein, *Tractatus Logica-Philosophicus*

Employees do not leave their problems aside as they turn to face their working day.

Michael Carroll, *Workplace Counselling*

It has been estimated that 80 per cent of the manager's working day is spent in face-to-face interaction.[1] Much of this time is taken up dealing with employee problems. The nature of such difficulties differs from worker to worker and the actual role played in handling them varies from manager to manager. Some take a more direct hands-on approach than others. But regardless of the strategy adopted for coping with them, these problems ultimately represent a management issue that must not be side-stepped.

Troubles experienced by employees in their job can be traced to a number of sources, one of which is the organization itself. Work generates difficulties of contrasting types and at different levels. Some are technical. For example, the chief engineer may see no immediate solution to designing a structure that will serve the purpose intended at the cost specified. Here the problem is centred in the lack of insight required to produce a creative but viable solution. It is highly unlikely that anyone without a detailed knowledge of either engineering or finance would be of much help in resolving the matter.

Other problems have more to do with oppressive, negative emotional states that have become dysfunctional. They need to be approached in an altogether different way with its own knowledge base, operating principles and set of skills. An employee, for instance, requests a meeting with management on account of the intolerable stress experienced since the departmental reorganization. Further work-based problems may emerge as a result of poor working relationships. A production worker, for instance, feels singled out and bullied by a victimizing supervisor and demands to see the section leader. Neither situation is likely to be solved satisfactorily by merely providing information or offering advice. What is required of the manager is knowing how to help by applying relevant skills and procedures.

The present chapter is concerned with counselling in the workplace, and offering help of this type. Its relevance to the manager is twofold. First, managers should be aware of the potential contribution that counselling provision in the workplace can make for both staff and the organization. Second, managers should have a grasp of the basic skills and procedures that form the helping process. We will outline what counselling is, its potential benefits in organizations and present provision in the workplace. Attention will be given to the extent to which the manager can and should counsel. Stages through which the helping process typically moves will be outlined and the qualities and skills of the effective helper presented. For the moment, however, we will return to the topic of problems at work.

EMPLOYEE PROBLEMS AT WORK

Work can inflict problems on workers. But these, unfortunately, do not represent the sum total of troubles that beset employees during work and that can adversely affect job performance. Some are brought in to the workplace from outside. Sources of these[2, 3] include:

- poor health, both physical and mental, and including anxiety and depression
- social relationship difficulties and family concerns
- financial worries
- substance abuse and drug dependency
- housing problems.

The important point is that, regardless of their source, these troubles inevitably find their way into the workplace to produce an insidious and often highly corrosive effect. The comment was made by a manager, having attended a counselling skills training course,[4] that one of its results was an altered vision, by the manager, of staff as 'not just people at work, but [as] human beings living their lives'. They must be accepted 'warts and all'. It is misguided and unreasonable to expect someone caught up in the throes of an acrimonious divorce or nursing a sick relative at home, not to be suffering at work the resulting emotional turmoil or sheer physical exhaustion. Overlooking this fact can often unfairly lead to the misattribution of sloppy performance to incompetence or poor motivation.[5]

The extent to which workers suffer from problems at work is often underestimated. Some of the conclusions reached by reviews of survey research[6, 7] are captured in the statistics that:

- in the UK, approximately 90 million working days are lost per annum as a result of mental illness at a cost of some £3.7 billion
- when asked the real reason for absenteeism, more than 50 per cent of those taking time off point to some form of emotional/personal problem or stress
- 33 per cent of workers feel so vulnerable in their job that they are afraid to take time off when sick
- 20 per cent of the US workforce suffer from problems that affect how they do their job. These include alcohol and drug dependence, conflicts at home and legal and financial complications.

Organizations that turn a blind eye to these statistics do so at their peril. The cost suffered can be measured[6, 7] in:

- *Work performance* – employees preoccupied with personal worries are unlikely to be in a fit state to make carefully thought-through decisions, or produce quality work.
- *Staff morale* – when workers sense that their concerns are ignored by the organization, they begin to feel undervalued. This lowers morale and dissolves commitment and loyalty to the organization.
- *Staff turnover* – staff unhappy at work are likely to seek employment elsewhere, at a high cost to the company. There is a growing appreciation that staff *really are* a company's most valuable asset.
- *Compensation claims* – employees whose job difficulties have gone unheeded are increasingly litigious in their quest for monetary compensation. This may be for an accident suffered while distracted due to emotional or mental turmoil, or for the effects of stress caused by unreasonable working conditions. In either case, it can be deemed that an employer, in ignoring the worker's plight, was in breach of a duty of care to that individual. The recent upsurge in US work-related stress claims may set a trend for the UK, verifying the prediction that 'Legal action against employers is expected to replace uncomplaining pill-popping as the remedy for occupational stress'.[8]
- *Corporate image* – gaining the reputation of an uncaring, Dickensian exploiter of a workforce forced to function in intolerable conditions of abject misery, will do little for the corporate image of any organization.
- *Profit* – the effects of all the above consequences are reflected in high rates of staff absenteeism and declining company performance.

WHAT IS COUNSELLING AT WORK?

The term 'counselling' has been used loosely in the workplace to refer to activities ranging from disciplining a member of staff, through offering advice, to providing emotional support. Many managers seem to regard it as simply akin to advising, guiding or instructing.[9] In its purest form in professional counselling circles, however, the essence of the practice takes on a more distinct hue. According to the British Association of Counselling (BAC):[10] 'Counselling includes work with individuals and with relationships which may be developmental, crisis support, psychotherapeutic, guiding or problem solving ... The task of counselling is to give the "client" an opportunity to explore, discover, and clarify ways of living more satisfyingly and resourcefully.'

There is no good reason, in principle, to prevent this definition of counselling being applied to the workplace. Indeed some even argue for a broader vision, which includes counselling not only as a mechanism for promoting the self-actualization of the individual worker, but as an agent of organizational change.[7] In practice, though, counselling at work is thought of much more circumspectly as:

- short term
- problem/crisis centred and work focused (e.g. stress)
- geared to restoring employee effectiveness and efficiency.[11]

Thought of narrowly in this way, as centring on problem management, counselling has been described as, 'helping someone to explore a problem, clarify conflicting issues and discover alternative ways of dealing with it, so that they can decide what to do about it; that is, helping people to help themselves'.[12] The process is underpinned by a set of values reflected in the following precepts:

- listen, for the most part, rather than tell
- always have the employee's best interests at heart
- help staff to clarify their thinking and understanding of the issues surrounding their problems rather than impose your constructions of those problems on them
- assist individuals to work through their difficulties to a resolution rather than attempt to solve their problems for them
- respect people's rights to their own values, judgements and decisions as to what is best for them
- accept that staff, despite their possible confusion or emotional turmoil at present, know much more about themselves and the circumstances of their predicament than the manager does
- acknowledge that managers will often not have ready or easy answers to the difficulties brought to them

- act to strengthen the autonomy and independence of the other
- recognize that this type of involvement, if poorly handled, can hinder rather than help
- be constantly mindful of the possible need to refer the individual to someone with greater expertise.

INCIDENCE AND EFFECTS OF COUNSELLING AT WORK

Counselling in the workplace is not a new phenomenon. It can be traced back in the UK to the late nineteenth century when large family-owned companies such as Rowntree, inspired by humanitarian values, introduced a workers' welfare service. Some time later, several US firms introduced schemes designed to reduce the effects of alcohol abuse amongst the workforce on productivity. In time, such provision evolved into Employee Assistance Programmes (EAPs) which are now one of the main providers of counselling for employees, particularly in the USA. It is estimated that there the number of EAPs has grown from about 50 programmes in 1950 to over 5 000 in the 1990s.[6] Most of the *Fortune 500* companies in the USA now offer a counselling service for employees.[13]

In the UK, the picture is somewhat different. In a survey by the Independent Counselling and Advisory Services[14] in 1993, only 4 per cent of the 1 500 companies with more than 100 employees, which were sampled, offered an EAP. However, counselling provision by other means was quite common:

- 85 per cent provided stress counselling
- 30 per cent provided retirement counselling
- 24 per cent provided redundancy counselling.

The effects of counselling interventions in the workplace have been largely positive:[6, 7, 11, 13]

- McDonnell Douglas estimated a total saving of some $5.1 million from their EAP over the four-year period of its evaluation.
- General Motors calculated that it returned $67 for every dollar invested in its EAP.
- The US Department of Health and Human Services reported that its EAP returned $7.1 per dollar of investment.
- Johnston and Johnston, in the UK, found its rate of absenteeism reduced by 41 per cent with savings of almost £250 000, attributable to its EAP over the first three years.
- The Post Office reported a 66 per cent reduction in days lost through absenteeism during a three-year period following the introduction of a stress counselling programme, with savings of about £5.7 for every £1 spent.

- A survey of UK workplace counselling programmes commissioned by the Health and Safety Executive and carried out by the Manchester School of Management, found a reduction in absenteeism. Workers also reported significant improvements in mental and physical health following counselling.

More general effects of workplace counselling programmes are given in Key point 11.1.

Key point 11.1   Potential benefits of counselling in the workplace

For the employee

- Less stress.
- Improved morale.
- Enhanced job satisfaction.
- Increased effectiveness and efficiency.
- Greater sense of being valued by the company.
- Fewer accidents.

For the employer

- Lower absenteeism rates.
- Reduced staff turnover.
- Less litigation.
- Better internal relations.
- Improved image for both internal and external customers.
- Better quality work.
- Increased profits.

WHO SHOULD COUNSEL THE WORKFORCE? THE ROLE OF THE MANAGER

Counselling is either provided internally by companies or is bought in from external agencies. It is really only the former arrangement that concerns us here since it brings into sharper focus issues to do with the direct helping role of managers. If counselling is offered in-house, should it be provided by someone with professional levels of training and in a specialized role, or become a sub-role of the manager? Arguments for both options can be found. Robert de Board[15] declared that 'It is my belief that the ability to counsel and to establish a counselling relationship is now a necessary addition to the managerial role ...'. On the other hand, ethical dilemmas surrounding the line manager in counselling mode have been strongly voiced.

One of the preconditions of the counselling relationship, as decreed by the BAC,[16] is that the counsellor be impartial, having no personal interest in any one particular outcome to the client's problem, other than what is believed to be best for the client. It has been vehemently argued that the line manager is unavoidably compromised in this respect by the other demands of the managerial role.[17] Indeed, in the USA there is legislation preventing managers engaging in formal counselling relationships with those whom they manage.[7]

There are clearly unavoidable difficulties surrounding the concept of line managers as counsellors. Formal counselling is a highly specialized activity to be left to those with special training. That said, there is widespread support for managers:[7, 17, 18]

- being familiar with the counselling process
- possessing at least basic helping skills
- being able to use these skills in a counselling-like way
- recognizing problems amongst staff that could benefit from such help
- knowing when and where to refer employees for more specialized assistance.

QUALITIES OF HELPERS

In order to deal satisfactorily with staff experiencing problems, the manager must be able to draw on certain personal qualities which should permeate the helping relationship. The three most important of these are associated with the views of Carl Rogers, one of the twentieth century's most influential figures in the counselling field. He labelled them empathy, genuineness and unconditional positive regard, and believed that they were the necessary ingredients of a successful counselling encounter.[19]

EMPATHY

This is commonly regarded as one of the most important qualities that a helper can display. Indeed, it is also an ingredient of effective communication, more generally.[20] 'Empathy' derives from the ancient Greek word 'empathea' meaning affection and passion with an attribute of suffering. It should not be confused with sympathy. Someone who empathizes with another makes an effort to enter the world of that person, to see things from that person's point of view: to look through that person's eyes. It is also important that the other person appreciates the fact they are being engaged with at this level of understanding.

Empathy then has three main elements:[21, 22]

- *Sensing and understanding.* The manager must be sensitive enough to accurately tap into the employee's concerns and be able fully to appreciate them from that person's point of view.
- *Feeling.* Empathy has also a 'feelings' component. It is not enough to merely be *au fait* with 'the facts of the case' in a detached, intellectual way. The manager must be constantly aware of the emotional experiences that the employee is undergoing: feeling *with* the other person is what counts, without losing your own sense of identity in the process.
- *Communicating.* Unless the other is made aware that they are being empathized with, empathizing is a futile exercise. The manager must, in what is said and done both verbally and non-verbally, *convey* empathy to the person seeking help. As stated by Carl Rogers, empathy 'includes communicating your sensing of his world as you look with fresh and unfrightened eyes at elements of which the individual is fearful. It means frequently checking with him as to the accuracy of your sensings, and being guided by the responses you receive'.[23]

Empathy, then, is being alongside people requiring help as they work through their difficulty, trying to appreciate the world from their perspective, sensing how this emotionally affects them and letting them know that this is happening. With this in mind turn to Exercise 11.1 and try to identify the empathic responses from among the alternatives on offer.

Behavioural manifestations of empathy include:[24]

- good eye contact
- close seating distance
- a forward-leaning posture
- the appropriate use of touch
- concerned facial expressions
- reflecting feeling (statements that capture and reflect back the emotional message just communicated by the other. They will be discussed in greater depth later in the chapter.)
- appropriate use of self-disclosure. (In self-disclosing, the helper discloses personal detail which resonates with that revealed by the other. This will be discussed more fully later in the chapter.)

Exercise 11.1 Responding empathically

Bill, a line manager in a manufacturing company which has recently undergone significant structural changes, is offloading some of his troubles at work over a drink with an old friend, Bob. This is a snippet of the conversation:

> *Bill*: It has reached the stage where I simply detest the thought of having to go to work in the morning. I used to really enjoy my work there, but since the take-over I seem to spend all my time trying to crawl out from under a mountain of paper. I seldom have time now to meet with the production staff on the shopfloor, the way I used to. The bloody phone goes non-stop. I'm there late most nights to try to clear my desk because if not the next day is just impossible ...

Beneath are a number of possible ways that Bob could respond to this disclosure. Pick those which you feel convey a strong sense of empathy.

- Why don't you employ some extra secretarial support?
- You're tired and frustrated because more and more paperwork is being piled on to the point where you can hardly cope while you don't have time to do those things that you feel really matter in the job.
- Sorry to hear that the old job has taken a turn for the worse, Bill!
- You never really could prioritize your commitments and now it's causing all sorts of stress.
- Come on, let me cheer you up. Have you heard the one about ...
- You mustn't just pack it in because things are becoming a bit rough.
- Don't feel too upset. These things have a way of sorting themselves out.
- I know exactly how you feel. Our place is a madhouse – I never see the day for paper, phone calls, meetings ...

If you turn to the end of the chapter you can compare your assessment with ours.

GENUINENESS

The helper should be 'real' in the helping relationship: a sincere, authentic person, not someone pretending to be who or what he or she is not, or merely playing a role.[24, 25] Being naturally oneself means being what you appear to be. Since the intention is to encourage others to enter into a relationship of trust in which they are expected and encouraged to be open and honest, the helper must be no less so. Being prepared to self-disclose, as we shall see in the next section, is a way for the manager to manifest genuineness. (See Key point 11.2.)

Key point 11.2   Being genuine

Genuineness requires managers to:

- be themselves rather than taking refuge behind a role or some such mask
- have sufficient self-knowledge to ensure than there is no lack of consistency between feelings held, experienced and expressed
- be spontaneous rather than merely mouthing the empty words of a well-rehearsed routine
- remain open and receptive to what staff have to say and avoid becoming defensive, even if under attack from them
- ensure consistency between their thoughts, feelings and actions
- be prepared to share feelings and life experiences if this is thought to be appropriate.

UNCONDITIONAL POSITIVE REGARD

This involves being receptive to, and accepting of, other people regardless of who they are or the nature of their difficulties. It has to do with recognizing and responding to the inalienable 'personhood', the spark of human dignity, at the core of each of us. There are three components to this quality:[22]

1. *Experiencing a warm, caring but non-possessive acceptance of the other.* Indeed Carl Rogers went further, describing it as a 'prizing' of others, not because of *who* or *what* they are, but rather *that* they are. It is the celebration of a shared humanity. While valuing another in this way, though, there should be no attempt to take away their independence or diminish their sense of autonomy: no desire to 'take them over'. This is what is meant by acceptance being 'non-possessive'.
2. *Constancy of acceptance.* This entails that the individual seeking help must be accepted without 'ifs', 'buts' or 'maybes'. This is where the *unconditionality* of positive regard comes into play. It implies no judgement of that person by external standards: no approval or disapproval.
3. *Respect.* People must be respected as unique autonomous individuals with the right to decide how to live their lives. Respect entails that what they have to say is worth listening to and that they deserve courtesy and consideration.

CONCRETENESS

Those in trouble seldom are able to sit down to rationally and logically work through the details of their predicament. If they were, they could probably reach an acceptable solution on their own. Rather, their thinking is often clouded by emotion so that what they say becomes confused, vague and sometimes contradictory. Feelings themselves are notoriously difficult to articulate. Much of their disclosure is obscure, abstract and imprecise. In working towards understanding and beginning to tease out ways of assisting in a possible resolution of a problem, it is helpful if the manager can introduce a level of precision and specificity in discussing information and making decisions.[26]

FLEXIBILITY

Difficulties that perplex people are seldom neatly packaged, nor do they have ready-made solutions. While we will come on to consider the stages through which the helping process can move, that route is rarely clear cut. It is important to feel comfortable accommodating other people's agendas, being prepared to move at the pace they dictate, dealing with the issues that they raise when they raise them.

SENSITIVITY AND SELF-KNOWLEDGE

Managers who are good helpers possess considerable awareness both of self and of others. Unless you have some insight into your own needs, values, motives, fears, abilities, attitudes and biases, you probably will not be able to assist others to strike the match that will illuminate theirs.[27] In addition to awareness of self, self-acceptance is an important requirement. This does not rule out change through growth and self-development, of course, but unless managers feel positive about themselves, it is unlikely that they will be accepting of others either.

DISCRETION

The importance of trust at the basis of the helping relationship has already been mentioned. Part of this trust lies in having confidence in the helper not to disclose information given in confidence.[28]

HELPING SKILLS

A range of skills involved in helping have been identified.[18, 25, 26, 29] Regardless of whether or not managers should contemplate personal involvement in a helping relationship through playing a formal counsellor role, it is advocated that they should be able to draw on these skills.[17, 18] Indeed, many have a wider applicability beyond the narrow helping context. The skills which will be considered here are: active listening, reflecting feeling, paraphrasing, open questioning, and self-disclosure.

ACTIVE LISTENING

Active listening requires considerable sensitivity, but does not just involve hearing and seeing. It is much more demanding than that. It is about being as fully tuned in as possible to the totality of the message being delivered, and in turn communicating back that level of comprehension. Listening in this concerted way has been described as listening with a 'third ear'.

Two components are therefore involved:

1. Tuning in to and picking up the deep meaning and significance for the other of what has been conveyed.
2. Making that person feel accurately understood.

Both of these components will now be briefly elaborated.

Tuning in

Sensing what the employee is struggling to get across, or on occasion even actively trying to avoid disclosing, is a challenging task. It requires:

- Listening carefully to what is being said and asking oneself, 'What does it mean from this other person's point of view, to have said this?' 'What is its significance at this time, at this juncture in the conversation?' 'Has this issue been mentioned before?' 'Does it fit into a theme or does it seem, on the other hand, to have "come from nowhere, out of the blue"?'.
- Being sensitive to *how* what is said, is said. Strong emotional cues can be picked up through paralanguage, in the tone of voice, voice inflection, speed of speech and voice quality.
- Observing other bodily cues accompanying the utterance. Important emotional and attitudinal information can be revealed in this manner. Does the body language signal discomfort or unease with the topic? Does it complement or contradict what is being said?
- Being mindful of what is *not* being said. Is there significance in the fact that the employee has not mentioned something that you would have expected under the circumstances? Could this be due to a bad experience with that which is being avoided, or does it indicate a lack of trust and confidence in the relationship with you?

Conveying understanding

This is where the active bit of 'active listening' comes in. The manager may pick up more than is appropriate to communicate at that particular point. The employee may not yet be comfortable dealing with those issues at that depth of consideration. That apart, it is important that the manager conveys back to the staff member a sense of being listened to, a commitment to grasp as firmly as possible what is problematic for that individual and a resolve to work with the person to, hopefully, achieve new insights for both. What is important is not that helpers must be unerringly accurate in what they pick up during the interview, but that they are dedicated to getting it right and that this commitment is appreciated by the other.

Active listening can be conveyed both verbally and non-verbally, by the counsellor.[30] Verbal components are outlined in Key point 11.3 and non-verbal components in Key point 11.4.

Key point 11.3   Verbal components of active listening

These include:

- *Verbal encouragers.* These are brief expressions like 'Right', 'Yes' or 'I see', together with vocalizations such as 'Uh-huh' or 'Ah-hah' that provide feedback, conveying attention and understanding. They encourage the speaker to continue. Listen to any telephone conversation and you will pick them up. Remove verbal encouragers and the quality of the conversation inevitably suffers.
- *Verbal following.* Good listeners conversationally follow the speaker rather than attempt to hijack the discussion. They avoid cutting across the speaker's line of talk by introducing new topics. Rather, in responding, they follow on in a coherent fashion from what has just been said, thereby making it possible for the speaker to extend the previous point and perpetuate the line of conversation.
- *Reference to past statements*. Bringing in some point made earlier in this or a previous conversation, is a very palpable way of demonstrating that effective listening is going on.
- *Linguistic matching.* It was pointed out in Chapter 2 that non-verbally matching the other in posture, gestures and such like, is a way of establishing rapport. Likewise using similar forms of expression as the speaker can create a sense of being listened to and engaged with.
- *Summarizing.* Being able to neatly and succinctly summarize the main points covered by the speaker in a segment of the conversation, or in a more comprehensive way at the end, is a further tangible demonstration of effective listening.

Key point 11.4   Non-verbal components of active listening

These include:

- *Mirroring the facial expressions of the speaker.* This suggests that feeling states are being recognized and empathised with.
- *Direct eye contact.* Averted gaze often indicates a lack of interest and involvement with others and what they have to say.
- *Appropriate paralanguage.* As with other aspects of non-verbal communication, mirroring the paralanguage of speakers in tone of voice and speed of speech is a way of showing engagement with them and their concerns.
- *Head nods.* These signal attention, interest and agreement and as such are examples of non-verbal encouragers, facilitating speakers to continue with their line of conversation.
- *Attentive posture.* A relaxed, open, and forward-leaning posture is commonly regarded as indicative of deep involvement with a conversational partner.

SELF-DISCLOSURE

In order to help others gain a full appreciation of what is troubling them, it is necessary to encourage them to openly and honestly disclose personal details about their situation and circumstances. Self-disclosure is also a way for helpers to constructively share some of their own experiences. In this sense, self-disclosure can be thought of as the act of verbally and/or non-verbally communicating to others some dimension of personal information. Thus, self-disclosure can be non-verbal, given that it is possible either to hide feelings such as happiness, sadness and anger or to express them through the use of facial expressions, gestures and so on. The verbal component of this skill is very important since this aspect is less prone to misinterpretation, whereas we can be mistaken in our judgements about the non-verbal behaviour of others.[30]

A knowledge, and skilled use of self-disclosure is important for managers for two main reasons:

1. They should be aware of the factors which encourage others to fully present, and openly express, their concerns.

2. They need to be sensitive to situations in which it is apt for them to self-disclose to those seeking help.

Elements of self-disclosure

There are three features which should be considered when evaluating the effectiveness of this technique:

1. *Informativeness*. This relates to the amount (total number) of disclosures made and to their depth (or intimacy). Too much disclosing by the manager should definitely be avoided as it may shift the focus from the needs of the employee to those of the manager. The depth of self-disclosure offered is also important. It is common for people to reveal themselves in greater depth as relationships develop.
2. *Appropriateness*. Manager self-disclosures that are said merely for some sort of self-serving effect are inexcusable.[25] Self-disclosures are most frequently used between people of equal status, followed by disclosures from low-status to high-status individuals. The least frequent usage is from those in high-status to others in low-status positions. This may make it more difficult for a manager to self-disclose, at any more than a superficial level, to a junior member of staff. That said, the truly helping relationship is one where differences in status are not played up.
3. *Accessibility*. Certain individuals are more inhibited than others when presenting personal information. This may be due to:
    a) personality differences (e.g. extroverts disclose more than introverts)
    b) upbringing (i.e. children may be taught not to reveal too much of their private business)
    c) culture (some cultures encourage greater disclosure than others).

People usually find it more awkward discussing embarrassing, intimate problems. In addition to personal characteristics of the people and information content concerned, other factors that shape the likelihood and appropriateness of self-disclosure relate to the nature of their relationship and the particular situation in which they find themselves.[30]

Effects of self-disclosure

Self-disclosure serves a number of important functions in the helping setting, including to:

- Open conversations. ('Hello. I am the manager and I will introduce you to ...')
- Encourage reciprocation. Self-disclosure by one interactor often leads to a similar response by the other.

- Provide reassurance. Knowing that the helper has experienced and overcome similar difficulties can be immensely reassuring.
- Share common experiences. It demonstrates that you are 'on the same wavelength', and can make the other feel empathized with.
- Express concern. ('I am really worried about you and I want to help.')
- Facilitate self-expression. It can frequently be a relief just to be allowed to talk things through. There is truth in the adage that 'a problem shared is a problem halved'.
- Develop relationships. Self-disclosure plays a significant role in the development and maintenance of relationships.

Guidelines for using self-disclosure

A number of recommendations to increase the effectiveness of the use of this technique in the helping process have been advanced.[25] Self-disclosures should:

- Be appropriate. The guideline here is, does it assist people to explore and understand their problems and find a way to manage them successfully?
- Be selective and focused. The revealed experience or feeling should resonate in harmony with that of the other, be offered for a specific purpose and with a particular effect in mind. A long self-indulgent ramble down memory lane will only serve to abandon that person until your return.
- Not burden the individual being helped. Managers should be careful when disclosing their own feelings and concerns. These may merely impose further pressure on those seeking help who are already struggling to cope with their own difficulties.
- Be flexible. Not everyone will expect managers to self-disclose, want them to do so or benefit from the experience.

REFLECTING

Reflective statements depend on careful listening and are a further means of listening actively. They can be thought of as statements, in the manager's own words, that encapsulate and re-present the message conveyed in what the employee has just said. In doing so, they are a way of showing empathy.[31] Additional functions can be found in Key point 11.5.

Key point 11.5   Functions of reflections

Reflections are a means of:

- demonstrating an interest in and involvement with the employee
- indicating close attention to what is being communicated
- showing that the manager is trying to understand fully the employee and what the latter is saying
- checking the manager's perceptions and ensuring accuracy of understanding
- facilitating the employee's comprehension of the issues involved and clarity of thinking on those matters
- bringing attention to particular aspects and encouraging further exploration
- communicating a deep concern for that which the employee considers important
- placing the major emphasis upon the employee rather than the manager in the situation
- indicating that it is acceptable for the employee to have and express feelings in the situation and to facilitate their expression
- helping the employee to 'own' feelings
- enabling the employee to realize that feelings can be an important cause of behaviour
- helping the employee to scrutinize underlying reasons and motives for feelings and actions.[30]

Reflections can either address the factual content of what the employee has just said, in which case they are called paraphrases, or focus on the feelings conveyed in the form of reflections of feeling.

Paraphrases

In paraphrasing the other's preceding statement, managers should:

- use their own words rather than simply repeat, parrot fashion, the other's statement
- precis the message in what was said rather than attempting to cover everything
- include the factual content, the thoughts, ideas and descriptions given, rather than the emotional melody behind the words.

To illustrate how this could work, let us take the example of a conscientious supervisor under stress through trying to be everywhere at once, making sure that everything and everyone is closely and constantly monitored.

> *Supervisor*: I know that some of the other supervisors are inclined to be slack, but that is not my way. You need to be about the floor and be seen to be about all the time. I seldom take a break, apart from lunch. I'm on my feet constantly, making sure things are being done as they should be. But is it appreciated? No way! I know that the staff talk about me behind my back.

A suitable paraphrase of this could be:

> *Manager*: You constantly check what is happening on your floor, even to the extent of missing breaks, but the staff don't value your efforts.

Reflections of feeling

The difference here is that feelings hinted at, rather than factual content, are picked up and mirrored back. Returning to the above example, the manager could have reflected the affective part of the message as follows:

> *Manager*: You feel frustrated, despondent and devalued because all your hard work is rejected by the staff.

Responding in this way reveals that the emotional impact of the supervisor's experience has been recognized. The supervisor is thereby encouraged to continue exploring feeling states surrounding the problem.

Reflections can, of course, embrace elements of fact *and* feeling, if the helper senses that it is important for the other to consider both together.

Guidelines for using reflective statements include:

- Use your own words.
- Do not go beyond the information just received by including your own interpretations of it.
- Be concise – remember it is only the core message that you are trying to catch and reflect.
- Be specific, it usually aids understanding.
- Be accurate.
- Do not overuse reflections – doing so may restrict the exploration of issues.
- Keep to the immediate message received, although more wide-ranging summaries of what has been communicated can also be useful.

OPEN QUESTIONING

The excessive use of questions of any type is sometimes frowned on in counselling circles because it is felt that questioning has to do with helpers pursuing their own agendas, rather than allowing people with problems to tell their stories as they see fit. However, open questioning in particular can be a beneficial tool. Open questions are ones that place few restrictions on how they should be responded to. In the extreme, they merely offer a topic for comment: for example, 'What are your views on work, generally?'

Open questions tend to:

- Be broad in nature.
- Leave the answer given entirely up to the respondent.
- Encourage the other to talk at length.
- Be particularly helpful in getting at more than just limited pieces of factual information. As such they are especially facilitative in exploring opinions, emotions and attitudes.
- Impose minimal control on the interaction.

Closed questions, by way of contrast, are better at getting at limited pieces of factual detail while the questioner retains firm control over the proceedings. Examples of open and closed versions of questions are given in Key point 11.6.

STAGES OF THE HELPING PROCESS

Helping typically evolves through processes of initial engagement with employees seeking help, exploring and fully understanding their problems, facilitating them in reaching decisions as to what best to do about managing these difficulties, to finally helping them firm up on, and implement, strategies to achieve these goals. We can think of four main phases involved: attending, exploring, understanding and action.

ATTENDING

At the outset, careful attention must be paid to the employee by demonstrating an active listening style. In particular, the manner in which the interaction is opened will have an important bearing on how that person responds. If the manager conveys the impression of having the time, disposition and energy to devote to it, the employee is more likely to be prepared to risk entering into a supportive relationship.

Since troubled individuals frequently open the discussion with a 'presenting' problem, and will often only reveal their real concerns when encouraged to do so later, the manager needs to be aware of verbal and non-verbal cues which may indicate a desire for a deeper level of involvement.

Furthermore, the portrayal of warmth, acceptance and respect which involves communicating a liking for the other person and an indication of being willing to engage fully, is necessary to the establishment of a good rapport conducive to a helping encounter. The use of verbal and non-verbal encouragers communicates warmth.

Key point 11.6 Closed and open questioning

'Were you delighted when you discovered that you would be fronting the whole restructuring operation from the production end?' (*Closed question*)

'How did you feel when you discovered that you would be fronting the whole restructuring operation from the production end?' (*Open question*)

'Did the fibre get caught in the bearing just before the machine jammed?' (*Closed question*)

'Could you take me through what exactly happened just before the machine jammed?' (*Open question*)

'Do you have a mortgage, personal loan, or overdraft at the moment?' (*Closed question*)

'What are your other financial commitments at the moment?' (*Open question*)

'Are you and Rebecca getting on any better than you were when we last spoke?' (*Closed question*)

'How have things been with you and Rebecca since we last spoke?' (*Open question*)

'Do you think that you won't get the job because of your age?' (*Closed question*)

'What makes you think that the job won't be offered to you?' (*Open question*)

EXPLORING

Following the initial relationship-development phase, the next step is to attempt to gain a full and accurate understanding of the member of staff's situation. This necessitates allowing freedom to talk, with as few restrictions as possible imposed by the manager. One way this can be achieved is through the use of reflections which, to a large extent, permit the employee to control the flow of the discussion.

Where questions are used, these should be open rather than closed, again placing minimum restrictions on the respondent. Another technique which is useful at the exploration stage is the use of spaced reviews. By employing this type of intermittent summary, the manager can ensure that both parties are in agreement about the information presented, before moving on to explore further issues at greater depth.

UNDERSTANDING

Before progressing to the final stage, make sure that both parties are fully appreciative of issues, thoughts and feelings raised during the exploratory phase. The manager should demonstrate empathy. Self-disclosure can also be introduced. This can either be about experiences which the manager has had, or has dealt with, which are similar to those being described by the employee, or it can involve commenting on how the latter's situation is viewed. The employee also needs to feel fully accepted and the manager therefore must visibly convey positive regard and respect. The manager must be accepted as genuine and without façades, and not simply playing a role. There should ideally be consistency between how the manager feels about and relates to the employee.

Two important techniques that come into play at this stage are reframing and normalizing.[32]

Reframing

Here the manager metaphorically puts a new frame round the picture being presented by the other so that it can be viewed in a different way – one which offers possibilities for constructive action. This is particularly important where others get fixed into a particular viewpoint, seeing the world from a position of depression, anxiety or low self-esteem. Let us go back to the earlier example of the conscientious supervisor over-stressed trying to be everywhere at once, making sure that everything and everyone is closely and constantly supervised:

> *Supervisor*: I know that some of the other supervisors are inclined to be slack, but that is not my way. You need to be about the floor and be seen to be about all the time. I seldom take a break, apart from lunch. I'm on my feet constantly, making sure things are being done as they should be. But is it appreciated? No way! I know that the staff talk about me behind my back.

The manager could reframe this as follows:

> *Manager*: Could it be that you come across to your section, not as conscientious and hard-working, but perhaps as having little trust or confidence in them, because they see you as always checking up?

Note how in responding in this way, the manager moves outside the supervisor's frame. However, in reframing, the manager must not deny the supervisor's point of view but merely offer an alternative for consideration. It therefore needs to be presented in a sensitive and tentative fashion.

Normalizing

The purpose is to normalize the other's emotional state by giving an assurance that it is not uncommon or inexplicable, under the circumstances. This is useful in response to questions such as: 'Am I going crazy?' 'How could I feel like this?' 'Is it only me?' For example, those who have been recently bereaved may experience a mix of feelings, including anger, depression, guilt and despair. It can be made clear that this is part of a normal grief reaction, without diminishing the personal pain involved. Learning that one's emotions are experienced by others in similar circumstances can serve to reduce anxiety. At the same time, such feelings should not be denied and the need for them to be worked through should be recognized.

ACTION

By this stage, the problem should have been fully explored, and a thorough understanding of it achieved, placing the employee in a position to consider the final phase of taking action to alleviate it. The employee should be the decision-maker, knowing what needs to be achieved and the steps which have to be taken to do so, with the manager acting in a supportive role. A range of possible ways to achieve the goal can be formulated and the one most likely to succeed selected. The employee should also be aware of those factors which will both facilitate (benefits) or hinder (barriers) goal realization. Success usually occurs where the benefits can be engineered to clearly outweigh the barriers. Action may also include educating the employee to increase resources to bring about the chosen goal. Teaching and training can therefore be a part of the helping process at this stage. A final aspect of the action stage may necessitate referring the person elsewhere for specialist advice and guidance.

SUMMARY

Employees experience problems and difficulties that can have an adverse effect not only on the quality of their work but on their lives. Some of these difficulties are caused by work, others have to do with personal matters, while yet more have family, social or financial concerns at their root. Nevertheless, none are left at the door as the worker enters the workplace each day.

Counselling at work is not a new provision, but is becoming much more common. Research carried out, especially in the USA, attests to its benefits for both the company and the individual member of staff. Cost-benefit analyses show that generally monies invested pay a very acceptable dividend. The precise role of the manager in a counselling service is a more contentious issue, however. Some hold that counselling should be an additional sub-role of the manager: others that it is ethically unacceptable for a line manager to contemplate entering into a true counselling relationship with an employee. All are in agreement, nevertheless, that it is important for managers to be familiar with the helping process and to possess some of the core skills involved.

People who are able helpers tend to possess qualities of empathy, genuineness, warmth, acceptance, respect, concreteness, discretion, flexibility, sensitivity and self-knowledge. Basic skills and techniques through which these qualities are displayed include active listening, reflecting feeling, paraphrasing, open questioning and self-disclosure.

Answers to Exercise 11.1

- Why don't you employ some extra secretarial support?

(*This response offers* ADVICE *and as such reflects Bob's, rather than Bill's frame of reference.*)

- You're tired and frustrated because more and more paperwork is being piled on to the point where you can hardly cope while you don't have time to do those things that you feel really matter in the job.

(*This is an* EMPATHIC *response. It attempts to convey an understanding to the experiences of the job that Bill has disclosed from within his frame of reference.*)

- Sorry to hear that the old job has taken a turn for the worse, Bill!

(*This is a* SYMPATHETIC *response. It conveys how Bob feels about Bill's predicament.*)

- You never really could prioritize your commitments and now it's causing all sorts of stress.

(*This is an* INTERPRETATIVE *response in that it offers an explanation of the problem as Bob sees it.*)

Answers to Exercise 11.1 *continued overleaf*

Answers to Exercise 11.1 (Cont'd)

- Come on, let me cheer you up. Have you heard the one about ...

(*This is a* BLOCKING *response. Although it may be intended to chivvy Bill along and lift his spirits, it has the effect of blocking further consideration of the topic. It can also be perceived as dismissing or trivializing the problem.*)

- You mustn't just pack it in because things are becoming a bit rough.

(*This is a* JUDGEMENTAL *response in which Bob is imposing his values upon Bill and telling him what he ought and ought not to do.*)

- Don't be too upset. These things have a way of sorting themselves out.

(*This is an attempt at* REASSURANCE. *However, genuine problems need solutions, not glib reassurances.*)

- I know exactly how you feel. Our place is a madhouse – I never see the day for paper, phone calls, meetings ...

(*This is a* ME TOO *response which takes the focus back to Bill. It can be helpful at times to know that others are under similar pressure, but such a reaction often undermines the person seeking help.*)

Some of these other responses may be helpful depending upon circumstances, but only the second one is properly empathic.

---

12 'Our most important asset': selecting people

Scene 1

Manager enters interview room ahead of applicant, while reading her application form. Her handwriting, particularly her 'Is', is illegible:

Manager: 'I see you have very funny Is.'

Manager sits down, faces applicant and discovers that she has a squint.

Scene 2

Manager makes long speech in favour of safety in the workplace, describes recent legislation (in detail), and then asks applicant: 'So, would you say that safety in the workplace is important?'

Interviewee: 'Yes.'

The above stories, both derived from interviews in which we have been involved, show some of the traps into which we commonly fall when conducting selection interviews. Yet, even with its shortfalls, the interview remains the most widely used selection tool, despite many years of research which has questioned its validity as an instrument capable of predicting job performance. A survey of 220 UK organizations by Reed Accountancy Personnel found that 80 per cent regarded interviews as the most important part of their recruitment process, while 22 per cent said that they were a more important factor when picking someone to fill a post than they would have thought three years earlier.[1] The problem with this is that most of us exaggerate our own competence as interviewers, imagine that we have a better insight into how personality can be assessed than most other people and believe, quite wrongly, that our ability to predict how well people will do improves with time and experience.[2]

As countless studies have demonstrated, future performance is best predicted from past performance, aptitude tests or other information which can be quantified into statistical models, than from short face-to-face and unstructured interviews.[3] This overcomes the problems caused by our ability to see the defects of others extremely well, but our own as a distant blur. The tenacity of such self-serving biases, in the face of the evidence, is simply explained:[2]

- *People tend to look for positive feedback on decisions which they have made.* There is no merit attached to being acclaimed as an inexpert interviewer. We therefore look for evidence that most of our appointment decisions have worked, and ignore or belittle those instances where this is contradicted. We also trumpet our successes to colleagues, while suppressing any suspicion that such successes were exceptional. This is termed 'selective recall'.

- *Instances where are our judgement is correct tend to be vividly remembered.* The rarer such judgements are the more vivid our recollections of them are likely to be. As the number of 'rare' instances accumulates during our career they become embellished in the telling. The process is similar to what happens when fishermen exchange tales about 'the one that got away'. The size of the fish grows in proportion to the number of times the story is told. This is called 'selective interpretation'.

- *It is often difficult for managers to obtain honest feedback from subordinates on decisions which they make.* Research shows[4] that ingratiation is the most commonly deployed tool of impression management, and that the greater the status differential between two people the more likely it is to be used by the junior partner in the interaction. Ingratiation involves pumping up the ego of the message recipient with the hot air of flattery. Critical feedback is therefore limited. In this context, staff rarely tell managers when hiring decisions are wrong.

- Attribution theory (discussed in Chapter 13) suggests that perception is distorted by the *fundamental attribution error.* In interview terms, this means that desirable outcomes are attributed to oneself, and undesirable ones to the situation. Thus, an interviewer reasons that 'I appointed Joe and he is excellent. This shows what good interviewer I am.' If the same interviewer appointed someone who fails, the likely reasoning will be: 'Fred didn't work out – it's a pity that he was so lazy, and that Department needs a review anyway.' We like to claim the credit for success, but put the blame for failure on someone else's shoulders. Perception is distorted by a powerful self-serving bias.

The purpose of this chapter is to look critically at selection interviews, bypassing these four cul-de-sacs. The selective hiring of new personnel has been identified as one of the seven main characteristics of high-performing organizations, and typically absorbs an enormous amount of senior management time.[5] A common mantra, chanted in some management circles, is that 'there are no bad soldiers – only bad generals'. We disagree. Many people are capable of making an outstanding contribution to industry, science, politics or the arts. However, in the event of a compulsory career change, they would make appalling soldiers, even if led by Alexander the Great. They should be weeded out before combat commences, and found a more appropriate niche for their talents. The role of selection is to put the right person in the right place at the right time for the right job.

This chapter explores the most common interview errors found in the selection process. In particular, a promising new field of research into selection interviewing is outlined, concentrating on what is known as 'behaviour description interviewing' (BDI). The evidence suggests that this relatively new approach is an enormous improvement on the unstructured methods of the past. The main stages involved in such interviews are outlined, and the skills which managers need in order to improve their effectiveness in them are addressed. We will also look at how such insights can help managers improve their effectiveness in their frequent role as interviewees.

THE PROCESS OF SELECTION INTERVIEWS

In general, selection interviews involve an encounter between a panel of interviewers and a solitary interviewee, during which questions will be asked to determine whether the personality, skills and experience of the interviewee means they are the best applicant for a particular job. Common issues raised during interviews include the following:[6]

1. Are candidates' qualifications relevant, adequate and genuine?
2. Is their alleged experience relevant and real?
3. Can they motivate people?
4. What have they improved (changed, prevented, stopped, started) in their previous jobs?
5. Do they communicate enough?
6. Do they communicate well in writing?
7. Are they assertive (but neither submissive nor aggressive)?
8. Do they have the ability to succeed in this organization?
9. What sort of personality do they have, and do I like it?

It is difficult to probe any of these issues, let alone all of them. As a result, many interviews are directionless, omit what is important, concentrate on the inconsequential and climax in poor decisions. In effect, we do the wrong thing, but we do it very carefully. A number of important biases have been identified in interviewer behaviour, which further confound the selection process. Some of the most important are discussed below:[7]

THE 'SIMILAR TO ME' EFFECT

Candidates with similar biographical backgrounds, attitudes and perceived personalities to the interviewer are rated more favourably than candidates who are in some way different. This leads to what is known as 'clone recruitment', in which only people identical to the interviewer have a chance of employment. There are two main problems with this. First, it enhances the process, discussed above, in which managers receive only positive feedback from subordinates and eventually come to believe in their own publicity, as do film stars surrounded by a paid entourage. Secondly, if two people in an organization do very little but agree with each other one of them is in effect redundant. Minority dissent improves decision-making (see Chapter 3), and selection interviews should facilitate the recruitment of people prepared to challenge the organization's 'conventional wisdom'. This is also a necessary pre-condition for innovation.

PERSONAL LIKING BIAS

Positive correlations have been found between the interviewer's personal liking for the candidate and the evaluations which they receive. Thus, it has been shown that people who are more physically attractive have a much better prospect of impressing an interview panel. In reality, there is no connection between merely liking someone (for whatever reason) and their actual ability to do a job.

PROTOTYPE BIAS

Interviewers often possess notions of occupation-specific stereotypes of suitable personalities for particular job functions, and screen applicants against the extent to which they match these notions. Consider, for a moment, how you feel when you advertise a secretarial position. You write the job description, you draw up the personnel specification, you visualize your ideal applicant in post, you turn up to the interview – and as you read this sentence you most probably imagine a woman holding down the job. It is obvious that screening along such lines distracts us from the central task – determining who is the best applicant for the particular job.

THE HALO ERROR

The assumption is that a desirable characteristic, skill or job success in one area indicates the same in all areas. This explains our constant surprise when we find that sporting heroes are incompetent at managing either money or their romantic lives, or find themselves in a court charged with murder. We have made the quite unreasonable assumption that their prowess on the sports field translates into equal competence in everything else which they do. Similar errors proliferate during selection interviews.

THE ERROR OF EXPECTATION

Expectations are formed on the basis of documentary biographical information. This predisposes interviewers towards a decision, in advance of either the interview or of any other form of evaluation. It increases the possibility that someone with good communication skills (or easy access to desktop publishing) will appear more job proficient than they actually are, and so bamboozle the panel into making an inappropriate appointment.

PRIMACY BIAS

Interviewers often boast of their ability to know whether a candidate is 'the right stuff' at an early stage of the interview. Research supports the view that decisions are often made within the first four minutes. Interviewers then spend the rest of the time justifying the decision which they have already reached. For example, one investigation has found that when negative impressions were formed during the first five minutes of an interview, 90 per cent of those applicants were not appointed. When positive impressions were formed during those five minutes applicants were hired 75 per cent of the time.[8] However, such practices are the result of pure bias. Opinions formed early in an interview are generally based on irrelevant criteria (such as physical attractiveness, or similarity to the interviewer), rather than criteria related to job effectiveness.

UNFAVOURABLE INFORMATION MAKES MORE OF AN IMPRESSION THAN FAVOURABLE INFORMATION

It is difficult to set aside a negative impression, once it is formed. One study[9] of interviewing found that on average 8.8 items of favourable information were required to change an initially unfavourable impression, but only 3.8 items of unfavourable information were required to alter an initially favourable impression. A possible explanation for this, in the context of selection interviews, is that interviewers perceive their main task as being to select a good candidate and reject those who are poor. No one will really know if good candidates are rejected. However, they will know if we employ someone incapable of doing their job. This will damage the reputation of the interviewer, and other employees will grumble about poor interview decisions. In short, the costs of false positives are greater than the costs of false negatives.

The traditional reliance on unstructured interviews has allowed such biases free

239

rein. The evidence suggests[3] that the more planned, structured, systematic and consistent the interview becomes, the easier it is to eliminate the defects discussed above. In particular, interviews that dwell on past behaviours as a means of predicting future performance have been shown to work relatively well. We now look at this approach and how it might be more widely applied.

THE BEHAVIOUR DESCRIPTION INTERVIEW

Traditionally, standard questions have been asked during interviews, which probe the candidate's personality, family and educational background, past job performance and future career intentions. Such questions usually *obtain applicant opinions and generalities as opposed to what the applicant has actually done in the past*. Since we tend to reduce uncertainty and ambiguity in our own minds by resorting to stock preconceptions, social stereotypes and unfounded social categorization, the effect of this is to further activate the interviewer biases already discussed.

One study found that interviewers operating with traditional methods obtain *vague generalities* in about 80 per cent of the responses to such questions.[10] Consider for a moment a question such as, 'What is your biggest weakness?' Responses typically vary along a continuum from 'I can't think of any' to 'I work too hard.' In neither case is real information about past performance likely to result: any useful information obtained is almost an accidental by-product of the question asked.

By contrast, behaviour description interviews *are based on past behaviour.*[11] The underlying assumption is, as Lord Byron once remarked, that 'the best prophet of the future is the past'. Research into this approach suggests that it is much better than traditional methods of interviewing, as a predictor of future job performance. Table 12.1 lists estimates of validity[12] which demonstrates that the behaviour description interview is a more valid selection tool than traditional approaches.

Table 12.1 Selection interview validity

Selection tools	Mean predictive validity
Traditional one-to-one interview	.20
Reference check	.26
Assessment centres	.36
Traditional board interview	.37
Cognitive ability testing	.53
Structured behaviour interview (i.e. behaviour description interview)	.70

The main principles of behaviour description interviewing are:

1. Interviewers are fully conversant with the job specification and person specification for each position being filled.
2. All questions are job related. Panels do not rely on a generic stock list of set questions. They develop job appropriate questions for each vacancy that arises.
3. The same questions are asked of all applicants, and follow-up questions are not permitted. This ensures a consistent interviewer approach, which promotes inter-rater reliability in assessment and validity in terms of final panel decisions.
4. Questions relate explicitly to past performance. They should also be designed to obtain information for assessment against job-related criteria. Questions which could be construed as unduly personal, or potentially discriminatory (including those relating to age, gender, marital status or ethnic or religious background), are avoided and where information is requested for monitoring purposes, this is made clear to the applicant.
5. Rating scales should be anchored scales. This means that each item has precise weightings, determined through discussion with personnel and job experts. Such an approach ensures that each part of the job is assessed for its importance, with more weight attached to its most important function and so on, in descending order of importance. An example is provided in Key point 12.1.
6. Panels should include at least three people, familiar with the job and trained in this method of interviewing. People are not permitted to drive a car without passing a test: why allow them to determine your organization's future without appropriate training?
7. All candidates should experience the same process, and panel members should not discuss questions, answers or candidates between interviews. In this way, premature judgements are avoided.
8. The process should be as job related as possible. Full documentation should be maintained. This ensures that each candidate is treated fairly and the reliability of the interview is improved.

Good practice would also suggest that recruiters must ensure that:

9. Candidates are kept fully informed of changes in interview times and consideration is given to their time constraints.
10. Applicants are informed of the interview process, test procedures where applicable, the terms and conditions of employment, the time scale of the recruitment process and the appointment procedure.
11. All members of the organization with whom the interviewee comes into contact are kept fully aware of recruitment procedures and policies.

Key point 12.1 Example of behaviour description interview rating scale

Name of applicant:

Position:

Skill	Very poor	Poor	Satis-factory	Good	Very good	Weight (%)
Written communication skills	1	2	3	4	5	25
Verbal communication skills	1	2	3	4	5	25
Ability to diagnose problems	1	2	3	4	5	15
Attention to detail	1	2	3	4	5	10
Team-building skills	1	2	3	4	5	10
Oral presentation skills	1	2	3	4	5	5
Knowledge of Pacific Basin	1	2	3	4	5	5
Marketing expertise	1	2	3	4	5	5

Recommendation

Hire/Not hire

Additional comments:

Signature of panel chairperson:

Date:

CONSTRUCTING A BEHAVIOUR DESCRIPTION INTERVIEW

The above principles can be turned into practice by following a number of important steps:[10, 11, 12]

ANALYSE THE JOB AND DETERMINE ITS KEY RESULT AREAS

This means asking the following questions:

- What are the job's core areas?
- What additional activities would you expect the post holder to undertake?
- What value do you see it adding to the organization?
- What does the job 'look like', in terms of the day to day activities the employee will engage in?
- How will you assess performance?

The answers to such questions should then be turned into a *skills profile* of the ideal candidate. The profile might include reference to numeracy, leadership skills, writing ability, creativity, team-building skills, interpersonal skills or other performance areas directly pertinent to the job concerned. The result areas identified should relate directly and specifically to the job in question, and to the strategic goals of the organization. The fundamental questions are: what does success in this job look like? How will we know whether the person appointed is helping or hindering us to achieve our strategic goals? What precisely do we want them to do, and how will we measure their performance?

The interview involves more than compiling a 'hit list' of desirable qualities, which most people would compile for almost any job. It presumes that each of the component areas will be analysed in depth. As an example, let us consider the area of interpersonal skills – cited as of great importance in many jobs. A BDI approach would develop the notion of interpersonal skills so that it becomes specific for each vacancy being filled. Thus, a panel might decide that a high level of interpersonal skills in Case A would mean that a candidate is well versed in:

- conflict and conflict resolution
- relationship-building
- influence
- presentation
- listening
- selling
- empathy, awareness, sensitivity.

The panel can then spend time during the interview looking for solid evidence that the candidate has, in their previous career, demonstrated the effective use of precisely these skills. In consequence, interviews become a precision search rather than a stab in the dark.

Exercise 12.1 is designed to enable you to apply the above principles to the task of analysing core result areas.

Exercise 12.1   Assessing your core result areas

The job you know most about is the one which you currently do.

- Analyse your job and identify its key result areas, as if you were about to embark on a job search for your successor.

- How would such a person's success or failure be identified?

- What would they actually do?

- What gains would you expect from their appointment?

Be as detailed and as precise as possible.

IDENTIFY EVIDENCE THAT APPLICANTS HAVE IN THE PAST DEMONSTRATED AN ABILITY TO PERFORM AND PRODUCE IN THESE CORE RESULT AREAS

At this stage, core result areas are detailed further, so that clear pictures emerge of what successful activities in these areas look like. One example is the area of written communication skills. The task is to identify the precise form successful written communication would have taken in the past, so providing evidence that the candidate is capable of fulfilling the needs of the job in the future. For some jobs evidence of having produced press statements would be appropriate; for others, the evidence might take the form of written reports; for still others, the evidence might be a number of summaries of various strategic reports produced by outside agencies. In terms of influence (one of the key interpersonal skills identified above), the panel could look for evidence of successfully introducing a significant reorganization; convincing an organization to compete in challenging new markets; or resolving an industrial dispute.

The task is to identify *critical incidents* in which an individual performed a key task and exhibited one or more of the behaviours regarded as necessary for success. What the person did, how they did it and the results obtained are all identified. During the resulting interview, such behaviours are then ranked in terms of their effectiveness (see Key point 12.1 again, for one suggested rating method).

FORMULATE THE JOB ANALYSIS AND NOTION OF EVIDENCE INTO APPROPRIATE JOB-RELATED QUESTIONS

Most people prefer to rely on questions as a means of obtaining information during interviews. However, as one researcher[13] has pointed out in relation to the interview process: 'we ask too many questions, often meaningless ones. We ask questions that confuse the interviewee, that interrupt him. We ask questions the interviewee cannot possibly answer. We even ask questions we don't want the answers to, and, consequently, we do not hear the answers when forthcoming'.

In contrast, consider designing questions which address the real needs of the organization and the job under consideration. Key point 12.2 (page 246) contains examples of questions which are widely recognized[11, 14] as meeting the criteria of behaviour description interviewing. *We are not suggesting here that these be used in all interviews for all candidates.* However, they demonstrate a different approach to interviewing which dwells in detail on past performance. They are therefore useful in suggesting a different approach, and offer the prospect of interviewers receiving answers which assist them in making effective employment decisions.

Having studied the questions in Key point 12.2, it might also be useful to devise your own, for a post you are very familiar with – your own! Exercise 12.2 (page 247) will assist you with this process.

It has been suggested here that behaviour description interviewing represents a means of improving the recruitment decisions which result from selection interviews, by concentrating on the past behaviours and achievements of applicants. In addition, there are a number of phases common to most interviews. These complement the approaches outlined above, and it is to an exploration of these phases that we now turn.

PLANNING AND PREPARATION

Success in selection interviewing is largely dependent on preparation, as the above discussion of behaviour description interviewing has shown. Arriving without a script and with no previous rehearsal sets the stage for disaster. Further preparatory steps are involved.[4, 15, 16]

CONSIDER WHETHER A REPLACEMENT IS REALLY NECESSARY

The job might now be superfluous for many reasons. Has computerization eliminated the need for it? Is the main project that formed its core now complete? Appointing a direct replacement is sometimes like hiring a new architect when you have reached a stage where what you really need is a bricklayer. Thus, job

Key point 12.2 Behaviour description interview questions

Questions about effort/initiative

- Tell me about a project you initiated. What prompted you to begin it?
- Give an example of when you did more than was required.
- Give an example of when you worked the hardest and felt the greatest sense of achievement.

Planning and organizing skills

- What did you do to prepare for this interview?
- How do you decide priorities in planning your time? Give examples.
- What are your objectives for this year? What are you doing to achieve them? How are you progressing?

Interpersonal skills

- Describe a situation where you wished you had acted differently with someone at work. What did you do? What happened?
- Can you describe a situation where you found yourself dealing with someone whom you felt was over-sensitive. How did you handle it?
- What unpopular decisions have you recently made? How did people respond? How did that make you feel?

Sales ability/persuasiveness

- What are some of the best ideas you ever sold to a superior/subordinate? What was your approach? Why did it succeed/fail?
- Describe your most satisfying (disappointing) experience in attempting to gain support for an idea or proposal?

Diagnosing problems in complex situations

- Tell me about the last time you recognized a problem in an organization in which you were involved.
- How did you recognize the problem?
- How did you study the problem?
- How did you determine a solution to the problem?

Key point 12.2 (Cont'd)

Leadership skills

- What are some of the most difficult one-to-one meetings you have had with colleagues? Why were they difficult?
- Have you been a member of a group where two of the members did not work well together? What did you do to help them to do so?
- What do you do to set an example to others?

Exercise 12.2   Devising BDI questions for your own replacement

Working from your job analysis, your key result areas and the evidence which you have decided is needed in order to appoint your own replacement, identify detailed questions for each of the key areas. Remember:

- You need questions which can be asked of all candidates.

- Follow-up questions during the interview are not allowed.

- Your questions must therefore be as probing and precise as possible – you will not have a second and third chance to cover the ground required.

---

descriptions in many organizations are often works of fiction. They disorient staff by providing the wrong signal of what the job's priorities should be, confuse managers during the selection process and, most importantly, send misleading messages to the organization's customers.

COMPILE THE JOB SPECIFICATION

The need is to compile a detailed picture of what the post holder will actually do, where they fit into the organizational hierarchy, to whom they will be accountable and what their core result areas will be. Such a review is time-consuming, and the temptation is to use the job specification drawn up ten years ago for the previous post holder's predecessor. However, all jobs evolve over time – or they should do. Jobs which remain static serve yesterday's market rather than tomorrow's. Organizations that do not change go out of business. An updated job specification is a vital means of ensuring a relevant, probing and appropriate interview. This stage should not be missed.

TRANSFORM THE JOB SPECIFICATION INTO A PERSONNEL SPECIFICATION/PERSON PROFILE

Normally, this covers the following dimensions:

1. *Physical requirements.* Issues of legislation and equal opportunity must be borne in mind here. It is inappropriate (and may be illegal) to exclude people from jobs on grounds of disability, height, age, race, colour, religion or other distinguishing characteristics: the sole criterion must be their ability to do the job. It is, however, necessary to identify whatever physical attributes are necessary in order to ensure that the job can be done. Thus, it is reasonable to assume that applicants for a university lectureship should not have a severe speech dysfunction, that those who work in warehouses possess a minimum level of physical strength and that florists have a sense of smell.
2. *Educational attainments/other qualifications.* The guiding principle is to specify the lowest possible level of qualifications that are required, thereby ensuring that a sufficient pool of people capable of doing the job apply. A university degree is not required to collect rubbish, but might be justified for a research assistant. A clean driving licence may not be needed for a director of human resources, but will be needed for a sales representative.
3. *Work attainments.* This is a question of specifying the required level of previous experience that candidates must hold. Should the applicant have served an apprenticeship? Must they have had five years' previous experience at a senior management level? Should they have been the main budget holder in their last job? Ought they to have already guided a large organization through fundamental restructuring?
4. *Intelligence.* The difficulty with this is clear. Intelligence, like beauty, is hard to define, even though we know the real thing when we encounter it. It is even more difficult to explore during an interview, and yet it is necessary for most jobs. (A colleague of ours once discovered a factory administering aptitude tests to a host of eager job applicants, all of whom invested their best effort in doing well. Unknown to them, the company was planning to employ only those who achieved the lowest scores, thinking that the jobs concerned were so menial that no one with any intelligence could tolerate them. We trust that such circumstances are rare.) The per-

sonnel specification should turn the general notion of intelligence into specified attainments and outcomes which will be evident from the candidate's past record.

5. *Disposition*. This is as difficult but important to assess as intelligence. The key, again, is to identify what the candidate should have accomplished in the past in terms of team-building skills, leadership skills and interpersonal skills in general. It might be appropriate to look for evidence of team-building successes under adverse conditions – a candidate who held together a team which conquered Everest would certainly be worth a second glance, while someone who always seems to be working alone might not suit the post concerned. All such considerations need to be made explicit. The challenge is to identify those attributes necessary to the job, but no more.

A personnel specification would normally list under each criterion the personal attributes of the ideal candidate incorporating two headings – that which is 'desired' and that which is 'essential'. For example, a university degree might be desirable for a particular post and attract a correspondingly higher weighting, but it might not be essential.

EXAMINING THE CV/APPLICATION FORM

CVs and application forms should be rigorously examined before the interview begins.[16] In the first place, the task is to ensure that prospective interviewees match the personnel specification already drawn up. If they do not meet all of the essential criteria outlined the applicant should not be invited for interview. Applications should also be probed for weak areas which might either influence the interview or be discussed by the panel during its final decision making meeting. Key point 12.3 suggests what should be looked for.

CONDUCTING THE INTERVIEW

The opening phase of most interactions is generally regarded as instrumental in its success or failure (see Chapters 5 and 11). Interviewers tend to make up their minds about applicants during the first few minutes of an interview. It is therefore important to manage the opening stage so that premature decision-making is delayed, a supportive atmosphere conducive to self-disclosure is created and clear expectations about the progress of the interview are established for both sides.

This is best accomplished[17] by attending to the following.

SOCIAL OPENING

At this stage, rapport is built and the climate of the interview established. Non-task statements are employed, such as comments about the weather, traffic congestion

Key point 12.3   Main issues in evaluating CVs

- Be aware of 'functional' CVs – look out for general statements with little content, no dates of employment, missing employer addresses.
- Be aware of 'qualifiers' – phrases such as 'knowledge of', 'assisted with', rather than evidence of solid achievement and real responsibilities.
- Look for signs of bitterness about past jobs, previous managers or work colleagues, rather than evidence of team-building skills and a problem-solving orientation.
- Notice sloppiness – misspelled words, a copy of the CV rather than an original, wrong addresses. Minor errors here show the lack of attention to detail which derails bigger projects.
- Don't read more into a CV than is there – assume that if a skill, attribute or experience is not listed that the applicant doesn't have it. It is the applicant's job to sell themselves, not yours.
- Look for a willingness to work hard. What evidence is there that this applicant goes beyond the minimum threshold of satisfactory performance? What added value do they habitually bring?
- Do not be dazzled by CVs which have been expensively produced. Format should not overshadow content. Look hard for evidence of substantial achievement rather than access to desktop publishing.
- Look for skill and logic in providing information on an applicant. How much effort has been spent in emphasizing those aspects of the applicant's career which are directly relevant to the job in hand?
- Look for an ability to write intelligently on an application and résumé.
- Search for signs of self-reliance and initiative. Is this the sort of person who always waits for direction from others, or do they routinely take the initiative themselves?
- Review reasons for leaving previous jobs. Is there evidence of seeing things through and positive career progression? Tell-tale signs include long lists of jobs held for a few weeks or months.
- Do not pass final judgement in advance. In short, use your evaluation of the CV as a guide to interviewing rather than a determinant of your eventual decision. The most important task still lies ahead.
- Check. For many people embroidering CVs is a hobby. One or two phone calls may save you enormous trouble in the future.

or the length of time the applicant has had to wait. The task is one of meeting, greeting, seating and exchanging small talk. Although short in duration, this gives everyone the opportunity to relax, become acclimatized to the interpersonal atmosphere and exchange supportive non-verbal cues.

FACTUAL OPENING

The nature, purpose and format of the interview is explained. The candidate is told how long the interview will last, which members of the panel will be asking questions and in which order, and when the applicant will be able to ask questions of his or her own.

SHAPING PERCEPTIONS

This involves manipulating the environment so that favourable and constructive first impressions are created. We make instant judgements about whether we like people, want to work with them and whether we will be able to give of our best in the interview situation. Positive favourable initial impressions are created by comfortable chairs, a pleasant decor, the smell of coffee, the presence of flowers, soft lighting and the absence of chaos. We know of specially set aside interview rooms in some organizations where flip charts litter the room, the interview panel sits with its back to windows so that light shines in the applicants' faces, where there is no air-conditioning in summer and poor heating in winter. The message here is: this interview is not important. Such situations predispose applicants to leave feeling aggrieved by what they have been through. It also prevents them giving of their best in the interview. This is in no one's interests.

LISTENING

Ninety per cent of talk in an interview should come from the interviewee. The following principles of effective listening are particularly pertinent to selection interviews:[18]

1. *Provide an environment that permits concentration*. There should be privacy and quiet. For example, there should be no distractions such as the sound of a lawn mower outside or a worker attempting to drill through the wall.
2. *Give applicants your full interest*. This means that note taking should be explained in advance but kept to a minimum. Interviewers should look at the applicant rather than at paperwork or at each other. In no circumstances should the panel whisper to one another or break into subgroups, while one of them engages in a private dialogue with the applicant.

3. *Questions should be asked in their proper sequence* – that is, in the sequence originally agreed by the panel. Private hobby-horses and pet obsessions should remain private. (For example, we have observed an interview for a senior position in which one panel member asked a candidate only one question: 'Are you related to the X family in London?')

4. *Listen for the meaning behind the words.* Note signs of anxiety about future performance, or evasion in accounting for the past.

5. *Avoid the fast rebuttal.* Listen objectively, with a deliberate attempt to postpone judgement. Give the applicant time to assimilate your questions, think what they mean and formulate a reply.

6. *Listen for basic ideas.* What is most important in the answers given? What is not said as well as what is said?

7. *Welcome and utilize pauses.* Do not rush in to fill a silence: when an interviewer allows a pause to occur, most interviewees resume talking within an acceptable period of time.

INTERVIEWER CLOSURE

This stage is short, but important. A final opportunity is usually afforded to the candidate to raise any issues which they feel are outstanding. Interviewers might ask: 'Is there anything that you wanted to tell us about yourself which you haven't had the chance to say?' The candidate is thanked for attending, informed when a decision will be made, when they will hear the outcome and is escorted from the room. Some interviewers find such closure difficult, and are inclined to retread familiar ground by asking new questions even as the candidate vacates the room. Such practices are essentially symptoms of poor preparation. Using the BDI format, the closure stage is reached when ground has been covered, and should be devoted to straightforwardly terminating the interaction.

POST-INTERVIEW ACTION

This is decision time. Normally, a panel should reach a decision as soon as the interview is over. The general rule is that each panel member individually completes the interview evaluation schedule. This leads to each member producing a weighted score. The scores are then added up, and divided by the number of panel members to produce a mean score for each candidate. Discussion takes place on those candidates with a tied top score, if such a tie takes place, until agreement emerges on the best candidate for the job. Again, such discussion should be of job-related characteristics, experiences and statements made by the candidates, rather than of idiosyncratic personal tastes of panel members.[19] At this stage, if the BDI format has been followed, the panel should be in the happy position of choosing between a number of people all eminently capable of satisfactorily filling the vacancy.

At this point, having considered all the ramifications of the interview process, we want to return to the principles of behaviour description interviewing. Exercise 12.3 encourages you to reconsider some basic interview questions, often used, and assess whether they accord with the guidance which we have offered in this chapter.

Exercise 12.3   Devising questions that produce answers

Read carefully the questions below. Tick those that you think are questions which follow guidelines for BDI questioning and mark a cross against those that are not. (Answers can be found at the end of this chapter.)

Typical interview questions

1. Why did you leave ... ?
2. How are/were ... as employers?
3. What are your greatest strengths/weaknesses?
4. What have been your best achievements?
5. What are the qualities needed in a good (job title)?
6. If we offer you a job what can you bring to our organization?
7. What area of work do you feel least confident about?
8. What would colleagues see as your greatest weakness?
9. How would you describe your career progress to date?
10. What do you see yourself doing in 5/10/15 years time?
11. Why did you become a ... ?
12. How do you take direction?
13. Why do you want this job?
14. Why should we offer you this job?
15. Are you being interviewed for any other jobs? Which one do you want?
16. How would you expect your results to be judged if you were appointed to this job?
17. What is the best measure of performance in this job?

AN INTERVIEWEE'S PERSPECTIVE

All interviewers are also, on many occasions, interviewees. However much experience we have, most of us still approach this role with great anxiety. How, therefore, can the insights into the interview process outlined above also help us in our role as interviewees?

One psychologist[20] has proposed that people remember short anecdotes, packed with detail, very well. Such information is usually specific to a particular individual, and is stored in what has been termed episodic memory. On the other hand, interviewees often provide information of a very general kind which is either readily known to everyone or shared with all other applicants. For example, many interviewees will claim in their CVs that they enjoy 'reading'. However, they do not identify precisely what it is that they read. The information offered is therefore something that is shared by most applicants, and by failing to stand out as a unique selling point confers no competitive advantage on the interviewee. Interviewers find it more difficult to connect such information to particular individuals: it is stored in what has been called semantic memory. Thus, a vivid account of a fire in corporate headquarters which concluded with the interviewee bodily carrying the Chief Executive from the engulfing flames will be memorable (it is stored in episodic memory) – and will favourably influence a panel. On the other hand, someone who merely claims to 'keep my head in a crisis' will make little impression on interviewers (this account is stored in semantic memory).

The conclusion is that, to prepare for interviews, you should:

- Identify incidents that relate to the main achievement areas of the job for which you are applying.
- Ask yourself questions about what you found easiest, most difficult, and about what you liked most and least in your previous career.
- Think of examples, relating to job successes. Concentrate on those associated with powerful feelings, and which are therefore likely to be particularly vivid.
- Ask whether the stories identified are illustrations of the qualities required for the job being sought.

Having done this, answer as many questions as possible in the actual interview with specific examples of compelling achievements in your previous career. Now is the time to cast all modesty aside.[14] Key point 12.4 contains some examples of typical interview questions, and the beginnings of interviewee answers which correspond to this method of approach.

Applicant questions themselves serve many important purposes in the interview.[21] Recruiters have ranked these questions as third in an inventory of 12 important factors which influence the final interview decision.

254

Key point 12.4 Responding to interviewer questions

Q. *What is your greatest strength?*

A. This position requires someone capable of X. In my last job when I was Xing, I did the following ...

Q. *What is your greatest weakness?*

A. Perhaps I can best answer this by referring to Crisis X last month, when I initially found that I had Y problem. This led to Z difficulties, which eventually I managed to overcome by ABC methods ...

Q. *How would you feel about moving to New York?*

A. Well, my present job meant that I had to move from X to Y. What happened was ...

Q. *What do you think about your current job?*

A. My best moment recently was when ...

Interviewee questions should relate to the tasks of the job rather than vague generalities, and show a concern for how the candidate can contribute to the organization's effort. Conversely, applicant questions which concentrate on promotion prospects, pay or how the job will better position the applicant in the wider job market, suggest someone whose mind is more on their next move than the present task.

It is clear that this approach also corresponds to the BDI format discussed previously in this chapter. The challenge for interviewees, as much as for interviewers, is to generate specific examples of successful past performance. These will be seen as the best predictor of future performance, and will determine whether the job, promotion and opportunities being sought will be attained.

Finally, interviewees need to pay careful attention to impression management techniques. The interview is a game and both sides are expected to play by set, yet unspoken, rules. Individuals who act in a manner which does not conform to expected norms are regarded as 'bad applicants'. In particular, successful candidates have been shown[17] to:

- self-disclose freely
- present fluently and with few hesitations

255

- give direct and relevant answers to questions
- use powerful speech ('I would' rather than 'I might')
- employ intensifiers (such as 'extremely', 'absolutely', 'definitely')
- maintain high levels of eye contact with all members of the panel
- use smiles and other positive facial expressions
- be in control of gestures and posture
- dress smartly and appropriately.

SUMMARY

Selection interviews show no sign of losing their prime importance in business life. However, as this chapter has demonstrated, they have often been a ramshackle vehicle for achieving their intended objectives. Unstructured interviews allow free rein to a variety of disabling interviewer biases and result in many poor appointment decisions. This has not been in the interests of either managers or those appointed: there are few fates more miserable than accepting a job for which one's talents, abilities and interests are ill suited. Thus, interviewers and interviewees have often found themselves dancing back to back, in the vague but unrealistic hope that each of them is performing the same moves.

More recently, the development of the BDI has transformed the conduct of selection interviews and led to much more satisfactory outcomes. The key principle is that the best predictor of future performance is past performance. Interviewers should systematically probe the past experiences of candidates for evidence of job behaviours which are in line with those needed in the job for which they have applied. Given such an approach, high validity scores have been reported in the research literature, which translates into satisfied managers, fulfilled employees and successful organizations. As this chapter shows, considerable effort needs to be invested in making such a process work. It remains true that for most businesses their most important asset is their people. Second-class appointments prepare the ground for failure in the marketplace, and relegation to the ranks of the bankrupt. First-class appointments signal success, achievement and increased profitability. Time spent on improving selection interviews is an important investment in the future of your organization.

Answers to Exercise 12.3

None of these questions fall within a behaviour description format. The main rule is that such questions always ask candidates 'What did you do *when?*' The emphasis throughout is on what people did in the past, rather than what they think or what they might do in the future.

13 Feedback time: appraising performance

(Appraisal) leaves people bitter, crushed, bruised, battered, desolate, despondent, feeling inferior, some even depressed, unfit for work for weeks after receipt of rating, unable to comprehend why they are inferior. It is unfair, as it ascribes to the people in a group differences that may be caused totally by the system they work in.

Edward Deming, the inventor of statistical quality control

A modest little man, with much to be modest about.

Winston Churchill, commenting on the Labour Prime Minister, Clement Attlee

All of us enjoy passing judgements on other people. For this reason, gossip is the gravity of human communication. The informal appraisals in which we routinely engage are often concerned with making ourselves feel better at the expense of someone else, rather than honestly examining the facts. Such judgements are frequently based on flimsy evidence: in effect, a verdict is pronounced before any testimony has been heard. This was well demonstrated by a newspaper report on the appointment of General Boonthin Wrongakmit as Assistant Police Director in Thailand some years ago.[1] Speaking after his appointment he said 'I shall be introducing an all-round shoot-to-kill policy towards our criminals. As police chief of North-East Thailand for 37 years I always used this policy'. Asked how he could be sure his men always shot the right people, the General replied: 'You could tell by the look of them.'

Once such judgements have been formed (even if on a less terminal level) they are difficult to abandon. We have a tendency to seek out and remember information which confirms our prejudices, while ignoring or forgetting anything which suggests we might be wrong.[2] For example, if we expect someone to be a poor performer in their job it is likely that we will see only evidence of this when we

259

examine what they do. Furthermore, this perception is communicated to the person concerned by our bearing, and the tension created results in actual poor performance. Our expectation has created a self-fulfilling prophecy, which of course only confirms our view that what we thought at the beginning was right all along.[3]

Performance appraisal, when run well, is a powerful defence against these dangers. First, it promotes open and honest two-way communication between managers and staff. This reduces the risk that opinions will be formed on the basis of the manager's personal prejudices, through gossip or through an inadequate scrutiny of insufficient information. These are real dangers. With an expanding span of control in more and more organizations, most managers are no longer familiar with every detail of what their people do. Second, open and honest communication ensures that when misunderstandings occur an opportunity is provided for their resolution. This prevents disagreement festering into destructive and deeply embedded conflict. Third, open communication means that both sides discuss their expectations of the other. There is less scope for hidden agendas, and more space for a constructive work on main business issues. An appraisal scheme should therefore liberate people's sense of creativity, empower them, promote involvement and result in greater cohesion.

We would define appraisal as: *A means for managers to identify and reward positive performance, promote a unified concentration on the achievement of business goals and provide support for the personal development needs of employees.*

As defined above, appraisal has three commonly agreed functions:[4]

1. To provide adequate feedback to staff about their performance.
2. To serve as a basis for changing behaviour towards more effective working methods.
3. To provide managers with information which they can use to judge future job assignments.

Appraisal, in one form or another, has been widely used in industry since the 1930s, although the formal monitoring of performance is as old as commerce itself. Robert Owen in the nineteenth century used what were called 'silent monitors', a piece of wood above machines with one of four colours attached to show daily performance. A Superboss report,[5] which surveyed over 120 businesses in the UK, found that 89 per cent of them had a formal performance appraisal system in place. The scope of appraisal is also developing rapidly. It has been estimated that over 94 per cent of US companies use some form of formal performance appraisal.[6] A survey of 280 Midwest companies in the USA carried out in the 1990s found that 25 per cent used annual upward appraisals, 18 per cent peer appraisals and 12 per cent used what are known as 360-degree appraisals, in which people evaluate themselves, and then receive feedback from their immediate peers, managers and subordinates.[7] Companies such as AT&T, the Bank of America, Caterpillar, GTE and General Electric have been pioneers with this latter approach.

For these reasons, we would argue that managers should eliminate the term 'appraisal' in favour of the word 'feedback'. The former implies one-way communication, and never entirely escapes the judgemental connotations of a courtroom. The latter term suggests dialogue, partnership and participation. It also emphasizes the importance of continual feedback, rather than on one formal occasion. These are emerging as core challenges for staff–management relationships. Although we use the expression 'appraisal' at intervals during this chapter, since it is still the term most familiar to readers, it should be read as interchangeable with 'feedback'.

But we are still a long way from a position where appraisal is generally conducted well. In the words of the Superboss report,[5] many appraisals are 'demotivational, divisive, pseudo-scientific and counter-productive'. They consume vast amounts of time and use up acres of forest in paperwork, raise expectations that cannot be met, place emphasis on negative behaviours while forgetting to reward the positive, and produce a boiling resentment towards all those associated with the process.

However, as suggested above, the assessment of behaviour is *unavoidable*. An official appraisal/feedback scheme should merely formalize what is already an informal process. Unless carefully prepared, formal schemes may simply become a means of apportioning blame, shame and disgrace. This will not promote business success or organizational cohesion.

This chapter seeks to guide you past such quicksands. We start by examining some of the biases in interpersonal perception which lead appraisal astray, outline the principles of effective feedback, look at some of the things which go wrong most often and then explore how our knowledge of best practice can be applied to create feedback systems which identify good performance, celebrate it, and so reward and enhance achievement.

BIASES IN INTERPERSONAL PERCEPTION

It is said that when Sir Walter Raleigh was imprisoned in the Tower of London in the sixteenth century he wrote a history of the world. While he was doing so, a fight broke out between some workmen under the window of his cell and one of them was killed. Raleigh himself witnessed the fight and tried to find out what had caused it. But despite being an eyewitness and despite making extensive inquiries he never could discover what had sparked it off. Legend has it that this failure caused him to burn what he had written and abandon the whole project.

What this story shows is that facts rarely speak for themselves – we have to interpret them. And the problem is that no two people interpret a set of facts in the same way. This is particularly true when our own self-interests are at stake. Most of us possess a powerful reflex of self-justification, which would put us in the running for a gold medal if blaming others were to become an Olympic event. Many of the biases discussed in Chapter 12 pertaining to selection interviewing also apply here, along with many others. How might such biases create problems in a feedback interview?

THE PERSPECTIVE OF THE INTERVIEWEE

- A survey of British drivers found that 95 per cent thought they were better than the average driver. This explains why so many relationships founder when we try to give driving lessons to our friends or, worse still, our spouses. In general, we have a high opinion of our own behaviour, and a correspondingly poor opinion of that of others. Furthermore, we tend to assume that others see us in the same rose-tinted light in which we see ourselves. Thus, critical feedback is generally seen as threatening. Those messengers offering it are more likely to be shot than greeted with applause.

- Another study found that people were 100 per cent confident of the correctness of their answers in a series of tests, even when they were correct only 78 per cent of the time.[8] People tend to be particularly certain of their decisions when they have been made in a group. By the same token, we are acutely aware of defects in the decision-making of others, particularly in that of other groups.

- Most of us think that we contribute more to group discussions than the average input of everyone else involved, and that more people agree with our opinions than is actually the case.[8] A main reason for this might be that we are intrinsically motivated to develop a positive evaluation of ourselves, as a means of shoring up our sense of identity.[9] This is easily achieved when we exaggerate our role, general level of influence and contribution to group discussions. Each of us becomes our own spin doctor. In short, success has many fathers, while failure is an orphan.

- We are inclined to explain the behaviour of the people around us as the result of global (i.e. what is true of them in one situation is true of them in all) personality characteristics which are also assumed to be permanent, while we excuse our own behaviour as the result of the situation we find ourselves in.[10] People often feel that their organization is mired in the mud despite their own superb navigational skills, while everyone else is viewed as an incompetent driver. The tendency to overestimate the role of personality in the behaviour of others while exaggerating the role of situation in our own has been termed 'the fundamental attribution error'. This also tempts us into a process of what could be called 'blame realignment', in which our primary concern is to plead innocence of all charges while putting complete responsibility for disaster on someone else's shoulders. An interesting illustration of this comes from Oscar Wilde, who on being asked by a friend how the opening night of his new play had been received responded: 'My play was a complete success, but the audience was a disaster.'

- Organizations are often uneasy coalitions of conflicting professional tribes. Research shows[2] that intense prejudice between groups is induced when they compete with each other, especially if valued rewards are at stake. When people have a pride in their group they tend to denigrate other groups, thereby exaggerating the virtues of their own. Furthermore, bad behaviour is more easily noticed in minority groups than in majority ones. This is because we associate bad behaviour with minority groups, since both bad behaviour and the minority group itself are rare. This suggests that if appraisal is introduced into an organization with a history of poor working relationships it will, initially at least, exacerbate rather than ease the tension.

The above, in short, inclines most of us to exaggerate the extent of our contribution to organizational success. It also renders us resistant to critical feedback. A study in the 1960s found that attempts to assist people by identifying improvement needs in their work were perceived as threatening to employees' self-esteem and resulted in defensive behaviour.[7] Seventy five per cent of people in any event saw the evaluations they received as less favourable than their own self-estimates and therefore regarded appraisal as a deflating experience. Furthermore (and this is the crux) follow-up studies found that aspects of performance most criticized showed the least improvement. It seems that negative feedback creates resentment and places obstacles in the path of personal development. Thus, when criticisms have to be made they should concentrate on specific behaviours, and be linked to realistic action plans capable of achieving improvements. Positive feedback, on the other hand, is more likely to create concentration, clarity and a bias in favour of action to secure significant change.

PERSPECTIVE OF INTERVIEWER

- We tend to slot people into categories based on immediately obvious *stereotypical traits*, such as the colour of their skin, height, accent and mode of dress.[11] If you doubt this, consider why you never arrive for an executive job interview dressed in jeans and T-shirt. First impressions count. This inevitably means that we perceive many people based on our own personal prejudices, rather than as they really are. For example, studies have found that those rated as more physically attractive are assumed to possess a range of other desirable attributes, such as intelligence, power and charisma (see Chapter 2).
- We frequently fall victim to the *halo effect*.[12] This has already been identified, in the previous chapter, as a fundamental problem in selection interviews. In the context of appraisal, we tend to assume that a positive attribute or a job-related success in one area automatically implies success in others. An example of this occurred recently when a colleague of ours was assessed by students on the

effectiveness of her teaching. Among the scores obtained was a rating of 'excellent' for her use of flip charts. However, the colleague concerned never uses flip charts. Evidently, students considered her to be effective overall, and assumed that she must be excellent in this category too. Of course, this also illustrates the power which results from a significant job-related success – one initial triumph may well provide enough lift-off to sustain a whole career. In short, glossy bodywork can blind us to serious defects under the bonnet. (Many romantic relationships run aground from precisely this sort of miscalculation!)

- The *horn effect* arises when a problem in one area is assumed to be representative of defects elsewhere.[12] If we see a scratch on the bodywork of a new car it might well be that everything else is perfect, but it is unlikely that we will be able to set aside our initial poor impression. As an old Russian proverb puts it: 'A spoonful of tar spoils a barrelful of honey.' In turn, we feel compelled to concentrate our attention on such negatives rather than positives. One consequence is what has been termed the 10–90 effect, in which 90 per cent of time in an interview is spent discussing the 10 per cent of the job where the employee is performing badly.

- The *consistency error* suggests that we have an exaggerated need to feel consistent in our opinions and judgements, and to assume that people and circumstances are more stable than they actually are.[13] Thus, when we form an initial impression of someone it is very difficult to change it. This predisposes us to interpret new evidence in the light of our existing assumptions, while ignoring anything which contradicts our most cherished beliefs.[3] Thus, if we assume that Rico is a lazy and incompetent employee, Rico will have to do much more than his more fortunate colleagues to convince us otherwise.

- The *fundamental attribution error*, discussed above, means that an appraiser tends to attribute poor performance to the personality of the interviewee, rather than to the situation.[14] The employee, meanwhile, is likely to have exactly the opposite perception. This replaces discussion with trench warfare. Peace becomes progressively more elusive, since each side uses the same words but attaches different meanings to what is said. In truth, managers and staff are often two sides divided by a common language.

- The *similarity* bias means that we are attracted to people who look like us, sound like us and form a convenient echo chamber for our own ideas.[13] In appraisal terms, this leads to a *crony effect*, in which acquiescent workers have a natural advantage in the competition for promotion, and the *doppelgänger effect*, in which appraisal ratings reflect the similarities between the person being appraised and the appraiser. The challenge here is to seek out, cherish and reward difference. If five people on a team do nothing but agree with each other at least four of them are, for all practical purposes, redundant.

These perceptual biases suggest that we have a high confidence in our judgements of other people, but that many of these judgements are inaccurate. However, we find it difficult to pay attention to anything which suggests that this might be the case. Thus, giving feedback often leads to communication roadblocks, multiple pile-ups and outbreaks of road rage. But if approached with an awareness of the various pitfalls discussed here appraisal becomes an invaluable means of institutionalizing two-way feedback into all relationships within the workplace. Managing feedback is like cycling on a tightrope, stretched across a pit of crocodiles: survival depends entirely on achieving a sense of balance.

THE PRINCIPLES OF APPRAISAL

We began this chapter with a quotation from Edward Deming, denouncing the whole notion of performance appraisal. Clearly, many feedback systems fully deserve Deming's scathing assessment. However, a fall from the tightrope can be averted if our movements are guided by a number of fundamental principles:[15, 16]

- Organizations work better when they have clear business goals, widely disseminated and understood by everyone. The chief saboteur of efficient performance is secrecy.
- Employees are entitled to know how well they are contributing to the achievement of important business goals, and should feel able to communicate how they feel about the support they receive to this end. Open, honest communication and all-round feedback are important ingredients of business success.
- Managers should regularly sit down with each member of their staff and discuss (a) how well the organization is doing (b) how the individual concerned is contributing to the organization's effort, and (c) what else the organization in general and the manager in particular could do to enhance the employee's effort.
- These discussions should be frequent, informal, simple and free of paperwork. Paperwork is an organization's cholesterol. For many of us a diet is in order. Less is best.
- Managers are entitled to have opinions about the individual's performance, and should communicate such opinions during these informal discussions. This feedback should concentrate on behaviours rather than personalities, be highly specific and emphasize successes which the person has had as well as areas where performance could be improved.
- Similar opportunities to comment on the manager's performance should be afforded to staff. Securing accurate upward feedback is the biggest single problem faced by many organizations. Critical upward feedback is so often met with a hostile response that most people simply give up. The problem is well illustrated in

Sam Goldwyn's fabled comment to his staff, after his studio had produced a string of six flops: 'I want you to tell me what's wrong with me and MGM – even if it means losing your jobs.' Effective appraisal creates two-way feedback and clears this arterial blockage.

- Informal appraisal/feedback should focus overwhelmingly on examples of excellent performance. Excellent performance, publicly appreciated, is emulated. Poor performance, publicly upbraided, promotes an atmosphere of defeat, resignation, fear and resentment. It creates a context for failure. Managers should praise publicly, but criticize privately.

- Poor performance should be discussed with the individuals concerned, privately and at once. The purpose should be to agree an action plan to prevent its recurrence, rather than to secure confessions, convictions and public floggings.

- A culture of openness, honesty and trust is necessary if feedback schemes are to succeed. Otherwise, public compliance is combined with private defiance. An organization at war with itself conquers no new markets.

- Training must be given to help both managers and other employees accept and offer feedback. Most organizations train managers in appraisal: very few train staff in how to respond.

These principles suggest that appraisal is concerned only with *the management of two-way feedback*. This should be unthreatening, action oriented and supportive. However, it will help us to understand how these principles should be applied if we also look at how appraisal so often goes wrong.

THE PERILS OF FEEDBACK

A variety of problems with appraisal have been identified:

1. *Appraisal is often restricted to small numbers of staff in key managerial positions.* The Superboss report,[5] already referred to, found that only 14 per cent of organizations appraised all their employees, with front-line employees mostly left out of the loop. The rationale for such restrictions is invalid if appraisal is reconceptualized as the promotion of feedback.

2. *Appraisal has often been linked to evaluation of performance in the form of 'rating systems'.* Performance is graded on a scale of one to five, with five representing excellent performance and one representing grounds for dismissal. Problems with this are legion, and are worth examining since so many appraisal schemes still make use of rating schemes. They include:

   a) The grave difficulty in accurately assessing the details of someone's performance. Results are frequently a team effort. How do we disentangle the extent of Ahmed's contribution from Jill's? What happens if we credit Ahmed with all the achievement, when Jill will think that she put in more effort than him? If ratings are awarded which people think are unfair, the 'unfair rating' will become the issue, rather than necessary improvements in performance.

b) How does one measure intangible factors such as motivation, creativity, team spirit, responsibility and loyalty? Subjective impressions of performance on these issues tend to govern the ratings that we award. However, the impossibility of escaping subjective assessments makes the eventual 'grade' appear arbitrary to the person receiving it, and so leads to destructive conflict over the assessment awarded.

c) When everyone knows that a grade is at stake, the emphasis of the meeting shifts from an open discussion of performance (in which both strengths and weaknesses can be honestly discussed) towards the optimum presentation of the self, the covering up of errors and inflated claims for one's own performance. Naturally, this will also involve a greater reluctance to accept feedback on where performance needs to improve.

3. *Appraisal has often been linked to the award of performance-related pay.* Many of the points made in opposition to the use of rating schemes also apply here. Linking appraisal to pay transforms feedback into confrontation. It heightens status differentials between managers and employees, and threatens working relationships. It also signals that it is management which is in control, rather than the staff in the organization. This lowers people's sense of both their own competence and self-determination, and thus undermines attempts to create intrinsic feelings of reward based on the work itself.[17] For these reasons, the evidence suggests[18] that such innovations as performance-related pay demotivate rather than motivate people, that it does not help organizations to retain high performers, does not encourage poor performers to leave and creates widespread perceptions of unfairness.

In short, the research on appraisal suggests two hard won lessons:[5]

- Do not use rating systems for the evaluation of performance.
- Do not link appraisal interviews to performance-related pay.

Both of these are landmines, primed to disable the whole feedback process. If they are disarmed the territory to be covered is immediately made safer. What steps characterize the competent conduct of appraisal schemes?

MANAGING THE FEEDBACK INTERVIEW

All good interviews start before the interview begins: success is 90 per cent preparation.

267

ELIMINATING THE MYSTERY

As discussed above, informal feedback should be a routine part of relationships between managers and employees, all year round. The final interview then becomes nothing more than the formal climax to a continual informal process. It will be helpful for employees to receive a feedback preparation form, well in advance of the scheduled meeting. Key point 13.1 contains a sample of what this could look like, derived from a variety of such forms commonly in use. This is not intended to be either prescriptive or exhaustive. It can, however, be used as a template, which organizations should amend so that the documentation used meets their own unique needs. As will be seen, the issues which the form covers attempt to create an agreed agenda which identifies successes, areas where further personal development is indicated and how both the feedback recipient and organization can co-operate to achieve these ends. The completed form should be received by the manager in advance of the feedback interview, so guarding against unpleasant and unnecessary surprises.

Key point 13.1   Feedback preparation form

1. What aspects of your job give you the greatest satisfaction?

2. Are there additional skills you have developed in any other job or organization which you feel you aren't getting to apply here?

3. What have been your most important objectives over the past 12 months?

4. In which objectives have you done well? Why?

Key point 13.1 (Cont'd)

---

5. Which objectives have been the most difficult? Why?

6. What could the organization do to help you achieve your objectives more effectively?

7. What sort of problems make it more difficult for you to perform your work (deadlines, type of manager, bureaucratic obstacles, teamwork etc.)

8. What are your key job skills and areas of strength?

9. What skills or knowledge do you feel you lack? What extra training would be of help?

10. How, if at all, has your job changed significantly over the past 12 months?

11. What are your main development needs?

12. What are your key job priorities over the next 12 months?

13. Is there any further information we need to discuss to help you make a realistic action plan for the coming year?

STEPS TOWARDS PREPARATION

Appraisal/feedback is all about recognizing job achievement, identifying areas for further improvement, and agreeing action to improve job effectiveness.[19] More broadly, it is also an opportunity to improve staff–management relationships, standards of communication and organizational climate. A feedback preparation form contributes to this, by setting a supportive tone. However, it is imperative that everyone approaches the actual interview in a similar spirit.

Consider the following dialogue. What do you think the intentions are of those involved? What would be the likely outcome of an interview approached in this spirit?

Mrs Jones: Well, I'm seeing Ted tomorrow.

Personnel Director: How do you think it will go?

Mrs Jones: Just great. I've been collecting evidence all week. He won't know what's hit him. The figures are really appalling. Did you know that production was down 5 per cent last week alone? He doesn't have a leg to stand on.

The guiding motivation in this example is the desire for revenge. In the short term, it might well make the manager feel better, but it is unlikely to improve performance. You cannot come in peace, while armed and prepared to fire. It is also certain that such hostile attitudes will be reciprocated on the shopfloor. Thus, we could imagine that those ranged on the other side might gird themselves for a feedback interview as follows:

Worker 1: Well, Ted, I hear you're seeing Mrs Jones tomorrow. Are you all ready?'

Ted: I can't wait. When she hears about the state that new machine she bought is in she won't know what to do. I told her it was a daft idea. It lost us more production last week. She won't have a leg to stand on.

On the other hand, the gains derived from having a constructive feedback preparation form can be consolidated if managers approach the interview in the following spirit:[15, 20]

- *Prepare your mind.* Here, you need to consider how you feel about the person you are meeting, what you think of their work, and how you normally communicate with them. You also need to reflect on the balance you usually strike between positive and negative feedback, particularly where this person is concerned. Of course, this requires some ability to recognize and to set aside your own prejudices and biases.
- *Understand the job.* The world expert on any particular job is the person doing it. They live with it, day in and day out. In particular, job descriptions are often a poor guide as to what a job consists of. Each job has a core area, consisting of activities which the organization insists must be carried out. Beyond that, many

270

of us have considerable latitude as to what we do and in which direction we can develop our work. It is not unusual for jobs to change radically over time, as a person stamps their own authority and personality on what they do. You must therefore consider the purpose of the job and its core result areas, both as originally defined and as they might now be. How clear are these to everyone? Is there a possibility that you might think Janet's core area of responsibility is still developing the new computer system, while she now feels that it is running so well she can move on to a new marketing strategy? *How much do you really know?* Of course, if informal and continuing feedback is working well the scope for misunderstanding is reduced. In any event, both sides should be clear about such issues before a formal interview begins.

- *Highlight training and development needs.* An attempt should be made to anticipate the training and development needs of the individual concerned. Obviously, these must be linked to the business goals of the organization. A desire to learn fluent Mandarin Chinese or win a ballet competition might well boost individual self-esteem, but prove irrelevant to the development of a marketing strategy for Latin America. Nevertheless, the more that both sides can anticipate here, and the more the manager may be primed to offer in advance, the smoother the feedback interview will proceed. As with the rest of the process, the main objective is to eliminate unpleasant surprises.
- *Consider the discussion.* Finally, the manager needs to consider the logistics of the discussion. An appraisal/feedback interview, like all interviews between managers and staff, requires a set time, a designated venue, a relaxing atmosphere and creature comforts (such as warmth, suitable chairs, coffee and biscuits). There should be no distractions, such as ringing telephones or secretaries bustling in with 'important' messages. Attending to these elementary needs communicates interest, concern and respect. Ignoring them sets the stage for disappointment and conflict.

HANDLING THE INTERVIEW

The opening of an interview is very important, and determines the prospects for success or failure. This is because the opening triggers further expectancy effects – we tend to assume[21] that how people behave when we first meet them will be typical of how they behave the rest of the time. This forms an expectation which may be positive or negative. Such an expectation then governs our own behaviour, and creates self-fulfilling prophecies which often determine the outcome of the interaction. Our first concern at the beginning of an interview (especially if we approach it in an anxious frame of mind) is to reduce feelings of uncertainty. This predisposes us all the more to pay attention to the other person's opening behaviours, and use them as a framework within which to organize our perceptions of what is happening. The following approaches will therefore be particularly appropriate at the beginning of a feedback interview:[13]

- Arrange for relaxed, informal seating. Avoid sitting behind a desk, imposing a physical barrier between yourself and the interviewee.
- People bring social needs into the interview context with them. A short period of social chat is appropriate, possibly combined with tea or coffee. If this period becomes too extended the interview loses its purpose: social talk should not become an extended gossip. However, some social talk reinforces the informal and human connection which underlies the staff–manager relationship.
- Review what both of you already know and have agreed about the process – for example, the amount of time available, the forms that the interviewee will have filled in and returned to you, the main issues that you want to discuss. Make positive statements such as 'This is a very important discussion for me. I've been looking forward to hearing how well your last project is doing'. Describe the interview, stress its positive purpose, explain how you intend to conduct it, and invite comments from the interviewee. In this way you are shaping and agreeing an agenda for action.

The rest of the interview time is spent reviewing the issues covered in the feedback preparation form. The key is to ask lots of open questions, thereby allowing the interviewee the maximum amount of space and opportunity to raise issues which concern them. Some of the most typical questions asked in such interviews are included in Key point 13.2.

Key point 13.2 Typical questions asked in feedback interviews

1. What was the most interesting task you had to do this year?
2. What was the most successful thing which you accomplished in the past year?
3. How do you feel you handled X in retrospect?
4. What areas of your work would you say require most attention?
5. What extra help do you need to improve in these areas?
6. What do you think you need to learn now to develop the job further?
7. How have you found dealing with X?

Key point 13.2 (Cont'd)

---

8. How do you see your future in this company?
9. What are your priorities for the next 12 months?
10. What have you most enjoyed working on recently?
11. Where did you have the most fun?
12. What was most difficult project you've worked on since our last meeting?
13. What have you most disliked in the last year about working here?
14. Where do you think you could most improve in your work?
15. What could I improve as your manager that would make things better?

The emphasis throughout should be on supportive, two-way communication. The interview should be regarded as an opportunity not only to give feedback but receive it. Key point 13.3 identifies some communication approaches which will achieve this end.

Key point 13.3 Developing supportive communication

- Listen more than talk.
- Seek the interviewee's views rather than impose your own.
- Give information, but keep it limited and do so only as necessary.
- Seek the other person's views, feelings, proposals, suggestions and opinions.
- Test understanding by frequently summarizing what has been said or agreed. Pause and repeat, if an issue is causing difficulty.
- Propose rather than impose. Action plans which are not mutually agreed create resentment. Plans genuinely agreed through open discussion are more likely to be internalized, owned and acted upon.
- Encourage self-assessment by the interviewee.

AGREEING OBJECTIVES

Part of the interview will be concerned with agreeing objectives for the forthcoming year. There are two points to be made about this. First, too many objectives creates disorientation. A hundred priorities equals no priorities. Therefore, a small number of agreed objectives which should be restricted to the most important business requirements of the organization is sufficient. Second, these objectives should be as specific as possible. Key point 13.4 explores how one well-known acronym (SMART) can be adopted in this context.

Key point 13.4 Agreeing specific objectives

Specific Can the objective be visualized? What will success look like? Will everyone recognize dry land when they get there?

Measurable Suggesting that 'new product launches will improve' is not the same as saying 'we will have ten new products launched in Japan by Christmas'. The figure ten makes the objective measurable – we will either be there, or we won't.

Agreed All parties crucial to the objective's success should be openly committed to it, and convinced that it is achievable. Imposed objectives inspire dejection rather than achievement.

Realistic It must be genuinely within the person's and organization's capacity to achieve the goals concerned. Targets set and missed suggest failure, and undermine the credibility of future business plans.

Time-bounded The objectives should have a time frame attached. Otherwise, they always find their way to the bottom of everyone's 'to do' lists.

Exercise 13.1 contains a list of objectives, and it is worth going through it to ascertain how many of them fit the 'SMART' description above. How could each of them be improved, so that they meet all of the criteria suggested here?

Exercise 13.1 Setting objectives

Study each of the following objectives carefully. How many of them do you think fit the 'SMART' criteria outlined in Key point 13.4?

Now, take each objective which you think does not meet the criteria we have suggested, and adapt it so that it does. Ensure that each of the criteria is met as fully as possible. How much more likely is it that the new objectives you have developed at the end of this exercise could be implemented and evaluated in your organization? (We list those objectives that meet the criteria at the end of this chapter. Only refer to it once you have completed this exercise!)

1. Absenteeism in the human resources department will be reduced.
2. Sales will improve over a ten-year period by a significant percentage.
3. Morale will improve.
4. Inventory will be reduced by 30 per cent by the end of the current financial year.
5. Budget savings will be made on consumables.
6. We will eliminate waste, cut costs and improve profits by 300 per cent within six weeks of this action plan being agreed by the senior management team.
7. Staff resistance to the reorganization plan will be overcome and the new structure will be in place by the new financial year.

OFFERING CRITICAL FEEDBACK, AND GIVING INSTRUCTIONS

As stated above, the overwhelming purpose of the feedback interview should be to offer positive feedback and agree actions for the future. In some cases serious problems will exist which must be dealt with. How this is done is very important. If handled well, the underlying relationship can actually be improved, and the person concerned will emerge with a much clearer picture of what needs to be changed. Mishandled, the manager's feedback becomes the issue, rather than the job performance of the employee. In general, critical feedback should be accompanied with precise instructions designed to solve the underlying problem. The following guidelines should help:[22, 23]

1. *Give the employee plenty of opportunity to raise the issue themselves.* Most people are well aware of problem areas in their performance, although they may be slow to appreciate their full significance. If managers are always the first to raise such

problems they undermine self-confidence and are viewed as aggressive: the messenger is contaminated by the bad news delivered. Few undertakers enjoy a parallel career on the comedy circuit. However, if employees get the chance to raise problems first managers will be viewed as coaches engaged in joint problem-solving, rather than unpopular oracles of doom. Ask questions such as:

a) 'Are there any difficulties in your job that you wish to discuss?'

b) 'Where do you need most help to improve in the year ahead?'

c) 'Is there anything that has proved more difficult than you expected in the last year?'

d) 'We certainly had some successes with that project, but is there any way that we could have done even better?'

2. *When your feedback is critical, let the person know what is wrong in clear and unambiguous language.* When you have done this, explain why you think the issue is a problem. This is particularly important if the employee has shown little sign of anticipating the criticism made. You should then summarize and repeat back to the person their response to the criticism, so that it is clear it is being heard. You should also reassert the underlying point that is being made.

3. *Concentrate your criticism on specific behaviours which can be changed, rather than on personality traits which are more resistant to change.* People perceive judgements of their personality as an attack.[24] However, they are likely to see comments on specific behaviours as constructive feedback which they can use to make things better. The key here is to assess feedback in terms of the 'video' test. Can the person actually 'see' in their mind's eye the behaviour that you are describing? The statement 'You are always aggressive' is a judgement on the recipient's personality. It is also hard to 'see'. What exactly does this aggression look like, and what can be done to change it? On the other hand, you could say: 'At yesterday's meeting you walked out and slammed the door behind you, and that was the second time this week.' Such behaviour can certainly be visualized, and immediate steps taken to avoid its recurrence.

4. *Couple criticism with guidelines to solve the problem.* Criticism by itself changes nothing. People need to know what you now expect them to do, and believe that what you are suggesting is fair, viable and possible to implement. The SMART acronym, discussed above in relation to setting objectives, applies fully in this context as well. Give instructions which can be obeyed (rather than which are desirable, but impossible), which are within the employee's range of competence, which relate to specific behaviours and which you are both committed to reviewing within a specified time frame.

HANDLING CRITICAL FEEDBACK

Inevitably, in at least some feedback interviews, the manager will also receive criticism. This will often be emotional, wrong-headed, highly personalized and aggressive. It will also sometimes be constructive, specific, well intentioned and accurate. Managers must themselves model effective approaches to handling criticism. Otherwise, it will be even harder for them to offer it to others.

The normal rules of supportive communication, as discussed in Chapter 4, still apply in this context. Critical feedback should be listened to and examined honestly to see whether there is any substance to it. The four R method[25] is one useful means of using criticism to strengthen the relationship, and ensure that the channels of communication remain open in the future. This proposes that we should:

1. *Receive* the other person's comments without interruption, denying the validity of the criticism, launching immediate counter-attacks or engaging in other defensive behaviours. This shows an openness to discussion, and an interest in what the other has to say.
2. *Repeat* what has been said as objectively as possible. This is a core means of building empathy, and shows that what has been said has been understood.
3. *Request* the other person's ideas about how the difficulty should be dealt with. This helps prevent a spiral of defend/attack, and moves the critic into the constructive position of helping to identify solutions. It also ensures that the discussion deals with specifics rather than generalities.
4. *Review* at the end the different options available and agree the best way forward.

CLOSURE

Research suggests that we are inclined to remember very well the beginning of an interaction and its end – but lose most of what occurs in the middle. This has been termed the primacy/recency effect (see Chapter 7). Therefore, the main points which have been agreed should be summarized at the end. Pause after each point until the other party involved signifies their agreement.

It has also been shown that when people make a public commitment to a particular course of action it is more likely that their attitudes will shift to agree that it is indeed appropriate.[26] This prepares the way for future actions in line with the agreement reached. Therefore, one option is for both parties to formally 'sign off' on any documentation used during the interview. This is an important symbolic gesture and a very useful point of departure for what is ultimately at stake – the securing of significant improvements in work performance, in the ability of the organization to achieve its goals and in the relationships between managers and staff.

SUMMARY

Appraisal is now widely used in business, and is rapidly growing to embrace both upward appraisal and 360-degree appraisal. Therefore, managers need to hone their skills in giving and receiving feedback. The lack of such feedback, in both directions, is a recipe for communication breakdown and organizational dysfunction. We have argued that, where possible, the term 'appraisal' should be dropped in favour of 'feedback.' This is much less threatening.

The benefits of such two-way feedback are increasingly confirmed in the literature. For example, Ricardo Semler[27] reports the following innovations in his organization, Semco, based in Brazil:

- Factory workers set their own production quotas.
- Employees set their own salaries, with no strings attached.
- Before people are hired or promoted into management positions they are interviewed and approved by those they will be managing.
- Managers are reviewed on their performance every six months, by those who work under them.
- Semco has grown sixfold, despite serious recessions.
- Productivity has increased sevenfold.
- Profits have risen fivefold.

Feedback interviews are an integral part of innovative new management styles (such as those adopted by Semler), and more traditional management approaches. In whatever context they occur, they should only be the formal conclusion of an informal and continuing process. They should be conducted in as supportive a manner as possible, with their main emphasis being on successful behaviours, which can be praised publicly and thus are perceived as having been rewarded. Where negative issues are raised, feedback must be on specific behaviours which can be changed and must be constructive, linked to important business goals, highly specific and conducted in private.

With these approaches in mind feedback becomes a tool for improving relationships, strengthening organizational cohesion and achieving business success. Everyone's efforts will be geared towards common goals, and a perilous journey across the tightrope will have reached a safe conclusion.

Answer to Exercise 13.1

NONE of the objectives listed meets ALL of the criteria identified in the SMART acronym. For example:

1. This contains no *time scale* as to when the objective will be met.
2. This does not *specify* the percentage improvement which will be attained within ten years.
3. How will we *measure* the improvements in morale, when will we do it and who has *agreed* to implement this plan?
4. This looks good, but by not mentioning who will be responsible for reducing inventory it conveys the impression that the objective has not really been *agreed* with anybody, and therefore will probably become *unrealistic*.
5. *How*, by *whom*, and *when* will budget savings be made on consumables?
6. It is highly questionable whether the objective of improving profits by 300 per cent within six weeks could be a *realistic* objective for any organization!
7. This last objective suggests that managers see themselves on a collision course with staff, and that therefore the objective has not been *agreed* by anyone, least of all those capable of implementing it.

14 More than words can tell: communicating non-verbally

There's language in her eye, her cheek, her
  lip,
Nay, her foot speaks; her wanton spirits
  look out
At every joint and motive of her body.

William Shakespeare, *Twelfth Night*

By a man's finger-nails, by his coat-sleeve, by his boot, by his
trouser-knees, by the callosities of his forefinger and thumb, by his
expression, by his shirt-cuffs – by each of these things a man's
calling is plainly revealed.

Arthur Conan Doyle, *The Adventures of Sherlock Holmes*

Communicating face to face is something that we tend simply to do, for the most part. We seldom step back from the activity to reflect on what it is that we actually do, when we do it, or on how it operates. No doubt this is one of the reasons why communication is frequently fraught and periodically problematic.

But if we do take that step back to distance ourselves sufficiently from the activity of communicating to enable us to bring it into sharper focus, we no doubt begin to mull over what was *said*. Was a particular point put rather indelicately? Could a word have been misconstrued? Was a choice of topic ill-judged? In short, we are inclined to concentrate on *verbal* communication, on words used and their sequencing and structure. How we looked at the other person as those words were uttered, the expression on our face, a dismissive gesture of the hand, or the tension in our body, will most probably escape our attention. Yet it is often such *non-verbal* communication (NVC) that proves decisive in conveying information and making judgements about others. Abercrombie,[1] one of the earlier contributors to the field, asserted, 'We speak with our vocal organs, but we converse with our whole body'.

THE IMPORTANCE OF NON-VERBAL COMMUNICATION

The point has already been made that the non-verbal dimension of communication tends to be overshadowed by the verbal when we think about interaction and how it operates during formal meetings and interviews, as well as informal conversations. But much of relating to others is non-verbal and is in response to non-verbal cues picked up from the other, albeit often with little conscious awareness. To begin to obtain some sort of idea of what interaction might be like if it were possible to strip the non-verbal part away and rely solely on the verbal, think of the difference between simply reading these words on the page, as you are doing now, and hearing them delivered in a talk. How much more information about the authors would be potentially available in the presentation? How would that extra information be conveyed? Relying on the written word confines communication to the verbal medium, presentations include both the verbal and the non-verbal.

In some ways, NVC can be thought of as playing a more pivotal role than the verbal in our social dealings, although it is not sensible to regard them as two totally distinct systems in competition. Arguments supporting the importance of NVC include the following:

- Non-verbal communication is a more primitive form of communication than language. Fossil records show that our early ancestors would have been unable to command language in the way that we do. Again, in terms of the evolution of the individual, as distinct from the species, NVC is primitive in the sense that it predates language. Being more primitive, however, does not necessarily mean being more necessary.
- Most social meaning is conveyed non-verbally rather than verbally. Research suggests that in some cases non-verbal cues contribute more than half to the meaning of the overall message received.[2] This is particularly so in cases where there is marked incongruity between *what* is said and *how* it is said. Where the manager bellows at his secretary that he is *not* angry, it is true to say that greater weight is placed on the non-verbal and paralinguistic message sources.
- We tend to be less aware of the non-verbal accompaniment to much of what we say, than we are of the actual words spoken. While we often carefully monitor what is said to achieve the desired effect, how we say it may escape our inner censor thereby 'leaking' the reality of the situation despite our best efforts to keep it hidden. In other words, NVC is a more 'truthful' form of communication through the insights that it affords into what may lie behind the verbal message.

Of course, skilled interactors can learn to control what their bodies say as well as the messages sent in words. The work of 'spin doctors' with politicians and other influential people in the public eye does not stop merely at verbal manicure. Appropriate facial expressions, looks, gestures and tones of voice are all included in the packaged end-product. Part of the 'repackaging' of Mrs Thatcher, as she became one of the most formidable politicians of her generation, included the use of a lower vocal register and altered hairstyle. Formerly, her rather high-pitched voice was thought to create an unfavourable impression suggesting feminine hysteria rather than assured gravitas.

- Language is particularly suited to conveying ideas and information about our environment, together with our understandings and intentions in respect of it. Through the use of language *homo sapiens* have succeeded in such spectacular feats of joint endeavour as building the pyramids and putting a man on the moon. Only through language can we access and discuss the philosophy of Wittgenstein, the plays of Chekov or the novels of Proust. Non-verbal communication, in contrast, tends to convey information of a different type to do with such matters as feelings and attitudes towards those we meet. It is largely on the basis of this sort of detail that interpersonal relationships are built, sustained and sometimes terminated. These relationships are the bedrock of institutions such as marriage, family and work, which go to make up society as we know it.

- When communicating with people from differing cultural backgrounds who do not share a common language, we can often make ourselves known in a rudimentary way through signs and gestures. Non-verbal communication has therefore a greater universality than language. This is true but only to a certain extent. As we shall see later in the chapter, failure to appreciate the non-verbal nuances of cultural diversity can lead to miscommunication and interactional breakdown in just the same way as failure to use the proper words. Many people beginning a career in international business know this, often at some considerable cost!

NON-VERBAL COMMUNICATION IN MANAGEMENT

The significance of NVC in developing effective relational skills in the workplace must not be overlooked. The conclusion reached from a review of literature on the topic,[3] was that, 'interest in non-verbal communication within the business world is broad-based'. Furthermore, up to 50 articles per year concerning NVC are published in business periodicals. There is also an ever increasing stock of personal development/self-help type books for the committed businessperson keen to find out how a greater knowledge of both our own and other people's NVC could help them operate more effectively.

In a survey[4] of 550 managers and staff in 50 organizations involved in manufacturing, health care, finance, retail and government, 92 per cent of respondents rated non-verbal aspects as either important or very important in group settings such as committee or departmental meetings. Importance in dyadic (one-to-one) situations was rated even higher. Additionally, those who regarded themselves as being particularly sensitive to the non-verbal cues of others, when compared to colleagues who felt their abilities in this quarter were only average, placed greater importance on NVC in both dyadic and group situations. Incidentally, more than 50 per cent of those surveyed noted that their supervisors' verbal communication and NVC were either occasionally or frequently in conflict. It would seem that when managers attempt to disguise or mask their true feelings, all they succeed in doing is to send conflicting signals which may readily be decoded by staff as confusion, subterfuge or duplicity and lead to the erosion of trust. Small wonder that what Carnevale[5] calls the ability to 'people read' is hailed as a skill on which depends the imaginative management of diversity in large companies and consequent success in the new global economic order.

FUNCTIONS OF NON-VERBAL COMMUNICATION

Just why we should make use of NVC is a legitimate question. We are the only species with this marvellously abstract and sophisticated means of communicating that we call language. Other species communicate, of course, but they all do so by means of various forms of non-verbal behaviour. Through changes in, for example, real or apparent size, posture and movement, odour and skin colour, and in a myriad of grunts, screams and roars, they convey information about bodily and emotional states, social status and territorial ownership. But language is different. It frees us from the here and how, from the physical and actual. Without it we would find it difficult or impossible to refer to, never mind take into account:

- abstract concepts such as love, loyalty or honour
- happenings at this point in time in another place
- happenings in the past
- happenings in the future
- things that have never happened and probably never will (including the whole literary genre of fiction).

So why do we bother with NVC? It seems that NVC serves a number of functions, although some of these are not unique to it. These are summarized in Key point 14.1 and elaborated in the remainder of this section.

- *Replacing verbal communication.* Some forms of NVC, especially gestures, are used as direct substitutes for words under circumstances where speech is either not feasible or desirable. In the Lancashire cotton mills, in days gone past when that working environment was particularly noisy, workers signalled when management was on the factory floor, by patting the top of the head.

Key point 14.1   Main functions of NVC

- Replacing verbal communication.
- Complementing the spoken word.
- Contradicting the spoken word.
- Expressing emotions and interpersonal attitudes.
- Conveying personal/social/cultural identity.
- Negotiating relationships.
- Regulating conversations.
- Contextualizing interaction.

- *Complementing the spoken word.* Non-verbal communication is used alongside what is said, especially when material is difficult to communicate, in order to accentuate the message (e.g. drawing an imaginary map in the air while giving directions). Tone of voice may also add impact to the verbal message as witnessed by a skilled orator rousing a crowd.
- *Contradicting the spoken word.* Devices of discourse ranging from sarcasm to humour often rely on something being said 'in a particular way'. The words suggest one interpretation but tone of voice and body language something different. The NVC provides a frame for interpreting what was said.
- *Expressing emotions and interpersonal attitudes.* How we feel, and how we feel about others, is revealed through NVC. Again the extent to which this is done intentionally and with awareness can vary. Some emotional cues such as pupil dilation in response to heightened arousal are largely outwith our control. Others suggesting anger or sadness are more manageable. Likewise we can convey attitudes about others non-verbally with little awareness of having done so, or on the other hand deliberately decide to, for instance, give somebody the 'cold shoulder'.
- *Conveying personal/social/cultural identity.* In a complex of subtle (and not so subtle) ways involving habitat, dress, deportment and accent, we send messages about ourselves to do with who and what we are, and how we wish to be received and reacted to by others. *Impression management* is the term used to refer to this process of projecting an image that we want ratified by those with whom we deal. In business organizations with hierarchically ordered structures of authority, projecting suitable images of status forms an inevitable part of dealings with others both within and outwith the company. Features such as size of office space and opulence of furnishings take on a special significance in this process. Many

firms have standards stipulating the minimum size and type of office for employees at a particular level in the management pecking order.

- *Negotiating relationships.* Communication is a multifaceted activity. Two people discussing an issue are never *just* discussing that issue. They are doing other interpersonal things at the same time, both in what they say and how they say it. One of these 'other things' has to do with the relationship shared. Is it positive or negative? Is there an equal or unequal sharing of power and control? In largely non-verbal ways, both parties establish, sustain or indeed terminate a particular type of interpersonal association. Generally those who relate well engage in more eye contact and interact at closer interpersonal distances, as will be explained later.

- *Regulating conversations.* How do we manage to conduct conversations so that we don't keep interrupting each other but, at the same time, avoid awkward silences between speech turns? Non-verbal communication helps to regulate turn-taking. Conversationalists are able to anticipate when they will have an opportunity to take the floor. The next time you are talking to someone, think of the cues that they give off that suggest to you that it would be acceptable for you to speak at a particular point. You will probably note changes in tone of voice, gestures and eye-contact.

  While there are important cultural differences, someone from a North American/ North European background, in coming to the end of a speech turn, will typically introduce a downward vocal inflection (unless they have just asked a question), stop gesticulating and look at their partner. This information can be used in situations where one is keen not to hand over the floor. Since high status and interpersonal influence are usually positively correlated with extent of verbal contribution, there are occasions when retaining the floor in this way can promote a positive image.

- *Contextualizing interaction.* In the ways that people interact and communicate they, in a sense, create social situations. Again NVC has an important part to play. Through chosen dress code and layout of office space, opportunities are created for a meeting to become, for example, a formal interview or a more casual chat. As we shall see later, some managers organize their offices to include formal work space and separate social areas more conducive to informality.

FORMS OF NON-VERBAL COMMUNICATION

We have taken a look at the main uses to which NVC seems to be put. But *how* are these achieved? What are the most important forms of non-verbal communication by means of which these various interactive outcomes are reached?

PERSONAL SPACE

We all occupy an envelope of space that we move around in and like to think is in some sense 'ours'. This is our personal space. We feel very uncomfortable, even aggrieved, if it is invaded without our express permission. In other words, we like people to 'keep their distance'. The extent to which they do, depends on a complex of factors including culture, personality, age, sex, status and dominance. It is more common, and 'permissible', for a person of high status to encroach on the personal space of someone of lower status than the other way around. For example, a production manager, on a visit to the shopfloor may move largely unannounced into the personal/work space of a machine operator. Such tactics can be used intentionally for the purposes of impression management to stamp one's authority and gain an upper hand. Indeed, there is evidence[6] to suggest that managers and other high-status members can actually *enhance* their credibility and attractiveness by violating spatial norms in this way. For the machine operator to reciprocate in a visit to the manager's office, though, would be regarded as very bad form and have completely the opposite effect.

There may also be benefits for sales personnel, on occasion, in infringing the personal space of the customer. The received wisdom in selling has tended to be that this is bad practice and is to be avoided. It has been found,[7] though, when put to the test, that such behaviour can pay dividends, but only under certain circumstances. Moving very close to the customer can aid the sale when both involved in the transaction are female. Adverse effects occur when both seller and customer are male. This finding is in keeping with a range of findings about gender and NVC. Women tend to make greater use of a range of cues including:

- eye contact
- closer interpersonal distance
- direct orientation
- touch.

All of these suggest positive interpersonal qualities of engagement, openness and warmth. Women have also been found to be much more sensitive to the non-verbal behaviour of others, than the average man. Perhaps this explains why, in part at least, female sales representatives, when compared with their male counterparts, have been reported to earn more sales awards at Prudential and higher commissions at Exxon Qyx typewriters.

INTERPERSONAL DISTANCE

Interpersonal distance is the distance people maintain while interacting. It might be thought to be totally coincidental and largely insignificant. Neither assumption would be correct. Interpersonal distance, like personal space, is shaped by multiple factors as shown in Key point 14.2. One of these is culture. Northern European and North American cultures tend to adopt relatively large interpersonal distances compared to those from Southern Europe, Latin America and the Middle East. These differences can lead to unfortunate consequences.

Key point 14.2   Factors shaping interpersonal distance

- *Cultural/ethnic background.*
- *Sex* – females typically adopt closer distances than males.
- *Personality* – extroverts adopt closer distances than introverts.
- *Interpersonal relations* – friends adopt closer distances than strangers.
- *Age* – the very young and old adopt closer distances than those from puberty to old age.
- *Topic of conversation* – topics that are thought to engender discomfort promote greater interpersonal distance.
- *Physical features of the other* – people stigmatized through disfigurement or deformity evoke greater interactive distances.
- *Physical/social setting* – the location places constraints on how far apart people can be, e.g. crowded cocktail party.

The story is told of a group of British businessmen who formed a trade delegation to one of the Arabian countries at a time when wealth was pouring into that part of the world in the wake of the oil boom. A banquet was held in their honour, at which Arab and British had an opportunity to meet and make contacts. But something strange seemed to be taking place. All those present were seen circling the large banqueting hall, mostly in pairs, with the British businessmen in retreat, hotly pursued by their Arabian hosts. What on earth could account for this rather bizarre 'dance'. The answer was down to interpersonal distance. An Arab would approach a member of the delegation to introduce himself. Of course he did so in keeping with his culturally determined interpersonal distance, moving right up close to his guest. Somewhat taken aback, his uncomfortable guest, in responding, would take a few steps back to maintain his culturally determined interpersonal distance for such occasions. The Arab would, once more, close the distance and so it continued.

Apart from the humorous side, the incident had rather unfortunate consequences in terms of each group's perceptions of the other. British businessmen were seen to be cold, distant, aloof and unfriendly. (Notice how we use expressions to do with distance, such as 'stand-offish' and 'approachable', to describe how friendly or unfriendly people are!). The Arabs, in turn, were thought to be pushy, aggressive and domineering. Needless to say, that particular trade delegation met with little success.

With the onward march of international business, it is now increasingly accepted that simply knowing the language is not enough, if one is to succeed abroad. A wider appreciation of communication and culture is required. As Richard Mead,[8] an authority on cross-cultural management communication, points out, 'Different cultures invest different meanings in non-verbal signals when sending, and also interpret signals differently. The manager needs to understand the extent and importance of variations'.

But differences in interpersonal distance exist *within* a culture denoting contrasting relationships and social activities. Based on observations of predominantly white, middle-class American males from business and professional backgrounds, four distinct categories of distance have been recognized, characterizing the range of interpersonal contacts engaged in:[9]

1. *Intimate* (ranging from physical contact to about 18 inches). Reserved for very close friends and family.
2. *Casual-personal* (from 18 inches to 4 feet). Typifies informal chat with friends and acquaintances.
3. *Social-consultative* (from 4 to 12 feet). Used for more impersonal business transactions.
4. *Public* (from 12 feet to the furthest range of sound and vision). Used for making speeches and addressing large groups at formal gatherings.

SPATIAL ARRANGEMENTS

The ways in which work space is arranged and utilized can send strong signals about the status and authority of occupants, the sorts of tasks and activities being implicitly proposed, and the desirability and appropriateness of focused communication in that situation.

Promoting/inhibiting interaction

Interaction can be made more or less likely in the way that the seating in a room is set out. A layout that encourages interaction is called *sociopetal*; one that has the opposite effect, *sociofugal*. It is imperative, therefore, that a manager arranges seating for a meeting accordingly by, let us say, using a sociopetal grouping to make it easier for those present to become acquainted with each other and share ideas in free and open exchange or, on the other hand, a sociofugal variant if the intention is to play a dominant role making more use of one-way communication. Examples of types of seating varying along the sociopetal-sociofugal continuum can be found in Figure 14.1.

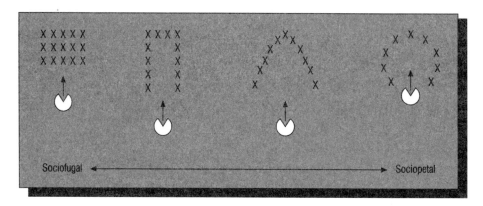

Figure 14.1 Seating arrangements and interaction

Denoting status and authority

Those in authority and control in organizations commonly have their status acknowledged by the way they position themselves *vis-à-vis* other staff. As a rule they tend to adopt positions that are more elevated, isolated and 'head-of-table', than their lesser ranking colleagues. This is particularly marked in hierarchically structured organizations that tend to be more status conscious. Indeed it is common for the seats of power in organizations to be located in the top floors of buildings. It was said of Harry Cohn, the one-time president of Columbia Pictures, that he had his desk placed on a raised platform at the far end of a long, spacious room as a way of not only marking status but intimidating those who came to do business with him!

Office design conveys messages about the position and personality of the manager. According to Michael Korda,[10] a recognized authority in this area of NVC, one of the factors that determines the power afforded by an office arrangement is the extent to which the manager can control space and readily restrict access to visitors. Furthermore, he believes that the organization and use of office space is more impactful in this sense than the size of the office, or how it is furnished. Other factors such as not being exposed, being able to look directly at visitors, and seeing visitors before being seen, are also held to be important. Having access monitored on one's behalf by someone of lesser status, a gate-keeping secretary, elevates this art to an even higher level.

Considering the office plans in Figure 14.2, it can be seen that A communicates most power, B next, with C the least power. What about your own office? How is it organized at present? What impression of you and your position in the organization does it possibly convey? How could it be changed to be more effective?

In larger offices, separate areas are often set aside for distinct purposes, enabling temporary adjustments to be made to suggested power and control. What Korda

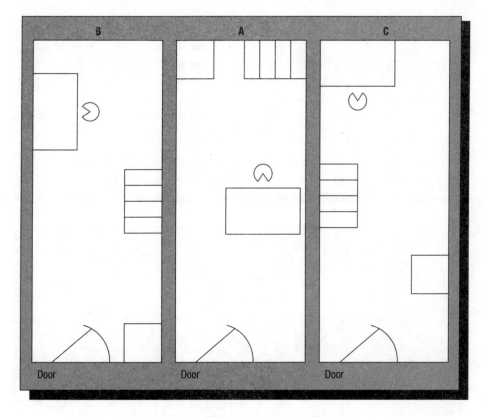

Figure 14.2 Office designs communicating power

calls the 'pressure area' is centred on the desk and is the site of formal business transactions. It is here that hard bargaining and difficult decision-making takes place. The 'semisocial area' is set apart and furnished differently with, for example, a sofa or easy chairs, coffee table and drinks cabinet. Here visitors can be stalled, ingratiated or mollified, as necessary.

Furthermore, it seems that apart from impressions of power and authority, personality judgements are frequently based on how managers make use of their office space. Comfort in dealing with others, friendliness and extroversion tend to be attributed to occupants of more open office arrangements in which, for example, the desk is moved against a wall rather than used as a barrier.

Conducting tasks

It seems that people have firm notions of the sorts of seating arrangements appropriate to carrying out certain types of task. In one piece of research, workers in various organizations were asked how they would position themselves at a rectangular table with six chairs, if required to carry out a series of tasks with a friend of the same sex.[11] The tasks were:

- conversation (sitting chatting for a few minutes before work)
- co-operation (sitting doing a crossword)
- co-action (sitting at the same table reading)
- competition (competing to see who would be first to solve a number of puzzles).

The majority responded as shown in Figure 14.3.

Note how often managers adopt what many would see as a non-co-operative seating pattern when supposedly working collaboratively with colleagues, especially junior colleagues. Failing to move physically 'alongside' someone with whom one

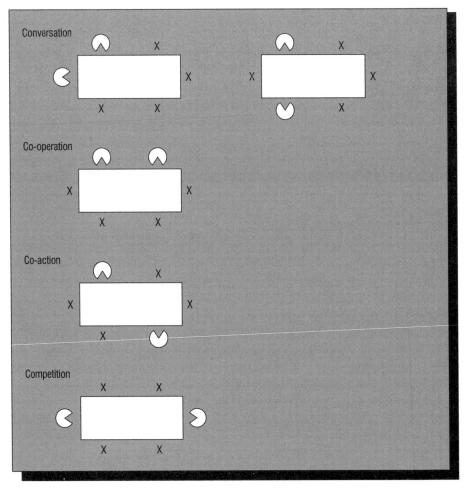

Figure 14.3 Types of task and seating arrangement

is supposedly sharing a task may suggest a lack of harmony in the working relationship.

FACIAL EXPRESSIONS

The face is without doubt the most expressively significant area of the body, particularly the regions of the eyes and the mouth. It is through co-ordinated movements of brows and mouth that we encode and decode non-verbal messages to do with emotional state. Even with simplified schematic faces such as those in Figure 14.4, reading the primary emotions displayed, such as fear, anger, happiness and sadness, comes easily. Yet the only differences in the 'faces' are in the lines representing the brows and the mouth. More subtle emotional states such as *affect blends* are

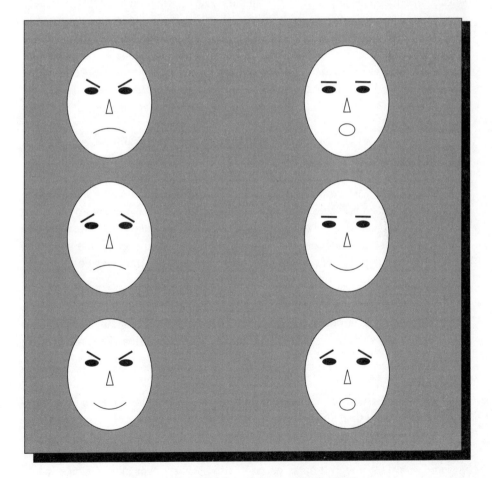

Figure 14.4 Facial expressions and emotional states

293

expressed when part of the face suggests one emotional state (e.g. surprise) but another region something different (e.g. anger).

E-mail users will be familiar with adaptations of these faces, using combinations of key strokes, to relay emotional messages. These represent faces on their side so you will have to turn the page horizontally to appreciate them e.g.:

:-)   = smile

:-(= displeasure

We have already mentioned how different cultures use NVC in different ways. It seems, though, that facial expressions of primary emotional states, by contrast, are quite universal. In other words, everyone looks happy, angry or sad, in more or less the same way. But cultural norms dictate when and with whom it is appropriate to display emotion. The Japanese, for example, are renowned for their inscrutability. They tend to conceal emotion in situations where others would freely express it. In a clever (if ethically questionable) experiment,[12] members of different nationalities were asked to watch a rather gruesome video, in some cases alone and unaware that they were being videoed, in others in company. Whilst in the presence of others, the Japanese showed no emotion, unlike the Americans who took part, who readily revealed their revulsion facially. When alone, however, the Japanese let their masks slip.

Smiling is one of the most readily recognizable and universal facial expressions. It is regarded as a positive cue suggesting friendliness and affiliation. It is also one of a complex of behaviours that tends to be used more frequently by women than men. But people who smile a great deal in power situations can sometimes be looked on as weak and seeking to appease. This can serve women poorly who are striving to establish themselves in managerial positions. Indeed, the conclusion to be reached from a piece of research into job interviewing concluded that smiling is more likely to suggest lower status for female than for male interviewees.[3]

Gaze

Gaze (i.e. looking at another) and eye contact (i.e. both parties looking each other in the eye), plays several important roles in face-to-face interaction. They are used to:

- *Initiate contact.* Catching someone's eye is a first step to engaging them in conversation.
- *Define the interpersonal relationship.* Friends and those who like each other typically gaze more than strangers or those who feel negatively. However, extreme negativity can be marked by a gaze becoming a stare.
- *Regulate the flow of conversation.* We have already seen how turn-taking is regulated, in part, through the use of gaze, with speakers typically engaging in eye contact as they come to the end of their speech turn.

- *Monitor feedback.* Speakers gaze at listeners in order to gain feedback on the success or otherwise of their message.
- *Orchestrate discussion.* In group situations a speaker, or someone in a chairing role, may use gaze to invite certain members to speak at particular junctures, and tactfully discourage others. This is a useful tactic for chairpersons to employ.
- *Reflect thinking activity.* Speakers frequently engage in patterns of gazing with breaks at points in their speech turn when they are concentrating on what to say next. According to proponents of neurolinguistic programming, the direction in which a person looks away can reveal fascinating insights into what is going on at that point 'inside their head'. Depending on a person looking up, to the side, or down and to the left or right in each case, you can gain an idea of whether that person is remembering or constructing visual, auditory or tactile representations of events real or imagined. Hard research evidence in support of these claims, however, has yet to be provided. There may be some individual variations in patterning with left-right reversal for left-handed people. Still, this theory can be put to the test by asking a friend or colleague the questions in Figure 14.5 and noting if the eye responses correspond to those given.

GESTURES

Gestures are normally thought of as movements of the hands and arms, but can also be made with the head as when nodding approval. The extent to which they are put to use varies, depending on such factors as culture and situation. Italians are notorious users, while in Britain, newscasters would seem to find little need for them at all. There are three main types of gesture:

- *Semantic gestures.* These are also called emblems and are one of the few non-verbal cues that function, to all intents and purposes, like words. Examples include the signs used by police officers to direct the flow of traffic, by those communicating with the deaf and by bookmakers at racetracks. In all cases, the gesture has a direct verbal translation which can differ, of course, from culture to culture. Since some have obscene meanings, one must be careful. The sign with the thumb touching the tip of the index finger forming a ring and palm facing out, that in the UK means exquisite and is used as a compliment, in France and Belgium means that the thing referred to is worthless. In Turkey and Malta the gesture is an obscene insult with the ring representing the anus!
- *Baton gestures.* If you spend time watching people speak, especially to large public gatherings, you will notice that gestures are often used to add emphasis and create impact. But this is usually against a backdrop of continuing gesticulation that seeks to simply mark out the beat of the delivery. It is as if speakers are conducting the orchestra of their own voice with an invisible baton.

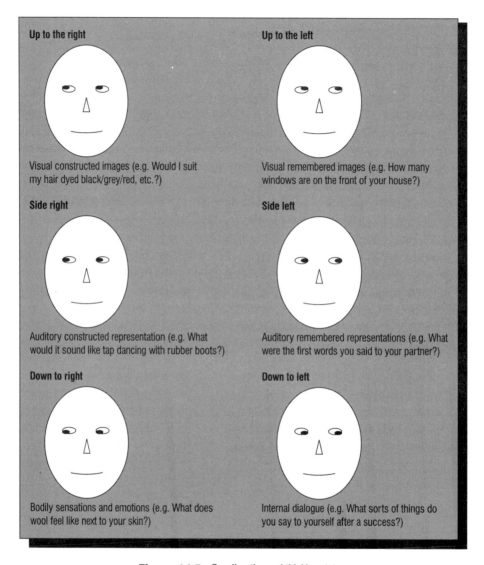

Figure 14.5 Eye direction and thinking states

- *Self-manipulative gestures.* These are also called adaptors and include such things as scratching, rubbing, hand-wringing, and hair-preening. One school of thought suggests that they are signs of anxiety or unease. Others proffer a more Freudian interpretation and hold that they represent the acting out of deeper psychic conflicts. As such, excessive scratching or hair-tugging becomes a form of symbolic self-mutilation. In either case, self-manipulatory gestures are quite different in function from the previous two types mentioned and are decoded accordingly.

POSTURE

It was once thought that the primary communicative function of posture was to carry information about the *intensity* of emotional experience and, to a lesser extent, status and bearing. But attitudes can also be revealed in this way. Watch how people sit in chairs at meetings, for example. It is usually reasonably easy to tell from their posture who is riveted and who is virtually comatose, who is in enthusiastic agreement with what is being said, who implacably opposed, who is relaxed with those around them and who uneasy.

The matching or mirroring of postures can also take place. This is where one interactor adopts a similar or mirror image posture to that of another. This may change to maintain congruence as the other's changes. Neurolinguistic programmers place great store by this process of matching as a way of establishing empathic rapport. Likewise, it is often possible in meetings to spot the cliques and coalitions by noticing the members who are matched. Those 'on the same side' will frequently adopt matched postures, especially if they have a well co-ordinated strategy.

VOCALICS

The point has already been made that NVC includes parts of speech as well as body language. These are the parts that accompany the spoken word, but are not verbal.

Paralinguistics

The general term 'paralinguistics' includes such features as speech rate and intensity, pitch, modulation and quality of voice, and vocal lip, articulation and rhythm control. Other non-verbal sounds like moaning and sighing, speech dysfluencies, and vocalizations such as 'uh-huh', 'er' and 'ahh' are also included.

By means of paralinguistics, judgements can be made (with varying degrees of accuracy) about:

- *The speaker* (e.g. age, sex, size, personality, emotional state, and to some extent occupation).
- *The presentation of the message* (e.g. enthusiasm, excitement, competence).
- *How the message should be received* (e.g. 'tongue in cheek', soberly, respectfully). In *The Selling of the President 1968*, McGinniss[13] relates how before a broadcast, the announcer who was about to do the introduction, asked if his voice was too shrill. 'Yeah, we don't want it like a quiz show', he was told, 'He's going to be presidential tonight so announce presidentially'.

Image and personal impressions are not the only factors. How information is delivered paralinguistically has important consequences for how much of the message is understood, recalled and acted on.

297

Extralinguistics

Accent, an extralinguistic aspect of speech, is an important marker of social identity and a rich source of opinions and value judgements about people. Once a person is located, by accent, according to ethnic background, culture or class, corresponding stereotypes can be triggered that evoke favourable or unfavourable attributions. Accent is a powerful catalyst for prejudice. So, Glaswegians are aggressive, Yorkshire men doggedly determined but unimaginative, Essex women stupid, Irish drunken, and so on.

One management context where this can become particularly problematic is in staff recruitment. You may want to complete Exercise 14.1 at this point. In the presence of a poor interviewer, such thinking can lead to inferior selection decisions. It has been found,[14] for example, that a foreign accent leads to lower ratings of suitability for a high-status job, but higher ratings for one of low status.

Exercise 14.1 Accents and stereotypes

Imagine that you have just picked up the phone. The caller wants to find out how your company recruits, as he is keen to apply for a job in sales. As he begins to speak you notice his strong accent. Write down (truthfully) images and qualities that are triggered if the person was obviously from:

Birmingham

Glasgow

Kensington

Liverpool

Exercise 14.1 (Cont'd)

Pakistan

Belfast

Melbourne

Jamaica

Texas

If you are unfamiliar with any of these accents, or if they do not trigger any stereotypes in your mind, select alternatives that do.

Interestingly, it seems to have become fashionable for some of the most successful in business to flaunt, rather than try to disguise, their regional accents! Perhaps it is seen as a further cue which sets them apart from the herd and promotes their individuality. Alternatively, it could be a way of saying, 'I have made it, despite my unfavoured background'.

ENVIRONMENTAL FEATURES

Modifiable features of the environment we inhabit send immediate and very strong personal and social messages that can have enormous impact in business and management. The communicative significance of office layout has already been discussed. How the office is furnished and decorated should not be overlooked.

Props

Physical 'props' in the office such as state-of-the-art computers, Sales Manager of the Year awards, wall-hangings and type of furniture, without doubt influence initial impressions of the manager, and more broadly of the organization. This is particularly so in situations where one has little prior knowledge of the person about to be met. Research has reported that such props generally shape impressions of comfort, warmth and friendliness, as well as status.[15] The presence of artwork is a particularly potent symbol of power and influence.

Certain props also influence impressions formed of the organizational climate.[15] Specifically, the presence of:

- *Authority symbols* (e.g. flags, logos, pictures of organizational leaders) lead to impressions of tight structure, restriction and lack of employee involvement in decision-making.
- *Empathic symbols* (e.g. plants, magazines, family photos) create images of autonomy and comfort.
- *Reward symbols* (e.g. trophies, plaques, medals, certificates) are thought to reflect an organization at pains to acknowledge and encourage excellence in its workforce.

A further finding is that an organization's props, on the whole, reflects its mission. Service organizations tend to be characterized more by humanizing artefacts such as plants, magazines and pieces of artwork, while authority organizations such as the police and the armed forces, display flags, photos of organizational or national leaders and logos. In which type of organization do you work? What are the artefacts on display? Are they in keeping with the organization's mission and image? What do they say to outsiders?

Colour of décor

Colour of décor, together with intensity and type of lighting, are further considerations. Executives seem to have a marked preference for organizations that have reception areas decorated in shades of blue.[15] Indeed, blue has generally been found by psychologists to be associated with moods of pleasantness, security, transcendence, calm and tenderness. Red, by contrast, is a more arousing colour, provoking intenser feelings of vitality, excitement and affection or, on the other hand, anger and hostility.

PHYSICAL APPEARANCE AND DRESS

Perhaps the one feature of appearance that, above all others, influences how we are received is attractiveness.

Interpersonal attraction

To the extent that we can make ourselves more attractive in the way that we present ourselves, we have a distinct advantage in most walks of life. Physically attractive people are seen as more personable, popular, persuasive, happy, interesting, confident and outgoing. In most work situations, attractiveness seems to be more influential in the advancement of women although, paradoxically, extremely attractive females may find their paths to the highest company positions blocked for that reason (among others). Perhaps they are thought to be too feminine for such a tough job. In any case, those who are not naturally gifted in this direction can compensate, to some extent, in how they dress. Several studies have shown that people are more inclined to take orders from, and accept the lead given by someone wearing 'high-status' clothing.[16, 17]

Dress

According to advice offered via the press by an image consultant to graduates looking for jobs, the single most important purchase they could make in going for interview is a new jacket.[18] There are few fixed rules though about dress. Fashions come and go shaping what is acceptable. Perhaps if a rule had to be framed it would be to dress in accordance with the codes that apply in different situations as followed by significant others in the company, unless one has the status to flout such expectations with alacrity. Many companies, such as IBM, have strict policies on dress, removing the option of individual choice.

Where less formal codes apply, look at what colleagues wear, especially if you are new to the organization, and particularly at those in positions just above yours. If you have aspirations to move up through the organization, are there some at the level of management just above who are more successful than the rest? Do they have particular styles of dress? If so, you may want to bear this in mind when you add to your wardrobe. Don't forget the old maxim, 'Dress for the job you want to be in, rather than for the one you are in'!

Despite the vagaries of fashion, in *Dress for Success*, John Molloy[19] believes men in business and managerial positions command greatest credibility when wearing a dark-blue suit. In the often cited television debate between Richard Nixon and John Kennedy as part of the 1960 presidential campaign, Nixon appeared in a grey suit that contrasted poorly with the drab grey background of the studio. Kennedy, on the other hand, wore a stylish dark suit. While Nixon's failure to win the battle of image in this debate has been commonly put down to his infamous 'seven o'clock shadow', this sartorial contrast is also thought to have played a big part. Likewise Nancy Golden,[20] author of *Dress Right for Business*, believes that the darker the suit, the greater the authority suggested.

As far as women are concerned, John Molloy[21] favours a business 'uniform' of blazer and skirt, although from casual observation, suits now seem to be the preferred option in many quarters. However suitability will depend ultimately on the type of profession and the corresponding image being cultivated. *In Looks That Work*, Janet Wallach[22] suggests three categories:

- *Corporate.* The corporate woman wants to be seen as competent, rational and objective (for example, banker, accountant, lawyer). Formal dress such as a suit is preferred and expected by customers.
- *Communicator.* This woman wants to project an image of warmth, sincerity and approachability (for instance, reporter, teacher, social worker, media worker). Less formal attire, such as a skirt and blouse, tends to be selected for this.
- *Creative.* The image is one of flair, originality and innovation (examples include, musician, artist, writer, fashion designer). The dress code in this instance favours flamboyance and above all individuality.

In summing up, the points of advice tentatively offered in Key point 14.3 are based on those by Cheryl Hamilton and Cordell Parker[16] in *Communicating for Results*.

Key point 14.3   Dress rules in business

These tentative rules apply for both men and women in typical business environments:

- Always follow formal dress codes.
- Pay attention to others going places in the company.
- If unsure, dress conservatively.
- Simple, classic lines are usually best.
- Neutral colours (e.g. grey, blue, beige etc.) work well.
- Dark colours command greater authority.
- Dress as expensively as you can afford.
- Do not dress wildly above your stratum in the organization.
- Wear real products rather than simulations.

SUMMARY

The main uses to which NVC is put and how this is done by gestures, posture, facial expressions, gaze, personal appearance and environmental features, together with the relevance of this to business and management practice, has occupied us in this chapter. Without a firm appreciation of NVC both from the point of view of sending messages and being sensitive to the total message received from others, the quality of management communication is bound to suffer. Non-verbal behaviour plays an inescapable part in the activities that form the core of almost all of the other chapters of this book. This fact must not be overlooked. While we have isolated this dimension of communication from the verbal, it must be stressed that operationally the two are inextricably interwoven in almost every instance of face-to-face interaction.

This does not mean that the verbal and non-verbal channels carry meaning in exactly the same way. For the most part they do not. Apart from those specific instances, such as semantic gestures, which have dictionary definitions in much the same way as words, most non-verbal cues carry meaning less precisely. The sociologist Erving Goffman[23] described the process as 'giving off' rather than 'giving' meaning. Cues are offered enabling judgements to be made about, for example, emotional state, interpersonal attitudes, information processing, status, occupation and personality. As we have seen, conversations are also regulated in part non-verbally.

15 Ethics and audits: doing things right and doing the right thing

A gentleman takes as much trouble to discover what is right as the lesser men take to discover what pays.

Confucius

The time to fix the roof is when the sun is shining.

John F. Kennedy

The subject of this book has been communication in organizations and, in particular, the pivotal role played by managers in maintaining communicative flow within the workplace. In the previous chapters we provided a comprehensive analysis of a wide range of managerial skills and strategies which are necessary to beneficial interpersonal interaction. Following a general introduction in Chapter 1, each of the following chapters examined a separate dimension of managerial communication, as follows:

- persuading
- team-building
- leading motivated teams
- making presentations
- negotiating
- selling
- using the telephone in business
- writing skills
- asserting oneself
- helping
- selecting staff
- appraising and giving feedback
- non-verbal communication.

The manager who has mastered these dimensions of communication will undoubtedly be skilful across a wide range of one-to-one and group situations. Exercising these skills on a day-to-day basis helps the organization to achieve its main goals. Good communication serves a number of important functions in the workplace and it is to an examination of these that we turn in the next section. Then, given that communication is not a neutral, value-free process, we will discuss core ethical issues associated with the world of work. Finally, we recommend that managers measure and develop a strategy for internal communications. The methods for so doing are discussed in relation to the process of communication audit.

THE FUNCTIONS OF COMMUNICATION IN ORGANIZATIONS

Communication is necessary to organizational functioning,[1] and has been shown to serve five key functions:[2]

1. *Task/work function*. The completion of tasks on time and to a high standard depends on a steady flow of co-ordinated communications. Staff need to know the goals and objectives of the organization, information must be shared widely, instructions must be given in a meaningful and comprehensible way, inter-departmental co-ordination of assignments has to be facilitated, and problems have to be openly identified and shared. Smooth two-way communication between managers and staff ensures that the job is done efficiently and *productively*.
2. *Social/maintenance function*. In harmonious organizations, staff are friendly and colleagues become *workmates*. If this is not the case, then there is likely to be disharmony, and reduced output. The workplace is not just somewhere we go to do a job, it becomes an important and valued part of our life and helps to shape our sense of self-identity and worth. Good organizations develop this function through activities such as staff outings, social evenings, clubs, family days, parties, and staff newsletters.
3. *Motivation function*. In all organizations, staff need to be motivated to perform at optimum level. In the military sphere, compliance with directives can simply be ordered – yet even here if the foot-soldiers are not motivated to carry them out there will be disaster on the field of battle. However, in most organizations staff have to be encouraged and supported to ensure they produce their best efforts. While salary is one aspect of this, people are not primarily motivated by money. Rather, they appreciate good line managers who take an interest in what they are doing and who listen to their ideas and concerns.
4. *Integration function*. Employees should feel they are an integral part of their organization, and be proud to tell others who they work for. The more they experience a sense of belonging, the greater will be their commitment to work.

Conversely, when staff feel dislocated from the organization, they devalue their work and the organization, so that output and quality are reduced. *Branding* and *bonding* are very important processes in achieving integration. The name of the organization, its logo, mission statement and reputation, all facilitate brand identity. Bonding to the brand is achieved through measures such as involving staff in the development or review of its mission statement and logo, having a system of team meetings, ensuring maximum upwards communication, engaging in outreach and community activities, as well as through aspects of the social function discussed above.

5. *Innovation function*. All businesses must move with the times, since there is truth in the old maxim 'innovate or die'. New products need to be developed or more profitable ways of producing the current ones must be found. The workplace is a potential seed bed of sprouting ideas. However, the seeds need to be nurtured, rather than smothered by bureaucracy or poisoned by the harmful herbicide of apathetic, antagonistic or autocratic management. Suggestion schemes, quality circles, focus groups, 'idea of the month' awards, and problem-solving forums, are all methods whereby innovation can be fostered.

All five of these functions are important, and the role of communication in achieving them equally so. However, it is also paramount that the objectives of any company should be pursued in an ethical fashion.

COMMUNICATION ETHICS

Some cynics regard the term 'business ethics' as an oxymoron.[3] They believe that most managers in the commercial world equate ethics at best with what is legal, and at worst with what they can get away with. This view was colourfully epitomized by the lubricious Gordon Gecko character, as depicted by Michael Douglas in the film *Wall Street*, whose maxim was 'Greed is good'. Indeed, some two-thirds of the American public regard business executives as having suspect ethical codes of practice.[4] This is not surprising, given that many managers themselves view business as analogous to a game of poker, where a certain degree of bluff and deceit is acceptable.[5]

This perspective on business morality is reinforced by highly publicized tales of company fraud, dark dealing, deceit and subterfuge. For example, we selected at random one edition[6] of the *Sunday Times*, the UK's leading broadsheet, and found that the first six pages revealed the following stories.

- A leading bank had sent a memorandum to all branch staff instructing them forcefully *not* to tell account-holders that their money would earn more interest if they moved it to a higher-interest account. This would mean that the bank could then save some £160 million a year in interest payments.

307

- A corrupt policeman was convicted of accepting £16 000 in bribes from criminals. As partial justification, he argued that such corruption was widespread in the police force and known to be so by senior officers.
- An estimated 1 000 opticians were making fraudulent claims for spectacles they had not supplied and eye tests they had not carried out (including claims for work on people who were dead), at a total cost to the National Health Service of £25 million per year.
- Water companies were engaging in a publicity blitz to convince the public they were doing a good job, while at the same time saving money by diverting storm waters into sewers that were too small, resulting in polluted beaches.

These practices are both ethically dubious and financially damaging. In her book on business ethics,[7] Sternberg shows how: 'most dramatic business failures and the most significant business losses of the last decade have been the result of unethical conduct. In almost all cases "bad ethics is bad business": the short-term gains which may be won by unethical conduct seldom pay in the end'. This is graphically illustrated by Punch in his analysis[8] of numerous case studies of organizational misbehaviour which have resulted in financial catastrophe for the companies involved.

The other side of the coin is that there are many thousands of ethical companies employing honest managers. There is also an increasing public desire for scrupulous practices in companies, as evidenced by the growth in corporations which publicly proclaim their ethical commitments in written codes of practice,[9] and the linked expansion (and financial success) of ethical investment trusts which deal only with such firms. A moral approach is also required when dealing with employees. As expressed[10] by the Chairman and Chief Executive of the Rover Group:

> If there is one thing I have learned in my career as an industrialist which I would wish to share with others, it is that business should always strive to operate to the highest moral standards. This has a wide meaning, but in particular it means treating your people properly, and with respect.

Knowledge of interactive skills should be used to *good* effect. By this we mean that managers should have moral principles to mediate their interactions. For example, it would be possible for a manager to use skills of selling, negotiating and persuading in a Machiavellian fashion to manipulate staff. This would be unethical, and in the long run counter-productive, since staff who have been manipulated against their true interests will bear a grudge – once manipulated, twice hostile. Managers therefore need to be guided by higher-order values. In communicating with staff and with external publics, the following ethical considerations[11, 12] should be borne in mind:

LYING

The basic principle here is that *you should not attempt to deceive others*. This is easier said than done. 'White lies' are ubiquitous. When asked, we are more likely to say 'Yes, I really like that new hat', than 'No, actually it is hideous' or that we are glad to see someone, when in truth we are so busy we wish we hadn't! Indeed, studies[13] have shown that some form of deception occurs in 25 per cent of all conversations. Social rules dictate that we do not always say what we think, but say what is polite. There are sins of commission and sins of omission. As well as telling overt falsehoods one can, as the former UK Cabinet Secretary Sir Robert Armstrong put it, be 'economical with the truth' by omitting particular facts. Other euphemisms include 'putting a different spin on it', 'creative accounting', 'accentuating the positive' and 'massaging the figures'. In relation to the latter, as Mark Twain famously noted, 'There are lies, damned lies and statistics'.

In the business world, where rival companies are working on similar projects, it is obviously not prudent to be always open with information and trade secrets when communicating with another company. Furthermore, within organizations, legal constraints may mean that certain information cannot be disclosed to staff before specified procedures have taken place. As a rule, however, with one's own staff honesty is the best policy, and where employees cannot be given certain information, they should be told why.

HARM

The rule that your communication should not purposefully harm other members of staff is referred to as the *non-maleficence* (literally 'do no harm') *principle*. Engaging in scurrilous gossip about a colleague is an example of how this principle might be broken. However, as with many things in life, non-maleficence is not simple. For example, at a disciplinary interview it may be necessary to relate some home truths which the other person may find hurtful or even harmful. The important dimension here is that the *intention* should not be to cause harm.

JUSTICE

Most people would not usually dispute the rule that *you should treat others justly*. The principle of justice is concerned with affording others their just rights and dues. Again, however, this is not always easy to apply. For example, is it just that some individuals earn more than others? Is it right that downsizing means that some staff lose their jobs while others do not? Is it moral to have some workers on short-term contracts while others are in permanent positions? In theory we should value all humans equally, but the effort factor enters the equation. Those who carry a managerial load or perform at a higher rate of output may be paid more than their colleagues. However, justice dictates that staff should be kept informed about what is happening within the organization on the basis of having a *right to know*, rather than only being told what management ordain they *need to know*.

WHISTLE-BLOWING

This occurs when people release information in the interests of the greater good, even though it may be detrimental to the company. When *should an employee break written or unwritten codes of loyalty to the organization* by going public about some aspect of its operation which may be dangerous or immoral? As a rule, this should only occur once internal attempts to remedy the problem have been rebuffed. So how can managers circumvent and obviate the need for whistle-blowing? An open-door policy and a culture where criticism is seen as positive are conducive to problems being accepted and resolved in-house. Contentious issues should be recognized, accepted, and openly debated.

The converse of whistle-blowing is what is known as 'swallowing the whistle' where the employee keeps silent about identified problems. This is often through fear of telling the truth, and again can be overcome through a conducive communication climate. However, in the UK the importance of workers being able to reveal damaging organizational practices, and being protected in law while so doing, has been recognized in the Public Interest Disclosure Bill.

LEAKS

Someone in the organization may decide to release information through informal channels, and on a confidential or anonymous basis. Leaks are often used to sabotage plans, or force changes in direction. Trade unions may initiate leaks to frustrate possible management decisions. Likewise, managers may use deliberate leaks to assess staff reactions to proposed initiatives. Leaks are similar to whistle-blowing, but the difference is that information is leaked simply to serve selfish personal interests rather than the wider public good. But *are leaks ethical*? The answer is 'No'. They represent subterfuge and dark dealing, and in general should be avoided. The remedies proffered to avoid whistle-blowing can be applied to help prevent leaks.

RUMOURS

There are two ethical questions about rumours. First, *should you start or spread a rumour*? Second, *should you listen to rumour*? The ethical answer to both is 'No', but in relation to the latter question it is difficult to avoid hearing the rumour mill as it grinds relentlessly. Organizations are fertile breeding grounds for gossip and hearsay. Some of this is harmless. However, where it goes beyond that, to the discussion of unsubstantiated matters which may be harmful to particular individuals or the company as a whole, then it is wrong to be part of it. Rumours are almost always more fascinating and engrossing than reality, and so they spread rapidly along the grapevine like some form of viral infection. They are more likely to occur in ambiguous situations or where there is an information shortfall. They can be shut off by the rapid dissemination of credible information across all levels.

AMBIGUITY

Politicians are very good at obfuscation, equivocation and vagueness, but should managers use these tactics? There is an old expression that in certain circumstances the best advice is 'Whatever you say, say nothing'. In other words, no direct or forthright information should be given. However, *while there may be occasions when ambiguity could be justified, it should certainly not be policy*. Likewise, while euphemisms play a useful role in everyday communication (for example 'passed away' sounds less harsh that 'died'), they can also distort reality. Thus, rightsizing is often a euphemism for getting rid of staff. Overuse of ambiguity and euphemism will result in a decrease in trust in the communicator.

APOLOGY

Where a manager, or indeed an organization, makes a mistake, then there is an ethical issue as to *whether an apology is in order*. In everyday social encounters apologies are widely used and are expected. When we accidentally bump into someone, spill their drink or commit some other form of *faux pas*, we say we are sorry and the apology is usually graciously accepted. These are norms of politeness and manners, which also serve to prevent aggression. From a moral standpoint, where a mistake has been made, resulting in someone feeling offended or hurt, then the proper form of communication is a genuine apology. In the business context, some managers are loath to apologize to staff because they fear a loss of face. However, there is evidence that public apology is an effective tactic[14] both for managers and for organizations, leading to improved perceptions of the person or the organization.

These are the main ethical issues which need to be borne in mind. It is also important to recognize that we sometimes have to face considerable ethical conflict. Such occasions have been termed[15] 'defining moments'. An ethical decision typically involves choosing between an option that is right and one that is wrong. A defining moment involves choosing between two options both of which you believe to be right. They are so called because the decisions we make help us to define who we are and what exactly we stand for. An example is provided in Key point 15.1. There is clearly no simple answer to such dilemmas. With good planning, collisions between two rights can be minimized, but where they occur there will inevitably be moral debris of some sort left behind in the emotional wreckage at the scene of the crash. Sometimes we also have to decide on the lesser of two evils. For instance, should you make a few workers (all of whom are very conscientious) redundant in the hope of saving the jobs of the rest of the workforce? Again, there are no easy solutions.

Key point 15.1 Defining moments: an example

Your colleagues are depending on you as the key member of the team making a specially arranged Saturday afternoon presentation to the company's biggest client. A large contract is at stake. The team has worked on this for weeks, with you as keynote presenter. The Chief Executive keeps reminding you all about its importance. To your horror, you then discover you promised your ten-year-old son that on the same afternoon, and at the same time, you would be at his school's cup final since he is captain of the team, and every other parent will be there. There has been considerable excitement in the family about this for weeks. You cannot fulfil both commitments. What do you do? Is your duty to your employer and colleagues higher than your moral responsibilities to your son and family?

- You could go down the unethical road by *lying* either to your colleagues (by saying you are ill) or to your family (pretending your car broke down on the way to the game). The ultimate destination of this road is Tensiontown! Relational breakdown is very probable, and lying is therefore not an option to be recommended.
- An alternative is to take the *apology* trail. Explain to the company that your family must come first and prepare others fully to stand in for you (not good for your future promotion prospects!). Or, try to explain to your child that work must come first (the emotional and loyalty damage is probably immense) and you will make up for it (how?).
- You could try to *compromise* by, for example, attending the first part of the presentation and the end of the cup final. Neither party will be entirely satisfied.
- A better solution is to try to *avoid* such occasions through good forward planning. Once they arise, there is never an easy solution to such ethical dilemmas.

AUDITING COMMUNICATION

While it is important for managers to know how to communicate and to do so ethically, they also must be keenly aware of the current state of communications generally within the workplace. Just because all seems well on the bridge and the ship is moving ahead, this does not mean that the journey will be smooth. The *Titanic* operated successfully for most of its only voyage. It is better to chart and circumvent the icebergs than to hope that your ship will miss them. Just as a vehicle operates best when serviced regularly, so do organizations need frequent check-ups. Prevention is always preferable to cure.

In analysing the nature of organizational communication, Church[16] illustrated how: 'when systems of communication begin to deteriorate within a given organization, the likelihood increases that the collective set of individuals will fragment into subgroups whose structures reflect their own internal communication needs and dynamics, rather than those of the total organization'.

It is therefore necessary for managers to know the current state of communication within their organization so that they can take rapid steps to rectify identified problems. They cannot simply rely on their own perceptions, or on what others tell them, to give them a comprehensive, objective and true picture of the current state of communication. Indeed, managers are often told what subordinates think they want to hear – no one wants to be the bearer of bad news (i.e., a dead messenger). This results in a process known[17] as 'the boss's illusion', whereby managers mistakenly believe that this defective feedback is honest, well meant and accurate. To avoid this vicious circle, steps need to be taken to ensure that staff can openly express what they really think, as opposed to what they believe is politically correct or safe to express. This necessitates an objective, confidential and anonymous mechanism for accessing and assessing employee views.

The best method for obtaining accurate information about the state of internal communications is through the use of a *communication audit*. An audit has been described[18] as providing 'an objective picture of what is happening compared with what senior executives think (or have been told) is happening'. Such knowledge empowers managers to realistically evaluate how communication relationships can best be transformed to meet the needs of the organization. The results of an audit shed bright light on the dark back alleys of organizational dysfunction, and enable managers to see clearly where they should be going.

The term 'audit' is used widely in the world of business.[19] Financial audits are long established, and terms such as medical audit, clinical audit and organization audit have all filtered into the lexicon in various sectors. All forms of audit have the following common characteristics:

1. *The accumulation of information* – the *diagnostic* phase of the auditing process. Managers need information about who they are communicating with, through what channels and with what productive and qualitative effect.
2. *The creation of management systems* – the *prescriptive* phase of the audit. Once information has been obtained, systems must then be developed to overcome identified problems and to build on existing best practice.
3. *Accountability* – the *functional* aspect of auditing. Specific individuals should be made accountable for different aspects of the flow of information within the

313

organization. At a practical level, this means that if vital information is not getting through to its audiences the blockages in the channels of communication must be identified and dealt with.

Organizations require all three of these strands to be applied to their internal and external communication systems. An audit is the organizational equivalent of a medical check-up, since it examines the health of the company. It highlights where the corporate body is functioning well, but also ascertains if some communication arteries are clogged, if blood pressure is high in certain departmental organs, and whether signs of growing malignancy are evident. Accurate diagnosis then informs decisions about an exact prescription tailored to cure the identified problems.

AUDIT MEASURES

The measures employed in any particular audit will vary depending on its exact objectives. In general terms, however, the following are the main tools.

QUESTIONNAIRES

There are existing validated questionnaires which can be readily adapted for use in any specific communication audit context.[2, 20, 21] Questionnaires:

- obtain the views of a large sample of respondents
- allow for a high degree of control over the focus of the research
- provide quantitative data to act as benchmarks against which future performance is measured
- produce approval ratings[22] for each element of the organization.

At the same time, the use of open questions provides freedom of expression for respondents to air their wider views.[23]

INTERVIEWS

The structured interview is a tried and tested approach to data collection.[24] It is also a very time-consuming, and therefore costly, method especially where large numbers of people are involved in the audit. Another drawback of interviews as opposed to questionnaires is that the responses obtained are not anonymous and, so, respondents may be reluctant to give certain information or express particular opinions. However, given a trusting relationship between interviewer and interviewee, coupled with firm guarantees of confidentiality, interviews tap a rich and deep seam of valuable information.

FOCUS GROUPS

These are, in some respects, an extension of interviews, being defined[25] as 'a discussion based interview that produces a particular type of qualitative data'. Between five and eight representative staff participate in a small group discussion. The general 'focus' of the discussion is led by a facilitator, although the emphasis is on allowing members as much freedom as possible to verbalize their opinions. The discussion is recorded, either on tape or by a colleague of the facilitator, and the content analysed for recurring themes. The chief advantages of focus groups are that they encourage staff to:

- spark ideas off one another
- attempt to reach a consensus on identified concerns
- produce creative solutions to problems.

Two main disadvantages are that more introverted staff are reluctant to participate, and some staff may be unwilling to express honest views in the presence of colleagues.

DIARY ANALYSIS

A simple and readily available method for obtaining information concerning communication contacts is to analyse diary entries over a set period of time. This provides an overview of meetings that have occurred, how often, about what topics and for what duration. The problem with this is that usually it is only formal meetings and contacts which are entered into diaries, and so other information will not be included.

SELF-REPORTS OF INTERACTIVE EPISODES

Here, a pro forma or schedule is used to allow participants to itemize all their communicative activities over a set period.[26] An entry is made as soon as possible after each communicative episode. Respondents are asked to list the source of the communication, the topic, the channel (telephone, face to face, letter, memo, fax, e-mail), the length of the communication (in pages) or the duration (in minutes), whether it was one- or two-way and, finally, to rate the effectiveness of the communication using a scale from one (totally ineffective) to seven (totally effective).

EPISODIC COMMUNICATION CHANNELS IN ORGANIZATIONS (ECCO) ANALYSIS

This is a specially designed questionnaire which tracks the progress of a specific piece of information through the organization. Respondents are asked to list whether or not

315

they know of the information, if so when they received it, where they were when they first heard it, through which channel (memo, phone call, grapevine), and from what source (manager, colleague). From the results, a pattern emerges of where communication is flowing well and where blockages are occurring. An ECCO questionnaire only takes a few minutes to complete and its ease of analysis means that it can be administered to a large sample of the workforce.[2] Drawbacks are that some staff are reluctant to identify sources, while others are loath to admit that they have not heard what is perceived to be an important piece of information.

These, then are the main methods used to audit organizational communication. Decisions about which to employ depends on a range of factors including the purpose and scale of the audit, the accessibility of respondents and their responsiveness to being recorded. The audit results should then feed in to a communication strategy.

DEVELOPING A COMMUNICATION STRATEGY

A communication strategy is a process which enables managers to evaluate the communication consequences of the decision-making process, and which integrates this into the normal business planning cycle and psyche of the organization.[27] There are four stages in the development of such a strategy:

1. *Secure senior management commitment.* This is the cornerstone of change in any organization. Without the backing of the chief executive nothing concrete will be achieved. The senior management team should clearly endorse the importance of a strategy of effective internal communications, and cascade this down the hierarchy.
2. *Identify current practice.* Managers need to start from a clear picture of where the organization is in communication terms. This means that some form of objective audit of existing communication practices must be carried out. To be credible,[2] it should be carried out by independent auditors. It should not be conducted by anyone within the organization, since this will result in the related twin problems of perceived vested interest and staff suspicions of the results.
3. *Set standards to measure success.* This operates on two levels. First, explicit links between communication and organizational outcomes should be made by all business units. Second, staff 'satisfaction with communication' targets should be set. Ongoing audit research will track the extent to which these standards are being achieved.
4. *Incorporate this process into the business planning cycle (and psyche) of the organization.* A genuine communication strategy means involving all managers and ultimately all staff in identifying goals, standards of good practice and methods of evaluation. When business plans are being drawn up, their communication consequences should be highlighted.

316

A communication task force and a communication committee can both be useful in regulating strategy.[1] The task force is given a short-term remit, usually to investigate specific problems identified by an audit and to make recommendations about how these can best be resolved. The communication committee is a more permanent structure, comprising managerial and non-managerial staff from across the different sections of the organization. It has the remit of continually monitoring communication practices, diagnosing issues of concern and taking steps to rectify these. One useful technique is for membership of the task force to be rotated, so that as wide a range of staff as possible recognize communication as a core area of interest and carry this perspective back into their working practice.

SUMMARY

Organizational communication has become a vast field of study with a voluminous amount of literature being published in recent years. This is not surprising given that, as shown by Frank and Brownell in their text[1] on organizational behaviour: 'Effective communication is crucial to almost every aspect of operating and managing organizations.'

In this book, we have attempted to extract from this burgeoning work the key points of effective managerial communication. Managers have to decide which strategies to employ within the given context in which communication is taking place, and bearing in mind the nature of those with whom they are interacting. This text provides detailed guidelines to help managers to shape better behavioural decision-making across a broad range of situations. As emphasized in this chapter, two broader aspects which are important for managers to keep in mind are:

- doing what is right, in terms of communicating ethically
- knowing exactly how you are doing, by regularly auditing your communications.

In concluding, we recognize that life is not always within our control and sometimes, regardless of how well we communicate, the result is not as we would have hoped. As the Scottish poet Robert Burns once put it:

> The best-laid schemes o' mice an' men
> Gang aft a-gley.

In other words, circumstances can conspire to frustrate even the most carefully worked-out plans. This has been humorously depicted variously as Murphy's Law or Sod's Law, and we have developed a version called 'The Pessimist's Charter' (Key point 15.2). However, it remains true that the more skilled we are in the realm of communication and the more carefully we plan what we intend to do, the more likely we are to be successful in life.

317

Key point 15.2 The Pessimist's Charter

- If anything can go wrong, it will go wrong.
- Every silver lining is part of a much larger cloud.
- Most enjoyable things in life are either illegal or unhealthy.
- Just when you have mastered a computer system it becomes obsolete and is replaced by a new one.
- The light at the end of the tunnel is likely to be the headlamp of a huge train coming at speed towards you.
- Everybody has a scheme for getting rich that is sure to fail.
- People who tell you that appearance doesn't matter, always look much better than you do.
- Races may not always be won by the swift, nor battles by the strong, but that is the way to place your bets.
- The other queues will always move faster than the one you decide to join.
- Any repairs you decide to make will always take much longer and cost far more than you anticipated.
- The probability of the toast falling buttered-side down is directly proportional to the cost of the carpet.
- A friend in need is a real pest.
- To secure a loan you first must prove that you do not really need it.
- Life does not begin at 40 – it is half over by then.
- When anything breaks down the repair shop will tell you 'It is impossible to get parts for this nowadays'.
- A short cut is the longest distance between two points.
- People who see the glass as half empty and not half full, have just watched some other sod drinking the first half.
- Only winners will tell you 'You can't win all the time'.
- No matter how carefully you shop for an item, after you've bought it you will see it cheaper elsewhere.
- Those who look at life through rose-tinted spectacles are only happy because they do not see things as they truly are.
- If everything seems to be going very well, you haven't a clue about what is really going on.

Organizations are like families. Those in trouble are characterized by dysfunctional communication, while successful ones have harmonious relationships. Managers are similar to the heads of the family. They need to lead by example and encourage an atmosphere in which all members can achieve their potential. The outcome will be success and stability. Conversely, where managers rule like tyrannical parents, the consequence is typified by constant strife and ultimate breakdown. By judiciously employing the skills and strategies discussed in this book, managers will achieve much more positive results from their staff. In the end, it is the workforce who determine the success or failure of any business. We will therefore end with a quotation taken from Pfeffer's text[28] *The Human Equation*:

Capital and Machinery Make It Possible – People Make It Happen.

References

CHAPTER 1 Introduction: the communicating manager

1. Schermerhorn, J.R. (1996) *Management and Organizational Behavior*, New York: Wiley, p. 2.
2. O'Hair, D. and Friedrich, G. (1992) *Strategic Communication in Business and the Professions*, Boston: Houghton Mifflin, p. 4.
3. Scase, R. and Goffee, R. (1989) *Reluctant Managers: their Work and Lifestyles*, London: Unwin Hyman.
4. Buchanan, D. and Huczynski, A. (1997) *Organizational Behaviour*, 3rd edn, Hemel Hempstead: Prentice Hall, p. 9.
5. Parsons, T. (1963) *Structure and Process in Modern Societies*, New York: Free Press.
6. Clampitt, P. (1991) *Communicating for Managerial Effectiveness*, Newbury Park: Sage.
7. Clampitt, P. and Downs, C. (1993) 'Employee Perceptions of the Relationship between Communication and Productivity: a Field Study', *Journal of Business Communication*, **30**, 5–28.
8. Tourish, D. (1996) 'Internal Communication and the NHS: the Results of a Fieldwork Analysis, and Implications for Corporate Practice', PhD thesis, University of Ulster, Jordanstown.
9. Berger, B. (1994) 'Revolution at Whirlpool', *Internal Communication Focus*, November, 8–11.
10. Forrest, A. (1997) *5 Way Management*, London: The Industrial Society.
11. Lee, J. and Jablin, F. (1995) 'Maintenance Communication in Superior-Subordinate Work Relationships', *Human Communication Research*, **22**, 220–57.
12. McGregor, D. (1960) *The Human Side of Enterprise*, New York: McGraw-Hill.
13. Quirke, B. (1995) 'Internal Communication', in N. Hart (ed.) *Strategic Public Relations*, London: Macmillan.

14. McKeans, P. (1990) 'GM Division Builds a Classic System to Share Internal Information', *Public Relations Journal*, **46**, 24–41.

15. Smith, A. (1991) *Innovative Employee Communication: New Approaches to Improving Trust, Teamwork and Performance*, Englewood Cliffs: Prentice Hall.

16. Hargie, O., Tourish, D., Waldrop-White, C. and Marshall, B. (1994) 'Did You Hear It on the Grapevine?' *Health Service Journal*, **104**, 26–9.

17. Hargie, O. (ed.) (1997) *The Handbook of Communication Skills*, 2nd edn, London: Routledge.

18. Caulkin, S. (1998) 'How that Pat on the Back can Mean Money in the Bank', *The Observer: Work Section*, 19 April, p. I.

19. Hargie, O. (1992) 'Communication: Beyond the Crossroads', monograph, University of Ulster, Jordanstown, p. 10.

20. Hargie, O., Dickson, D. and Saunders, C. (1994) *Social Skills in Interpersonal Communication*, 3rd edn, London: Routledge.

21. Goleman, D. (1997) *Emotional Intelligence*. London: Bloomsbury.

22. Kreps, G. (1990) *Organizational Communication: Theory and Practice*, 2nd edn, New York: Longman, p. 126.

23. Deal, T. and Kennedy, A. (1982) *Corporate Cultures: the Rites and Rituals of Corporate Life,* Reading, MA: Addison-Wesley.

24. Thompson, P. and McHugh, D. (1995) *Work Organisations: a Critical Introduction*, 2nd edn, London: Macmillan Business.

25. O'Shea, J. and Madigan, C. (1997) *Dangerous Company: the Consulting Powerhouses and the Businesses They Save and Ruin*, London: Nicholas Brealey.

26. Hargie, O. and Morrow, N. (1995) 'An Evaluation of a Presentation Skills Course for Pharmacists', *International Journal of Pharmacy Practice*, **3**, 101–5.

CHAPTER 2   The gentle art of persuasion: influencing others

1. Reardon, K. (1991) *Persuasion in Practice*, Newbury Park: Sage.

2. Turner, J. (1991) *Social Influence*, Buckingham: Open University.

3. Perloff, R. (1993) *The Dynamics of Persuasion*, Hillsdale, NJ: Lawrence Erlbaum.

4. Buchanan, D. and Huczynski, A. (1997) *Organizational Behaviour*, 3rd edn, London: Prentice Hall, p. 695.

5. Barry, B. and Bateman, T. (1992) 'Perceptions of Influence in Managerial Dyads: the Role of Hierarchy, Media and Tactics', *Human Relations*, **45**, 555–74.

6. Seibold, D.R., Cantrill, J.G. and Meyers, R.A. (1994) 'Communication and Interpersonal Influence', in M. Knapp and G. Miller (eds), *Handbook of Interpersonal Communication*, 2nd edn, Thousand Oaks, CA: Sage.

7. Goldsmith, W. and Clutterbuck, D. (1997) *The Winning Streak Mark II*, London: Orion Business Books.

8. Cialdini, R. (1993) *Influence: Science and Practice*, 3rd edn, Glenview, IL: Scott, Foresman and Co.

9. Gibb-Clark, M. (1997) 'People with "Hot Skills" Can "Call the shots" on Wages, Survey Finds', *The Globe and Mail*, 29 October, p. B6.

10. Dillard, J.P. (1995) 'Rethinking the Study of Fear Appeals: an Emotional Perspective', *Communication Theory*, 4, 295–323.

11. Pratkanis, A. and Aronson, E. (1992) *Age of Propaganda: the Everyday Use and Abuse of Persuasion*, New York: Freeman.

12. Garko, M.G. (1992) 'Physician Executives' Use of Influence Strategies: Gaining Compliance from Superiors Who Communicate in Attractive and Unattractive Styles', *Health Communication*, 4, 137–54.

13. Craig, O. (1997) 'Focus', *Sunday Telegraph*, 29 June, p. 21.

14. Kleinke, C. (1986) *Meeting and Understanding People*, New York: Freeman, p. 179.

15. McCall, M., Lombardo, M. and Morrison, A. (1988) *The Lessons of Experience: How Successful Executives Develop on the Job*, New York: Free Press.

16. Schweiger, D. and Denisi, A. (1991) 'Communicating with Employees: a Longitudinal Field Experiment', *Academy of Management Journal*, 34, 110–135.

17. Bennett, H. (1996) 'Communicating Change – a Case for Multiple Methods', *Corporate Communications: an International Journal*, 1, 32–9.

18. Tourish, D. and Hargie, O. (1998) 'Communication between Managers and Staff in the NHS: Trends and Prospects', *British Journal of Management*, 9, 53–71.

19. Hargie, O. (ed) (1997) *The Handbook of Communication Skills*, London: Routledge.

20. Duck, S. (1995) 'Repelling the Study of Attraction', *The Psychologist*, 8, 60–63.

21. Feeley, T.H. and Barnett, G.A. (1997) 'Predicting Employee Turnover from Communication Networks', *Human Communication Research*, 23, 370–387.

22. Rackham, N. and Morgan, T. (1977) *Behaviour Analysis in Training*, London: McGraw-Hill, p. 233.

23. Smith, D. and Higgins, S. (1997) 'Call me "Sir", Demand British Bosses', *The Sunday Times*, 13 July.

24. Marsh, P. (1988) 'Raising a Smile', in P. Marsh (ed.), *Eye To Eye: your Relationships and How They Work*, London: Sidgwick and Jackson, p. 113.

25. Kipnis, D. and Schmidt, S. (1990) 'The Language of Persuasion', in I. Asherman and S. Asherman (eds), *The Negotiation Sourcebook*, Amherst, MA: Human Resource Development Press, p. 50.

26. Huczynski, A. (1996) *Influencing Within Organizations*, London: Prentice-Hall.

CHAPTER 3 Team-mates: building teams that work

1. Katzenbach, J. and Smith, D. (1993) *The Wisdom of Teams*, Cambridge, MA: Harvard Business School Press.
2. Tourish, D. (1997) 'Transforming Internal Corporate Communications: the Power Of Symbolic Gestures, and Barriers to Change', *Corporate Communications: an International Journal*, **2**, (3), 109–116.
3. Reichfield, F. (1996) *The Loyalty Effect*, Boston: Harvard Business School Press.
4. Fukuyama, F. (1995) *Trust: the Social Virtues and the Creation of Prosperity*, London: Hamish Hamilton.
5. D'Aprix, R. (1996) *Communicating For Change*, San Francisco: Jossey-Bass.
6. Pfeffer, J. (1998) *The Human Equation*, Boston: Harvard University Press.
7. Banker, R., Field, J., Schroeder, R. and Sinha, K. (1996) 'Impact of Work Teams on Manufacturing Performance: a Longitudinal Field Study', *Academy of Management Journal*, **39**, 867–90.
8. Kanter, R. (1983) *The Change Masters: Innovation and Entrepreuneurship in the American Corporation*, New York: Simon and Schuster.
9. Parker, G. (1990) *Team Players and Teamwork: the New Competitive Business Strategy*, San Francisco: Jossey-Bass.
10. Kharbana, O., and Stallworthy, E. (1990) *Project Teams: the Human Factor*, Oxford: Blackwell.
11. Arnott, M. (1987) 'Effective Employee Communication', in Hart (ed.), *Effective Corporate Relations*, London: McGraw-Hill.
12. Papa, M. and Tracy, K. (1988) 'Communicative Indices of Employee Performance with New Technology', *Communication Research*, **15** (5), 524–44.
13. Coles, M. (1997) 'Firm Plays It by Ear', *Sunday Times*, 19 October, p. 28.
14. Tuckman, B. and Jensen, M. (1977) 'Stages of Small Group Development Revisited', *Group and Organization Studies*, **2**, 419–27.
15. Brown, K., Klastorin, T. and Valluzzi, J. (1990) 'Project Performance and the Liability of Group Harmony', *IEEE Trans Eng Management*, **37** (2), 117–25.
16. Peters, T. and Austin, N. (1985) *A Passion for Excellence*, Glasgow: Collins.
17. Hayes, N. (1997) *Successful Team Management*, London: Thomson Business Press.
18. Meyer, C. (1994) 'How the Right Measures Help Teams Excel', *Harvard Business Review*, May–June, 95–103.
19. Evans, R. (1997) 'Hollow the leader', *Report on Business Magazine*, November, p. 60.
20. 'Boss Buys 600 Workers Free Drinks', *News Letter*, 30 April 1998, p. 13.
21. Whetten, D. and Cameron, K. (1991) *Developing Management Skills*, 2nd edn, New York: HarperCollins.
22. Brown, R. (1988) *Group Processes*, Oxford: Blackwell.

23. Janis, I. (1972) *Victims of Groupthink*, Boston: Houghton Mifflin.
24. Tobias, M. and Lalich, J. (1994) *Captive Hearts: Captive Minds: Freedom and Recovery From Cults and Abusive Relationships*, Alameda, CA: Hunter House.
25. Ingham, A., Levinger, G., Graves, J. and Peckham, V. (1974) 'The Ringlemann Effect: Studies of Group Size and Group Performance', *Journal of Experimental Social Psychology*, **10**, 371–84.
26. Yeatts, D. and Hyten, C. (1998) *High Performing Self Managed Work Teams*, Thousand Oaks, CA: Sage.
27. Sinclair, A. (1992) 'The Tyranny of a Team Ideology', *Organization Studies*, **13** (4), 611–26.

CHAPTER 4   Team-meets: managing productive meetings

1. Seibold, D. (1979) 'Making Meetings More Successful: Plans, Formats, and Procedures for Group Problem Solving', *Journal of Business Communication*, **16**, 3–20.
2. Mintzberg, H. (1973) *The Nature Of Managerial Work*, New York: Harper and Row.
3. Smith, D. (1997) 'Managers Lack Proper Skills', *The Sunday Times*, Business Section, 14 September, p 12.
4. Wilke, H. and Meertens, R. (1994) *Group Performance*, New York and London: Routledge.
5. Pfeffer, J. (1992) 'Understanding Power in Organizations', *California Management Review*, 34, 29–50, esp. 41.
6. Kotter, J. (1988) *The Leadership Factor*, New York: Free Press, p. 5.
7. Messé, L., Kerr, N. and Sattler, D. (1992) '"But Some Animals are More Equal than Others": the Supervisor as a Privileged Status in Group Contexts', in S. Worchel, W. Wood, and Simpson, J. (eds), *Group Process and Productivity*, London: Sage.
8. Napier, R. and Gershenfeld, M. (1989) *Groups: Theory and Experience*, Dallas: Houghton Mifflin.
9. Hunt, J. (1991) *Leadership: a New Synthesis*, London: Sage.
10. Doucouliagos, C. (1995) 'Worker Participation and Productivity in Labor-Managed and Participatory Capitalist Forms: a Meta-Analysis', *Industrial and Labor Relations Review*, **49**, 58–77.
11. Tourish, D. and Hargie, O. (1998) 'Communication between Managers and Staff in the NHS: Trends and Prospects', *British Journal of Management*, **9**, 53–71.
12. Tourish, D. and Mulholland, J. (1997) 'Communication between Nurses and Nurse Managers: a Case Study from an NHS Trust', *Journal of Nursing Management*, **5**, 25–36.

13. Schweiger, D. and Denisi, A. (1991) 'Communication with Employees Following a Merger: a Longitudinal Field Experiment', *Academy of Management Journal*, **34**, 110–35.

14. Tropman, J. (1996) *Effective Meetings: Improving Group Decision Making*, 2nd edn, London: Sage.

15. Evans, R. (1997) 'Hollow the leader', *Report on Business Magazine*, November, p. 66.

16. Whetten, D. and Cameron, K. (1991) *Developing Management Skills*, 2nd edn, London: HarperCollins.

17. Locke, M. (1980) *How to Run Committees and Meetings: a Guidebook To Practical Politics*, London: Macmillan.

18. Huber, G. (1980) *Managerial Decision Making*, Glenview, IL: Scott Foresman and Co.

19. Rackham, N. and Morgan, T. (1977) *Behavior Analysis in Training*, Maidenhead: McGraw-Hill.

20. Whittington, D. (1986) 'Chairmanship', in O. Hargie (ed.), *A Handbook of Communication Skills*, London: Routledge.

21. Jarboe, S. (1996) 'Procedures for Enhancing Group Decision Making', in R. Hirokawa and M. Poole (eds.), *Communication and Group Decision Making*, 2nd edn, London: Sage, p. 356.

22. Bennis, W. (1989) *On Becoming A Leader*, London: Century Business.

CHAPTER 5   Stand and deliver: making effective presentations

1. Maes, J., Weldy, T. and Icenogle, M. (1997) 'A Managerial Perspective: Oral Communication Competency is Most Important for Business Students in the Workplace', *Journal of Business Communication*, **34**, 67–80.

2. Cosnett, G. (1990) 'A Survival Guide to Public Speaking', *Training and Development Journal*, **44**, 15–19.

3. Guirdham, M. (1996) *Interpersonal Skills at Work*, Hemel Hempstead: Prentice Hall Europe.

4. Hamilton, C. and Parker, C. (1990) *Communicating for Results*, Belmont: Wadsworth.

5. Mandel. S. (1987) *Effective Presentation Skills: a Practical Guide for Better Speaking*, Los Altos, CA: Crisp Publications.

6. DeVito, J. (1990) *The Elements of Public Speaking*, New York, Harper and Row.

7. McCarthy, P. and Hatcher, C. (1996) *Speaking Persuasively*, St Leonards, NSW: Allen and Unwin.

8. O'Hair, D. and Friedrich, G. (1992) *Strategic Communication in Business and the Professions*, Boston: Houghton Mifflin.

9. Hargie, O., Saunders, C. and Dickson, D. (1994) *Social Skills in Interpersonal Communication*, London: Routledge.
10. Steven, M. (1989) *Improve Your Presentation Skills: a Complete Action Kit*, London, Kogan Page.
11. McDaniel, R. (1994) *Scared Speechless: Public Speaking Step by Step*, Thousand Oaks CA: Sage.
12. Turk, C. (1985) *Effective Speaking: Communicating in Speech*, London: Spon.
13. Wood, J. (1988) *Speaking Effectively*, New York: Random House.
14. Dickson, D., Hargie, O. and Morrow, N. (1997) *Communication Skills Training for Health Professionals*, London: Chapman and Hall.
15. Brown, G. (1997) 'Explaining', in O. Hargie (ed.) *The Handbook of Communication Skills*, London: Routledge.
16. Brosius, H. and Bathfelt, A. (1994) 'The Utility of Exemplars in Persuasive Communications', *Communication Research*, **21**, 48–78.
17. Knapper, M. (1981) 'Presenting and Public Speaking', in M. Argyle (ed.) *Social Skills and Work*, London: Methuen.
18. Nadeau, R., Jablonski, C. and Gardner, G. (1993) *Speaking Effectively in Public Settings*, Lanham, MD: University Press of America.
19. Hargie, O. and Morrow, N. (1995) 'An Evaluation of a Presentation Skills Course for Pharmacists', *International Journal of Pharmacy Practice*, **3**, 101–5.

CHAPTER 6   I think we've got ourselves a deal: negotiating and bargaining

1. O'Hair, D. and Friedrich, G. (1992) *Strategic Communication in Business and the Professions*, Boston: Houghton Mifflin, p. 358.
2. Bolton, R. (1986) *People Skills: How to Assert Yourself, Listen to Others, and Resolve Conflicts*, Brookvale, Australia: Simon and Schuster, p. 206.
3. Thomas, K. (1976) 'Conflict and Conflict Management', in M. Dunnette (ed.), *Handbook of Industrial and Organizational Psychology*, Chicago: Rand McNally.
4. Lawyer, J. and Katz, N. (1985) *Communication and Conflict Management Skills*, Dubuque, IA: Kendall/Hunt.
5. Pruitt, D. and Carnevale, P. (1993) *Negotiation in Social Conflict,* Buckingham: Open University Press.
6. LePoole, S. (1991) *Never Take No for an Answer: a Guide to Successful Negotiating*, London: Kogan Page.
7. Thompson, L. (1992) 'Negotiation Behaviour and Outcomes: Empirical Evidence and Theoretical Issues', *Psychological Bulletin*, **108**, 515–32.
8. Brandenburger, A. and Nalebuff, B. (1996) *Co-opetition*, New York: Doubleday.
9. Berlew, D. (1990) 'How to Increase your Influence', in I. Asherman and S. Asherman (eds), *The Negotiating Sourcebook*, Amherst, MA: Human Resource Development Press, p. 33.

10. Putnam, L. and Roloff, M. (1992) 'Communication Perspectives on Negotiation', in L. Putnam and M. Roloff (eds), *Communication and Negotiation*, Newbury Park, CA: Sage, p. 3.
11. Fisher, R. and Ury, W. (1981) *Getting to Yes: Negotiating an Agreement without Giving in*, London: Hutchinson, p. 64.
12. Morley, I. (1986) 'Negotiating and Bargaining', in O. Hargie (ed.), *A Handbook of Communication Skills*, London: Routledge.
13. Scott, B. (1988) *Negotiating: Constructive and Competitive Negotiation,* London: Paradigm Press.
14. Lewicki, R. and Litterer, J. (1985) *Negotiation*, Homewood, IL: Irwin.
15. Karrass, C. (1970) *The Negotiation Game*, New York: Thomas Y. Crowell.
16. Roloff, M. and Jordan, J. (1992) 'Achieving Negotiation Goals: the "Fruits and Foibles" of Planning Ahead', in L. Putnam and M. Roloff (eds), *Communication and Negotiation*, Newbury Park, CA: Sage.
17. Mattock, J. and Ehrenborg, J. (1996) *How to be a Better Negotiator*, London: Kogan Page.
18. Rackham, N. and Carlisle, J. (1978) 'The Effective Negotiator – Part 2', *Journal of European Industrial Training*, **2**, 2–5.
19. Mills, H. (1991) *Negotiate: The Art of Winning*, London: BCA.
20. Berry, W. (1996) *Negotiating in the Age of Integrity: a Complete Guide to Negotiating Win/Win in Business*, London: Nicolas Brealey.
21. Pruitt, D. (1981) *Negotiating Behaviour.* New York: Academic Press.
22. Rackham, N. and Carlisle, J. (1978) 'The Effective Negotiator – Part 1', *Journal of European Industrial Training*, **2** (6), 6–10.

CHAPTER 7   Selling the idea: the manager as salesperson

1. O'Hair, D. and Friedrich, G. (1992) *Strategic Communication*, Boston: Houghton Mifflin, p. 453.
2. Hersey, P. (1988) *Selling: a Behavioral Science Approach*, Englewood Cliffs, NJ: Prentice Hall.
3. Lund, P.R. (1987) *Compelling Selling: a Framework for Persuasion*, London: Macmillan Papermac.
4. Doyle, S. and Roth, G. (1992) 'Selling and Sales Management in Action', *Journal of Personal Selling and Sales Management*, **12**, 59–64.
5. Hayes, H.M. and Hartley, S.W. (1989) 'How Buyers View Industrial Salespeople', *Industrial Marketing Management*, **18**, 73–80.
6. Miles, M., Arnold, D. and Nash, H. (1990) 'Adaptive Communication: the Adaptation of the Seller's Interpersonal Style to the Stage of the Dyad's

Relationship and the Buyer's Communication Style', *Journal of Personal Selling and Sales Management*, **10**, 21–7.

7. Comstock, J. and Higgins, G. (1997) 'Appropriate Relational Messages in Direct Selling Interaction: Should Salespeople Adapt to Buyers' Communicator Style?' *Journal of Business Communication*, **34**, 410–18.

8. Hawes, J., Mast, K. and Swan, J. (1989) 'Trust Earning Perceptions of Sellers and Buyers', *Journal of Personal Selling and Sales Management*, **9**, 1–8.

9. Hargie, O. and Morrow, N (1987) 'Interpersonal Communication: the Sales Approach', *Pharmacy Update*, **3**, 320–24.

10. Kossen, S. (1982) *Creative Selling Today*, New York: Harper and Row.

11. Rackham, N. (1995) *Spin Selling*, Aldershot: Gower.

12. Poppleton, S.E. (1981) 'The Social Skills of Selling', in M. Argyle (ed.) *Social Skills and Work*, London: Methuen.

13. Davis, W. (1986) *The Supersalesman's Handbook*, New York: Sidgwick and Jackson.

14. Williams, A. (1983) *All About Selling*, London: McGraw-Hill, p. 99.

15. Marks, R. (1985) *Personal Selling: an Interactive Approach*, Boston: Allyn and Bacon.

16. Miller, R. and Heiman, S. (1988) *Conceptual Selling*, London: Kogan Page.

17. Hayward, S. (1998) 'Sales Executives Still Struggle to Sell Themselves', *Sunday Times*, 11 January, p. 36.

18. Ehninger, D., Gronbeck, B. and Monroe, A. (1984) *Principles of Speech Communication*, Glenview, IL: Scott, Foresman and Co.

19. Yoder, D., Hugenberg, L. and Wallace, S. (1993) *Creating Competent Communication*, Madison, WI: Brown and Benchmark.

20. Brown, G., Boya, U., Humphreys, N. and Widing, R. (1993) 'Attributes and Behaviors Preferred by Buyers: High Socializing Vs. Low Socializing Industrial Buyers', *Journal of Personal Selling and Sales Management*, **13**, 25–33.

21. Crosby, L., Evans, K. and Cowles, D. (1990) 'Relationship Quality in Services Selling: an Interpersonal Influence Perspective', *Journal of Marketing*, **54**, 68–81.

CHAPTER 8   Making the right connections: the telephone in business

1. Office of Population Censuses and Surveys (1992) *General Household Survey*, London: OPCS.

2. Irwin, A. (1998) 'Calls to Mobile Phones "a Rip Off"', *Daily Telegraph*, 6 March, p. 6.

3. Jagoda, A. and de Villepin, M. (1993) *Mobile Communications*, Chicester: Wiley.

4. Kennedy, D. (1998) 'Millions Call for Privacy', *The Times*, 14 February, p. 10.

5. Freephone, *Daily Telegraph*, Special Supplement, 4 July 1997.
6. Advertising feature by Kent County Constabulary and BT, *The Times*, 24 December 1997, p. 5.
7. Short, J., Williams, E. and Christie, B. (1976) *The Social Psychology of Telecommunications*, Chichester: John Wiley.
8. Frey, J.H. (1989) *Survey Research by Telephone*, 2nd edn, Newbury Park, CA: Sage, p. 16.
9. Hargie, C. and Tourish, D. (1997) 'Relational Communication', in O. Hargie (ed.) *The Handbook of Communication Skills*, London: Routledge.
10. Argyle, M. and Henderson, M. (1985) *The Anatomy of Relationships*, Harmondsworth: Penguin.
11. Rutter, D.R. (1979) *Communicating by Telephone*, Oxford: Pergamon Press.
12. Argyle, M. (1988) *Bodily Communication*, 2nd edn, London: Methuen, p. 118.
13. Beattie, G. (1983) *Talk: an Analysis of Speech and Non-verbal Behaviour in Conversation*, Milton Keynes: Open University.
14. Hargie, O. (1997) 'Interpersonal Communication: a Theoretical Framework', in O. Hargie (ed.) *The Handbook of Communication Skills*, London: Routledge.
15. Goddard, J. (1973) *Office Linkages and Location*, London: Pergamon Press.
16. Hargie, O. and Tourish, D. (1996) 'Auditing Communication Practices to Improve the Management of Human Resources: an Inter-Organisational Study', *Health Services Management Research*, **9**, 209–22.
17. MacErlean, N. (1997) 'How to Deal with Rudeness on the Telephone', *Observer*, 31 October.
18. Barry, B. and Bateman, T. (1992) 'Perceptions of Influence in Managerial Dyads: the Role of Hierarchy, Media and Tactics', *Human Relations*, **45**, 555–74.
19. Lyman, G.C. (1984) 'Voice Messaging Comes Of Age', *Speech Technology*, **2**, 45–9.
20. 'Don't Touch that Phone', *Wall Street Journal*, 25 July 1989, p. A1.
21. Kleinke, C. (1986) *Meeting and Understanding People*, New York: Freeman.
22. Feldman, R. and Rime, B. (eds) (1991) *Fundamentals of Nonverbal Behaviour*, Cambridge: Cambridge University Press.
23. Rosenfield, R. (1997) *Counselling by Telephone*, London: Sage.
24. Schegloff, E. (1987) 'Identification and Recognition in Interactional Openings', in I. Pool (ed.) *The Social Impact of the Telephone*, Cambridge, MA: MIT Press.
25. Roman, E. (1993) *How to Use the Telephone Effectively and Economically*, London: Business Books.
26. Shafiroff, M. and Shook, R.L. (1982) *Successful Telephone Selling in the '80s*, New York: Harper and Row.
27. Pool, I. (ed.) (1987) *The Social Impact of the Telephone*, Cambridge, MA: MIT Press.

CHAPTER 9　The word made permanent: putting it in writing

1. Mabrito, M. (1997) 'Writing on the Front Line: a Study of Workplace Writing', *Business Communication Quarterly*, **60**, 58–70.
2. Hobson, R. (1997) 'Getting the Message: We Value your Custom', *The Times*, Special Supplement: Communicating with your Customer, 18 February, p. 2.
3. Jones, T. (1997) 'Retaining the Thrill of the Letter', *The Times*, Special Supplement: Communicating with your Customer, 18 February, p. 8.
4. Jones, T. (1997) 'Create the Write Impression', *The Times*, Special Supplement: Communicating with your Customer, 18 February, p. 8.
5. Sutherland, S. (1992), *Irrationality*, London: Constable.
6. Peters, T. (1988) *Thriving on Chaos*, London: Macmillan.
7. Hargie, O. and Tourish, D. (1996) 'Auditing Communication Practices to Improve the Management of Human Resources: a Regional Study', *Health Services Management Research*, **9**, 209–22.
8. Huettman, E. (1996) 'Writing for Multiple Audiences: an Examination of Audience Concerns in a Hospitality Consulting Firm', *Journal of Business Communication*, **33**, 257–73.
9. Ley, P., Flaherty, B., Smith, F., Martin, J. and Renner, P. (1985) *A Comparative Study of the Effects of Two Warning Messages about Volatile Substances*, Sydney, NSW: New South Wales Drug and Alcohol Authority.
10. Young, L. and Humphrey, M. (1985) 'Cognitive Methods of Preparing Women for Hysterectomy: Does a Booklet Help?' *British Journal of Clinical Psychology*, **24**, 303–4.
11. Tourish, D. and Hargie, O. (1998) 'Communication between Managers and Staff in the NHS: Trends and Prospects', *British Journal of Management*, **9**, 53–71.
12. Pratkanis, A. and Aronson, E. (1991) *Age of Propaganda*, New York: W.H. Freeman.
13. Suchan, J. and Colucci, R. (1989) 'Analysis of Communication Efficiency between High-Impact and Bureaucratic Written Communication', *Management Communication Quarterly*, **2**, 454–84.
14. Ogilvy, D. (1987) *Confessions of an Advertising Man*, London: Pan.
15. Ogilvy, D. (1983) *Ogilvy on Advertising*, London: Pan.
16. Poulton, E., Warren, T. and Bond, J. (1970) 'Ergonomics in Journal Design', *Applied Ergonomics*, **13**, 207–9.
17. Roman, K. and Raphaelson, J. (1981) *Writing That Works*, New York: Harper and Row.
18. Orwell, G. (1970) 'Politics and the English Language', in I. Angus and S. Orwell (eds), *The Collected Essays, Journalism and Letters: Volume 4*, London: Penguin.
19. Padget, P. (1983) *Communications and Reports*, London: Cassell.
20. Ley, P. (1988) *Communicating with Patients*, London: Croom Helm.

21. Bailey, E. (1990) *The Plain English Approach to Business Writing*, Oxford: Oxford University Press.

22. Hartley, J. (1992) 'Return to Sender: Why Written Communications Fail', *The Psychologist*, **11**, 477–80.

23. Bowman, J. and Branchaw, B. (1983) *Business Report Writing*, Chicago: Holt-Saunders, p. 7.

24. Adair, J. (1988) *The Effective Communicator*, London: The Industrial Society.

25. Baig, E. (1994) Ready Steady – Go On-Line, *Business Week: the Information Revolution*, Special Issue, 18 May, 124–33.

26. Globe and Mail (1997) 'Are you Ready for E-business?' *Globe and Mail*, Advertising Supplement, 30 October.

27. Kiesler, S. (1986) 'Thinking Ahead', *Harvard Business Review*, **64**, 46–60.

28. Utley, A. (1997) 'Abusive E-mails Ignite Work Fury', *Times Higher Education Supplement*, 30 May, p. 1.

29. Angell, D. and Heslop, B. (1994) *The Elements of E-mail Style*, London: Addison-Wesley.

30. Quirke, B. (1996) *Communicating Corporate Change*, Maidenhead: McGraw-Hill.

31. Goodworth, C. (1986) *The Secrets of Successful Business Letters*, London: Heinemann.

CHAPTER 10   It's your right: communicating assertively

1. Rakos, R. (1997) 'Asserting and Confronting', in Hargie, O. (ed), *The Handbook of Communication Skills*, London: Routledge.

2. Lazarus, A. (1971) *Behaviour Therapy and Beyond*, New York: McGraw-Hill, p. 38.

3. Lange, A. and Jakubowski, P. (1976) *Responsible Assertive Behaviour*, Champaign, IL: Research Press.

4. Zuker, E. (1983) *The Assertive Manager: Positive Skills at Work for You*, New York: American Management Association.

5. Alberti, R. and Emmons, M. (1975) *Stand Up, Speak Out, Talk Back: the Key to Assertive Behaviour*, San Louis Obispo, CA: Impact, p. 13.

6. Hargie, O., Saunders, C. and Dickson, D. (1994) *Social Skills in Interpersonal Communication*, London: Routledge, p. 270.

7. Gillen, T. (1992) *Assertiveness for Managers*, Aldershot: Gower.

8. DeGiovanni, I. (1979) 'Development and Validation of an Assertiveness Scale for Couples', *Dissertation Abstracts International*, **39** (9-B), 4573.

9. Burley-Allen, M. (1995) *Managing Assertively: a Self-Teaching Guide*, New York: John Wiley.

10. Back, K. and Back, K. (1992) *Assertiveness at Work*, Maidenhead: McGraw-Hill.
11. Willcocks, G. and Morris, S. (1996) *Putting Assertiveness to Work: a Programme for Management Excellence*, London: Pitman.
12. Stubbs, D (1985) *How to Use Assertiveness at Work*, Aldershot: Gower, p. 15.
13. Bandura, A. (1997) *Self-efficacy: the Exercise of Control*, New York: Freeman and Co.
14. O'Brien, P. (1992) *Positive Management: Assertiveness for Managers*, London: Nicholas Brealey.
15. Fry, L. (1983) 'Women in Society', in S. Spence and G. Shepherd (eds), *Developments in Social Skills Training*, London: Academic Press.
16. Mullinix, S. and Galassi, J. (1981) 'Deriving the Content of Social Skills Training with a Verbal Components Approach', *Behavioural Assessment*, **3**, 55–66.
17. Solomon, L., Brehony, K., Rothblum, E. and Kelly, J. (1982) '"Corporate Managers' Reaction to Assertive Social Skills Exhibited by Males And Females", *Journal of Organizational Behaviour Management*, **4**, 49–63.
18. Sigal, J., Branden-Maguire, J., Hayden, M. and Mosley, N. (1985) 'The Effect of Presentation Style and Sex of Lawyer on Jury Decision-Making Behaviour', *Psychology: a Quarterly Journal of Human Behaviour*, **22**, 13–19.
19. Bryan, A. and Gallois, C. (1992) 'Rules about Assertion in the Workplace: Effects of Status and Message Type', *Australian Journal of Psychology*, **44**, 51–9.
20. Fensterheim, H. and Baer, J. (1975) *Don't Say Yes When You Want to Say No*, New York: David McKay, p. 14.

CHAPTER 11   A problem shared: helping communication

1. Hughes, J. (1991) *Counselling for Managers: An Introductory Guide*, London: Bacie.
2. Sworder, G. (1977) 'Counselling Problems at Work: Where Do We Go from Here?', in T. Watts (ed.), *Counselling at Work,* Plymouth: Bedford Square Press.
3. Pont, T. and Pont, G. (1998) *Interviewing Skills for Managers*, London: Piatkus.
4. Martin, P. (1997) 'Counselling Skills Training for Managers in the Public Sector', in M. Carroll and M. Walton (eds), *Handbook of Counselling in Organizations*, London: Sage, p. 245.
5. Tysoe, M. (1988) *All This and Work Too: the Psychology of Office Life*, London: Fontana.
6. Green, C. (1997) 'Employee Counselling: Historical Developments and Key Issues', in C. Feltham (ed.), *The Gains of Listening: Perspectives on Counselling at Work*, Buckingham: Open University Press.
7. Carroll, M. (1996) *Workplace Counselling*, London: Sage.

8. Buckingham, I. (1992) 'A Headache that Won't Go Away', *Guardian*, 31 October, p. 38.

9. Wheeler, S. and Lyon, D. (1992) 'Employee Benefits from the Employer's Benefit: How Companies Respond to Employee Stress', *Personnel Review*, **21**, 47–65.

10. British Association for Counselling (1984) *Code of Ethics and Practice for Counsellors*, Rugby: BAC, p. 2.

11. Bull, A. (1997) 'Models of Counselling in Organizations', in M. Carroll and M. Walton (eds), *Handbook of Counselling in Organizations*, London: Sage.

12. Hopson, B. (1981) 'Counselling and Helping', in D. Griffiths (ed.), *Psychology and Medicine*, London: Macmillan, p. 267.

13. Highley-Marchington, C. and Cooper, C. (1997) 'Evaluating and Auditing Workplace Counselling Programmes', in M. Carroll and M. Walton (eds), *Handbook of Counselling in Organizations*, London: Sage.

14. Reddy, M. (ed.) (1993) *EAPs and Counselling Provision in UK Organisations*, London: Independent Counselling and Advisory Services.

15. de Board, R. (1983) *Counselling People at Work*, Aldershot: Gower, p. x.

16. British Association for Counselling (1992) *Code of Ethics and Practice for Counsellors*, Rugby: BAC.

17. Nixon, J. (1997) 'Line Management and Counselling', in M. Carroll and M. Walton (eds), *Handbook of Counselling in Organizations*, London: Sage.

18. Reddy, M. (1987) *The Manager's Guide to Counselling at Work*, London: Methuen.

19. Rogers, C. (1957) 'The Necessary and Sufficient Conditions of Therapeutic Personality Change', *Journal of Counselling Psychology*, **21**, 95–103.

20. DeVito, J. (1992) *The Interpersonal Communication Book*, New York: HarperCollins.

21. Northouse, P. and Northouse, L. (1992) *Health Communication: Strategies for Health Professionals*, Norwalk, CT: Appleton and Lange.

22. Irving, P. (1995) 'A Re-conceptualisation of Rogerian Core Conditions of Facilitative Communication: Implications for Training', unpublished PhD thesis, University of Ulster, Jordanstown.

23. Rogers, C. (1975) 'Empathic: an Unappreciated Way of Being', *The Counseling Psychologist*, **5**, 2–10.

24. Dutfield, M. and Eling, C. (1990) *The Communicating Manager: A Guide to Working Effectively with People*, Longmead: Element Books.

25. Egan, G (1998) *The Skilled Helper*. New York: Brooks/Cole.

26. Murgatroyd, S. (1985) *Counselling and Helping*, London: Methuen.

27. Nurse, G. (1975) *Counselling and the Nurse*, Aylesbury: HM&M Publications.

28. Dickson, D., Hargie, O. and Morrow, N. (1997) *Communication Skills Training for Health Professionals*, London: Chapman and Hall.

29. Brammer, L. (1993) *The Helping Relationship: Process and Skills*, Englewood Cliffs, NJ: Prentice-Hall.

30. Hargie, O., Saunders, D. and Dickson, D. (1994) *Social Skills in Interpersonal Communication*, London: Routledge.

31. Authier, J. (1986) 'Showing Warmth and Empathy', in O. Hargie. (ed.), *A Handbook of Communication Skills*, London: Croom Helm.

32. Geldard, D. (1993) *Basic Personal Counselling*, 2nd edn, Sydney: Prentice-Hall.

CHAPTER 12 'Our most important asset': selecting people

1. *Belfast Telegraph* (1997) Business Section (news item), 10 February, p. 9.

2. Dawes, R. (1994) *House of Cards*, New York: Free Press.

3. Anderson, N. and Shackleton, V. (1993) *Successful Selection Interviewing*, Oxford: Blackwell.

4. Jones, E. (1990) *Interpersonal Perception*, New York: Freeman.

5. Pfeffer, J. (1998) *The Human Equation*, Boston: Harvard Business School Press.

6. Levant, J. (1995) *Selecting The Right People*, Hertfordshire: Technical Communications.

7. Anderson, N. and Shackleton, V. (1990) 'Decision Making in the Graduate Selection Interview: a Field Study', *Journal of Occupational Psychology*, **63**, 63–76.

8. Hamilton, C. and Parker, C. (1990) *Communicating For Results*, 3rd edn, London: Wadsworth.

9. Bolster, B. and Springbett, N. (1981) 'The Reaction of Interviewers to Favourable And Unfavourable Information', *Journal of Applied Psychology*, **45**, 97–103.

10. Janz, J. (1982) 'Initial Comparisons of Patterned Behaviour Description Interviews Versus Unstructured Interviews', *Journal of Applied Psychology*, **67**, 129–34.

11. Roth, P. and McMillan, J. (1993) 'The Behaviour Description Interview', *CPA Journal*, December, 76–9.

12. Van Clieaf, M. (1994) 'In Search of Competence: Structured Behaviour Interviews', *Business Horizons*, **34** (2), 51–5.

13. Benjamin, A. (1981) *The Helping Interview*, 3rd edn, New York: Houghton Mifflin, p. 17.

14. Hornby, M. (1991) 'How to Succeed in Recruitment Interviews', *Training and Development*, **9**, 17–20.

15. Institute of Personnel Management (1991) *The IPM Recruitment Code*, London: IPM, p. 7.

16. Hackney, M. and Kleiner, B. (1994) 'Conducting an Effective Selection Interview', *Recruitment, Selection and Retention*, **3**, 10–16.

17. Millar, R. and Gallagher, M. (1997) 'The Selection Interview', in O. Hargie (ed.), *A Handbook of Communication Skills*, 2nd edn, London: Routledge.

18. Black, J. (1982) *How To Get Results From Interviewing*, Malabar, FL: Robert Krieger.

19. Cooper, D. and Robertson, I. (1995) *The Psychology of Personnel Selection*, London: Routledge.

20. Fisher, P. (1995) 'I'm Glad You Asked That', *The Guardian*, Careers Supplement, 4 February, p. 2.

21. Dillon, J. (1990) *The Practice of Questioning*, London and New York: Routledge.

CHAPTER 13   Feedback time: appraising performance

1. Hargie, O. (1992) 'Communication: Beyond the Cross-roads', monograph: University of Ulster, Newtownabbey.

2. Tourish, D. (1999) 'Communicating beyond Individual Bias', in A. Long (ed.), *Advanced Interaction in the Health Care Setting*, London: Macmillan.

3. Manzoni, J. and Barsoux, J. (1998) 'The Set-up-to-Fail Syndrome', *Harvard Business Review*, **76**, 101–13.

4. Levinson, H. (1976) 'Appraisal of *What* Performance?', *Harvard Business Review*, **54**, 30–46.

5. Freemantle, D. (1994) *The Performance Of 'Performance Appraisal' – an Appraisal: a Superboss Research Report*, Windsor, Berks: Superboss, p. 4.

6. Latham, G. and Wexley, K. (1994) *Increasing Productivity through Performance Appraisal*, 2nd edn, Reading, MA: Addison-Wesley.

7. DeNisi, A. (1996) *A Cognitive Approach to Performance Appraisal*, London: Routledge.

8. Sutherland, S. (1992) *Irrationality*, London: Constable.

9. Wilke, H. and Meertens, R. (1994) *Group Performance*, London: Routledge.

10. Hewstone, M. (1989) *Causal Attribution*, Oxford: Blackwell.

11. Leyens, J., Yzerbyt, V. and Schadron, G. (1994) *Stereotypes and Social Cognition*, London: Sage.

12. Philp, T. (1983) *Making Performance Appraisal Work*, London: McGraw-Hill.

13. Millar, R., Hargie, O. and Crute, V. (1992) *Professional Interviewing*, London: Routledge.

14. Pettigrew, T. (1979) 'The Ultimate Attribution Error: Extending Allport's Cognitive Analysis of Prejudice', *Personality and Social Psychology Bulletin*, **5**, 461–76.

15. Wynne, B. (1995) *Performance Appraisal: a Practical Guide to Appraising the Performance of Employees*, Hertfordshire: Technical Communications.

16. Randall, G., Packard, P. and Slater, J. (1984) *Staff Appraisal: a First Step to Effective Leadership*, 3rd edn, London: Institute of Personnel Management.
17. Pfeffer, J. (1998) *The Human Equation: Building Profits By Putting People First*, Boston: Harvard Business School Press.
18. Institute of Manpower Studies (1993) *Pay and Performance – the Employee Experience*, Report, No. 258, London: IMS.
19. Anstey, E., Fletcher, C. and Walker, B. (1976) *Staff Appraisal and Development*, London: Allen and Unwin.
20. Lawson, I. (1989) *Notes For Managers: Appraisal and Appraisal Interviewing*, 3rd edn, London: The Industrial Society.
21. Eden, D. (1993) 'Interpersonal Expectations in Organisations', in P. Blanck (ed.) *Interpersonal Expectations: Theory, Research and Applications,* Cambridge: Cambridge University Press.
22. Goodworth, C. (1989) *The Secrets Of Successful Staff Appraisal And Counselling*, Oxford: Heinemann.
23. Hunt, N. (1994) *How To Conduct Staff Appraisals*, 2nd edn, Plymouth: How To Books.
24. Rakos, R. (1991) *Assertive Behaviour: Theory, Research and Practice*, London: Routledge.
25. Kolt, W. and Donohue, R. (1992) *Managing Interpersonal Conflict*, London: Sage.
26. Cialdini, R (1993) *Influence*, 3rd edn, New York: HarperCollins.
27. Semler, R. (1993) *Maverick*, London: Century.

CHAPTER 14   More than words can tell: communicating non-verbally

1. Abercrombie, K. (1968) 'Paralanguage', *British Journal of Communication*, **3**, 55–9.
2. Mehrabian, A. (1972) *Non-verbal Communication*, Chicago: Aldine-Atherton.
3. DePaulo, P. (1992) Applications of Non-verbal Behaviour Research in Marketing and Management, in R. Feldman (ed.), *Applications of Non-verbal Theories and Research*, Hillsdale, NJ: Lawrence Erlbaum, p. 63.
4. Graham, G., Unruth, J. and Jennings, P. (1991) 'The Impact of Non-verbal Communication in Organizations: a Survey of Perceptions', *The Journal of Business Communication*, **28**, 45–62.
5. Carnevale, A., Gainer, L. and Meltzer, S. (1991) *Work-place Basics: the Essential Skills Employers Want*, San Francisco: Jossey-Bass.
6. Burgoon, J., Buller, D. and Woodall, W. (1989) *Non-verbal Communication: the Unspoken Dialogue*, New York: Harper and Row.

7. McElroy, J. and Loundenback, L. (1981) 'Personal Space and Personal Selling: Customer Reactions to Personal Space Invasion', *Proceedings of the Educator Seminar*, **38**, 52.
8. Mead, R. (1992) *Cross-Cultural Management Communication*, New York: Wiley.
9. Hall, E. (1966) *The Hidden Dimension*, Garden City, NY: Doubleday.
10. Korda, M. (1975) *Power! How to Get It, How to Use It*, New York: Random.
11. Cook, M. (1970) 'Experiments on Orientation and Proxemics', *Human Relations*, **23**, 61–76.
12. Ekman, P. and Friesen, W. (1975) *Unmasking the Face*, Englewood Cliffs, NJ: Prentice-Hall.
13. McGinniss, J. (1969) *The Selling of the President 1968*, New York: Simon and Schuster.
14. Kalin, R. and Raydo, D. (1978) 'Discrimination in Evaluative Judgements against Foreign-Accented Job Applicants', *Psychological Reports*, **43**, 1203–9.
15. Ornstein, S. (1989) 'Impression Management', in R. Giacaolone and P. Rosenfeld (eds), *Impression Management in the Organization*, Hillsdale, NJ: Lawrence Erlbaum.
16. Hamilton, C. and Parker, C. (1990) *Communicating for Results*, Belmont, CA: Wadsworth.
17. Knapp, M. and Hall, J. (1992) *Non-verbal Communication in Human Interaction*, Fort Worth: Holt, Rinehart and Winston.
18. Grattan, G. (1997) Telegraph Education, *Belfast Telegraph*, 1 July, p. 18.
19. Molloy, J. (1975) *Dress for Success*, New York: Peter H. Wyden.
20. Golden, N. (1986) *Dress Right for Business*, New York: McGraw-Hill.
21. Molloy, J. (1977) *The Women's Dress for Success Book*, Chicago: Follett.
22. Wallach, J. (1986) *Looks that Work*, New York: Viking Penguin.
23. Goffman E. (1959) *The Presentation of Self in Everyday Life*, New York: Anchor Books.

CHAPTER 15 Ethics and audits: doing things right and doing the right thing

1. Frank, A. and Brownell, J. (1989) *Organizational Communication and Behavior: Communicating to Improve Performance*, New York: Holt, Rinehart and Winston.
2. Downs, C.W. (1988) *Communication Audits*, Glenview, IL: Scott, Foresman and Co.
3. Green, R. (1994) *The Ethical Manager: a New Method for Business Ethics*, New York: Macmillan College Publishing.

4. Freeman, R. (ed.) (1991) *Business Ethics: the State of the Art*, Oxford: Oxford University Press.

5. Donaldson, T. and Gini, A. (1990) *Case Studies in Business Ethics*, Englewood Cliffs, NJ: Prentice Hall.

6. *The Sunday Times*, 29 March 1998.

7. Sternberg, E. (1994) *Just Business: Business Ethics in Action*, London: Little, Brown and Company, p. 19.

8. Punch, M. (1996) *Dirty Business: Exploring Corporate Misconduct*, London: Sage.

9. Hoffman, W. and Moore, J. (eds) (1990) *Business Ethics: Readings and Case Studies in Corporate Morality*, New York: McGraw-Hill.

10. Hasselkus, W. (1998) 'Manager's Maxim', *Observer*, Work Section, 29 March, p. I.

11. Clampitt, P.G. (1991) *Communicating for Managerial Effectiveness*, Newbury Park, CA: Sage.

12. Kreps, G. (1990) *Organizational Communication: Theory and Practice*, 2nd edn, New York: Longman.

13. Buller, D. and Burgoon, J. (1996) 'Interpersonal Deception Theory', *Communication Theory*, **6**, 203–242.

14. Clampitt, P. and Benson, J.A. (1988) 'Crisis Revisited: an Analysis of Strategies Used by Tylenol in the Second Tampering Episode', *Central States Speech Journal*, **39**, 49–66.

15. Badaracco, J.L. (1998) 'The Discipline of Building Character', *Harvard Business Review*, March–April, 115–24.

16. Church, A.H. (1994) 'The Character of Organizational Communication: a Review and New Conceptualisation', *International Journal of Organizational Analysis*, **2**, 18–53, esp. 19.

17. Baumeister, R. (1989) 'Motives and Costs of Self-Presentation in Organizations', in R.A. Giacalone and P. Rosenfeld (eds) *Impression Management in the Organization*, Hillsdale, NJ: Lawrence Erlbaum.

18. Hurst, B. (1991) *The Handbook of Communication Skills*, London: Kogan Page, p. 24.

19. Tourish, D. and Hargie, O. (1998) 'Communication between Managers and Staff in the NHS: Trends and Prospects', *British Journal of Management*, **9**, 53–71.

20. Goldhaber, G. and Rogers, D. (1979) *Auditing Organisational Communication Systems*, Texas: Kendall-Hunt.

21. Lount, M. (1997) *Interpersonal Communication Processes in the Pastoral Ministry Of Catholic Clergy*, PhD thesis, Jordanstown: University of Ulster.

22. Hargie, O. and Tourish, D. (1996) 'Auditing Internal Communication to Build Business Success', *Internal Communication Focus*, November, 10–14.

23. Tourish, D. and Hargie, O. (1996) 'Communication in the NHS: Using Qualitative Approaches to Analyse Effectiveness', *Journal of Management in Medicine*, **10**, 38–54.

24. Millar, R., Crute, V. and Hargie, O. (1992) *Professional Interviewing*, London: Routledge.

25. Millward, L. (1995) 'Focus Groups', in G. Breakwell, S. Hammond and C. Fife-Shaw (eds), *Research Methods in Psychology*, London: Sage, p. 275.

26. Hargie, O. and Tourish, D. (1996) 'Auditing Communication Practices to Improve the Management of Human Resources: an Inter-Organisational Study', *Health Services Management Research*, **9**, 209–22.

27. Hargie, C. and Tourish, D. (1996) 'Corporate Communication in the Management Of Innovation and Change', *Corporate Communications: An International Journal*, **1**, 3–11.

28. Pfeffer, J. (1998) *The Human Equation*, Boston: Harvard Business School Press, p. 305.

Subject index

appraisal interviews 21, 259–79
  biases in 261–5
  definition of 260–261
  functions of 260
  interviewee's perspective 262–3
  interviewer's perspective 263–5
  managing the interview 267–7
  preparation for 268–71
  principles of 265–6
  problems in 266–7
assertiveness 20, 38, 187–210
  and aggression 192–6
  and submissiveness 196–200
  benefits of 208–9
  elements of 201
  impinging variables 206–7
  in management 188–92
  non-verbal behaviours of 205–6
  rationale for 187–8
  rights and beliefs 200–203
  verbal behaviours of 203–5
attribution 236, 262, 264
authoritarian leaders 69

bargaining 19–20, 105–29
behaviour description interviews 237,
  240–245, 246–7
bullying 31–2

chairing meetings 75–80
chairing skills 78–9
cognitive dissonance 145
college graduates 1
communication
  auditing 312–6
  channels of 16
  context 17

definition of 13
elements of 15–18
ethics 307–12
functions of in organizations 306–7
interpersonal 14
intrapersonal 14
mass 15
messages 16
network 15
noise 16–17
strategy of in organizations 316–17
communication audits 71, 170, 181,
  312–16
  definition of 313
  functions of 313–14
  measures 314–16
communication skills training 12
communication strategy 316–17
communication task force 317
conflict 106–7
consistency error 264
counselling 211–34
  definition of 214–15
  effects of 215–16
  importance of in organizations 211–13
  qualities of helpers 217–21
  role of the manager in 216–17
  skills of 221–9
  stages of 229–32
culture 17, 207, 289

democratic leaders 69
door-in-the-face technique 29

e-mail 181–3
emotional intelligence 15–16
empathy 217–19

Employee Assistance Programmes (EAPs)
    215
enthusiasm 80
Episodic Communication Channels in
    Organizations (ECCO) 315–16
ethics 307–12
expectancy effect 51

feedback 17
focus groups 315
foot-in-the-door technique 29
future shock 152

gender 207
genuineness 219–20
groupthink 58–9

halo error 238–9, 263–4
horn effect 264
helping skills 20–21, 211–34
humour 39

information fatigue syndrome 152
Internet 181

job specifications 248–9

laissez-faire leaders 69
leadership 19, 66–71
    of meetings 72–3, 75–80
    roles 66
    styles of 67–71
listening 222–4

management
    definition of 67
    style of 8–9, 67
manager
    definition of 7
Maslow's hierarchy of human needs 136–7
meetings
    blocks to effectiveness of 73–5
    planning of 76–8
    role of 71
    when to call 72–3
Monroe's motivated sequence 146–7
multiphrenia 152

negotiation 19–20, 105–29
    and bargaining 122–4
    characteristics of 107–10
    exploration phase 119–20
    importance of 105–6

making concessions 124–5
    making proposals 121– 6
    opening phase 118–19
    planning for 113–18
    reaching settlements 124–6
    skills of 126–9
    stages in 112– 26
    strategies of 110–12
neurolinguistic programming 295–6
non-verbal communication 21, 281–303
    appearance and dress 300–302
    environmental aspects of 299–300
    facial expressions 293–4
    functions of 284–6
    gaze 294–5
    gestures 295–6
    importance of 282–3
    interpersonal distance 287–9
    in management 283–4
    personal space 287
    posture 297
    spatial arrangements 289–93
    vocalics 297–9

organizations
    best communication practices in 6,
        316–17
    culture of 17
    definition of 2–4
    ethical issues in 307–12
    functions of communication in 306–7
    goals of 3
    metaphors for 4

performance-related pay 267
persuasion 19, 23–43
    and the boomerang effect 25
    and the sleeper effect 25
    central and peripheral routes to 41
    definition of 23
    emotional proofs 31–4
    in presentations 87
    logical proofs 27–31
    outcomes of 24–5
    personal proofs 34–9
    purposes of 24
    sequence of 25–6
    strategies of 39–42
    written strategies of 171–2
Pessimist's Charter 317–18
Plain English Campaign 175
positive regard 220–21
power 34–7

presentations 19, 83–103
  anxiety in 90, 92–3
  audio-visual aids in 95, 99
  content of 91–8
  delivery of 98–101
  features of successful presenters 88–9
  importance of 83–4
  structure of 95–8
  the audience 91, 94
  the role of the presenter 88–90
  the setting 102
  types of 86–9

selection interviews 21, 235–57
  behaviour description interview 240–45,
      246–7
  biases in 238–40
  closing phase 252
  interviewee's perspective 254–6
  listening skills of 251–2
  planning and preparation 245–9
  post-interview action 252–3
  process of 237–40
  opening phase 249–51
  role of the CV in 250
self-disclosure 224–6
self-serving bias 236
self-monitoring 17
selling 20, 131–49
  closing techniques in 144–5
  establishing needs 135–8
  making a sales presentation 138–41
  opening techniques in 132–5
  overcoming objections 141–4
  role of additional sales suggestions 144
similarity bias 264
sleeper effect 25, 98
social loafing 60–61

speech dysfluencies 155–6
staff views on communications 11–13

teams 19, 45–63, 65–81
  achievements of 47
  barriers to team development 55–61
  celebrations within 53–4
  characteristics of success in 50–55
  functions of 45–7
  goals of 50–51
  productivity of 60–61
  social rewards in 53–5
  stages of development of 48–50
  symptoms of team ruination 48
techno stress 152
telephone 1, 151–66
  communication problems on 161–2
  differences between telephone and face-
      to-face interaction 155–9
  disliked behaviours on 159–61
  making and answering calls 162,
      164–5
  norms of telephone behaviour 154–5
Theory X and Theory Y 9
training 12–13

upward communication 11–12

whistle-blowing 310
written communication 20, 167–85
  and complaints 183–4
  dynamic writing 177
  e-mail 181–3
  evaluation of 170–72
  high impact style 172–6
  letters and memos 176
  reports 177–81
  strategic role of 168–70

Name index

Apple Computers 182
Argyle, M. 154
Aristotle 23, 27
Armstrong, Sir Robert 309
AT&T 5, 152, 260
Auden, W.H. 39
Austin, N. 50

Balmford, C. 185
Bank of America 260
Bass, B. 1
Beatles, 138
Bell, A.G. 151
Blair, T. 39
Body Shop 54
Bolton, R. 106
Brandenburger, A. 107
Branson, R. 18
British Association of Counselling (BAC)
    214, 217
British Telecom 159, 161
Brownell, J. 317
Burke, E. 37
Burns, Robert 317

CableTel 5, 7
Cameron, K. 56, 73
Carnegie, D. 39
Carphone Warehouse 54
Carroll, M. 211
Caterpillar 260
Church, A. 313
Churchill, Winston 91, 105, 259
Citibank 160
Clampitt, P. 172
Cohn, H. 290
Columbia Pictures 290

Conan Doyle, Arthur 281
Confucius 167, 305

Davis, W. 138
Decca Recording Company 138
Deming, E. 259, 265
de Board, R. 217
deVito, J. 86
Dickens, Charles 187
Direct Line 160
Direct Marketing Association 152
Disney World 7
Douglas, M. 307

Exxon Qyx 287

Federal Express 4
Financial Mail 159
Fisher, R. 109
Ford, Henry 80
Ford Motor Company 18, 35, 46
Forrest, A. 8
Francis, D. 1
Frank, A. 317
Frey, J. 153
Friedrich, G. 105, 131

Gallup 13
Gates, B. 18
General Motors 10, 215
Goffman, E. 303
Golden, N. 301
Goldwyn, Sam 173, 266
Goleman, D. 15
General Electric 260
GTE 260

Hamilton, C. 302
Hare Krishna 58
Health and Safety Executive 216
Henley Centre 152, 168, 169, 183
Hewlett-Packard 46, 47

IBM 4, 161, 301
Independent Counselling and Advisory
    Services 215
Information on Hold 161

Jakubowski, P. 189
Janis, I. 58
Janner, G. 83
Jensen, M. 49
Johnston and Johnston 215

Kanter, R. 47
Kennedy, John F. 58, 301, 305
Kipnis, D. 39, 41
Klaus, R. 1
Korda, M. 290
Kossen, S. 135
Kotter, J. 67

Lange, A. 189
Lao-Tzu 67, 68
Lazarus, A. 188
Lincoln, Abraham 23, 37, 113, 167

Machiavelli, N. 37
Mandel, S. 87
Marriott 169
Marx, Groucho 30
McDonald's 7
McDonnell Douglas 215
McGinniss, J. 297
McGregor, D. 9
McGuire, W. 26
McKeans, P. 10
Mead, R. 289
MGM 266
Microsoft 18
Mills, H. 122
Mintzberg, H. 65
Molloy, J. 301
Morgan, T. 39

Nalebuff, A. 107
National Health Service 308
Nixon, Richard 301
Nissan 47
NOP 160

Office of Consumer Affairs 169
O'Hair, D. 105, 131
Owen, R. 260

Paisley, W. 26
Parker, C. 302
Parsons, T. 3
Peters, T. 50, 133, 169
Petronius, Gaius 45
Pfeffer, J. 67, 319
Post Office 215
Prudential 287
Punch, M. 308

Quirke, B. 182

Rackham, N. 39
Rakos, R. 189, 202
Raleigh, Sir Walter 261
Reed Accountancy Personnel 235
Rice, R. 26
Ridge Consultants 106
Ringlemann, M. 60
Rogers, C. 217, 218, 220
Rowntree 215
Rover Group 308
Royal Mail 168

Sartre, J-P. 45
Schmidt, S. 39, 41
Scott, B. 112
Seabury, D. 187
Semco 278
Semler, R. 278
Shakespeare, William 281
Simpson, Homer 48
Sinclair, A. 62
Slater, T. 169
Smith, A. 10
Smith, Adam 105
Sternberg, E. 308
Stevenson, R.L. 131
Sunday Times 307
Superboss 260, 261, 266

Tao-Te-King 65
Taylor, B.F. 151
Thatcher, Margaret 283
Tuckman, B. 49
Twain, Mark 309

Ury, W. 109
US Department of Health and Human
    Services 215

Virgin 18

Wallach, J. 301
Warner Brothers, 138
Waterman, R. 133
Weihenstephan Brewery 2
Whetten, D. 56, 73

Wilde, Oscar 56, 262
Williams, A. 142
Wittgenstein, L. von 211, 283
Wriston, W. 73

Xerox 4, 47

The Complete Guide to People Skills

Sue Bishop

As a manager wanting to get the most out of your team, you need to practise 'people-focused leadership'. You need to encourage your people to contribute fully to the success of your organization, and to do that, you need an armoury of people skills.

Sue Bishop's book provides a comprehensive guide to all of the interpersonal skills that you need to get the best from your team. Skills that you can apply in formal settings, such as recruitment interviews, or appraisals, as well as less formal, such as coaching or counselling. Team skills to help you communicate with, and develop, your people. Skills to handle disciplinary matters, or emotional crises, or to resolve conflict. And skills that you can use when you are just chatting with and enthusing individuals and the team.

The Complete Guide to People Skills is divided into two parts. Part I gives an overview of the core skills, and offers a brief explanation of some self-development and communication theories.

Part II shows how to apply these skills in different situations. It is arranged alphabetically by topic - from appraisals to teamwork. Each section includes an exercise to help you learn more about the skills and techniques and to apply them in your work.

Gower

50 Essential Management Techniques

Michael Ward

Are you familiar with the concept of product life-cycle? Of course you are! Does the prospect of a SWOT analysis bring you out in a cold sweat? Probably not. But what about the Johari Window? Or Zipf's Law?

Michael Ward's book brings together a formidable array of tools designed to improve managerial performance. For each entry he introduces the technique in question, explains how it works, then goes on to show, with the aid of an entertaining case study, how it can be used to solve an actual problem. The 50 techniques, including some never before published, are grouped into 11 subject areas, ranging from strategy to learning.

For managers in every type of organization and at any level, as well as for students and consultants, *50 Essential Management Techniques* is likely to become an indispensable source.

Gower

The Gower Handbook of Management

Fourth Edition

Edited by Dennis Lock

'If you have only one management book on your shelf, this must be the one.'

Dennis Lock recalls launching the first edition in 1983 with this aim in mind. It has remained the guiding principle behind subsequent editions, and today *The Gower Handbook of Management* is widely regarded as a manager's bible: an authoritative, gimmick-free and practical guide to best practice in management. By covering the broadest possible range of subjects, this handbook replicates in book form a forum in which managers can meet experts from a range of professional disciplines.

The new edition features:

- 65 expert contributors - many of them practising managers and all of them recognized authorities in their field
- many new contributors: over one-third are new to this edition
- 72 chapters, of which half are completely new
- 20 chapters on subjects new to this edition
- a brand new design and larger format.

The Gower Handbook of Management has received many plaudits during its distinguished career, summed up in the following review from *Director*:

'... packed with information which can be used either as a reference work on a specific problem or as a guide to an entire operation. In a short review one can touch only lightly on the richness and excellence of this book, which well deserves a place on any executive bookshelf.'

Gower

Gower Handbook of Management Skills

Third Edition

Edited by Dorothy M Stewart

'This is the book I wish I'd had in my desk drawer when I was first a manager. When you need the information, you'll find a chapter to help; no fancy models or useless theories. This is a practical book for real managers, aimed at helping you manage more effectively in the real world of business today. You'll find enough background information, but no overwhelming detail. This is material you can trust. It is tried and tested.'

So writes Dorothy Stewart, describing in the Preface the unifying theme behind the Third Edition of this bestselling *Handbook*. This puts at your disposal the expertise of 25 specialists, each a recognized authority in their particular field. Together, this adds up to an impressive 'one stop library' for the manager determined to make a mark.

Chapters are organized within three parts: Managing Yourself, Managing Other People, and Managing the Business. Part I deals with personal skills and includes chapters on self-development and information technology. Part II covers people skills such as listening, influencing and communication. Part III looks at finance, project management, decision-making, negotiating and creativity. A total of 12 chapters are completely new, and the rest have been rigorously updated to fully reflect the rapidly changing world in which we work.

Each chapter focuses on detailed practical guidance, and ends with a checklist of key points and suggestions for further reading.

Gower

Impro Learning

How to Make Your Training Creative, Flexible and Spontaneous

Paul Z Jackson

Likely to be on the bookcase of organisational classics, the book encourages potitive self-development in a nondirective, councelling style. *Impro Learning* is the first training book to treat creativity as the doorway to success - and provide the keys to unlock it. Drawing on sources as diverse as theatre, accelerated learning, sports, co-operative games and psychology, Paul Z Jackson reveals practical methods for enhancing all aspects of training, from joining instructions and bonding to detailed course design and evaluation. The emphasis throughout is on participation and results, and the text is packed with warm-ups, energizers, team exercises and innovative processes. As Peter Kline says in the Foreword, '... what Paul Jackson has to offer us is probably the most essential and basic ingredient of the new approach to corporate training that is beginning to emerge all over the world'.

This pioneering book will enable you to:

• design and deliver training programmes that achieve demonstrable results
• improve your skills as both a platform presenter and a group facilitator
• apply the principles of learning to broaden the range of training you can offer
• enhance your confidence and the ways you project it.

In short, *Impro Learning* offers simple yet powerful techniques for developing both yourself - as a trainer and a person - and those you train.

Gower

Winning Presentations

David Gilgrist with Rex Davies

The Learning Point Presentations School, in the City of London, caters mainly for senior people in banking, insurance, accounting, consultancy, law and financial services. Its highly successful courses on presentations are based on a radical new approach derived from extensive research into what actually works.

Now, for the first time, the essence of those courses has been made available in book form. The result is an eminently practical guide that, in brisk, no-nonsense fashion, shows you how to construct and deliver a winning presentation. The topics covered include:

- analysing your audience
- effective opening and closing
- delivering the correct messages
- key visual aid templates
- handling questions and negative reaction.

The text is supported by numerous checklists and planning formats. There is even a 'fast track' for anybody wanting to master the key points with a minimum of study.

If you are pitching for serious business or otherwise dependent on the quality of your formal presentations, then this is the book that will make the difference.

Gower